When Right Makes Might

A VOLUME IN THE SERIES

Cornell Studies in Security Affairs

Edited by Robert J. Art, Robert Jervis, and Stephen M. Walt

A list of titles in this series is available at cornellpress.cornell.edu.

When Right Makes Might

Rising Powers and World Order

Stacie E. Goddard

Cornell University Press

Ithaca and London

First published 2018 by Cornell University Press

Printed in the United States of America

Library of Congress Cataloging-in-Publication Data

Names: Goddard, Stacie E., 1974– author.
Title: When right makes might : rising powers and world order / Stacie Goddard.
Description: Ithaca : Cornell University Press, 2018. | Series: Cornell studies in security affairs | Includes bibliographical references and index.
Identifiers: LCCN 2018013753 (print) | LCCN 2018017539 (ebook) | ISBN 9781501730313 (pdf) | ISBN 9781501730320 (epub/mobi) | ISBN 9781501730306 | ISBN 9781501730306 (cloth : alk. paper)
Subjects: LCSH: Great powers—History—19th century. | Great powers—History—20th century. | Middle powers—History—19th century. | Middle powers—History—20th century. | World politics—19th century. | World politics—20th century. | International relations—Case studies.
Classification: LCC JZ1310 (ebook) | LCC JZ1310. G73 2018 (print) | DDC 327.1/1209034—dc23
LC record available at https://lccn.loc.gov/2018013753

To Sophie and Stella

Contents

Tables

Acknowledgments

This book looks at the ways actors attribute meaning to events, and like the events discussed in the book, the meaning of this study emerged from a lot of talk, conversations with colleagues and friends in which I attempted to justify my interest in nineteenth-century Prussia. I owe a huge debt to Lynn Eden for advice on turning my initial thoughts about this case into a full-blown book, and I was fortunate that Dan Nexon and Patrick Thaddeus Jackson invited me to present my work on Prussia at a forum on "realism-constructivism" at the Mershon Institute at The Ohio State University. After getting initial, incredibly insightful, and always skeptical input from participants in the workshop, I was hooked on a project about legitimacy and rising powers. I'm particularly thankful to Jennifer Mitzen, Randy Schweller, Bill Wohlforth, and Alex Wendt for pushing me on the project.

While writing the book, I had several opportunities to present chapters, and I am grateful for participants in workshops at the University of Chicago, George Washington University, MIT, Harvard University, University of Washington, Princeton University, and UCLA. Thanks especially to Charlie Glaser, Alex Downes, John Mearsheimer, Jon Mercer, Barry Posen, Elizabeth Saunders, Art Stein, Rob Trager, and Keren Yarhi-Milo for pushing me to think more deeply about my arguments. I cannot begin to name the debts I owe to all of the participants; the comments I received were invaluable. I was also fortunate to participate in the Lone Star National Security Forum in 2016, where participants gave me their close read of several chapters. I'm particularly grateful to Josh Rovner for the invitation and to Steven Lobell for the careful and thoughtful reading of my manuscript.

This book was written while I was an assistant professor and then associate professor at Wellesley College, and I am grateful for the support I've received from colleagues and students. I thank Jane Bishop for the research support I received as the Jane Bishop '51 Associate Professor of Political Science. I had invaluable research assistance from students, including Marsin Alshamary, Kendall Bianchi, Tiffany Chung, Charlotte Hulme, Poe Oo, and Judy Yao. And for years I've subjected my undergraduate seminar to my thoughts on rising powers, and I thank them for continuing to humor me. Julia Munemo provided outstanding editing in the final stages of the book.

I had a wonderful experience with Roger Haydon and all of the editors at Cornell University Press. I am hoping that the external reviewer of this book is reading these acknowledgments and understands all of the difference his or her thoughtful and constructive comments made in revising the book. That reviewer did more than what the job demands, for which I offer my thanks. Earlier versions of this work were published in *International Security* and *Security Studies*. I thank those journals for giving me permission to use the material here, and the reviewers and editors who helped make my arguments better, especially Kelly Greenhill, who shepherded my empirical discussion of Hitler's Germany through the process. For providing me with the time to develop my argument and cases, I am also grateful to the Smith Richardson Foundation for financial support.

I am especially thankful for the colleagues and friends who read the entire manuscript, sometimes multiple times. Bob Jervis and Jack Snyder must have thought they had gotten rid of me after graduate school, yet they proved willing, once again, to read their advisee's manuscript and give comments that were integral to the revisions of the book. The further I get into this career, the more I can see the imprint of my mentors, and I am thankful for it. Joe Parent gave me the blunt talking to I needed after the first full draft, and this is my chance to tell him that he was right. Dan Nexon doesn't think he read a draft, but without his conversations and work on what he thought was a "side" project, my own work never would have gelled. Fiona Adamson housed me while I dug away at the archives, and then even put up with me working out my empirical narratives out loud at her house. And then there is Ron Krebs, who has been my constant intellectual companion since our first days in graduate school. He read the manuscript and, when I just wanted the damn thing off my desk, told me to make it better.

During the course of writing this book, I lost two important role models. I was lucky enough to take a seminar from Ken Waltz as a graduate student, and it was conversations with him that helped me bridge the "realist-constructivist" gap in my own mind. In 2013, I lost my dear friend, Warner Schilling. While at Columbia, Warner taught a class on American foreign policy, which traced the rise of the United States from vulnerable nation to great power. It was Warner who put in my head that the rise of the United States was not inevitable, that all of the European powers were in a position to undercut the upstart revolutionary. Warner's classes, rich with detail and narrative, his ability to point out puzzles, and his uncompromising approach to scholarship sat with me every day as I wrote this book. I wish he were here to read it.

There is also the support that comes outside the academic world. I owe much to the teachers and staff at the Wellesley Community Children's Center, particularly my girls' "primary" teachers—Karen, Patti, Brad, Cindy, and Marlene. I would not have been able to work on his book if you had not given such care to my girls. My sister and her family, my father and my mother, all provided support and good humor throughout (although I could have done without the "you're still working on that?"). A special thank you to my mother-in-law for holding my newborn daughter while I finished up a chapter on a deadline.

My biggest debt, of course, is to my family. Paul MacDonald read this manuscript more times than I want to count and yet somehow managed to play the role of both a critical colleague and a supportive husband. It is to my daughters, Sophie and Stella, that I want to express my greatest thanks. Without you, I'm pretty sure I would have finished this book three or four years ago. My life, however, would have been poorer for it.

When Right Makes Might

CHAPTER 1

The Great Powers' Dilemma

Uncertainty, Intentions, and Rising Power Politics

Why do great powers accommodate, even facilitate, the rise of some challengers, while others are contained or confronted, even at the risk of war? What explains a great power's strategic response to rising powers in the international system? The conventional wisdom suggests that a great power's response to a rising power rests on how it perceives the challenger's intentions.[1] When a rising power has limited aims, it is unlikely to pose a threat. Rising powers with limited aims may seek minor adjustments to territorial boundaries, but not engage in extensive expansion; they will still abide by the rules and norms that govern sovereignty and regulate conquest. They may demand more economic resources, but not threaten the existing great powers' livelihood. They may seek recognition of their growing prestige, but accept the legitimacy of an existing status hierarchy.

Under these conditions, great powers should turn to accommodation as the best way to manage a new power's rise. In the nineteenth century, Britain was willing to cooperate with the United States because that rising power seemed likely to play by the emerging rules of the liberal international order: the American power might seek security within its own boundaries, and influence in the Western Hemisphere, but would not threaten Britain's core interests. Likewise after resisting German unification for over half a century, in the 1860s the European powers—Britain, Austria, and Russia—decided that Prussia's aims were ultimately benign. For this reason, the great powers allowed Prussia to overturn the political and territorial status quo on the continent, uniting the states of the German Confederation under Prussian leadership, and cementing Germany's position as a European power.

A rising power with revolutionary aims, in contrast, poses a significant threat and must be contained or confronted, even if doing so risks war between the great power and its emerging adversary. Revolutionary powers will seek to upend existing territorial boundaries and advance new and even hegemonic sovereign claims. They will overhaul the existing economic order, demanding changes to terms of trade and spheres of influence. The political and normative order, too, may come under attack, as rising powers demand changes to global governance that better reflect their increased influence in world politics. For this reason, great powers must mobilize against a revolutionary challenge. After appeasing a rising Germany for almost a decade, in late 1938 Britain came to see Hitler and the Nazi regime as an existential threat that had to be confronted even at the price of war. Japan's quest for a new order in the Asia-Pacific met a catastrophic end when the United States committed to containing, and then confronting, Japanese expansion. When it became clear that the Soviet Union harbored revolutionary intentions, the United States and its European allies rightly joined forces against their adversary. In each of these cases, great powers, believing they faced a revolutionary threat, mobilized their military, economic, and political resources to contain a rising challenger. They stood willing to sacrifice blood and treasure to check their adversary's ambitions.

The decision to accommodate, contain, or confront a rising power turns on how great powers gauge the ambition of a challenger's aims. Yet determining the intentions of a rising power is a process fraught with uncertainty. How do great powers know the intentions of rising challengers? How do great powers decide that they are *certain enough* about their potential adversaries' ambitions to commit to a strategy of containment, confrontation, or accommodation? My fundamental argument in this book is a straightforward one: great powers divine the intentions of their adversaries through their legitimation strategies, the ways in which rising powers justify their aims. To make judgments about a challenger's intentions, great powers look not only to what the rising power does; they listen to what a rising power *says*—how it justifies its foreign policy. When new powers rise, their leaders recognize that they operate in an atmosphere of uncertainty in which their adversaries are unsure of aims and interests. The rising powers hope to convince the great powers that, even as they increase their might and make revisionist demands, they will do so within the boundaries of what is right: that their growing strength will reinforce, not undercut, the rules and norms of the international system. If a rising power can portray its ambitions as legitimate, it can make the case that—far from being a revolutionary power—its advances will preserve, and perhaps even protect, the prevailing status quo. In contrast, if a rising power's claims are illegitimate—if they are inconsistent with prevailing rules and norms—then great powers will see its actions as threatening, making containment and confrontation likely.

To focus on rhetoric is not to deny that power transitions are a "material" phenomenon: new powers rise and old ones fall based on changes in wealth and military might. But whether a rising power is a threat is not only a material but a *social fact*: it is based not solely on the challenger's military and economic might but on understandings of whether its actions are right and consistent with the norms and rules of international politics.[2] The approach here bears a family resemblance to rationalist signaling theories, which focus on how states communicate their own intentions and interpret the ambitions of others. These scholars stress the role of costly signals—either capabilities or behavior—in shaping perceptions of a rising powers' aims. Some scholars, for example, suggest that great powers assess rising powers' ambitions based on the *politics of harm*. Accommodation may happen if a rising power can signal a limited ability to hurt the great power, if the challenger lacks the military capacity to threaten a great power's security.[3] For others, how great powers perceive a challenger's intentions depend on the *politics of interests*, with rising powers signaling not their inability to harm others, but their disinterest in doing so.

There can be no doubt that great powers worry about whether an emerging peer will use its newfound strength for good or ill, and whether a new distribution of power will undercut their interests. But I argue that these "costly signals" are actually indeterminate indicators of a rising power's intentions. Capabilities reveal only limited information about a state's intentions: it is not what a rising power has in terms of resources, but how it intends to use these resources that matters. Even what we commonly think of as costly behavior—invasion, conquest, aggression—often fails to reveal clear aims. Conquest can stem from offensive or defensive intentions. Aggression is often in the eye of the beholder. Legitimation is crucial because a rising power's behavior does not speak for itself. It is rhetoric that sets the meaning of these actions; in framing behavior as consistent or inconsistent with norms and rules, rising powers shape a great power's understanding of a rising power's intentions, and thus the choice for accommodation, containment, or confrontation.

The bulk of this book is devoted to four qualitative studies of rising powers, their legitimation strategies, and great power strategy: Britain's decision to accommodate the rise of the United States in early nineteenth century; the decision of the European powers to allow for growing Prussian power in the 1860s; Britain's appeasement of Hitler's rise in the 1930s, and its turn toward confrontation after the Munich crisis in 1938; and U.S. decisions to contain and confront the rise of Japan in the twentieth century. In each of these cases, I argue that the way in which rising powers justified their expansionist aims significantly shaped the reactions of the existing great powers. When great powers viewed challengers as willing to play by the "rules of the game," they were more likely to pursue accommodation, even at the price of relative power. In contrast, even weak rising powers were treated as existential threats when their claims seemed illegitimate.

While the focus of this study is historical, in the conclusion I take up the implications of the legitimation theory for contemporary power transitions, and relations between the United States and China. Whatever agreement exists over China's growing power, there is considerable debate over how China intends to use it. Some are increasingly concerned that China's ambitions are "growing in step with its power."[4] In this scenario, China's move toward a revolutionary strategy, one that upends the status quo in the Asia-Pacific, is inevitable, and the United States should be ready to contain or even confront this rising challenger. Others cast doubt on these concerns. As China's power has grown, its aims have remained relatively consistent; though it has become somewhat more assertive about its aims in the South China Seas, the substance of these claims has not changed, nor has it sought broader territorial or economic revision. For those who believe China has limited aims, a continued strategy of engagement is a wise choice, indeed the only way to avoid unnecessary conflict.[5] If the legitimation theory developed in this book is correct, the future of U.S.-China relations rests as much on rhetoric as reality: it will be how China legitimates its expansionist claims that communicate its intentions and shape the contours of U.S. foreign policy.

My aim in this book is to shed light on often-overlooked processes of legitimation in international politics. In this chapter, I lay out the core puzzle driving this study, beginning with a section looking at the traditional theories of power transitions. For the scholars discussed here, power transitions are a dangerous business: when new powers rise, they inherently threaten the existing great powers. A clash of catastrophic proportions is likely, if not inevitable.[6] In the next section, I unpack the two dominant explanations of great power responses: the politics of harm and the politics of interests. I conclude by introducing the book's core argument: that great powers look to a rising power's legitimation strategies as a way to divine the intentions of its adversary.

The Challenge of Rising Powers: Uncertainty, Intentions, and World Politics

All rising powers have some revisionist intentions.[7] As a state accumulates power, it will be tempted to seek changes in the territorial status quo, challenge existing economic rules, and demand revision of political institutions to reflect newfound status. As discussed above, a great power's response to a challenger should hinge on whether the challenger harbors limited or revolutionary aims. When an emerging power's intentions are relatively benign, accommodation should be the preferred strategy. There is no sense in aggressively balancing a state with limited aims: at best, it is a waste of resources; at worst, the policy provokes a security dilemma and a spiral toward war. Great powers believe, in contrast, that revolutionaries must be stopped. Without a firm policy of containment or confrontation, revolutionary states pose an existential threat to the international order.

How, then, do great powers divine the intentions of a rising power? For some, the task of assessing another state's intentions is a futile one. As Mearsheimer writes, "States can never be certain about other states' intentions. Specifically, no state can be sure that another state will not use its offensive military capability to attack [another state]."[8] Great powers can never be certain that they are facing a state with limited aims. To make matters more complicated, even if a great power can somehow figure out a rising power's intentions in the present—if it can reduce or eliminate current uncertainty about its ambitions—states are known to be mercurial, and intentions are likely to change in the future.[9] A benign power today can turn into an aggressive revisionist one tomorrow.[10]

Faced with this uncertainty, these scholars argue that existing great powers will always act assertively to secure their own survival. This means that great powers must deal with rising powers aggressively, deploying their own resources to check the emergence of the potential challenger. Some great powers may decide to *contain* a rising peer, allowing the developing state to amass some wealth and military might while at the same time making certain that this power cannot threaten the core interests of the status quo states.[11] To do so, great powers can mobilize their own domestic resources, building up their military to deter and check a challenger's increasing strength. Faced with a rising Russia, Wilhelmine Germany built up its manpower, invested in offensive strategies, and galvanized its economy. Another option is for great powers to build alliances, seeking partners abroad that can hem in a rising power's influence. Or states might seek to check challengers through economic measures. The Marshall Plan served as the original strategy of containment during the Cold War, an attempt to use economic investment to stem the tide of Soviet influence throughout Western European states.

If the rising adversary presents a significant threat, great powers will not only contain but *confront* a challenger, using their power to counter revisionist demands and roll back the rising adversary, thus preventing it from emerging as a potential competitor, even at the cost of war. In doing so, great powers strangle the baby in the cradle, so to speak, to eliminate the dangers of a new contender before those threats become reality.[12] A great power can crush a challenger's economy through sanctions, or by denying the rising power access to critical routes of trade. Great powers may use diplomatic tools to confront a challenger as well, excluding rising powers from key international institutions and alliances. At the extreme, when it still holds a significant advantage over the emerging opponent, an existing power will launch a preventive war against a challenger rather than face the costs of conflict later on, when the great power's own relative position may have weakened.[13] No doubt that preventive war is costly, but scholars contend that great powers often believe it is "the most attractive response" to a new power's rise.[14]

Power transitions are thus dangerous affairs. Unable to be certain of a rising power's intentions, great powers act on fear. But others question these grim predictions. The historical record suggests that great powers can and will accommodate rising powers, even when they cannot be entirely certain of a challenger's aims. Despite its uncertainty about American goals, Britain accommodated the United States' rise in the nineteenth century. Although they could not be entirely certain of Prussia's aims, the European powers accepted German unification, both in the nineteenth century and again in the twentieth. For decades, the United States has pursued engagement with a rising China. In each of these cases, these great powers chose neither containment nor confrontation, but a strategy of accommodation, making concessions to a state's expansionist demands that increase the power of that state in world politics.[15]

These great powers were not simply engaging in foolish appeasement. Great powers recognize that containment, even when limited, is not cheap. It requires building up military power, projecting this might abroad, and managing alliance partnerships. Containment may force great powers to engage in fierce economic competition, investing in costly trade deals or in potential allies. Confrontation is even more expensive in terms of casualties and costs, and may escalate into catastrophic war. Containment and confrontation also incur opportunity costs. Accommodation might allow for territorial expansion, but this might actually settle territorial disputes and create more stable borders. Accommodation might facilitate a power's economic rise, but it might also give a great power access to new markets and lead to an increase in wealth for all involved. The entrance of a rising power into institutions might mean diminished status for an existing great power, but it also might create more pillars to support international rules and norms. When faced with a new challenger, great powers do not make worst-case assumptions; they do not simply act out of fear. Rather, great powers will try to determine the intentions of the rising challenger, making predictions about what it will do with its growing might.

It is true that divining a rising challenger's intentions is no easy task. At the beginning of the nineteenth century, Britain closely watched the United States for signs that it was revolutionary or reformist. Whether the United States was a power to be feared or embraced, in other words, hinged on the question of America's status as a revolutionary state. A revolutionary America could overturn Britain's emerging economic regime in the Caribbean and South America, and threaten its position in Canada. But a United States with limited ambition might secure the Western Hemisphere and even aid the growth of British power. Likewise, in the mid-nineteenth century, the great powers sought to pin down the extent of Prussia's ambition. A revolutionary nationalist Prussia would have posed an existential threat to Austria and Russia's conservative governments. A German power with limited aims, committed to maintaining aristocracy, would prove an invaluable ally. Even when great powers eventually come to the "right" conclusion about their adversary's intentions, it is often a long and fraught process. In 1812, Britain fought a costly war with the United States before deciding it harbored limited aims. And Chamberlain and his government remained convinced Hitler's Germany could become a good European citizen up until the eve of World War II.

In each of these cases above, great powers struggled to determine whether a rising challenger's aims were revolutionary or limited. In each of these cases, the answer to this question drove critical choices in foreign policy, such as to accommodate, contain, or confront the rising power. In the midst of the uncertainty that is endemic in international relations, how did these great powers decide that they were certain enough about their potential adversaries to commit to a strategy of containment, confrontation, or accommodation?[16] Most scholars argue that it is through *costly signals* that rising powers reveal their intentions to potential adversaries.[17] Rising powers are not passive; they may invest their resources in particular behavior and policies in order to send a credible signal about their type. Great powers read these costly signals as credible indicators of their rivals' intentions, and thus a reliable way to distinguish "benign" from "revolutionary" challengers. When rising powers invest considerable resources in their behavior, moreover, this ties their hands, locking them into a benign course of action, now and in the future.[18] When these signals are sufficiently costly, they can solve both the information and commitment problems that hinder cooperation. As seen above, we can classify theories about this signaling process broadly into two schools of thought: the politics of harm and the politics of interest.

The Politics of Harm

When a rising power engages in the politics of harm, it sends signals that it is either building or limiting its capacity to hurt an existing great power.[19] Some scholars point to material capabilities—especially a rising power's military might—as the primary indicators of threat. Some of these indicators are structural, and thus cannot be manipulated by the rising power. Geography matters, and "neighboring states and world powers with substantial interests in the region of the rising power will be affected more than distant powers with minor or no interests in the area of its growth."[20] The distribution of power is significant as well. In a multipolar world, for example, rising powers might face numerous threats and may be less inclined to engage in offensive action.

But a rising power can also manipulate its ability to harm, and because of this, rising powers use their military might to signal their intentions, investing in behavior that decreases uncertainty about their aims. A rising power with limited aims, for example, can demonstrate its benign intentions through "restraint—that is, by reducing its military capability below the level that it believes would otherwise be necessary for adequate deterrence and defense."[21] In the 1920s, for example, Japan chose to participate in naval reductions that limited its ability to harm American and British interests in the Pacific. Likewise whether a rising power is able to harm a great power depends on its balance of offensive and defensive capabilities.[22] If a rising power invests heavily in offensive technology, seemingly building the capacity for force projection and conquest, then existing great powers should be fearful indeed, particularly if the rising power could rationally protect itself with defensive technology. In contrast, if a rising power looks to invest in defensive technology—if its capabilities are oriented toward protecting and not projecting its power—then the risks of cooperation are low, and accommodation is a more feasible choice.[23] Rising powers might also attempt to communicate information about their preferred military strategies: most notably, are there signs that the state is orienting its forces toward the offense, planning to project their forces outside of their borders, or to shore up their defenses at home?[24] The Soviets decision to maintain their forces after World War II, deployed outside of the country's borders, was taken as a strong signal that the power had expansionist aims far beyond what would be expected from a "defensive" power. Japan's invasion of Manchuria in 1931 demonstrated it had built the capacity to hurt not only China, but great power interests in the Pacific.

Information from military might effectively reveal intentions because it is costly. As Glaser argues, a state with limited aims can "communicate information about its motives only by adopting a policy that is less costly for it than the policy would be for a greedy state."[25] A rising power with limited aims incurs little cost by adopting defensive technology or maintaining forces at a level consistent with defending the homeland, but a state with revolutionary intentions must seek offensive capabilities. A rising power with limited aims is unlikely to engage in conquest even when its security is threatened, but a revolutionary state will seek out opportunities for expansion. Great powers rely on these signals, to reduce their uncertainty about a rising power's intentions, which allows them to commit to compromise or confrontation.

The Politics of Interest

States may also practice the politics of interest, with rising powers signaling not their inability to harm others with their newfound might, but a lack of interest in doing so. When a rising power engages in the politics of interest, it attempts to signal to other powers that its core aims are aligned with those of the existing great powers. Even if the rising power had the capacity to harm the existing powers, it would not do it. The thinking goes that revolutionary behavior would make little sense because it would hurt not only the interests of the other powers, but a rising power's own aims and ambitions.

Like the politics of harm, some of the signals that bring a rising power's interests into alignment with other states are akin to what Robert Jervis calls "indices," characteristics that a rising power cannot manipulate, and thus cannot use to dissemble its aims.[26] Democracies, for example, might inherently provide more reliable information about their interests than their autocratic peers. In "modern democracies," Kydd argues, "the policy-making process is transparent enough so that a wealth of information is generated about a state's motivations."[27] The restraints imposed by a democratic decision-making process, moreover, may allow great powers to conclude that revolutionary behavior would be difficult and costly to achieve, and not in the rising power's interests.[28] Some argue that when rising powers share ideologies with great powers, they are more likely to see this as a sign that their interests as aligned and will remain so in the future.[29] Others suggest that the content of an ideology is a reliable signal: if a rising power is driven by a hardline or "universal" ideology—the Soviet commitment to global communism, or the U.S. pledge to pursue democracy—this leads revolutionary tendencies in foreign policy.[30]

Rising powers can also signal whether their interests are aligned with the great powers in the system. For example, if a rising power invests substantial resources in existing economic institutions, this can be read both as a credible signal of intentions—the rising power is investing in the existing rules of the international system—and as a "binding" maneuver that locks the state into future cooperation.[31] It is for this reason that some scholars are optimistic about China's intentions: having linked its own interests with that of the liberal economic order, China no longer has any rational interest in pursuing revolutionary policies. Autocratic states might sign on to more liberal treaties as a signal that they will abide by international norms, even if their own internal values suggest otherwise. Rising powers can send costly signals that indicate revolutionary intentions as well. Transparency can be both a blessing and a curse. If it looks like a democratic rising power is rallying its domestic population around a program of expansion, for example, this can be read as a credible signal of a rising power's aggressive aims.

The politics of harm and the politics of interest are often treated like competing explanations about how great powers perceive rising powers and how they attempt to resolve their uncertainty about a challenger's intentions. In a world where the politics of harm guides state interactions, reducing uncertainty is a fundamentally dangerous and difficult task. If reducing uncertainty means limiting one's own capacity to harm, this is an inherently risky endeavor, one that could put a state's very survival at stake. A state that limits its arms in an attempt to signal its restraint risks vulnerability if attacked. A state that adopts only defensive technology might be unable to help an ally. For these reasons, even states with limited aims get locked into pernicious security dilemmas, when all of them pursue policies designed to increase their own security, yet end up threatening other states. For those that focus on the politics of interest, the signaling process is less fraught, and coping with uncertainty less dangerous. When a rising power accepts the status quo, signaling becomes a coordination game: given enough credible information, accommodation and cooperation is simply the optimal strategy.

But both of these approaches share fundamental assumptions about the way in which a rising power communicates its intentions, and the way in which great powers interpret those signals. Great powers begin with a set of prior beliefs about what "type" of rising power they are facing, assigning probabilities to whether that state has revisionist or benign intentions. A rising power's behavior gives them information that allows them to update these probabilities, and adjust their strategies accordingly. Both the politics of harm and the politics of interest assume that the meaning of the rising power's behavior is objective: what a signal means is given, stable, and universal.[32] Finally, for both approaches, these signals carry inherent material costs and thus reveal credible information about the challenger's type. Because signals are believed to reliably communicate information, then, they can reduce uncertainty about challenger's intentions, thus allowing great powers to decide whether accommodation, containment, or conformation is the best response.

In essence, both the politics of harm and the politics of interest are rationalist accounts of signaling. And there are significant silences in both accounts. First, neither approach explains how a signal acquires *meaning*: how and why its signals are interpreted as information. This would be fine if signals were truly objective, if the meaning of actions was inherent, stable, and uncontested. But, in reality, the meaning of actions "are not self evident, but contingent and open to interpretation."[33] Most signals are indeterminate: they can be interpreted in multiple ways by an audience. For example we can imagine a situation where a set of great powers is uncertain about a rising power's intentions, and while they are dithering, the rising power invades another country. Yet while "invasion" may seem like a fairly straightforward signal, in reality, its meaning is likely ambiguous. Was Prussia's invasion of Schleswig Holstein in 1863 an attempt to uphold a dynast's legitimacy? A defense of the rights of German speakers? The first step on the march to global hegemony? Is China's revisionist action in the South China Seas an attempt to challenge American dominance in the Asia Pacific? Or is it the return to the nineteenth century territorial status quo, as China claims? There may be brute facts in international politics, and expansion is not entirely what an actor makes of it. What is indeterminate in each of these cases—both to the scholar and to the contemporary observers of these events—is the meaning of these signals, and what they are supposed to say about intentions.

If a signal's meaning is indeterminate, then a rising power's behavior cannot be a stable and objective source of information. Rather, signals are social and intersubjective, and how actors interpret each other's behavior depends not on something inherent to the signal itself, but on social context, the understandings actors use to interpret the signal in question. Theoretically, if it signals a lack of inherent meaning, then the process of "Bayesian updating" is more complicated than rationalists suggest. Behavior does not seamlessly provide information; actors are not merely "sending" and "receiving" signals. Rather signals, as Jervis argues, "are not natural; they are conventional. That is, they consist of statements and actions that the sender and receiver have endowed with meaning in order to accomplish certain goals."[34] In practice, this means that how great powers understand a rising power's intentions depends on the meaning it attributes to its actions. It suggests that a rising power may have room to frame the meaning of its actions, and that how great powers interpret a signal's meaning determines how it will respond. Signaling becomes not an objective and given, but an intersubjective and contingent process.

Furthermore, both the politics of harm and the politics of interest assume that successful signals—those that are treated as credible indicators of intentions—are those that have inherent, material costs. The process of signaling works because actions provide costly information about intentions—it is the cost of the signal that makes the information a reliable indicator of intention. Yet it is not always clear what counts as a costly signal of a rising power's intentions. "Cost," on the face of it, should imply a significant investment of an actor's material resources. Given this definition, some of the signals that count as "costly" are somewhat mystifying. At times, actors seem to materially discount costly signals, privileging less costly appeals. Chamberlain took Hitler's appeals to European norms of self-determination as a costly demonstration of intentions, even as the Germans were investing in offensive military strategies. The United States seemed to ignore costly signals of Soviet constraint under Khrushchev, such as significant force reductions, and reacted more strongly to revolutionary pronouncements. A rising power's decision to join an institution or sign a treaty may be "costless," with little required of the state outside of what it would have normally done in order to join the institution, and few consequences if it were to leave.[35] We could add to the definition of "cost" more ephemeral concerns such as "reputation," but this would raise questions of under what conditions a state's reputation would be considered costly.

None of this is to say that cost is not a central component of effective signaling. Rather, what is problematic is determining what counts as a "costly" signal, when how states see costs is not self-evident.[36] This insight has already sparked a vibrant literature, especially in the literature on political psychology, on how cognitive filters shape whether actors perceive signals as costly or benign. These scholars point to mental mechanisms such as "selective attention," confirmation bias, and existing trust to explain how individuals attribute meaning to a given behavior.[37] Like cognitive theories, my argument suggests that how actors interpret the meaning of signals is critical to explaining great powers' management of uncertainty, and whether the subsequent response to a rising power is as a friend or adversary. But unlike adherents of cognitive theories, I maintain that how great powers understand a rising power's behavior is not simply in the mind of the beholder.

Rather than focus on individuals and cognition—the subjective evaluation of meaning and costs—I examine how social and intersubjective understandings shape the signaling process.[38] I follow rationalist and realist theories, arguing that rising powers will attempt to signal their intentions and convince others that they are status quo states, and that the existing great powers will attempt to use these signals to determine the veracity of that claim and the rising power's true type. Yet rather than assume that signals have objective costs and meaning, I begin with the assumption that events and behavior rarely speak for themselves. The process of signaling intentions must be understood and analyzed as a means of conveying information as well as a process of meaning making. Rising powers will strive to invest certain signals with meaning, relying on shared norms and understandings to define their aims to the other powers. Great powers, too, will rely on these social configurations to interpret the rising power's signals. The meaning and costs of signaling, in other words, cannot be reduced to a material and objective process; it is a rhetorical and intersubjective one.

And this leads us to the core argument of this book: if we are to understand how rising powers signal their intentions to great powers—and the strategies that great powers adopt as a response—we need a theory of how actors come to communicate and understand the meaning of signals. To gauge the nature of their potential adversary, I argue that great powers look to what a rising power does as well as to what it says, specifically the rhetoric it uses to justify its expansionist policies.

The Politics of Legitimacy

As argued above, all rising powers will adopt some expansionist aims. They will seek to modify the territorial status quo, demand economic institutions be reformed in their favor, and challenge those political rules that seem to restrain their growing power. The question for great powers is whether these actions are merely revisionist—do they seek to modify the rules of the game in minor ways—or are they revolutionary, an attack not merely on the interests of the other powers but on the system as a whole. I argue that to divine the intentions of their potential adversary, great powers look to a rising power's *legitimation strategies*, the rhetoric it uses to justify its policies. At its core, legitimation is a process through which rising powers explain their aims and motives—what they want and why they want it—in reference to existing norms and rules in the international system.[39] As states increase their power, they must justify their expansionist policies. Any territorial conquest, economic revision, or demand for a change in political institutions must be accompanied by rhetoric that explains why this change is legitimate. Russia, for example, has appealed to the norms of ethnic rights to justify its invasion of Crimea. China, likewise, has deployed a mix of historical and legal reasoning to explain its actions in the South and East China seas. The United States maintained that its 2003 invasion of Iraq was necessary in the name of self-defense. In each of these cases, states appealed to publicly accepted norms and rules to justify the coercive practice of power in the international system.

Legitimation strategies matter because, by giving meaning to behavior, great powers attribute intentions to the rising power. Justifying revisionist behavior as rule bound suggests that the rising power has limited ambitions. Flaunting the rules suggests a more revolutionary state. Rising powers' intentions will likely be seen as limited by great powers if their leaders invoke legitimate international norms to explain behavior, even if that behavior might otherwise be thought of as revolutionary. Conversely, states' intentions are deemed aggressive if their leaders fail to make legitimate sense of similar, and even more modest, actions. In essence, legitimation creates a rhetorical frame for a rising power's behavior, giving its actions meaning and allowing a great power to interpret material facts—military buildups, invasions, economic competition—as either threatening or benign.

To focus on the politics of legitimacy is not to deny the importance of power or interests. My theory takes for granted that great powers will care about the politics of harm, and consistently evaluate whether a rising power is capable of hurting its core interest. It assumes that great powers judge challengers based on their interpretation of shared interests. Yet a focus on legitimation fills crucial assumptions and silences in existing accounts. It explains what makes signals understandable and how they are invested with meaning. It explains how it is that certain signals are seen as "costly," even if they lack inherent material value. The politics of legitimation explains why certain actions are defined as "threatening" to a great power's core interests, and thus whether rising powers are seen as challenging or as upholding the international system.

Some scholars of international relations dismiss talk as cheap, arguing that it is the prater of politicians, not a serious object of political analysis. But talk is pervasive in social life, and it is arguably the primary way states practice international politics. This is why we see state leaders devote an inordinate amount of diplomatic resources to their rhetoric. Rising powers struggle to use language that defines the meaning of their expansionist attempts, hoping to persuade others to accept their benign intentions, or even to bludgeon possible opponents into silence. Rising powers pledge to abide by existing rules, make promises that any expansion will be limited, deny that they harbor revolutionary aims, and claim that any resistance to their expansion would be unjustified. This is all talk. Likewise, great powers look to rising powers' claims and make decisions about what is reasonable based on them. They look to the actions of a rising power, yes, but also for the *reasons* behind expansionist policies—to how they talk—as a guide to their strategic response.

By placing rhetoric at the center of this study, I owe much to the diverse literature that comprises the "rhetorical turn" in international politics.[40] Here I focus on a particular type of talk—legitimation—in a specific setting—a rising power's attempts to justify its behavior to great powers. The legitimation theory developed in this book rests on three analytical wagers about rhetoric and politics.[41] First, while the model assumes that both rising powers and great powers are strategic, legitimation cannot be reduced to self-interest. Actors are embedded in a social environment that simultaneously makes possible and constrains strategic action. No leader stands outside structures of discourse: they must operate within a given "cultural tool-kit," in Ann Swidler's words, that includes rhetorical resources.[42] This does not mean that discourse determines action. To conceive of speakers and audiences as social creatures is not to treat them as cultural dopes, mindlessly following established discourse. But as actors strive to explain their actions, and as they respond to others' efforts at justification, they are equally constrained and empowered by the resources embedded in discursive structures. Legitimation is thus no mere window dressing for interest.

This leads to the second assumption: while rhetoric is irreducible to interest, I argue that actors are less socialized and more strategic than in many constructivist accounts. For example, constructivists who draw from the discourse ethics of Jürgen Habermas have focused less on strategic action and more on processes of deliberation and the creation of consensus.[43] The legitimation theory here, in contrast, emphasizes how language is deployed strategically. Language thus remains tied to power and interest, marked by contestation, and central to politics. Finally, the model of legitimation here rests on a *dialogical* view of rhetoric and politics, in which a variety of actors' claims will compete for dominance. I will thus depart from an earlier postpositivist, often structuralist, linguistic turn in international relations.[44] Here the focus is not on discursive structures, but on the interaction and contestation among actors, as they deploy legitimation strategies in dialogue with one another. As they interact, these agents shift their arguments, strategically framing and reframing them in order to persuade and coerce their audiences. Because discursive structures do not determine signals, actors can choose their rhetoric during interaction, and even create new legitimation strategies in response to their opponents' actions. For this reason, existing discursive formations do not eliminate all space for choice and contingency. To the contrary, agency is at the core of legitimation theory.

Bringing together these three assumptions forms a theory that may be thought of as a social constructivist approach to strategic signaling. It accepts, like rationalist accounts, that communication is a strategic process, and that actors will deploy language that best suits their interest. But the point of communication is not merely to convey information. By legitimating their aims, these rising powers tell a story about what the state wants, why it wants it, and what it will want in the future. Certainty is achieved, not because this information is costly, but because the legitimation strategy makes sense of the rising power's actions to a great power audience.

When new powers rise, great powers face an unenviable set of choices. To contain or confront a rising power may seem the safe option, but those strategies carry considerable and potentially unnecessary costs. To accommodate a rising power might allow for peace, but it also carries the risk that one faces a wolf in sheep's clothing. To make the choice for accommodation or confrontation, great powers not only look to rising power behavior, but listen to what they say. In chapter 2, I put the flesh on the theoretical bones of this argument. I define what legitimation strategies mean and the assumptions a legitimation theory makes about the role of rhetoric and norms in world politics. I focus on two puzzles: *why* legitimation strategies matter for rising power politics, and *when* they are likely to be seen as credible indicators of a rising power's aims. I argue that legitimation strategies are a vital component in collective mobilization, both at home and abroad. By justifying its actions, a rising power hopes to manage its audience's understanding of its actions and, in the process, shape whether existing powers mobilize against—confront or contain—or allow revisionist behavior.

Fundamentally, then, legitimation strategies matter because they are a source of power politics.[45] If the argument of this book is correct, it has significant implications for academics and policymakers alike. It suggests that talk, so often ignored by academics, plays a critical role in the formation of grand strategy. It suggests that legitimacy is not peripheral to international relations, no mere window dressing for power and interests; it is an integral part of power politics. And it suggests, as the conclusion of this book discusses in depth, that the consequence of a future change in the balance of power is to be found not only in the realm of military and economic power, but also in the battle over the rules and norms of the international system.

CHAPTER 2

The Politics of Legitimacy

How a Rising Power's Right Makes Might

How a rising power legitimates its claims—how it justifies its demands to an international audience—significantly shapes how great powers understand its intentions, and thus affects whether great powers will accommodate or confront its increasing might. Power transitions are mired in uncertainty. If a rising power can portray its ambitions as legitimate, if it can argue that its aims and actions are and will remain consistent with existing rules and norms, it can make the case that, far from being a revolutionary power, its growing might will preserve and perhaps even protect the prevailing status quo. In contrast, if a rising power's claims are illegitimate—if they are inconsistent with prevailing rules and norms—then great powers will see even modest revisionist attempts as threatening, making containment and confrontation likely.

It may seem intuitive that legitimation is core to politics. It is through legitimation, as Weber famously argued, that the practice of power becomes palatable, turning brute coercion into authority and rendering the practice of power seemingly benign.[1] For this reason, scholars from diverse theoretical traditions argue that legitimacy is core to power politics. Constructivists have devoted the most attention to legitimacy in international relations, arguing that norms and rules can constrain states' pursuit of power and interest.[2] Martha Finnemore contends that even the most powerful states in the system must legitimate their actions, or else face condemnation and resistance, and Christian Reus-Smit contends that if the United States continues to flout norms of legitimacy, it will find its power gravely restricted as states work to counteract its wanton practice of power abroad. Realists and liberals stress the importance of legitimacy as well. According to Ikenberry, for instance, it was the United States' appeals to liberalism that made its dominance legitimate and have helped stave off attempts to mobilize against its might. In contrast, a rising power whose strategies appear illegitimate is more likely to provoke a balancing coalition. In a similar vein, Stephen Walt argues that if the United States continues to behave illegitimately, states will move to balance the once "benign" hegemon and bring an end to the unipolar moment.[3]

Yet we are left with important puzzles about legitimacy and rising powers. Why does legitimacy matter at all in world politics? Why, under anarchy, do states explain their actions, and why are some attempts to justify actions seen as convincing, while others are dismissed as disingenuous and deceptive? After all, *all* rising powers are likely to justify their actions to a great power audience. Very rarely do we see powers that admit they are violating existing international rules and institutions, and most states rationalize their behavior by appealing to shared norms and values. We need to understand under what conditions rising powers can successfully legitimate their actions and shape a great power's choice for confrontation, conflict, or accommodation.

In this chapter, I develop a theory of legitimation and rising power politics, explaining why and under what conditions legitimation can have such a profound effect on a great power's grand strategy. In the next section, I unpack the concept of legitimation, explaining why it is that legitimation is critical to how great powers come to interpret a rising power's ambitions. While all states try to justify their policies, rising powers must be particularly attentive to legitimation. Rising powers are likely to engage in behavior that demands legitimation: as their power grows, they will engage in some revisionist behavior. Because actions do not seamlessly reveal intentions, rising powers can shape the interpretation of their actions—and their intentions—through their legitimation strategies. Moreover a rising power—perhaps more than other states—must worry about *collective mobilization* in response to its behavior: a rising power legitimates its behavior because it understands that its audience, both at home and abroad, will either support or challenge its expansive behavior based in part on the reasons behind them.[4] By justifying its actions, a rising power hopes to manage its audience's understanding of its actions and, in the process, shape whether to mobilize against—confront or contain—or allow revisionist behavior.

Legitimation strategies are a vital component in collective mobilization, both at home and abroad. For this reason, they shape images of a rising power's intentions through three mechanisms. First, legitimation strategies can signal restraint and constraint, a willingness to abide by international norms and secure the status quo. Under these conditions, great powers believe that the rising contender will be bound to the existing normative order, even if they are undertaking revisionist actions. Second, legitimation strategies set rhetorical traps: when rising powers frame expansion as legitimate, they deprive opposing audiences grounds on which to mobilize against them.[5] Finally, legitimation strategies are likely to be successful when they appeal to a state's identity: a rising power can mobilize support for its demands by evoking principles and norms fundamental to a threatened state.

But the effects of a rising power's legitimation are not constant across time and space. The analytical challenge is thus not only to explain *why* legitimation influences great power strategies, but *when* legitimation is possible; in other words, the challenge is to identify the conditions necessary for legitimation processes to operate. For rationalist theories, variation in how rising powers legitimate their actions, and the great powers' response, rests on the inherent material costs of the signal. In these signaling models, it is the cost of a signal that gives it meaning: talk makes sense to the speaker and listener because it is connected to an expensive investment in the behavior or policy. In contrast, I argue that legitimation strategies are effective when they resonate, when they are seen as having "pertinence, relevance, or significance" with a targeted audience. This is possible under two conditions. First, the rising power must have the capacity to use a multivocal legitimation language, rhetoric that appeals to several legitimating principles, and thus appeals to multiple audiences simultaneously. Second, legitimation strategies resonate when the great power audience is institutionally vulnerable, when the great power believes the normative system it favors is under attack. Institutional vulnerability makes a great power more likely to listen to and accept a rising power's reasons for its aggression, to hear a rising power's reasons as a credible signal of limited and revolutionary aims. Combining these two conditions, I suggest that there are "four worlds of legitimation," explaining how vulnerability and multivocality either amplify or mute mechanisms of restraint, coercion, and identification.

The Logic of Legitimation

A state legitimates its actions when it appeals to recognized norms and rules to justify its demands to its audience.[6] All states engage in legitimation, attempting to explain their aims and motives—what they want and why they want it—to their audience. States justify their actions in order to get other nations to accept, if not support, them. If a state appears to have broken the rules, its leaders will hope that by making their actions understandable, they might escape punishment. For this reason, legitimation is particularly important when states adopt seemingly aggressive or expansionist policies: any territorial conquest, economic revision, or demand for a change in political institutions must be accompanied by rhetoric that explains why this change is legitimate.

The fact that states legitimate their actions points to some significant features of international politics. If the international system were purely "anarchic," operating only through the logics of power and interest, legitimation would be pointless.[7] The fact that states legitimate their actions implies that that the international system contains rules and norms that identify what counts as appropriate behavior, ascribe meaning to action, and set the boundaries of appropriate action in world politics.[8] While this assumption is most closely associated with constructivist approaches in international relations, liberals and realists both speak of a social international order, an international system governed by "settled rules and arrangements between states that define and guide their interaction."[9] Most international systems contain a dominant social system, composed of "legitimating principles," core norms that establish what counts as acceptable behavior and allow states to adjudicate the legitimacy of competing claims. "Keeping the balance" was arguably the core legitimating principle of the nineteenth century Concert of Europe; in contrast, some argue that "peaceful hegemony" guided the practices of China up through the late nineteenth century. In the early twentieth century, "self-determination" was arguably the dominant legitimating principle, by which territorial contestation and demands would be settled. In contemporary world politics, territorial conquest is strictly illegitimate, yet seizing sovereignty in the name of human rights remains acceptable.[10]

These dominant legitimating principles are socially constructed. Even legitimation strategies that seem natural and timeless—such as aggression justified in the name of "self-defense"—are contingent. States have long justified their expansion as a means to shore up their security and ensure their survival but, as Kratochwil argues, even claims of "self-defense" are not self-evident. These "natural rights, like moral principles in general, are a matter neither of simple intuition or cognition." They are embedded in a contingent and constructed legal order.[11] Nor are international social orders homogenous; most contain conflicting legitimating principles. During the Concert of Europe, nationalist claims challenged dominant norms of sovereign territoriality and the "balanced" order." Today, norms of sovereignty sit in tension with norms of humanitarian intervention.

Which norms become dominant legitimizing principles is a process inseparable from material power. More often than not, in the international system, it is great powers that are responsible for defining what counts as legitimate behavior in international politics. Often, this moment of definition comes in the wake of major power wars, where the great powers seek to impose a new world order designed to avoid the catastrophes of the recent past and to advance the interests of the victors. One cannot understand the origins of the Concert and the legitimacy of maintaining a "balance" without seeing it, in part, as the pursuit of Austria's and Britain's shared interest in maintaining peace on the Continent and preventing revolutionary change. The United States' support of liberal economic and political norms after World War II clearly reflected its belief that this system would advance its material wealth and military might in the shadow of a Soviet threat.

Because rules are determined by the powerful, some see "legitimacy" as little more than an ideational superstructure imposed on material resources.[12] If great powers respond when a state challenges the legitimate order, they are simply defending their interests, not the rules themselves. But while dominant legitimating principles may be rooted in power, the rules and norms of international society have a life of their own. At the very least, the great powers see them as instrumental in managing conflict and cooperation in the international system. More profoundly, the great powers often have a deeper connection to the rules and norms of an international order. Kissinger, for example, argued that the rules and norms of the international system are not simply cold abstractions or efficient procedures. They are reflections of a state's identity, and because of this, "no power will submit to a settlement, however well balanced . . . which seems totally to deny its vision of itself."[13]

While the rules and norms of the international system set the parameters of legitimate behavior, they do not determine the behavior of states. Within normative structures, there is a great deal of room for agency, both for the rising power to justify its actions, and for the great power audience to listen to a challenger's claims. This is because norms are not objective structures that neatly define what type of behavior is acceptable. Consider again the example of "self-defense." What constitutes appropriate self-defense is contested and ever changing.[14] Violations of the rule are never clear, and more often than not, states will argue that their aggression is consistent with the norms of self-defense. Rising powers, therefore, have room to interpret these norms in an attempt to coerce or persuade others that their actions are legitimate. Likewise, great powers have room to interpret the actions of a rising power, to decide whether they accept or reject a challenger's claims. This is why the focus of this book is not on whether a rising power's behavior is *legitimate*, but rather on the process of *legitimation*: how actors deploy rhetoric to frame their actions with meaning, and how great powers assess those claims.

Not only is there room for agency, there is room for the strategic use of legitimation claims.[15] Rising powers have a choice of how they legitimate their claims. They may appeal to dominant legitimating principles to persuade their international audience that expansion is not threatening, or to silence their opponents. Alternatively, they may appeal to other sources of legitimacy—principles that appeal to their domestic audiences, or to international revisionist coalitions—rejecting dominant norms as just constraints on expansion. Rising powers choose their reasons carefully, in order to strategically manage reactions to their aims, with the ultimate hope of increasing their power without challenge from opposing coalitions.

Legitimation is thus a strategic but simultaneously rule-oriented process of signaling. To focus on a rising power's legitimation is not to deny the importance of material power or interests in rising power politics. But by imbuing behavior with meaning, rising powers can strategically shape the perceptions of their intentions in world politics. Legitimation is thus a critical way rising powers attempt to mobilize support for their own expansion and undercut balancing efforts.

Legitimation and Collective Mobilization: The Dynamics of Rhetorical Politics

All states attempt to legitimate their behavior, especially when their actions seem to break the "rules of the game." Legitimation is ubiquitous in world politics, but for rising powers, it is particularly significant. To begin with, when new powers rise, the demand for legitimation is high.[16] Great powers pay a lot of attention to potential challengers, and rising powers are particularly likely to engage in behavior that demands legitimation. As I argued in the first chapter, all rising powers pursue some expansionist aims: they will seek to modify the territorial status quo, ask that economic institutions be reformed in their favor, and challenge those political rules that seem to restrain their growing power. This means that most rising powers—be they relatively benign or fully revolutionary—are going to break the rules.

Moreover the meaning of a rising power's revisionism is often indeterminate: it is unclear, on the face of it, whether a rising power's rule-breaking signals limited intentions or revolutionary ambitions. Because actions do not inherently reveal intentions, great powers will demand an explanation from the rising power: they will ask the challenger to give reasons for its troubling behavior. In so doing, great powers seek answers to two complex questions: is the rising power truly "breaking the rules," and if so, why. All rules have exceptions, and even rule-breaking can be legitimate, provided there is a good excuse. The second question—why is the power breaking the rules—is perhaps even more important because it gives great powers an indication of what the future will hold: if a rising power flouts the rules, it may signal revolutionary expansion is likely coming; if it embraces the rules, it may suggest that it remains contained within the rules and norms of the international system.[17] Great powers, in essence, look to a rising power's legitimation strategies to decrease their uncertainty about both current and future intentions.

Legitimation matters for rising powers because these states—perhaps more than others—must worry about *collective mobilization* in response to their behavior: a rising power legitimates its behavior because it understands that its audiences, both at home and abroad, will either support or challenge its actions based in part on the reasons behind them.[18] More often than not, rising powers cannot afford to go it alone, using brute force to grab what they want. Rising powers, especially those early in their rise, lack the might to confront the existing great powers. Even if they could manage a confrontation, expanding through coercion carries considerable cost. For this reason, rising powers must pay attention—and ideally manage—the collective mobilization of their adversaries.

By justifying its actions, a rising power hopes to manage its audience's understanding of its actions and, in the process, shape whether to mobilize against or to allow revisionist behavior. If the existing great powers are going to contain or confront a rising power, they have to convince both their domestic and international audiences that the challenger is a significant threat, one worth bearing the cost of containment or confrontation. If the rising power can give reasons that create questions about whether it is a threat or, better yet, assure its audience that its intentions are benign, then this should have significant effects. If a revisionist action looks legitimate, then alliances will become difficult to mobilize. If a revisionist action is justified, then domestic publics will not be willing to bear the costs of mobilizing against the rising power.

How do the justifications an actor offers shape the prospects of mobilization? A rising power's legitimations affect great power mobilization through three separate mechanisms. First, legitimation strategies can signal a rising power's restraint and constraint: they signal that the rising power is not mobilizing its own resources to pursue revolutionary demands and, as a consequence, that the great powers need not mobilize to check it. In contrast, illegitimate demands can provoke the great powers to see the rising power's actions as revolutionary, even if the revisionism is modest, and cause countermobilization. Second, by means of "rhetorical coercion," legitimation strategies can prevent an adversary's attempts to mobilize against it. When a rising power's demands appear legitimate, this shifts the burden of proof onto its opponent and can even silence more hawkish coalitions who support a confrontational policy. When a rising power's claims are illegitimate, however, opponents can use the challenger's revolutionary rhetoric as evidence of threat and a need for mobilization. Finally, legitimation strategies affect mobilization through identity politics as well. Whereas legitimate claims can assuage a state's sense of its own identity, illegitimate claims present an existential threat to a nation's identity and prompt an aggressive response.

SIGNALING LIMITED AIMS: RESTRAINT AND CONSTRAINT

When rising powers legitimate their actions to great powers, they hope to signal their limited aims and ambitions. This can, as Stein argues, "minimize the import of aggression" by explaining expansionist behavior in terms of the existing rules of the international system.[19] A rising power might insist that its revisionist behavior is not revisionist at all, but is instead consistent with the existing norms of international society; for example, invading a state is not an act of aggression if it is done in self-defense. Or, a rising power might concede that it has engaged in aggression—in rule-breaking behavior—but explain why this was an exceptional circumstance, one that won't be repeated in the future. By persuading other states that its aims are limited, a rising power attempts to increase certainty that it will not threaten its great power rivals. Because of this, there is no need for great powers to undertake costly containment or confrontation strategies; the normative system already serves as an effective constraint on a rising power.

Other scholars have suggested that rhetoric is integral in signaling limited aims, but it often remains unclear why rhetoric—mere talk—would effectively signal restraint, or how the words actors speak would produce such powerfully binding effects. Here I argue that legitimation effectively communicates restraint because of its role in collective mobilization, particularly in its power to mobilize public support. If a rising power intends to pursue revolutionary aims, it must mobilize massive domestic resources to pursue that foreign policy, and this requires a sustained program of legitimation.[20] A state may have the military capacity to conquer adjacent lands, but to galvanize the population to engage in conflict, it must justify the use of violence. A state may have the economic resources to pursue a revisionist agenda, but to ramp up and extract those goods, it must make legitimate appeals to its domestic audiences. It is through legitimation that rising powers produce the resources necessary for a revisionist foreign policy. When rising powers adopt the language of the status quo—when they make appeals to the existing normative order—they signal that they are avoiding these pathways of collective mobilization. For these reasons, language is taken as a credible indicator of restraint in the present: if the rising power eschews a revolutionary language at home, then it cannot possibly mobilize the capacity to challenge institutions on a large scale.

Note that the power of this rhetoric lies in its legitimacy, not in any inherent material cost to the rhetoric. Indeed, when a rising power appeals to status quo rules to justify its foreign policy, great powers may even come to see aggressive and expansionist behavior—what we would think of as "costly" signals of revolutionary aims—as limited and benign. The Monroe administration argued that U.S. incursions into Spanish Florida were consistent with both treaty law and international law governing the acceptable use of force. Bismarck argued that Prussia's invasion of Denmark in 1864 didn't undermine, but upheld Concert treaties. In both of these cases, the revisionist interests of the rising powers were not in dispute. Yet, the appeals to norms and rules still suggested restraint, that the rising powers recognized the boundaries of appropriate behavior.

Moreover, legitimation strategies are seen as having a constraining effect on rising powers, signaling not only what the rising power wants now, but what it will want in the future. Legitimation does not only signal intentions at the present; when rising powers give reasons about their actions, they also shape the future pathways of collective mobilization. As Elster notes, public legitimation creates consistency constraints, and if leaders appeal to the status quo in the present, future appeals to revolutionary principles become less likely because any attempt to switch rhetoric down the line will be costly. Legitimation creates concrete structural obstacles to future mobilization. Appeals to the status quo in the present, for example, can marginalize revolutionary coalitions, both at home and abroad, and remove them as a potential support for aggressive action in the future. These legitimations can activate alliances with status quo powers and sever ties with revisionists, thus sidelining these actors as potential partners in future expansion. The restraining and constraining effects of legitimation strategies, in other words, is no chimera. By defining actions as limited, legitimation suppresses collective mobilization at home and places very real constraints on a rising power's behavior.

DEMOBILIZING THE OPPOSITION: THE POLITICS OF RHETORICAL COERCION

Legitimation strategies work through rhetorical coercion: when rising powers legitimate their actions, they can deprive opposing actors of grounds on which to mobilize the resources for a strategy of confrontation or containment.[21] Rising powers do not legitimate their expansion in a vacuum. As argued in chapter 1, the process of legitimation is dialogical. When a rising power attempts to justify its foreign policies, it will face counterclaims, actors that hope to offer alternative explanations for a rising power's behavior. When Hitler's Germany began to rearm, "antiappeasers" desperately tried to undermine Hitler's arguments that his policies were justified by principles of self-determination, in hopes of mobilizing British support for containment or even confrontation. When the United States expanded into Spanish Florida, it provoked a debate among Europeans about the true reasons behind the aggression. If Spanish leaders could frame American expansion as an illegitimate attack on its territory, it could demand that its Concert allies mobilize against the illegal aggression. Legitimation is a rhetorical battle, and the stakes of the outcome are high. If a rising power's opponents can portray its aims as illegitimate, they will be more likely to pull together domestic coalitions that supports the cost of containment and confrontation.

When a rising power legitimates its claims, it aims to undercut the mobilization of its potential opponents against its expansion. If a great power hopes to contain or confront a rising challenger, it must muster its forces, both at home and abroad. Containment and confrontation, as Schweller argues, incur large domestic costs. As a result, elites must rationalize a program of containment and confrontation, giving good reasons for why the public must bear the cost of an active foreign policy. If a rising power claims it is acting in ways consistent with long-held policies—if it argues it is upholding the very principles the potential balancer claims to defend—the rising power can undermine domestic support for active balancing behavior. Legitimation strategies undercut international mobilization as well. Rising powers can use legitimation as a rhetorical "wedge strategy," using justifications designed to drive apart a potential balancing alliance. Bismarck's appeals, as described in chapter 4, successfully kept Austria and France from containing Prussia's growing power. In the early nineteenth century, the United States strategically used language with an eye toward separating Britain from the conservative continental powers. In each of these cases, by portraying their actions as legitimate, they prevented the great powers from mobilizing to constrain their growing might.

Legitimation strategies can thus deprive opponents of the reasons to bear the costs of containment and confrontation. At the very least, a rising power can shift the burden of proof to its opponent: portraying revisionist actions as legitimate removes the reasons for mobilizing against the challenger. In this case, if a rising power claims it is acting in ways consistent with long-held norms—if it argues it is upholding the very principles the potential balancer claims to defend—this invalidates any reason for mobilization against the rising power. At the extreme, rising powers can even silence their opponents, making it impossible to oppose a rising power's claims—which is key to setting a rhetorical trap.[22] This is when a rising power uses its opposition's rhetoric against it, speaking the same words as their potential adversary, but using them to justify its expansionist policies. Under these conditions, politicians fear that any attempt to contain or confront the rising power will create hypocrisy costs, which Kelly Greenhill defines as "symbolic political costs that can be imposed when there exists a real (or perceived) disparity between a professed commitment to . . . international norms, and demonstrated state actions that contravene such a commitment."[23] Because of this, potential balancers become trapped in their own rhetoric, unable to balance a rising state even if it is in their interests. In sum, by shifting the burden and trapping hawkish voices, rising powers can use legitimation to increase the cost of mobilization by making it difficult, if not impossible, to justify the costs of containment or confrontation to a domestic or international audience.

LEGITIMATION STRATEGIES AND THE MOBILIZATION OF IDENTITY: EXISTENTIAL PARTNERS, EXISTENTIAL THREATS

A rising power's legitimation strategies can shape collective mobilization by appealing to an existing great power's core identity, its "schemas that enable an actor to determine 'who am I/we are'" as it interacts with others.[24] Constructivists argue that a state's choice of strategy is not simply a matter of capabilities or interests. Rather, a state will strive to adopt strategies consistent with its identity, which allow it to project a coherent image both to its own population and to the international community. For this reason, identities are powerful determinants of strategy. Over time they influence not only what counts as legitimate governance within a state, but they will be transmitted "to the international arena, enshrining them as dominant standards of legitimate sovereignty and rightful state conduct."[25] For this reason, scholars suggest that great powers are less likely to be threatened by states with which they share an identity. For example, liberal democratic states are more likely to accommodate like-minded risers: Britain was inclined to support the United States in its rise as a hegemon, for example.

Like these constructivist accounts, the legitimation theory here argues that identities shape which strategies are viewed as appropriate, and which are inconsistent with a state's sense of self, as leaders will feel compelled to maintain "ontological security," to "choose a course of action comfortable with their sense of self-identity."[26] But this is not to say that identities determine behavior. Identities are neither fixed nor given; they are made and transformed through historical narratives and interactions with other states. Nor are identities easily defined. Most state identities contain myriad contradictions (Britain as a "liberal imperialist," for example) and these contradictions create space for multiple interpretations of a state's identity. What this means, in practice, is that "identification" is not a simple process whereby states easily discern who is friend and who a foe. It is, instead, a discursive process in which states attempt to persuade, or even manipulate, their image to an audience.

Rising powers are keenly aware of the role of identity in any state's foreign policy. Thus, they strategically deploy principles and norms fundamental to the existing great powers with an eye toward influencing the choice for confrontation, containment, or accommodation. In doing so, a rising power's legitimation can have two key effects. First, these identity appeals can be deeply coercive, and indeed operate much like the rhetorical traps described above. If a state identifies itself as a champion of nations, for instance, it will find it difficult to mobilize against a rising power expanding in the name of nationalism. Likewise, a liberal democratic state might find it impossible to mobilize against a challenger when "expansion" is framed as "liberation." In these cases, the rising power increases the chance that, if a great power adopts confrontation or containment, it would undermine its sense of self. While this mechanism might seem similar to rhetorical coercion, they are in fact different mechanisms. With rhetorical coercion, legitimation increases the political costs of mobilization. In contrast, with identity claims legitimation strategies raise not the rational but the *existential* costs of mobilization against a rising power. It is not simply that states incur domestic or international costs by acting hypocritically, although this certainly may be part of the problem. Some actions would contradict a state's reason for existence, creating an unmanageable sense of existential anxiety.[27] Under these conditions, accommodation is the only solution.

Identity appeals are not only coercive, however. When a rising power appeals to the identity of another state, the legitimation strategy carries a promise of partnership as well. By appealing to core principles of a state, the rising power communicates that it is willing to shore up rules and norms that are essential to a state's identity. By legitimating foreign policy in terms of a shared identity, the rising power suggests that it aspires to become a peer, not only in terms of power, but in terms of principle, and will work with the great powers to preserve and protect the existing content of the international system. The language of identity is thus a potent weapon in a rising power's rhetorical arsenal. But appeals to identity can have a dangerous side as well. If the model here is correct, then the use of illegitimate rhetoric should do far more than suggest a great power's material interests are under threat. If legitimate claims assuage a great power's ontological security, illegitimate claims can provoke an *existential* crisis among the great powers, a sense that its survival is at stake if the new challenger is allowed to rise. Indeed, if the legitimation process operates as detailed here, illegitimate claims should lead to extraordinary efforts to mobilize against the rising power, pursuing containment and confrontation even when a rising power's capacity for harm is anemic and its aims are objectively limited. If rising powers fail to legitimate their claims, their aims will be seen as nonnegotiable, aggressive, and insatiable. Under these circumstances, confrontation and containment is likely, even at a devastating cost to all involved.

All of this suggests that talk is not cheap. Rising powers use legitimation strategies to shape the meaning of events. In doing so, they shape the possibility of collective mobilization by signaling their constraint, coercing their opponents into silence, and appealing to identities so as to assuage the status quo powers' sense of identity. Through each of these pathways, a rising power can define the meaning of its actions as benign, which undercuts processes of mobilization. In contrast, revolutionary claims will signal aggressive aims, buoy opponents, and even give the appearance of an existential threat, and that gives proponents of confrontation cause to mobilize their publics.

Deft Language, Deaf Ears: When Do Rising Powers Win the War of Words?

Legitimation may be common, but not all justifications are equally effective at influencing collective mobilization. Some leaders of rising powers have effortlessly wielded legitimation strategies as a brutal weapon of *realpolitik*. Otto von Bismarck, in the years leading up to German unification, and John Quincy Adams, in the early years of American expansion have been hailed for their diplomatic acumen—for their ability to assure their friends and foes alike of their country's legitimate aims, even as their countries rose to positions of regional hegemony. When other rising powers attempt to legitimate their aims, their attempts seem clumsy, even absurd. In the wake of Russia's invasion of Ukraine in 2014, few states believed that Putin's appeals to self-determination were sincere. And then there are times that rising powers, even those with limited aims, flaunt international norms of legitimacy, instead adopting a revolutionary rhetoric that provokes international condemnation. Some rising powers seem surprisingly willing to flaunt international norms, justifying their aims with language that seems illegitimate to an international audience. Once a committed member of international institutions, during the 1930s Japan explicitly rejected the norms of a "Western" order as a constraint on expansion in the Asia Pacific.[28]

Under what conditions will rising powers successfully legitimate their aims? In other words, when does legitimation work? For rationalist theories, the ability of rising powers to legitimate their actions, and the great powers' response, should rest on the inherent material costs of the signal: talk makes sense to the speaker and listener because it is connected to a "costly" investment or behavior. The legitimation theory here turns this argument on its head: it is not cost that invests signals with meaning; it is the *meaning* of the signal that imbues it with cost. It was because the invasion of Manchuria in 1931 was framed as a challenge to the Western order that it became costly. It was because the American invasion of Florida in 1819 was justified as self-defense that it was costless. In these cases, talk was costly, but for reasons that conventional signal models do not explain.

I argue that whether legitimation strategies are effective depends not on their inherent material costs, but on their resonance. Resonance is defined as whether the rhetoric is seen as having "pertinence, relevance, or significance" with a targeted audience,[29] and it is a critical concept for theories of language and politics, particularly the literature on framing and collective mobilization.[30] In order for legitimation to matter, the appeals have to be heard: it is only when legitimation strategies resonate that they can signal constraint and restraint, set rhetorical traps, and appeal to a state's identity. Despite the concept's centrality, resonance remains an elusive concept. We know resonant rhetoric when we hear it. Indeed, that's the point. At times, a state's leaders attempt to legitimate its actions, but its language falls on deaf ears: the other powers dismiss justifications as ineffective, unimportant, or insincere. For example, the United States never found an effective justification for its intervention in Iraq, one that appeared as more than window-dressing on its interests. At other times, states struggle to cobble together an effective justification, even though everyone understands the rules of the game. It is tempting to establish the resonance of rhetoric after the fact: we know that a rising power's legitimation strategies "resonated" when they effectively signaled limited aims, or coerced opponents; those that failed were dissonant. Doing so obviously risks tautology.

Key to explaining resonance is treating it as a relational concept.[31] Resonance is not simply an attribute of the rhetoric itself. Someone might attempt to legitimate violence "in the name of God," but we cannot determine whether that claim resonates by analyzing the invocation of a divine being. Resonance depends, not only on what is said, but also on the characteristics of the speaker and the audience. In particular, whether a rising power's legitimation strategies resonate with a great power audience depends on two conditions: whether the speaker is multivocal, defined as having the ability to speak with authority across multiple audiences simultaneously; and whether the great power audiences are institutional vulnerable, and thus believe the normative order it favors is fragile and under attack.

THE RISE OF THE SPHINX: MULTIVOCALITY AND THE POWER OF AMBIGUITY

As argued above, rising powers must pay attention to how they legitimate their expansion. Great powers will demand explanations for revisionist behavior; the wrong response might increase their certainty that the emerging challenger is a threat, and mobilize the great powers against it. For this reason, it would seem that any rising power with limited intentions should appeal to international norms and rules to justify their expansion: with no need to mobilize their population, and with an identity that can assimilate easily within the existing normative order, such rising powers should always deploy the language of the status quo. In contrast, when a rising power's aims are expansive—when they are revolutionary by nature—their rhetoric should reflect these aims. Perhaps such powers might dissemble for a time, but they must ultimately turn to revolutionary language to mobilize the forces necessary to throw off the shackles of the international order. It seems then like there should be a tight link between intentions on the one hand and justifications on the other.

But the early life of a rising power is not so simple. For rising powers, even ones with limited aims, appealing to dominant international norms to legitimate their foreign policy can be a dangerous game. The government of a rising power—democracies and autocracies alike—often faces domestic opposition, factions that are eager to exploit opportunities to challenge, even overturn, the sitting government. These factions might be ideologically opposed to the international order. Both rising Prussia and the rising United States, cases discussed in later chapters, contained revolutionary factions deeply opposed to the international status quo. In interwar Japan, domestic factions charged that their government had bowed to "Western" institutions, forsaking Japan's history and culture as a source of world order. Other domestic factions might attack the existing normative order instrumentally, as a means to "outbid" the sitting government for domestic support. Regardless of their intent, radical factions will await their moment to challenge a sitting government. Thus, when a rising power's leaders appeal to international norms to justify their expansion to great powers, they run the risk of incurring significant costs to their legitimacy at home.

Further complicating matters, rising powers must appeal to a diverse audience abroad as well. Scholars often focus their attention solely on the signaling that occurs between the rising power and "status quo" great powers. But the international landscape is far more complicated than this. In any international order, there are multiple revisionist states, competing to attract allies who can assist them in their bid to upend the status quo. France under Napoleon III was certainly a member of the lingering Concert institutions, but it also hoped to transform this order into a forum for national rights.[32] There are important revisionists among "minor" powers as well. Eastern Europe of the 1930s was populated with revisionist states—Hungary, Romania, and Poland among them—eager to press irredentist claims.[33] Even "benign" or "limited-aims" rising powers will be reluctant to sever ties with these potential revisionist allies. Much has been made about great powers' uncertainty about a rising power's intentions, but rising powers are also uncertain about the intentions of their potential adversaries. Rising powers will want to keep potential revisionist allies close at hand, lest the "status quo" powers turn on it in the future. If a rising power's legitimations bind itself too closely to existing great powers, what started as a strategic asset can become a noose around the rising power's neck.

How to escape this dilemma? The answer is that rising powers must use legitimations that resonate across diverse and even opposed audiences. Only by doing so can they avoid containment and confrontation abroad without encountering fatal resistance, at home or abroad. To appeal to a broad audience, rising powers must be capable of what Padgett and Ansell call multivocal action: they must be able to speak with authority across multiple audiences simultaneously. Multivocality is a function of two factors: a rhetorical content that appeals to multiple legitimating principles, and a speaker positioned with ties to several ideologically diverse coalitions. On the one hand, multivocal legitimations rely on content that uses multiple and even contradictory legitimating principles at once, and thus "can be interpreted coherently from multiple perspectives simultaneously."[34] In the case of rising powers, the most important multivocal legitimations are the ones that appeal to existing international rules and norms, yet combine these appeals with revolutionary language that flaunts the status quo in the international system to its more revisionist factions.

Studies of domestic politics, especially in democracies, have stressed the importance of complex and ambiguous appeals. By appealing to multiple principles simultaneously, leaders attempt to forge winning coalitions among domestic coalitions, something crucial when politicians must craft a majority out of multiple factions with divergent interests. George W. Bush, for example, relied on "coded" phrases—such as "compassionate conservative"—that were designed to resonate across disparate—some would say almost entirely opposed—political factions.[35] To more secular and moderate audiences, "compassionate" appeared to be a check on "conservative" impulses, a suggestion that any far-right policies would be treated as illegitimate if they harmed the social fabric of the nation. To religious coalitions, his appeals to "compassionate conservatism" suggested a spiritual commitment that transcended politics and promised to bring sectarianism to the White House.[36] So too did Woodrow Wilson cloak his pleas to intervene in Europe in multivocal language. As Jack Snyder argues, Wilson's rhetoric—especially his appeals to a "League"—were explicitly designed to be heard differently by republican coalitions (who had first advocated a League to Enforce Peace), and by leftist progressives who heard a plan to fundamentally upend a corrupt international order.[37]

Appealing to multiple principles to legitimate their actions gives rising powers claims that resonate across diverse, even ideologically opposed audiences, both at home and abroad. Otto von Bismarck relied on such strategies to justify Prussia's territorial demands, appealing both to existing Concert norms and emerging standards of nationalism simultaneously. In doing so, Bismarck built an uneasy coalition between status quo and revolutionary coalitions, and staved off a formidable balancing effort from Russia, Britain, and Austria. Bismarck's contemporary, Napoleon III, also used multiple legitimating principles to justify France's revisionist demands. Indeed, so sphinxlike was Napoleon's rhetoric that an exasperated colleague remarked: "One is not at the same time the Son of the Revolution and the equal and beloved brother of the legitimate monarchs, the nephew of the Conqueror Napoleon I and founder of an 'empire which is peace,' the elect of the people and the hero . . . of a military conspiracy, one of the five guardians of the treaties which guarantee the existence of states and the Don Quixote of national principles which overthrow them. And yet Napoleon possessed something of each."[38]

Moreover, by resonating across both status quo and revisionist constituencies, rising powers can circumvent the constraints legitimation strategies typically impose. Multivocal legitimation strategies loosen binding effects on the rising power, both in the present and future, by keeping multiple paths of collective mobilization open and viable. By refusing to commit to one set of norms, politicians can circumvent charges of hypocrisy. And by presenting multiple visions of a rising power's identity, these legitimation strategies can elide the psychological and existential costs of legitimation strategies.

Multivocality is not only about content. Invoking multiple legitimations can be a problematic exercise. Actors who attempt to do so risk being labeled as hypocritical at best and deceptive at worst. To speak multivocally, a rising power must have leaders tied to multiple and ideologically diverse domestic and international coalitions: as Padgett and Ansell succinctly argue, "To act credibly in a multivocal fashion, one's attributed interests must themselves be multivocal."[39] From the early 1860s onward, Prussian elites—Bismarck in particular—straddled conservative aristocratic and revolutionary nationalist coalitions. The Hohenzollern dynasty was firmly embedded in dynastic political networks, but at the same time, actors within the Prussian monarchy held strong ties to the nationalist movement, ties Bismarck exploited to fulfill his program of a unified German state. Medvedev's Russia was a fragmented state, yet he himself (and Putin before him) maintained ties with both democratic-leaning liberals and revisionist nationalists and autocrats, leaving many unclear about on behalf of which faction Russian leaders were likely speaking. China's ties with core liberal institutions, such as the G20 and WTO, sit in tension with its centrality in institutions such as the Shanghai Cooperation Organization and the newly founded Asian Infrastructure Investment Bank.

Holding a position in multiple coalitions makes a rising power's legitimation credible. The Medicis were masters of multivocality, using their political resources to develop Florence's social networks into a nascent centralized city-state. Their multivocality depended on their complex position within coalitions. Embedded in multiple coalitions, the Medicis' intentions appeared inscrutable to their audience, and indeed most elites (mistakenly) thought the Medicis were acting on their behalf. Hitler's ability to invoke racist justifications to make territorial claims, and yet marry them to principles of European self-determination, worked precisely because he seemed both to have an interest in working with international coalitions, and an interest in mobilizing extreme, revisionist coalitions.

Moreover occupying a complex position gives a speaker the authority—the social capital—to appeal to different legitimation strategies.[40] For example, a rising power might claim that an intervention in another state's domestic politics is justified in the name of liberal, democratic values. But if the government rests entirely on the shoulders of illiberal autocrats, its leaders will lack the authority to make these claims. A leader advancing her aims in the language of ethno-national rights faces similar constraints: her authority to invoke nationalist tropes depends on her existing ties with nationalist coalitions. For actors to speak multivocally, they must be already associated with these ideological groups, relationships that give them the social capital to speak on behalf of the principles invoked. Bismarck's ability to persuade the French that he was a nationalist while also telling the Russians he was a legitimist stemmed from the fact that he actually was both of those things. China's ability to claim that it is acting both in the name of liberal capitalism and in the name of postcolonial resistance is grounded in the fact that it is positioned to make both of these claims effectively.

Multivocality, in short, is key to a rising power's ability to form resonant legitimation strategies, justifications that appeal to multiple coalitions at home and abroad. If a rising power cannot speak multivocally, it is left with a difficult choice: it can choose to appeal to status quo audiences and thus encourage accommodation during its rise, or it can turn to revolutionary rhetoric designed to mobilize its revisionist resources, even at the cost of conflict abroad. In most cases, these rising powers will choose the latter option: they will be forced to pay more attention to a domestic audience, especially if the leader's position is under fire. Only when a rising power's leaders face minimal internal opposition will they choose to ignore domestic pressures and appeal solely to international norms.

GREAT POWERS AND INSTITUTIONAL VULNERABILITY

Whether a rising power's legitimation strategy resonates also depends on the characteristics of the great power audience. Legitimation is not a one-way street: it depends not only on what is said and who says it, but on the listener as well. In particular, whether legitimation strategies resonate with a great power depends on institutional vulnerability: whether the great power is likely to believe that the norms and principles of order favored by the great powers are weak, under attack, and vulnerable to being overturned.

A great power's institutional vulnerability has two components. First, there is the state of the normative system itself, particularly whether that system is "settled" or "unsettled." As argued earlier, the international system contains a dominant set of rules that defines what constitutes acceptable action, and what will be treated as illegitimate. This order might range from informal understandings of appropriate behavior to more formal organizations of global governance. In a settled system, norms that establish legitimacy are widely accepted by the great powers. There is, as Krebs argues, a "common foundation for legitimation."[41] The early Concert was "settled": it rested on, as Paul Schroeder argues, a "mutual consensus on norms and rules, respect for law, and an overall balance among the various actors in terms of rights, security, status, claims, duties, and satisfactions."[42] By 1950, the Cold War consensus was a settled system, with the Western powers holding shared and institutionalized understandings about the nature of the enemy, their shared purpose, and the legitimate boundaries of behavior. In unsettled systems, the standards of legitimacy are deeply contested among the powers, and only loosely, if at all, formalized. In the years after the 1848 revolutions, Concert principles became increasingly unsettled, as actors turned to the principles of both nationalism and socialism to challenge the legitimacy of the dominant order. The early Cold War was an "unsettled" normative order: the liberal rules that would come to dominate the system were weak, the rules and principles of free trade and global democracy were not yet established.

To some extent, dominant norms of legitimacy are always vulnerable: it is difficult to think of any system devoid of some contestation over the "rules of the game." The measure is relative, and we can point to particular moments when dominant legitimating principles are more vulnerable. An institutional order in its infancy will be less robust than others: states are still investing in the treaties and organizations that will serve as instruments of global governance, and they are unlikely to have eliminated counternarratives of what counts as a "legitimate" order.[43] Likewise, institutional orders are only as strong as the number of great powers that support it. For two decades after the end of the Cold War, liberal legitimating principles were the only global order in town. As China, Russia, and even the United States waiver on these principles, the system becomes more fragile. The normative order may face an "exogenous" shock that unsettles the rules as well. The 1848 revolutions made clear the weaknesses of the conservative Concert order.

Further, "institutional vulnerability" is a characteristic not only of the system but of the great power. Not all states will see that a system is vulnerable or, if they see it, they may not care. Not surprisingly, the states that care most about dominating legitimating principles are those that believe they depend on these institutions for their own influence and security, states whose power relies in part on the persistence of these norms. As Gilpin and others have argued, the rules and norms of the international system are what give great powers their power, influence beyond what their own internal attributes would allow. In the nineteenth century, Britain cared about preserving norms of liberal trade in part because those standards were in its self-interest. Dominant normative systems both reflect and amplify a state's power.

Other states care about dominant norms for more ephemeral reasons. For example, the creators of an order may feel compelled to protect a dominant institution of rules and norms. Austria was a major force behind the Concert of Europe, and its leaders often identified its own interests with the persistence of those norms. A state might also become socialized into dominant norms over time, as a great power builds multiple ties to the order: as it joins organizations, signs treaties that cement the order's core principles, and take on a prominent place within institutional governance.[44] Britain was not the creator of the Versailles order, for example, but in the 1920s it became deeply embedded in its institutions and principles, coming to see itself as the key governor of the system.

The more institutionally vulnerable a great power, the more likely a rising power's appeals to dominant legitimating principles will resonate. The more a great power is institutionally vulnerable, the more likely these states will see a rising power's appeals to existing principles as an opening to shore up the status quo. Committed to protecting these institutionalized norms, these great powers are more likely to accept the rising power's legitimation strategies as significant. Indeed, these dependent states are less likely to recognize the multivocal nature of a rising power's legitimation strategy. Instead of focusing on the contradictions within the multivocal message, they instead hear a straightforward appeal to their preferred international norms. In the interwar period, Neville Chamberlain often seemed to focus on Hitler's appeals to self-determination and European stability, and dismiss his more militant appeals as mere pandering to the German public. Contemporary policymakers and scholars alike point to China's adherence to liberal economic norms, suggesting that these are more representative of China's "true" interests than its more nationalist and revisionist appeals.

For sociologists and psychologists, such interpretations are not surprising. Both have suggested that how an actor hears rhetoric depends on their social position. The example of "compassionate conservatism," is a case in point. Even when actors can see the ambiguous nature of the claims, they are likely to discount the dissonant message in favor of the resonant one. Actors have what psychologists would call "motivated bias": the great power hears what it wants to hear and accommodates demands accordingly. But the institutional account here suggests causal processes that go beyond selective hearing. The resonance of the rising power's legitimation rests not on cognitive pathologies, but on a great power's particular relationship with existing institutions.

Indeed, if this logic holds, when a great power feels institutionally vulnerable, illegitimate language is more likely to be *dissonant*: it will be heard as a wholesale rejection of international norms and rules. When a great power is institutionally secure—when it believes that the norms it favors have broad support from other powers—a rising power's claims are unlikely to prove troubling. But when great powers are institutionally vulnerable, illegitimate claims provoke significant concerns about the weakness of the normative structure. As described below, strong dissonance will likely provoke containment and confrontation, even when the great power has an interest in accommodation, and when the rising power seems to pose little objective threat to the great power. In these circumstances, rhetorical challenges to the status quo shape the perception of threat, so much so that even limited attacks on the status quo seem revolutionary. A realist might suggest that these dynamics are hardly surprising: of course a great power will act to protect or defend its interests against threats. What is threatened here, however, is not the great power per se, but the normative order the great power supports. While at times there might be direct ties between a state's material interests and the legitimate order, this connection is not necessary to produce perceptions of existential threat.

In sum, a legitimation strategy's resonance depends on the characteristics of both the rising power and the great power. Combining these two conditions—the rising power's capacity for multivocality and the great power's institutional vulnerability—give us four possible worlds of legitimation: a world of strong resonance; a world of strong dissonance; a world of weak dissonance; and a world of weak resonance. In each of these worlds, legitimation strategies' causal effects—their ability to signal restraint and

Table 1. Four worlds of rising power legitimation and great power strategies

Rising power's multivocality		Great power's institutional vulnerability: Low	Great power's institutional vulnerability: High
	High	**Weak resonance** *Great power believes legitimation unreliable, seeks additional information about intentions.* *May lead to infighting, policy paralysis. Hedging results.*	**Strong resonance** *Great power sees restraint, opposition is silenced, and sees rising power as partner.* *Accommodation is preferred strategy.*
	Low	**Weak dissonance** *Great power reads legitimation strategies as weak signal of type.* *Relies on existing order—institutions and allies—to contain the rising power.*	**Strong dissonance** *Great power sees challenger as revolutionary, hawks are emboldened, likely to see existential threat to normative order.* *Containment and confrontation are preferred strategies.*

constraint, their ability to rhetorically coerce, and their ability to shape identities—can be amplified, dampened, or even nonexistent. Table 1 links these conditions with how great powers should interpret and respond to rising powers' legitimation strategies.

High multivocality, high vulnerability. In this quadrant, the leaders of a rising power are multivocal, and their audience perceives their own institutional position as vulnerable. Here legitimation strategies are strongly resonant: the rising power is in the position to legitimate its claims to a broad audience, and the great power is particularly attentive to what the rising power has to say. It is in this world of power transitions that legitimation strategies have their most significant effects. On the one hand, the rising power can manage cross-pressures on its policies, convincing a wide array of audiences that it is acting legitimately. It can both appeal to norms that sound consistent with the existing dominant order and continue to mobilize domestic support at home and revisionist allies abroad. On the other hand, a great power's institutional vulnerability amplifies the effects of legitimation strategies, and rhetoric becomes more effective in signaling constraint, coercing opponents, and appealing to a great power's identity. When great powers are vulnerable, they are more likely to believe a rising power is signaling constraint, even when its strategies are multivocal. Caught in a "window of gullibility," these vulnerable states are especially inclined to take on risky gambles, to sate a rising power on the basis of ambiguous rhetoric and not much else.[45] They believe they can constrain the rising power in a web of institutions, even when that power gives only ambiguous signals that it will be bound, and more costly material signals suggest otherwise.

This means that even when rising powers are multivocal, their language ambivalent and contradictory, the great powers are likely to adopt conciliatory policies. Moreover, the more institutionally vulnerable the great power, the more effective a rising power's rhetorical coercion. When a great power is deeply embedded in the norms and principles of an international system, the more likely these norms are to dominate the security discourse of its politicians. Under these conditions, even disputes over grand strategy must be framed in the language of the dominant discourse: opponents might challenge the particulars of a foreign policy, but they cannot challenge the foundational norms on which they rest.[46] This means that these leaders face higher hypocrisy costs for abandoning these principles. Rising powers, for their part, must cross a lower bar of legitimation in order to silence their opponents. Finally, the more institutionally vulnerable the great power, the more potent the existential effects. As Alexander Wendt and Ian Johnston remind us, institutions are not merely material: they have a profound impact on how the great power defines itself as an actor in world affairs. If a great power identifies with the normative order, even multivocal language will appeal to the state.[47]

Overall, under these conditions, great powers are more likely to respond to a rising power's claims than other states in the international system. Indeed the great power becomes almost irrationally certain about its rival's intentions, believing that rhetoric is a clear signal of a commitment to the status quo. For this reason, in this quadrant legitimation strategies are likely to lead to strategies of accommodation, even when more objective factors suggest certainty about a challenger is premature or unwise.

Low multivocality, high vulnerability. In the lower right-hand quadrant, we have rising powers that lack the capacity for multivocal rhetoric and great powers that are institutionally vulnerable. In this world, legitimation strategies are likely to be dissonant: legitimation strategies will have a powerful negative effect on how a great power reads the intentions of the challenger. Here, rising powers are likely to reject the norms and values of the international system. As argued above, when rising powers lack the capacity to speak across multiple audiences, they will likely trend toward more revolutionary language, in order to sate revolutionary factions at home and abroad. Without the capacity to act multivocally, even rising powers with limited intentions might make revolutionary claims in order to appeal to a domestic audience.

Institutionally vulnerable great powers, in turn, are likely to take revolutionary talk seriously, even if the rising power poses little direct material threat to its security or interests. When a great power is institutionally vulnerable, it will be unwilling to risk waiting to see if the rising power has limited aims: it will see talk as an attempt to mobilize and overturn the international order. When a great power is institutionally vulnerable, moreover, there are likely hawkish opponents at home who will point to a rising power's illegitimate claims as a reason to quickly and fiercely mobilize against the revisionist state. And finally, when great powers are institutionally vulnerable, illegitimate claims appear not only menacing, but as an existential threat, one which must be met at any cost.

When legitimation strategies are dissonant, the outcomes are likely to be dangerous, even tragic. The rising power may not really have revolutionary aims: it may simply be wrestling with the dilemma of holding difficult cross-pressures in check. But vulnerable great powers will mobilize their resources against the challenger nonetheless. Indeed, under these conditions legitimation strategies will lead to containment and confrontation, even when a rising power's actions seems to pose little material threat to a great power's interest, and even if accommodation is the prudent choice.

Low multivocality, low vulnerability. In the lower-left-hand quadrant, legitimation strategies are weakly dissonant: the great power hears that the rising power's claims are illegitimate and inconsistent with dominant norms, but it does not take these claims as a significant signal of a rising power's intentions. As in the quadrant described above, rising powers are likely to turn toward language that seems illegitimate to justify their claims; in rare cases, the power might appeal to the status quo, but only when it is domestically secure. In this quadrant, however, the great powers occupy a secure position: they believe the institutional order is settled, and unlikely to be overturned through a rhetorical challenge.

This is not to say that legitimation strategies do not matter at all in this world. They are weakly dissonant. The great powers will be concerned that the rising power is mobilizing its own population beyond what limited aims will require. Hawkish factions will point to the rising power's rhetoric as evidence that the state should be on guard against a challenge. The rising power's attack on a great power's identity will be seen as evidence that the challenger is unlikely to become a suitable partner in protecting the existing order. Yet in this quadrant, the legitimation process is likely to resemble a more rationalist world of signaling and reassurance. The great power might see a threat, but it will be able to count on the resilience of the dominant order to secure its interests. It will assume that its allies will contain any threat to the order. It will count on international institutions to constrain significant challenges. There is no need, in these circumstances, for rash or costly behavior. Under these conditions, the great powers are likely to turn to strategies of containment, biding their time for other more costly signals of a rising power's aims.

High multivocality, low vulnerability. In this quadrant, the leaders of a rising power are multivocal, and are thus able to use multiple legitimation strategies simultaneously. But while this ability can appeal across a wide audience, it does not resonate as strongly as when the great power is institutionally vulnerable: although great powers will find some of the content of the legitimation strategies salient, great powers that are secure in their position are unlikely to see the rhetoric as a credible sign of intentions. They may even see the contradictions in the rising power's legitimation strategy as a sign that the rising power is attempting to sate both a status quo and a revolutionary audience. As in the "low multivocality, low vulnerability" quadrant above, legitimation strategies are not resonant enough to resolve certainty over a challenger's intentions.

Instead, great powers are likely to see this as a situation of "pooling equilibrium," where both limited aims and revolutionary rising powers are likely to use similar legitimation strategies, and thus talk is not a good indicator of type. It may be the case that a rising power that uses multivocal language is a threat, attempting to mobilize its population and challenge the status quo while avoiding punishment. It may also be the case that the rising power's leaders, concerned with their own vulnerability, are attempting to appeal to its own domestic population out of political insecurity. For this reason, in this world, legitimation strategies do little on their own to decrease uncertainty.

This is not to say that legitimation strategies have no effect, however. Even when a great power is secure, multivocality may be enough to maintain a useful uncertainty about a rising power's intentions. A rising power's ambiguous rhetoric may be used as evidence by both hawks and doves about the rising power's aims: those that wish to contain or confront a rising power will point to the revolutionary rhetoric as a sign of threat; others will argue that the rising power's appeals actually signal restraint. In the midst of this uncertainty, great powers may find it difficult to mobilize their own populations and alliances around a coherent strategy, and instead fall prey to dynamics of "underbalancing." Domestically, great powers will be unable to galvanize their own publics to counter an ambiguous threat. Internationally, allies will disagree over the intensity of the threat and see the situation as uncertain enough that "buckpassing" becomes the preferred strategy. While legitimation strategies are not completely resonant in this world, a rising power's multivocality allows it to maintain uncertainty about its intentions and undercut a forceful countercoalition.

Legitimation in Practice: Testing The Theory

The chapters that follow present four case studies of rising powers and the legitimation process. Chapter 3 looks at Britain's decision to accommodate the rise of the United States in the early nineteenth century. As argued in the chapter, the early nineteenth century, often ignored in international relations scholarship, was a critical moment in Britain's strategic response to America's rise. In 1817, Britain had already fought two wars with the nascent republic and had come to see the United States as a potential great power. While British leaders saw gains to be had in engaging the United States, it also feared buoying a revolutionary power on the continent. Whether to accommodate or contain American expansion depended on what type of power the United States would become: whether the rising challenger appeared as a liberal partner in the Western Hemisphere, or an unpredictable revolutionary, intent on spreading republican principles abroad. The chapter argues that it was U.S. leaders' careful use of multivocal rhetoric—its mix of legal and revolutionary rhetoric—that proved decisive. Because the Monroe administration appealed to norms and rules dear to the British, who were eager to institutionalize these rules in the Western Hemisphere, the rising power convinced its rival to see its expansion as legitimate.

Chapter 4 takes up the accommodation of Prussia in the late nineteenth century. From 1864 to 1871, Prussia mounted a series of wars that fundamentally altered the balance of power in Europe, yet no coalition emerged to check Prussia's rise. Rather than confront Prussian demands, the great powers allowed Prussia to unify the German states under Prussian rule. Not only did this upset the balance of power; it upended the Concert system, reorganizing the German states around principles of popular nationalism. While some have portrayed German unification as practically inevitable, this study argues that the European powers were poised to check growing Prussian power in 1863, as a crisis escalated over German claims to Schleswig-Holstein. Yet, although states like Austria and France had a profound interest in containing Prussia's expansion, ultimately they stepped aside, and even aided Prussia's invasion of Danish territory. Russia and Great Britain, two states that had stymied Prussian expansion in the past, decided to remain on the sidelines as well and not mobilize against the expanding power. Like much of the traditional historiography on German unification, the case focuses on the diplomacy of Prussian minister-president Otto von Bismarck as essential to Prussia's successful rise, noting particularly his skillful use of rhetoric that appealed to conservatives and nationalists alike. The chapter argues, however, that the power of rhetoric cannot be reduced to Bismarck's genius: it was the minister-president's multivocality, combined with the vulnerability of his audience, that made Prussia's expansion possible.

Chapters 4 and 5 take up failures of legitimation. The third case of the book, Britain's interwar policy toward Germany, is particularly valuable because it involves a substantial change in grand strategy, and the vast literature on this case makes it ideal for seeing whether legitimation theory adds value to conventional accounts of rising powers and accommodation. No doubt that, before 1938, British foreign policy was a seminal case of accommodation. Few grand strategies have been more scrutinized than Britain's decision to appease Nazi Germany. From 1933 to 1938, as Germany grew more belligerent, Britain eschewed confrontation and instead attempted to settle German demands through concession and compromise. But by late 1938 Britain came to the conclusion that accommodation of Nazi Germany was impossible, and that the expanding power must be met by force, even at substantial cost to the British Empire. The chapter here suggests that it was Hitler's shift from a multivocal strategy—one that combined legal justifications with German nationalism—to more militaristic appeals that rejected the legitimacy of the Versailles order, that drove the change in British strategy.

The final case—the rise of Japan—allows us to explore a case where a great power, the United States, adopted strategies of containment and confrontation. It is a clear case where attempts to legitimate expansion were unsuccessful. Japan, after a period where it had had expanded without much if any reaction from the great powers, found itself facing condemnation when it invaded Manchuria in 1931. An intense effort to legitimate this expansion proved futile, as Japan's revolutionary rhetoric unnerved the existing great powers, especially the United States. This case allows us to unpack why it is a power would use revolutionary rhetoric, and why the United States would respond so vehemently to Japan's claims when it arguably faced a more pressing threat in Europe.

These four cases were selected from the universe of all rising powers from 1815 to the present, outlined in table 2. I identified significant rising powers as those states that exhibited a *sustained* and *substantial* increase in their share of power relative to the other great powers in the system.[48] The table also identifies the great power's strategies in response to the emerging challenger, and whether the great power chose to contain, confront, or accommodate the rising power. There are some cases where great powers adopt a mix of strategies toward a rising power. States who choose to accommodate rising powers will not leave themselves entirely vulnerable, and will of course invest considerable resources in ensuring their own security. Containment, likewise, is bound to involve some moments of negotiation and compromise. What the table indicates, then, is a great power's dominant strategy over the period of a rise. If there are cases of hedging, these are explored in the empirical chapters. In multipolar systems, moreover, there might be multiple and divergent responses to a new power's emergence. For this reason, in those cases I break down responses dyadically.

The cases represent seminal cases of rising powers in international politics. Not only does this mean these cases are significant in their own right, but it also means that, in each case, the legitimation theory must address a number of specific alternative explanations. Each of the chapters engages with explanations consistent with the politics of harm and the politics of interest. But in each individual case, there are also unique historical

Table 2. Rising powers and great power strategies, 1815–2017

Rising power	*Period of rise*	*Great powers (most significant in bold)*	*Great power strategy*
United States	1783–1822	**Britain**, Russia, France	Britain: containment and confrontation, 1783–1817 Britain: accommodation: 1821–
Prussia	1860–71	**Britain, Russia, Austria, France**	Russia & Austria: accommodation Britain: mixed strategy (accommodation and containment) France: accommodation (1860–70) Confrontation (1870–)
Japan	1870–1917	Britain **United States**	United States: accommodation, 1905–17 United States: containment, 1917–20 United States: accommodation, 1920–31 United States: containment to confrontation, 1931–45
Germany, 1930s	1933–38	**Britain**, France	1933–38: accommodation 1938–45: confrontation
Soviet Union	1920–50	**United States**, Britain	Containment/Confrontation (with the exception of World War II, 1940–45)
Japan	1950–91	**United States**, Soviet Union	Accommodation
China	1980–present	**United States**, Soviet Union	1980–96: containment 1996–2012: accommodation 2012–present: hedging

explanations to contend with as well. Any attempt to explain accommodation of Hitler's Germany, for example, must wrestle with the argument that Britain simply had no capacity to confront or contain Germany.[49] Any attempt to explain the accommodation of the United States must show that this strategy was not simply determined by economic interests or shared liberal identity. If the legitimation theory can offer insight into these critical cases, then it increases the value-added of its claims.

The cases also allow for significant variation on choice of great power grand strategy, both within and across cases, and variation in the two factors that determine the resonance of legitimation strategies: the characteristics of the rising power (multivocality) and the great power's institutional vulnerability. As seen in table 2, the book provides cross-case variation on each of the conditions. There is in-case variation as well. While each of the chapters discusses rhetoric, chapter 5, in particular, contains an in-depth analysis of changing rhetorical strategy, tracing Hitler's reliance on a multivocal strategy in the years before the Munich crisis, to his abrupt shift in rhetoric in the fall of 1938. Likewise, while each of the chapters contains an analysis of institutional vulnerability, chapter 4 compares the different positions of the four great powers—Britain, Austria, Russia, and France—as a means to demonstrate how different positions affect the causal mechanisms of restraint, rhetorical coercion, and identification.

In each of the cases, the goal is to construct as hard of a test of the legitimation theory as possible. This is important because, although we refer to rising powers as unique cases, each historical instance of a rising power provides innumerable instances of legitimation. Indeed in some of these cases, powers are rising from twenty to fifty years. It might be possible to cover the entire course of a rising power's history in a chapter, but it would not allow for much in-depth analysis of legitimation strategies and their effects. To hone in on the signaling process, I looked at crises that are seen, both by contemporaries and historians, as turning points in the relationship between the great power and emerging challengers. To identify a turning point, I looked for moments where it was apparent that a state was significantly increasing its power, and where both the existing historiography and primary documents suggest that great powers perceived the rising power as a potential threat, but also believed the rising power was weak enough that they could have successfully contained or confronted the emerging challenger.

Table 3. Placing the cases

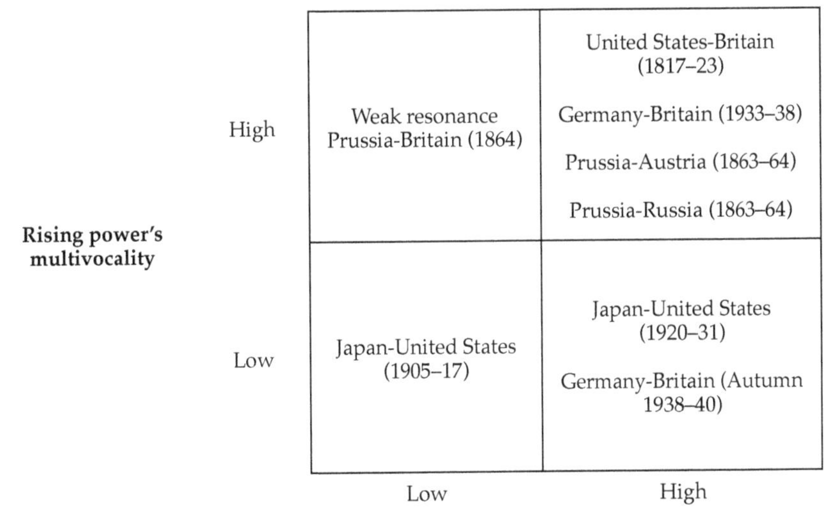

Rising power's multivocality	Great power's institutional vulnerability: Low	Great power's institutional vulnerability: High
High	Weak resonance Prussia-Britain (1864)	United States-Britain (1817–23) Germany-Britain (1933–38) Prussia-Austria (1863–64) Prussia-Russia (1863–64)
Low	Japan-United States (1905–17)	Japan-United States (1920–31) Germany-Britain (Autumn 1938–40)

In practice, I chose to focus on a specific crisis during each great power's rise. It shouldn't be surprising that crises present moments where legitimation efforts are likely to be most intense. It is precisely those moments when norms seem to be violated—in this case, when a rising power commits an act of aggression—that the power will be most likely to justify its actions to a broad audience.[50] It is also during a crisis when audiences are most likely to be listening to a rising power's reasons for its expansion. Crises are often difficult and chaotic affairs, where actors are searching for information in any place they can find it. In other words, if legitimation is going to matter, it's going to matter in a crisis. At the same time, crises also should also be "hard cases" for the theory here. During a crisis, rhetoric operates alongside extremely costly signals of aggressive intentions, such as mobilization and offensive military action. If legitimation shapes policies here—if cheap talk matters even at moments of conquest—then this should be particularly robust evidence of the theory.

No social science concept lends itself to easy operationalization. Yet, the concepts used in the theory here—legitimation, multivocality, and institutional vulnerability—may seem particularly slippery. Some messiness is unavoidable, but each chapter attempts to lay out the causal narrative in two parts: it identifies the rising power's legitimation strategy and whether or not it resonates, using evidence to establish the key factors of multivocality and institutional vulnerability; and, second, it uses process tracing to demonstrate the causal effects of legitimation, drawing from a variety primary and secondary sources to trace how legitimations restrain great powers, coerce opponents, and affect identities.

To establish a rising power's legitimation strategies and their resonance, I draw from published and unpublished diplomatic documents, transcripts a rising power's leaders' speeches, diaries and memoirs, biographies, and secondary historical sources. Legitimation, of course, cannot just be reduced to "talk." We are looking specifically at the justifications for action, for the appeals to public rules and norms that leaders deploy. These statements should be relatively public in nature. They need not be announced in front of large audiences, but they should be stated to a particular audience (in other words, statements of reasons that were entered in private entries in diaries, unless they described an instance of public legitimation, were not considered evidence for this theory). Finally, the study here is interested in *patterns* of legitimation, not one-off justifications of aims. To count as a legitimation, the rhetoric deployed had to occur consistently.[51]

To establish the resonance of legitimation strategies, I both needed to identify which rising powers had the capacity for multivocal action and to determine which great powers were institutionally vulnerable. To operationalize "multivocality," I relied on two techniques. First, to measure multivocal content, I drew from the toolkit of qualitative content analysis outlined above, looking to particular words and phrases to see if a rising power's legitimation strategies mixed "dominant" international principles with other contradictory reasons for its actions. Second, to establish whether leaders had the capacity to use multivocal legitimation strategies, I relied on methodological techniques drawn from qualitative network theory in order to map actors' connections with coalitions. Was the leader of a rising power, for example, credibly associated with multiple domestic constituencies? Did the rising power have strong institutional ties—treaties, economic relations, alliances—across multiple states and institutions in world politics?[52] The more a rising power's leaders had ties to multiple coalitions, the more certain I could be that the actor could speak multivocally.

Institutional vulnerability is designed to capture whether the norms and principles of order favored by the great powers are weak, under attack, and vulnerable to being overturned. For instance, are there "objective" indicators that the dominant normative system was vulnerable? As discussed in an earlier section, an institutional order in its infancy will be less robust than more "settled" others. Likewise, institutional orders are only as strong as the number of great powers that support it. For example, if there was heterogeneity among the great powers in the international system—variation in regime type, or in ideological commitments—then I treated this as evidence that the system was vulnerable.[53] Likewise, I looked to see if there were likely challengers in the great power ranks that could upset the status quo. Moreover, the cases looked for evidence that the great powers believed the order to be vulnerable? In contemporary U.S. politics, the pages of newspapers and journals are filled with speculation about the resilience of the current order. These debates are not unique to the current era: similar debates occurred, both in public and private, over the vulnerability of the Concert system, the Washington Treaty system in the 1930s, the League principles, and so on.

Finally I also needed to measure how legitimation strategies shaped collective mobilization through the three mechanisms of signaling constraint, rhetorical traps, and of existential threats and promises. Is there evidence of "signaling constraint"? Do we see politicians adopting different foreign policies in light of a rising power's rhetoric? Do politicians—in public debates or in private—refer to a rising power's rhetoric in justifying balancing or accommodating policies? Is there evidence of "rhetorical traps"? Do we find evidence of politicians saying they are locked into positions because of policies they have articulated in the past? Finally, what evidence is there of threats to a great power's identity? Do we see examples of politicians avoiding balancing policies, because they are afraid these would contradict deeply held principles and ideologies?

To trace each of these mechanisms, I relied heavily on diplomatic documents and contemporary media reports. Unpublished diplomatic documents proved to be particularly important because, not only did they include descriptions of policies, they often contained discussions and arguments among the actors in charge of formulating the policy. In these cases, I could look to see what role, if any, a rising power's rhetoric played in these assessments of the rising power's intentions. I also traced mechanisms through an analysis of major newspapers, and how they recorded the great power's response to the crisis. Newspaper editorials, in particular, provide significant insights into the interpretation of a rising power's intentions, particularly at moments of crisis. Through these sources, then, I could trace the public reaction to what rising powers claim about their demands, and whether these seem to mollify concerns about intentions or raise the specter of existential threat.

Although the research draws on primary documentation, each case is deeply embedded in a secondary historical literature. No project that attempts to compare cases over time and space can completely rely on primary sources, and each of the chapters rests on the shoulders of historians. Where there are departures from the historiography in these cases, I identify them, and give reasons why readers should support my interpretation. Where there are schisms in the historiographical literature, I make note of these as well, and explain where my argument is particularly dependent on a contentious interpretation of events.

If the cases here are successful, they will demonstrate that when a rising power can prove itself right, it is more likely to accumulate might and emerge as a new great power unchecked by potential rivals. How all of this plays out in the real world of rising powers is the subject to which we now turn.

CHAPTER 3

America's Ambiguous Ambition

Britain and the Accommodation of the United States, 1817–23

> We shall, if united, become a very dangerous member of the society of nations.
>
> —John Quincy Adams

In 1895 Henry Cabot Lodge declared that the United States had compiled "a record of conquest, colonization, and territorial expansion unequalled by any people in the 19th century."[1] In the decades following its independence the United States, propelled by a potent mixture of security, economic, and ideological motives, relentlessly pushed westward, subjugating once sovereign Indian tribes and dismantling European empires on the North American continent. Stymied only for a moment by its brutal Civil War, by the 1870s Americans were settling a vast continental frontier. By 1898, with the frontier closed, the United States would turn its focus outward, claiming a global empire in the Pacific and Caribbean. And in the wake of two world wars, the American leviathan would emerge as a world power, constructing a global order that persists through the present day.

So remarkable was the pace and scope of American expansion that many suggest that the United States was destined to rule the continent, the hemisphere, and perhaps even the world.[2] But at the beginning of the nineteenth century, it was unclear that the United States would emerge as a regional power, much less a global hegemon. In the years following its independence the United States was a vulnerable state, a weak and divided republic effectively hemmed in west of the Mississippi by the British, Spanish, French, and Russian empires. Yet from 1815 to 1823, the United States rapidly overturned the territorial, economic, and political status quo, not only on the American continent but also in the Western Hemisphere as a whole. In the years between 1817 and 1823, the United States settled its most pressing conflicts with Britain: it negotiated an end to its serious border disputes with the British and drove a wedge between that empire and its Native American allies. The United States wrested territory from Spain: in forcing the empire to accede to the Transcontinental Treaty, it claimed territory that stretched westward to the Pacific Ocean. Perhaps most famously, with the Monroe Doctrine in 1823, America announced that Western Hemisphere was no longer open to European colonization.[3]

By the end of the first quarter of the nineteenth century, the United States had not only expanded westward and settled much of its northern and southern boundary issues; it had laid the foundations for its regional hegemony, emerging as, as one historian writes, a "formidable actor in world affairs and nearly unassailable in the Western Hemisphere."[4] All of this was accomplished with only a limited use of force and without sparking a major conflict between America and the European great powers. Indeed, far from confronting or containing the expanding power, Britain—arguably the only power capable of unilaterally halting America's rise—chose to accommodate U.S. demands.

Why did Britain choose to accommodate the rise of the United States? For some, Britain's accommodation of the United States was inevitable, a strategy born less of choice than necessity. The United States was an ocean away, and Britain could not mobilize the military power or economic resources to contain or confront the rising challenger, especially when threats closer to home demanded more attention than those in the far-flung Atlantic. Yet at the beginning of the nineteenth century, containment and confrontation were not only real but likely options. For thirty years, Britain used Indian and European allies to hem in American power. It maintained a significant force in Canada and seemed poised to intervene on the side of Spain to buttress that power's empire in the Western Hemisphere. The War of 1812 had done little to change Britain's strategy of containment; indeed, in the years after the War of 1812, "fear, suspicion and recrimination hung over relations between Britain and the United States" and few believed that the countries were on the verge of permanent peace.[5]

Yet, in the years between 1815 and 1823, British strategy underwent a fundamental transition, from one that stressed containment and outright confrontation in the face of American expansion, to one that accommodated and even encouraged U.S. ambitions in the Western Hemisphere. It did so because Britain came to see U.S. ambitions, not as revolutionary, but as limited, that far from acting as a disruptive power, an American power would bring order and stability to the Western Hemisphere. This chapter examines how it was that Britain became *certain enough* that the United States was a benign rising challenger, one whose aims could be incorporated within the international order, to risk an accommodation strategy. Neither the politics of harm nor the politics of interest can fully explain this choice. Far from reassuring the British that the United States had benign intentions, American behavior from 1817 to 1823 often seemed a costly signal of revolutionary aims. Throughout its term, the Monroe administration worked relentlessly to expand its territory and influence at the expense of the faltering Spanish Empire. If the United States was a revolutionary power, the threat to Britain was significant: if the United States managed to expand into Spanish territory, it could close off the Western Hemisphere to British colonial rule and trade, threaten its interests in Canada, and disrupt Britain's hard-won Atlantic order.

Key to accommodation, this chapter argues, was how the British government came to understand the meaning of American actions. In particular, as it expanded into Spanish territory, the United States framed its expansionist actions as legitimate, consistent with international principles, persuading the British government that there was no need to mobilize against American might. Justifying American expansion was no simple task. The Monroe administration understood that it needed to convince British leaders that American revisionism was legitimate, that each of its actions was justified by norms of sovereignty, noninterference, and self-defense. Only by doing so could the United States stave off British mobilization against its expansionist aims. At the same time, however, the Monroe administration could not afford to lose the support of revolutionary factions at home, who demanded the United States not only expand, but build a new order steeped in revolutionary, republican principles.

To solve this dilemma, American leaders appealed to both revolutionary and European principles, deploying a heady mix of republican and legal language to justify their increasingly aggressive aims. Ultimately, the Monroe administration's legitimation strategies resonated with British politicians and its domestic public alike. In Britain, the rhetoric signaled constraint, the U.S. willingness to be bound by institutional rules, even as it pursued revisionist aims. Those skeptical of American intentions, moreover, found themselves silenced: as long as American elites appealed to existing rules and norms, opponents were stripped of reasons to confront U.S. power. And finally, the Monroe administration so effectively appealed to Britain's identity that supporting the Spanish empire in North America came to be seen as anathema to Britain's commitment to liberal principles. Through each of these mechanisms, the United States shaped its image as a rule-abiding "treaty worthy" nation, one that Britain could accept as a liberal partner in international politics.

American Expansion, British Accommodation: Crisis and Cooperation, 1817–23

Britain's accommodation of the rising power of the United States, its willingness to cede global leadership to the emerging leviathan, is a longstanding puzzle of international relations scholarship. These studies tend to focus on Anglo-American relations in the late nineteenth to twentieth centuries, when Britain concluded its "graceful decline," and allowed the United States to eclipse its hegemonic power in world affairs.[6] But what is often overlooked in these studies is that by the late nineteenth century, Britain had been practicing "appeasement" toward the United States for almost seventy-five years. Indeed it was not in 1898, but in the years between 1815 and 1823, that British strategy underwent a fundamental transition, from one that emphasized containment and outright confrontation in the face of American revisionist demands, to one that accommodated and even encouraged growing U.S. power in the Western Hemisphere.[7]

The British decision to accommodate American expansion came as the United States, under the administration of President James Monroe, attempted to expand into Spanish territory. During this period, the United States was not only expansionist, but often aggressive and violent in its strategies. In December 1817, in the midst of negotiations with Spain over what would become the Transcontinental Treaty, the United States seized the Spanish Islands of Amelia and Galveston; Spain declared American actions an act of war. Along its southern border, U.S. aggression was escalating.[8] In November 1817, U.S. forces attacked a Seminole settlement in Fowltown, burning it to the ground and forcing the Seminoles from the territory. The Indians retaliated against American settlements, prompting Secretary of War John Calhoun to order General Andrew Jackson to "adopt the necessary measures to terminate" the attacks. In January 1818, Jackson declared "the possession of the Floridas would be desirable . . . and in sixty days it will be accomplished."[9] In March, Jackson invaded Spanish Florida with a force of five thousand men, seizing St. Marks and Pensacola, capturing several Seminole leaders as well as two British citizens, Alexander Arbuthnot and Robert Ambrister, who were eventually court-martialed and executed. Throughout Jackson's invasion, the Monroe administration made it clear that if Spain continued to resist in the Floridas, or failed to accept U.S. claims in the west, then the United States would have no choice but to take these territories by force. Under pressure and without allies, Spain folded. In 1819, it agreed to the Transcontinental Treaty, ceding Florida and western lands that stretched from the Mississippi to the Pacific Ocean.

At the same time that the United States dismantled Spain's empire on the continent, it also worked to weaken its grip on South America. Beginning in 1808, opposition groups in South America had begun to challenge Spain's imperial rule. By 1815, South America was engaged in a full-blown struggle for independence. Before 1817, the U.S. government adopted a cautious policy toward the rebelling colonies, refusing to recognize the governments as independent republics, for fear that this would provoke conflict, not only with Spain, but with Britain as well.[10] At the same time, the Monroe administration insisted recognition of independence was inevitable, despite European resistance. In 1817, the United States sent a commission to South America, charged with gathering information about the rebellion and determining whether recognition was appropriate. By 1820, Secretary of State John Quincy Adams warned the British foreign secretary Lord Castlereagh that U.S. recognition of the colonies was imminent and urged Britain to lend its support to U.S. policy. In 1822, Monroe announced his administration's intent to recognize the Spanish colonies as independent nations. In 1823 the United States unilaterally declared the Western Hemisphere as off-limits to European colonization and interference.

From 1817 to 1823, then, the United States adopted a revisionist policy, pursuing some of its most ambitious efforts in its history. Historians rightly point to the period of 1817–23 as a critical moment in the growth of the United States. Strategically, U.S. expansion in the early nineteenth century made war with the rising power practically unthinkable. As Stagg argues, "By the 1830s . . . the rapid growth of the American republic . . . was such that it was almost impossible for Great Britain, even with its naval supremacy on the Atlantic Ocean, to contemplate the cost of a war with the United States."[11] With Florida and the Mississippi in hand, the United States could deny the Europeans access through the Gulf of Mexico and threaten British outposts in the West Indies and interests in Cuba. With its expansion to the Pacific, the United States virtually nullified British and Russian claims to the U.S. Northwest. Economically, as Samuel Flagg Bemis argues, 1817–23 laid the foundations for the great wealth of the United States, as the "Republic came to possess the favored expanse of territory that makes possible its varied history, its wealth, its power in the world for human freedom."[12] It was America's expansion westward that facilitated the immigration, settlement, and the population explosion that underpinned its rapid industrialization and growth in manufacturing and trade.

Moreover, British politicians understood this period as a significant strategic turning point in their relations with the United States. In the years following the end of the War of 1812, British policy took a purposeful turn from containment toward appeasement.[13] In 1817, Castlereagh began to publicly articulate Britain's policy of accommodation. As he wrote to Charles Bagot, the British envoy to the United States, Britain should seek "to smooth out all Asperities between the two nations, and to unite them in Sentiments of Good Will as well as of substantial Interest with each other."[14] To this end Britain would now seek the settlement of all outstanding territorial and economic disputes with the United States.[15] Arguably, the Treaty of Ghent (1815), which ended the War of 1812, laid the basis for more cooperative practices between the two states, but this was only a start. After Ghent, Castlereagh proposed a far-reaching convention between the states to settle the most serious disputes over the Canadian boundary, and allow the United States fishing rights off the Atlantic coast.[16]

To accommodate the United States, moreover, between 1817 and 1824, Britain abandoned two allies—the Indian tribes and Spain—that for decades had contained U.S. expansion in the west and south of North America.

As Elijah Gould details, Castlereagh's accommodation strategy represented a sea change in Britain's relations with their Indian allies.[17] While at Ghent the British had officially disavowed giving any formal support to Native American tribes, they continued to receive chiefs in court and bestowed distinctions among the British citizens who persisted in their efforts to funnel goods, arms, and ammunition toward their former allies, allowing them to contain U.S. efforts to expand into Spanish territory.[18] But shortly into Monroe's term Castlereagh shifted course. He severed Britain's ties with Native American tribes and proclaimed that any British citizen who continued to trade with or arm the Indians was acting contrary to British interests and international law.[19]

Britain withdrew support from its European allies as well. Most notably, Britain stepped aside as the United States expanded at the expense of the Spanish empire, both formally on the North American continent, and informally through its recognition of the South American colonies. When Spain attempted to protest American incursions at Aix-la-Chapelle in November 1818, in hopes of building a European coalition in support of its empire, Castlereagh ensured that Spain's request would go unanswered.[20] When Spain's more sympathetic friends in the Holy Alliance threatened intervention in South America, Britain made it clear that any European military action on Spain's behalf was unacceptable. When Spain asked Britain to mediate negotiations with the United States over the western territories, Britain replied that it would stand aside. When Spain demanded that Britain respond to the United States invasion of Florida, it denied that it had any reason to intervene.[21] And in 1823, when the United States recognized the independence of the South American colonies and declared the entirety of the Western Hemisphere closed to new colonization, Britain stood against its European allies and provided the United States tacit support.

From 1817 onward Britain, faced with American expansion, turned not toward confrontation but instead embraced a policy of accommodation of the rising American power. It held fast to this policy, even as the United States pursued significant territorial, economic, and political expansion, much of which came at the cost of British power. The United States may have still risen to great power status in the absence of British accommodation, but its rise would have likely been much more painful. With British accommodation, the United States could more easily pressure Spain and Indian tribes to cede land through treaty and not war. Once these actors realized that they would receive no aid from the British, they surrendered to the encroaching American power. Had British aid persisted, these foes to American expansion may have still conceded, but they would not have gone quietly.

Britain's decision to accommodate the United States also removed flashpoints between the great power and the rising challenger. Accommodation did not quell all conflict. Throughout the nineteenth century, the two powers would continue to contest territorial boundaries, especially in Maine and Oregon. Even as Britain adopted an accommodation strategy, it maintained the capacity to protect Canada from possible invasion.[22] During the Civil War, British officials contemplated a return to a balancing strategy, debating whether they should recognize the Confederacy in order to break up the American republic.[23] And as Sexton argues, "Far from ending great power rivalry in the New World, the diplomacy of 1823 kicked off what would be a near-century long struggle for hemispheric ascendency."[24]

But these conflicts were relatively minor. With the shift to accommodation, Britain ended its proxy wars with the United States. The Indian tribes, stripped of support, were now vulnerable to conquest. There was to be no major crisis over contested influence in South America. When crises did come, as they would in the late nineteenth century over Venezuela, they did not escalate. Britain guarded Canada, but contests over the United States' northern boundary were largely settled and no longer a potential flashpoint that could lead to a broader war. It is no wonder then that both historians of the period and contemporary British observers saw the Monroe administration's revisionist efforts as a critical turning point, that if the United States were allowed to expand, then it would lay the groundwork for its rise to great power status over the next decade—not just regionally, but globally. All of this raises the question: why would Britain adopt accommodation rather than contain or confront the rising power's revisionist aims?

Geography as Destiny: The Inevitable Rise of American Power

One popular answer to the puzzle of British accommodation is that structural factors made mobilization against the United States not only unwise but impossible. The costs of containing, much less confronting, the United States were simply too high for the British to sustain. The United States has always been "famously favoured by geography."[25] Keeping the United States confined to boundaries east of the Mississippi or confronting its incursions into Florida would have required projecting military power across an ocean, a far too costly task for the European powers. Certainly Spain, Russia, or France had no means by which to confront American demands on their own, but with an ocean separating the British from North America, even a superpower could not afford to expend its economic or military power in a confrontation with the United States. Moreover, Britain faced threats closer to home. France had threatened British interests at sea and on the Continent; in the wake of the Napoleonic wars, Britain needed to focus on its interests there. In Europe, Britain faced the possibility of a revisionist Russia and its coalition of conservative states, the Holy Alliance. Why invest in costly and futile efforts to contain a weak rising power, especially if other adversaries were looming on the horizon?

In this view, British accommodation of the United States' rise was inevitable. As seductive an argument this might be, it is deeply problematic. It is the case that by 1817, some British politicians began to think that projecting power to contain or confront the United States was an unwieldy and unnecessary burden. Yet while projecting power might be a costly strategy, it was a necessary one if the United States proved revolutionary and a threat to core British interests. If the United States would not respect its boundary in the north, then neither a drawdown in Canada nor a demilitarization of the Great Lakes was advisable.[26] If the United States were to threaten British interests in the Caribbean, then it would be forced to confront the rising power.

Moreover the British believed themselves capable of containing the United States. For thirty years Britain had demonstrated that, when the United States threatened its core interests, they could use a policy of containment and confrontation to hem in the United States. From American independence in 1783 to 1815, Britain had significantly constrained U.S. territorial claims. It refused to abandon its forts on the U.S. northwest frontier, as the Treaty of Paris mandated, and colluded with Spain to deny U.S. navigation rights on the Mississippi. Economically, Britain maintained its exclusive colonial trade practices, which locked the United States out of free trade and shipping in places like the West Indies. It continued to deny fishing rights off the Atlantic coast, threatening the economy of the New England states.[27] So significant was the conflict over fisheries that Adams had proclaimed the United States would "have to fight for this matter, in the end."[28]

The British believed they could mobilize resources to contain American ambitions. Part of the problem with structural approaches is that they assume that Britain would have to consistently project its own power to fight American battles, that British soldiers, sailors, and ships would pacify the Western Hemisphere. But Britain could limit the use of its own resources, provided it could rely on indigenous forces and European allies, a strategy of conquest that Britain used successfully throughout the nineteenth century.[29] In North America, during the eighteenth and early nineteenth centuries Britain had relied heavily on Native American allies to contain American expansion, maintaining what "looked like an informal Native American empire in the territory" it had ostensibly ceded to United States and Spain.[30] As Bourne argues, "British military power and diplomacy had tried between 1783 and 1814 . . . to contain American expansion and better protect Canada, first by pushing the frontier southward and then by the establishment of an Indian buffer state."[31] In the north, Britain funneled arms and ammunition to the Miami and Shawnee tribes, facilitating a constant state of war in the Northwest and Ohio territories. In the south, British maintained its alliances with the Creek Nation, whose numbers and organization made it a formidable bulwark against U.S. revisionist aims.[32] As late as 1815, it seemed Britain would continue to rely on its Native American allies. In the negotiations over the Treaty of Ghent in 1815, for example, Indian rights remained central to British demands, with the British demanding the United States recognize Indian territories as sovereign states.[33]

Britain could also use its European allies to contain the United States. Through the early nineteenth century Britain leaned toward an alliance with Spain, and as a result "at first the British government tried to discourage designs on Spanish territory."[34] Until 1817, the British considered mediating in both the Florida conflict and the dispute over the Transcontinental Treaty, in order to ensure a better deal for Spain and block U.S. expansion.[35] Castlereagh and his successor Canning also considered placing liberal monarchs on the thrones of the rebelling colonies, in hopes that this would block the spread of republican governments in the Western Hemisphere.

And when containment failed to work, the British had proved willing to confront the American challenger through the use of force. Even during the Napoleonic Wars—when the British might have reasonably concluded that threats at home trumped those in North America—the British saw American expansion as a significant threat. As the *Leeds Mercury* reported in 1812, "The question of Peace or War with America takes precedency in public importance of all other foreign news. . . . The happiness and tranquility of this country are much more closely connected with this subject, than with the victories in Spain, or the movements of contending armies in Russia."[36] When the Madison administration seemed ready to claim Florida in 1812, the British warned the administration that it must support its Spanish ally, even at the risk of war. The British refused to back down from the Orders of Council, and its insistence that the United States could not trade with French belligerents, risked war as a result.[37] As Castlereagh told his minister in the United States, if the United States would not yield on maritime conflict, "it will be your object to regulate the discussion in such a manner as to throw distinctly upon the United States the option of war."[38] It refused to cede ground on issues of impressment and stood ready to fight suspected incursions into Canada.

The War of 1812 did not disabuse Britain of the benefits of containment. True that, in the wake of 1812, Castlereagh bemoaned what he saw as London's overly aggressive strategies, policies that he believed were a central cause of the war. But at Ghent, Britain appeared determined to maintain a strategy of containment: it demanded strategic control of the lakes bordering Canada, the coastal islands of Maine, and for their allies, an independent Indian state. Arguably, in 1815 Britain was in a far better position to project power than it had been earlier in the nineteenth century. With Napoleon's defeat, Britain's resources could be directed toward stifling U.S. growth, and some observers argued that this was precisely what Britain should do.[39] Geography was thus not an insurmountable obstacle to containment. If the British thought it necessary to contain the United States, it would do so, just as it had for at thirty years. It was not then that the British *could* not mobilize its power to confront U.S. ambitions; it is that British leaders decided that they *should not*. Accommodation was not a necessity; it was a choice. And that strategic decision turned on Britain's growing certainty that the United States harbored only limited ambitions in the Western Hemisphere. How can we explain the turn to accommodation? As argued in chapter 1, many scholars see the politics of harm and interest as driving a great power's choice to accommodate, contain, or confront a rising challenger. Both of these explanations have guided international relations scholars' interpretation of Anglo-American relations in the nineteenth century. Taken together, they paint a picture of British accommodation as based on a rational assessment of American intentions: it was the limited American capacity to harm Britain, and a shared interest in building a political and economic relationship, that provided costly signals of benign aims.

As the sections below suggest, these explanations are right that both harm and interests made accommodation an attractive policy. But British leaders also believed accommodation was only possible if the United States was a reliable partner, one that would play by the "rules of the game" in the Western Hemisphere and not pose a threat to Britain's security or interests. Neither U.S. military power nor other "objective" indicators of American interest were sufficient to resolve Britain's uncertainty about U.S. intentions: while harm and interests made accommodation attractive, neither of these factors provided clear signals as to whether America was a benign power or revolutionary state.

THE FUTILITY OF CONFRONTATION: THE POLITICS OF HARM

As argued in chapter 1, leaders can look to a rising challenger's military might—both the composition of its forces and its strategy—to determine whether it is a threat that must be confronted or contained. From this perspective, in the early nineteenth century, there was little in U.S. military power that threatened Britain's security. Conventional measures suggest an embryonic American power unable to threaten the core interests of the European states. Excepting the period of the U.S. Civil War, from 1800 to 1898, U.S. military personnel hovered around 35,000 men, compared to European armies whose personnel numbered in the hundreds of thousands; from 1816 until 1830, the United States maintained a standing military composed of only about 11,000 personnel.[40] While the U.S. Navy claimed some victories in the War of 1812, it would only challenge British naval supremacy at the end of the nineteenth century.[41] Economically the United States fared better, but was still weak when compared to Britain's economic might. Its GDP from 1815 to 1830 was only a third of the United Kingdom's.[42] Without the ability to project power and threaten core interests, it is hardly surprising that Britain would accommodate American demands.

But whatever the United States' weakness, by 1815 British politicians were quite certain that the United States would eventually acquire the capacity to threaten British security. As Troy Bickham argues, many Britons recognized that the "sheer size" of the United States "would make it a global player—an awareness that stretched back well into the eighteenth century."[43] The United States was hardly the great power that it would become, but many in Britain believed that appeasing the United States in the present would *allow* it to grow into a great power in the future, and ultimately undermine Britain's position in the international system.[44] Arguments about a looming American threat appeared in major newspapers. "The Americans if they are not now humbled," declared the *Times*, "will not only rival us in Agriculture, in Commerce in naval force, but also in Manufactures."[45] An editorial in the liberal *Morning Chronicle*—often sympathetic to the U.S. government—warned that "we are actually trying to rear the pillar of American greatness higher and faster than otherwise would have happened, by giving up to them the resources of American wilderness, by regulations more favourable to trade than ours, and more especially, by improvidently allowing them to connect themselves early with the revolted provinces of Spanish America."[46]

It was not simply that the United States could potentially build up their military might at some time in the distant future; it was that there were increasing signs that the United States would pose a revolutionary threat to Britain's security. The U.S. attempts to annex Florida, British cabinet members argued, were a dangerous sign that it intended to upend British power in the Western Hemisphere. The United States' interest in Florida, for example, might be read as an indication that the challenger would block British power in the Caribbean, giving Britain's adversary access to the Gulf and lines of shipping that could result in Britain's ruin. As the *Courier* wrote, "If the United States occupy the Floridas, the whole navy of England, in the event of war, could not protect the trade of the Gulf stream."[47] The United States might also be tempted to expand its territory farther south, taking Cuba for its own.

The American interest in South America seemed even more telling of revolutionary intentions. As Lord Liverpool argued, "If we allow these new states to consolidate their system and their policy with the United States of America, it will in a very few years prove fatal to our greatness if not endanger our safety."[48] For this reason, in a series of memos, Canning declared his "apprehensions of the ambitions and ascendency of the U.S. of Am." He argued that America's growth in power was already prodigious and would threaten Britain, not only in the Western Hemisphere, but around the globe: "The great and favourite object of the policy of this country, for more than four centuries, has been to foster and encourage our navigation, as the sure basis of our maritime power. In this branch of national industry the people of the United States are becoming more formidable rivals to us than any other nation which has ever yet existed."[49] If the United States were allowed to expand its power in South America, it would be a grave threat: "I need not say how inconvenient such an ascendancy may be in time of peace, and how formidable in case of war."[50] Given the possibility of revolutionary intentions, Britain needed to recognize that it faced a final "opportunity (but it may not last long) of opposing a powerful barrier to the influence of the United States."[51]

The British were not alone in their beliefs that United States aggression signaled a revolutionary threat. In 1783, a Spanish diplomat argued that while "this federal republic is born a pigmy, a day will come when it will be a giant, even a colossus."[52] During the negotiations with the United States over the Transcontinental Treaty, the Spanish ambassador to the United States, Luis de Onís, warned his fellow European powers to recognize the United States as the dangerous nation that they were: "The Americans believe themselves superior to all the nations of Europe, and see their destiny to extend their dominion to the Isthmus Panama, and in the future to all the New World."[53] Likewise, as the U.S. pushed toward the Mississippi, the French declared the United States an "enemy to be feared." The Russians were concerned as well, and "the tsarist government reacted with alarm to the rapid American penetration of the northwest coast in the years after 1815."[54]

Overall, in the early nineteenth century America's military might was hardly reassuring. Its revisionist behavior signaled to many aggressive, even revolutionary intentions, and an interest in ultimately undercutting Britain's power and security in the Western Hemisphere. Despite these concerns, by 1823, there was growing certainty that the United States would not threaten British interests, that it in fact could be a reliable ally in staving off threats from other European powers.

THE PROMISE OF PARTNERSHIP? BRITISH ACCOMMODATION AND THE POLITICS OF INTEREST

There is perhaps no more plausible story about the roots of Britain's accommodation than the politics of interest. Here the story is not that the United States *could* not harm British interests, but that it *would* not, as doing so would prove too costly to its own interest. To begin with, given its own economic ambitions, the United States would be foolish to threaten British interests. By the early nineteenth century, the United States and Britain had become each other's largest trading partners.[55] "No two nations in the world are so strongly bound together in interest," claimed the *Times*, and "none are so identified in sound policy, as Great Britain and the North American Republic."[56] The American revolution had done little to undercut economic ties between Britain and the United States. The United States was Britain's primary export market. Britain relied on the U.S. agricultural and natural resources. It was American grain that "continued to feed African slaves in the Caribbean and American lumber was used for the casks that transported the sugar-based products the slaves produced."[57] The United States, too, relied on its trade relations with Britain. In the decade that followed the War of 1812, for instance, more than 40 percent of American agricultural exports went to Great Britain.[58]

By the early nineteenth century so intertwined were the Britain and American economies, so dependent was Britain on the United States for its trade, that confrontation seemed mutual suicide. As Bemis argues, "Hostilities with America had already become if not 'unthinkable' at least unwise, if only because the United States was one of Britain's most valuable foreign customers at a time when she was making every effort to recover from the Napoleonic wars."[59] Even before the War of 1812 the architect of accommodation, Castlereagh, recognized that "the friendship of the United States was a major asset," and that cooperation with the emerging power could bring much needed wealth to the war-exhausted country. Castlereagh too believed that the Americans would come to see cooperation with Britain as the only sensible policy.[60] As he wrote to Bagot, it was imperative that Britain "cultivate a good understanding with the Government of the United States" and seek a "Convention between the two Countries which I trust will have the effect of setting at rest for a considerable time to come, whatever feelings of Rivalry in Trade may still be entertained in America."[61]

Britain could also look to the U.S. democratic and liberal government as a reliable indicator of benign intentions. Britain could see in the United States a liberal partner, a state whose political and "cultural commonalities" provided a foundation for cooperation in world politics. As Charles Kupchan argues, "As Britain searched for adversaries that it could potentially convert into friends, it singled out the United States at least in part due to cultural commonality and the familiarity and comfort that it bred." Likewise, Stephen Rock suggests that Britain pursued a partnership with the United States for "reasons of geography, race, and ideology."[62] American democracy made it possible for Britain to gauge its adversary's interests as well: congressional debates, a free press, and presidential appeals made U.S. intentions to expand transparent to its friends and enemies.

Certainly economic interest made accommodation attractive, and as discussed extensively below, Britain did hope to find in rising American power a reliable partner in liberal international politics. But the possibility of shared interests did little to decrease Britain's uncertainty about U.S. ambitions. In 1817, it was far from clear that the United States would play by the rules of liberal economic trade: that it would not restrict trade arbitrarily, that it would not construct a closed economic system in the Western Hemisphere, that it would not move aggressively against vital British trading outposts in the West Indies. There were plenty of costly signals that, despite its own economic interests, the United States would not hesitate to play a revolutionary game. The United States had acted recklessly during the Napoleonic Wars, embargoing trade even though it devastated both states' economies.[63] The United States could use its position in Florida to disrupt the Atlantic free trade system and cut off vital British trading in the Caribbean. If this United States were to expand westward into Spanish territory, this meant turning over control of the Mississippi to the United States, and putting at risk the Gulf of Mexico, both of which contemporaries argued could lead to the "destruction of trade."[64] And while Britain benefited greatly from trade with the United States, it also had a prosperous and growing exchange—if an illegal one—with the South American colonies.[65] If the South American rebels established republican governments, the danger was particularly grave as the independent states could give "a decided preference in their ports to the people of the United States over ourselves," and trade with "these extensive dominions will be lost to us, and it will, in great measure, be transferred to our rivals."[66] Loud factions in the U.S. Congress were calling for a "closed Western Hemisphere" of trade, severed from European commerce, thus made Britain uneasy about its adversary's interests.

Likewise America's republican democracy provided little comfort to observers. Throughout the early nineteenth century Britain remained uncertain as to whether the United States would behave as a "normal" power or else conduct itself as a "dangerous nation," recklessly pursuing its republican principles and seeking to spread revolution beyond its borders. During the War of 1812, European governments argued that revolutionary urges drove the United States into expansionist projects that would "seem delirium to any rational person," as a Spanish minister remarked in 1812, and into acts of aggression that Liverpool condemned as "the most immoral acts recorded in the history of any country."[67] After the war ended, such concerns only grew more acute as the Americans pressed their claims on Spain. Many worried that the American government was volatile, prone to support republican revolutionary movements abroad, and likely to bend to the will of its most extremist and expansionist elements. "What with unpunished murderers and territorial acquisition, the Americans are drunk with exultation," the *Star* declared. "Of civilized nations, the Americans are unquestionably the most depraved in principles, and the duties of social relations, of any upon the face of the earth."[68]

In 1817, then, it was not at all clear that the United States would pursue its interests in a way that could be accommodated by the British power. If the United States could uphold liberal commerce, then, yes, accommodation was the preferred policy. But if the challenger pursued a revolutionary policy, it would strangle British trade, both on the North American continent and in South America. If the United States was not "treaty worthy," and willing to respect Britain's position in North America and the Atlantic world, then the British could not afford to step down their defenses along the Great Lakes and Canadian border, or find a modus vivendi in the Pacific Northwest.[69] If republican principles motivated the United States to seize Spanish territory, then the Americans could not be trusted to forgo conquest in the West Indies and Cuba, shut down trade in the Caribbean, and overturn Britain's economic and political order.[70]

Ultimately, the British did decide the United States was not revolutionary, that it indeed could act as a partner, preserving stability and order in the Western Hemisphere. While the politics of harm and the politics of interest might explain *why* Britain hoped to cooperate with the United States, neither can explain *why or how* the great power became certain enough of its challenger's intentions to risk a policy of accommodation. To understand how it was that Britain came to see the United States as a "limited aims" revisionist, we need to examine the politics of legitimacy.

"Among the Great Powers" or "Dangerous Nation"? The Politics of Legitimacy

At the start of the Monroe administration, American intentions remained murky at best. President Monroe, the British ambassador reported, was reaching out to "violent democrats," who sought domination of the western United States and to expand into Spanish territory in Florida and the west.[71] He reported that the Monroe administration maintained ties with devoted American republicans with deep sympathies toward the rebellion in the South American states. Monroe's appointment of John Calhoun, an ardent republican, to secretary of war seemed to signal pressures "that will endeavor to propel the government in the revolutionary direction."[72] Adams, appointed the administration's secretary of state, seemed inscrutable, equally likely to move in either a revolutionary or a conservative direction. Put simply, as Castlereagh remarked to Wellesley in 1817, having read "Mr. Adam's language before he left England, my impression is that the Cabinet in Washington *has not yet made up its mind to play a revolutionary game* in South America."[73]

Yet from 1817 to 1823, both British politicians and the public alike began to speak of the United States, not as a revolutionary power, but as a power with limited aims, indeed a liberal partner whose ambitions could and should be accommodated. The change, as historians argue, was pronounced, with Anglo-American relations moving from what Adams called a "warfare of the mind"—relations mired in nationalist outcry and mutual suspicion—to sustained, relatively peaceful cooperation.[74] Driving this change, I argue, were the Monroe administration's *legitimation strategies*, the reasons it gave for its expansionist behavior. As noted above, Monroe and his cabinet entered office in 1817 with equally if not greater revisionist aims than its predecessors. The administration was committed to seizing Florida and securing their northern and southern boundaries against encroachment from the European empires. With South American in rebellion, they saw the potential to dominate the Western Hemisphere, and reap the economic and political benefits that would come from recognizing the Spanish colonies as independent states. And, ultimately, they aspired to expand westward to the Pacific, laying claim to their "natural dominion" over the entire "Continent of North America."[75]

What was new were not the aims themselves but the reasons the administration used to justify expansion. Previous administrations had adopted revolutionary rhetoric: since at least Jefferson's presidency, officials had justified their expansion into Spanish territory through appeals to republican principles. In this narrative, the United States was expanding, not to reinforce a European order, but to overturn it and set in its place a fundamentally revolutionary, republican system, an "empire of liberty" that would stretch throughout the Western Hemisphere if not the globe.[76] It was in the name of a republican empire that Jefferson called on Americans to look westward in his inaugural address, to expand their "chosen country" where there could be "room enough for our descendants to the thousandth and thousandth generation."[77] Likewise, it was in the name of republican principles that the United States would challenge the existing colonial economic order and look to impose a "vision of a new world order based on free trade."[78]

In contrast, from 1817 to 1823 the Monroe administration, while still claiming to uphold republican principles, legitimated their expansion into Spanish territory as necessary to uphold Britain's vision of an international legal regime, taking particular care to invoke the norms of self-defense, treaty law, and nonintervention at the core of Britain's nascent "Atlantic system." In doing so U.S. leaders convinced British elites and their public that the United States was a rule-abiding nation: a revisionist power, to be sure, but one poised to uphold the institutional order of world politics. While these legitimation strategies dominated the Monroe administration's defense of expansion into Spanish territory from 1817 to 1823, two particular moments of crisis are noteworthy: Jackson's invasion of Florida in 1817 and 1818, and the U.S. decision to recognize the Spanish colonies as independent and declare the Western Hemisphere closed to colonization. Jackson's invasion provoked a crisis.[79] Regarding the invasion of Florida, the British government and public were furious over what it saw as flagrant violations of international law, not to mention the execution of its own citizens in a backwoods court-martial. No wonder that, as Adams wrote in his diary, to "justify the measures of this government . . . and as far as possible the proceedings of General Jackson" was a task "of the highest order: may I not be found inferior to it!"[80] In South America, the Monroe administration sought to recognize the rebels as independent nations without provoking mobilization from Spain and its European allies. If Britain believed the United States intended a republican revolution in South American, containment and confrontation were likely.

Why did American rhetoric proved so effective? Why would "cheap talk" exert such influence on British grand strategy? Rationalists might suggest that rhetoric was a costly signal, one that accurately conveyed that the United States was a "limited aims" revisionist and not a revolutionary power. On the face of it, this is an good description of the effects of American rhetoric: Britain did interpret American rhetoric as a credible signal, as an indicator that the United States would pursue limited aims and accept the British order. But it remains unclear *why* rhetoric would have these effects. Rhetoric was not a costly constraint on American ambitions. As argued below, the Monroe administration carefully calibrated its language to use both legal and republican principles, purposefully keeping republican and other expansionist coalitions sated at home. If anything, American legitimation strategies should have induced significant *uncertainty* among British leaders and their publics, providing evidence that the United States had not yet decided to abandon its revolutionary game.

American leaders' rhetoric was effective, not because of its cost, but because of its resonance. On the one hand, the United States leaders, especially Monroe and Adams, had the capacity for multivocal legitimation strategies: they had both the content and the position to frame their actions as legitimate to a diverse set of coalitions. On the other hand, British politicians were institutionally vulnerable, prone to listen to American claims, even if they were cheap and contradictory. It was this configuration of the characteristics of the speaker and audience, then, that gave American rhetoric its power, to tell the story of their expansion in terms that the British would understand, and ultimately accept as justified.

The analysis below uses primary and secondary documents to trace the development of the Monroe administration's legitimation strategies and their effects on British mobilization. Each of these crises had key moments of legitimation. In the case of the Jackson invasion, it was the Erving letter, written by John Quincy Adams with the purpose of explaining why the United States supported Jackson's invasion of Florida. In the case of the South American rebellions, Monroe's key addresses as well as a series of articles written by Adams in the *National Intelligencer* explaining U.S. policy are key to understanding this process.[81] To place each of these categories of statements in their larger context, I supplemented analysis of these specific communications with a content analysis of articles and editorials published by the *National Intelligencer* from 1817 to 1823 to establish the content of the Monroe administration's legitimation strategies. The *National Intelligencer* was not only the dominant paper of Washington, DC, but was considered the official outlet of the Monroe administration. Contemporaries in the United States and Britain treated legitimations in this paper as official justifications of U.S. policy.

To analyze the effects of legitimation on collective mobilization, I relied on both media accounts and unpublished documents in Britain's public records office. For the former, I looked at newspapers ranging from those sympathetic to the United States and a policy of accommodation (the *Morning Chronicle*) and those outlets pushing for a policy of containment and confrontation (the *Courier* and, under some circumstances, the *Times*). Parliamentary debates are also included in the analysis. Archival research focused primarily on the papers of Castlereagh, who both asked for and received intelligence about American statements through Charles Bagot, the British ambassador in Washington, as well as through other trusted intermediaries.

THE PRAGMATIC REVOLUTIONARY: THE MONROE ADMINISTRATION AND MULTIVOCAL RHETORIC

In chapter 2, I argued that rising powers often face a significant dilemma, that legitimation strategies designed to appeal to a great power audience will likely appear illegitimate to their domestic audience, and vice versa. To successfully expand, then, a rising power needs to undercut international mobilization against its efforts while at the same time mobilizing its own domestic resources behind its revisionist policies. Such was the dilemma faced by the Monroe administration. To Britain, leaders needed to frame U.S. expansion into Spanish territory as consistent with international norms and principles. In particular, the United States needed to look as though it was working within the norms of the "Atlantic system"—the economic, political, and social order Britain was constructing in the Western Hemisphere.[82] As in Europe, "Westphalian" principles provided the foundation of this system. States must recognize and respect norms of nonintervention, promising not to interfere in the domestic affairs of other states, to use violence, or pursue conquest without just cause. Trade was not "liberal" in the contemporary sense of the term—colonial and mercantilist practices continued to dominate—but it was governed through a set of rules that regulated shipping and protected against piracy. Much of the political order of the Atlantic remained colonial, with Britain claiming territories throughout the Caribbean. The British hoped to impose a normative order as well, particularly in its efforts to regulate and ultimately eliminate the slave trade.

To sate the British, the Americans had to frame their expansion in the terms of this Atlantic order. Yet appealing to only international principles was dangerous. If the Monroe administration hoped to justify its expansion to its domestic audience, it had to legitimate its actions as revolutionary, as driven by republican principles. Republican factions, led by Henry Clay, stood poised to condemn the Monroe administration if they appeared to kowtow to Britain and its Atlantic order. In concrete terms, Clay's expansionist aims differed little from those of the administration: he and his factions argued that the United States should press westward, and recognize the rebellious Spanish colonies. In other words, all the same material aims that Monroe's government embraced. But Clay's faction insisted that the United States pursue these aims *in the name of* revolutionary and republican principles, that the United States must create a unique *American* system. If expansion threatened to undercut Republican principles, then revisionist policies should be abandoned: expansion was not an end in and of itself.

To appeal across these audiences, the Monroe administration adopted a multivocal strategy, merging Atlantic world legal appeals with republican language to justify American ambitions. United States' leaders, Monroe and Adams in particular, were well positioned to make multivocal claims: both at home and abroad, these leaders bridged revolutionary and conservative coalitions and held ties with key republican and European actors. Monroe had impeccable republican credentials. He was a founding father, the last of the Virginia dynasty that epitomized republican principles. He served as secretary of state under Madison, so could claim to have defended those principles against British incursions with force. At the same time, Monroe had positioned himself as defender of international law, an advocate of squaring republican rights within, not outside, the European system. In Jefferson's administration, he served as the U.S. Minister to the Court of St. James, where his primary task was to negotiate an extension of the Jay Treaty and stabilize relations between the United States and Britain. While he succeeded in reaching an agreement, Jefferson refused to seek ratification of the treaty, believing it undermined core republican principles. From that point on, Monroe emerged as a vocal critic of radical, revolutionary elements in his party. Adams was perhaps even more of a Sphinx than Monroe. Here again, no one could doubt his revolutionary credentials: he was the son of the second president, and a defector from the Federalist to the Republican Party. But his republicanism was also "tempered by years of residence in Europe." Adams had spent two years in London during the negotiations to end the War of 1812, where he negotiated consistently with Castlereagh over the terms of the treaty. As a result of Adams's connections "he was never truly 'at home' anywhere. Ideologically Adams was neither democratic nor aristocrat. He never identified fully with any political party."[83]

These complex political positions gave Monroe and Adams the authority to appeal to multiple principles. In expanding into Spanish territory, leaders insisted that United States was acting both as a republican power and as a law-abiding "European" nation, its actions fully in line with existing norms in the international system. The use of multivocal appeals was both consistent and systematic. I used a qualitative content analysis program to look at articles in the *National Intelligencer* from 1817 to 1823 reporting U.S. policy in Spanish Florida and toward the South American colonies. I coded thirty-two articles published during the crisis, identifying sixty-nine "legitimating phrases" that offered reasons explaining U.S. actions in each of these territories. I classified these legitimating phrases into three categories: "law of nations," which included appeals to customary and treaty law; "self-defense"; and "republican principles." Appeals to the "laws of nations" accounted for about 40 percent of the legitimating phrases. Claims of self-defense accounted for another 39 percent of legitimating claims. The rest of the legitimating phrases refer to republican principles as guiding U.S. policies toward Spanish territories and colonies.[84]

These patterns of legitimation are apparent in each episode of U.S. efforts to expand into the faltering Spanish empire. In the defense of Jackson's invasion of Florida, Adams realized the necessity of a multivocal legitimation strategy. As he wrote in his memoirs, "The administration were [*sic*] placed in a dilemma from which it is impossible to escape censure by some, and factious crimination by many. If they avow and approve Jackson's conduct, they incur the double responsibility of having commenced a war against Spain, and of warring in violation of the Constitution without the authority of Congress. If they disavow him they must give offence to all his friends." To justify U.S. expansion, Adams crafted a multivocal legitimation that simultaneously proclaimed Jackson a republican patriot, but also insisted that his use of force—the brutal treatment of the Creeks, the occupation of Spanish territory, even the execution of British subjects—was justified both by treaty law and by norms of nonintervention. To a domestic audience, as Weeks argues, Adams cast Jackson as a hero in "the context of the mythic American struggle against the wiles of foreign intrigues and the 'uncivilized' natures of 'inferior' races.'"[85] Jackson's motives, Adams insisted, were beyond reproach, "founded in the purest patriotism . . . as well as in the first law of nature—self defense."[86]

To the British, Adam's public campaign took the form of a series of formal and informal statements, beginning with diplomatic notes in the summer of 1818 and culminating, most famously, in the "Erving letter," in November 1818, a letter circulated among all of the courts of Europe. His correspondence was published both in national papers, as well as in major British newspapers, such as the *Times*. In each of these cases, Adams insisted that far from violating international law the United States "identified the Union's expansion with the need to uphold the treaty law upon which the peace of Europe and America ultimately depended."[87] His legitimation strategies used three consistent appeals: justification of conventional law, customary law, and the laws of nature. First, Adams justified the invasion with reference to conventional law, as within the boundaries of existing treaties. The Seminoles, Adams argued, had rejected the "legitimate" Treaty of Fort Jackson signed between Jackson and the Creeks in 1814. They had conducted brutal attacks against unarmed American villages. Jackson's methods might be unsavory, but were they not, as Adams asked, "the dictate of common sense? Is it not the usage of legitimate warfare?"[88]

Second, Adams insisted that the United States was abiding by appropriate customary law, especially norms of nonintervention in its invasion of

Spanish territory. So long as Spain was truly sovereign in Florida, American intervention was unwarranted. Yet Spain, in failing to secure its territory, had failed both in its obligations as a sovereign state, and in its duties to uphold treaty law. Adams argued that Spain might have a right to nonintervention in theory, but it had abandoned its rights once it proved unable to enforce the peace. If Spain could not keep its territory free of "savages" and "pirates," then the United States use of force was vindicated by "every page of the law of nations."[89] Unable to control its American possessions, Spain had allowed the proliferation of "all the pirates and all the traitors to their country" to "wage an exterminating war against the portion of the United States immediately bordering upon this neutral and thus violated territory of Spain."[90] Under such conditions, force—even brutality—was clearly justified.

Third, Adams invoked the laws of nature, especially self-defense and preservation, to justify its claims. Jackson entered Florida in pursuit of an enemy intent on waging "an exterminating war" against the United States.[91] The Creeks and their allies, Adams argued, planned to seize Spanish forts in Florida as use them as base from which to attack the United States. In the face of this threat "by all the laws of neutrality and of war, as well as of prudence and of humanity, [Jackson] was warranted in anticipating his enemy . . . by the forcible occupation of the fort. There will need not citations from printed treatises on international law, to prove the correctness of this principle. It is engraved in adamant on the common sense of mankind: no writer upon the laws of nations ever pretended to contradict it; none of any reputation or authority ever omitted to assert it."[92]

This multivocal language pervaded the legitimation of U.S. policy toward South America as well. Here again, the Monroe administration faced cross-pressures from different audiences. Republicans demanded a new system to replace the European colonial order. "There could not be a doubt that Spanish America, once independent," Clay argued, "would obey the laws of the system of the new world."[93] That the system would be led by the United States, and devoid of European influence, was inevitable: the rebels of South America were "brothers. They adopted our principles, copied our institutions, employed the very language and sentiments of our revolutionary papers."[94] The Monroe administration could not reject revolutionary rhetoric; when they did so, republicans pounced, chastising their government for its "fear of insulting his Britannic majesty."[95]

Here again the solution was a multivocal strategy: the Monroe administration claimed that it would support republican principles in South America, but in ways consistent with existing international law, especially norms of nonintervention and Westphalian sovereignty. Early recognition of the colonies, the Monroe administration argued, would be illegitimate in the eyes of international law. In 1817 the Monroe administration argued that the rebels had not yet met the "essential prerequisites for carrying out the responsibilities and duties of a state under international law—the standard that Adams found it convenient to demand—did not yet exist in Latin America." As argued an editorial in the *National Intelligencer*, "The liberties of South America is indeed a theme well-fitted for the declamations of the demagogues of the day, admirably suited to the display of the oratory of our would-be Demosthenedes and Ciceros," but in reality it was unclear whether the revolutionaries were yet capable of forming a free government.[96] To recognize the South Americans was thus a profound violation of the Atlantic order, and the United States would not undercut "professed principles of non interference with foreign nations in questions of internal government."[97]

At the same time, the Monroe administration argued that its policy of nonrecognition was consistent with *republican* principles as well. Recognition without real self-determination, the administration argued, was tantamount to imposing rule on another people. As Adams wrote, "Among the most precious of the natural rights of man, is the right of the majority, in every political association, to decide for itself in adopting such form of government as it may deem most fitting to promote its happiness and prosperity. . . . To force the nations to be free, is beyond our power, as it is beyond our right."[98] If the United States were to disregard the laws of nations in pursuing revolutionary aims, then it would be behaving no better than Napoleon and he, as one writer intoned, was no "Friend of Liberty." The United States must, as argued in the *National Intelligencer,* "let our pride, as republicans, induce us to show the world, by our practice, that the faith of treaties is no where more strictly observed than under the laws of our republic."[99]

As the Spanish threat waned, so too did the United States see the opportunity for expanding its influence in South America. And if in 1817 the laws of the Atlantic order and republican virtue justified restraint, from 1818 onward this multivocal language could now justify a revisionist foreign policy. Once the South Americans could demonstrate that they were de-facto Westphalian states, recognition was now clearly justified. As Adams argued in 1819, "Now that we are convinced that the power of Spain cannot be restored, we desire Europe to consider how important it is that the new states should be recognized and held in their responsibilities as independent bodies." There was nothing "revolutionary" about this policy: recognition, Adams argued was "a mere acknowledgement of the fact of Independence."[100] Likewise recognition was, in Monroe's words, in strict accord "with the law of nations, that it is just and right as to the parties, and that the United States owe it to their station and character in the word."[101]

Finally, these norms of nonintervention and sovereign order justified more than just recognition of the South American colonies; the United States claimed that they mandated Europe no longer interfere in the Western Hemisphere. As Monroe declared in the doctrine of 1823: "With the *existing Colonies or dependencies of any European power,* we have not interfered, and *shall not interfere.*" Once again, Westphalian principles of nonintervention guided American policy. But the United States would uphold republican principles as well. "But with the Governments who have declared their Independence, and maintained it, and whose Independence we have, on great consideration, and on just principles acknowledged, we could not view any interposition for the purpose of oppressing them, or controuling [*sic*] in any other manner, their destiny, by any European power, in any other light, than as the manifestation of an unfriendly disposition towards the United States."

Here, as Britain and other European powers immediately recognized, was a significantly ambitious, revisionist proclamation: the United States was declaring its dominance over the Western Hemisphere. But as Weeks and others argue, the Monroe Doctrine relied on the same mix of legal and republican rhetoric that it used to justify the Florida invasion, the Transcontinental Treaty, and the recognition of the South American republics[102] The doctrine, Adams insisted, espoused republican principles in accordance with international law: it did not disturb the peace; it did not interfere with other nations; it respected sovereign rights.[103] Indeed, Adams demanded that any illegal, revolutionary language was struck from or at least watered down before Monroe delivered his famous message.[104]

In sum, from 1817 to 1823, the Monroe administration consistently legitimated American ambitions with a multivocal strategy. As argued in chapter 2, however, a capacity for multivocal rhetoric is not enough to stave off containment. Resonance lies not only in what the speaker says, but in what the audience hears a sympathetic audience is also necessary.

A PARTNER FOR PEACE? INSTITUTIONAL VULNERABILITY AND THE ATLANTIC ORDER

As the United States expanded into Spanish territory, the British proved willing to listen to American claims, even if they understood them as multivocal and ambiguous. Legitimations resonated because from 1817 to 1823, Britain was an *institutionally vulnerable* power, one that was eager to see the United States as a potential partner in building a liberal order in the Western Hemisphere. International relations scholars have written extensively on British institution building in the early nineteenth century, but have focused largely on British efforts in Europe, particularly Castlereagh's efforts to bring Britain into the Congress system.[105] But Britain's efforts in Europe to create institutions of liberal governance are only part of the story. In the late eighteenth and early nineteenth century, Britain also made strenuous efforts to construct an "Atlantic Order," attempting to pacify "zones of violence" by exporting a liberal legal framework into the Western Hemisphere.

Throughout the eighteenth century, the Atlantic world was a tumultuous institutional space. In certain places, such as North America, the laws of Europe—such as the Treaty of Utrecht—were argued to govern territorial disputes, commerce, and sovereign claims; in contrast, "zones of violence," such as Indian lands, African polities, and the high seas, existed outside of European legal boundaries. During most of the eighteenth century, moreover, Spain continued to claim "all lands and waters not explicitly ceded to other European powers," rejecting the application of international law to zones over which it perceived it held exclusive sovereignty.[106] As the Spanish Empire collapsed, Britain saw an opportunity to strengthen what Castlereagh referred to as the emerging "liberal system" in the Atlantic world.[107] As Onuf and Gould write, the British saw the possibility of governing the Atlantic "not as an inherently imperial space but as a region that could be organized as a system of independent states, an international regime defined by free trade and the rule of law."[108]

Britain was deeply invested in the success of these Atlantic institutions, believing that a stable Atlantic system was necessary for Britain's economic, security, and even moral interests. Castlereagh argued that only through an institutionalized order in the Atlantic could Britain ensure peace and material prosperity.[109] As a nation built on laws, leaders believed that a liberal, legal system must follow the path of Britain's expanding might. "Let an Englishman go where he will," argued the legal counsel of the Admiralty, and "he carries as much of law and liberty with him, as the nature of things will bear."[110] So essential was the order to British interests that elites were willing to implement it through "persuasion, coercion, or interest"—that is to say, through moral suasion, by providing economic incentives and, if necessary through punishment or the use of force.[111]

Britain thus was invested in building the institutional architecture of the Atlantic order. British leaders also perceived the order as extremely unsettled. It was, to begin with, a relatively new order, its norms deeply contested. As one historian argues, the revolutions of the Atlantic world—the American, Haitian, and now Spanish American rebellions—posed a "direct threat to the existing social order in the Caribbean."[112] In 1815, the British continued to view republicanism as an existential threat to its legal order, an expression of popular will with no respect for existing legal architecture. Britain was simultaneously threatened by a conservative, European threat to the legal order, as Russia, Austria, and Prussia—the Holy Alliance—were pressing against the legal norms of nonintervention that, to the British mind, formed the core of the Atlantic system, if not the international system as a whole.[113] Far from eschewing intervention in sovereign states, the Holy Alliance—especially Russia's Tsar Alexander—argued that the use of force to stem the rising tide of republican principles was both necessary and legitimate. In the Western Hemisphere, Britain's conflict with the Holy Alliance over the norms of intervention was no abstract affair; the Spanish decline in the Western Hemisphere following rebellions served as a crucible for this brewing conflict. From 1818 onward, Tsar Alexander pressed his European allies for military intervention wherever the forces of revolution were posed to unseat a legitimist government, and republican revolutionaries of the Western Hemisphere absorbed much of his attention. In the months leading up to the Congress of Aix-la-Chapelle, for example, Russian diplomats pressed to have Spain included among the great powers, so that the failing empire could plead its case for European intervention in South America. By 1823, the Holy Alliance was once again threatening to intervene in South America on Spain's behalf, with or without British support.[114]

Britain believed the consequences of intervention would be substantial. Its leaders feared that its European allies, including Spain, would use intervention to undercut the emerging liberal trade system in the Atlantic. As Castlereagh wrote to Wellesley in March 1817, Spain and its European allies had not made "any distinct avowal of the basis of the system upon it is willing to act" or articulated any "general principles of its own."[115] Without a clear commitment to liberal principles, Britain feared that Spain would seek to reinstate its own colonial order in the Atlantic world. The British also feared the European powers posed a moral threat to the Atlantic order. Castlereagh and Canning, for example, railed against Spain's refusal to abandon the slave trade in the Atlantic, fearing a Spanish victory would perpetuate the existence of "so odious a system as the Slave Trade" which "continued to disgrace the times in which we lived."[116]

In short, throughout the early eighteenth and nineteenth centuries, Britain was institutionally vulnerable. It was deeply invested in building a liberal international system in the Atlantic, a "region that could be organized as a system of independent states, an international regime defined by free trade and the rule of law,"[117] yet worried that this system was under increasing threat. Under these conditions, it is not surprising that American appeals to legal and liberal principles resonated with the great power. Even if the United States appeared a revisionist power, it looked like one inclined to support the Atlantic order. For this reason, the Monroe administration's rhetoric had powerful effects on British policy. Its multivocal appeals, with its promises to adhere to norms of noninterference, self-defense, and legal procedure, and yet not overturn republican principles, proved deeply resonant to the British audience.

Legitimation and the Politics of Collective Mobilization: Restraint, Coercion, and Identity

Between 1817 and 1823, the way in which the United States legitimated its ambitions proved strongly resonant: the U.S. capacity for multivocality, combined the British institutional vulnerability, proved a potent combination. By portraying its revisionist actions as legitimate, the United States drove the British away from policies of confrontation and containment, and persuaded the great power to accommodate American expansion into Spanish territory. British leaders and their public came to believe the U.S. justifications signaled restraint, that the United States would not mobilize to overturn the Atlantic order. Critics of conciliation in Britain, moreover, were silenced: both British elites opposed to accommodation, and European powers demanding containment of U.S. ambitions, found themselves stripped of reasons to mobilize against the emerging power. And finally, the normative appeals of Monroe's administration resonated with Britain's identity as a liberal power, a resonance that forced Britain to act, not merely on the basis of interest, but on the foundations of principle as well.

SIGNALING RESTRAINT AND CONSTRAINT

It was not a given that the British would view U.S. expansion as consistent with international norms, and both the case of the Florida invasion and the recognition of the Spanish colonies demonstrate the importance of American rhetoric in signaling constraint. Jackson's invasion, for example, sparked a fierce outcry, both within and outside of the British government. Britain and the European powers quickly condemned Jackson's invasion as an act of war against Spain.[118] The *Courier* seethed that "as the capture of Pensacola is no longer doubtful, we may now hope to know why it has been seized . . . the causes which reduced America to the necessity of seeking from war what she could not obtain by negotiation."[119] The *Caledonian Mercury*, a paper traditionally more sympathetic to the United States, condemned the "obscure Court-Martial of American officers, holding their sittings in the back woods of their half cultivated country. Who empowered them to constitute this new and capital offence in the law of nations?"[120]

At best, some argued that Jackson's invasion signaled a nation out of control, a weak state unable to contain its most extreme, violent, and expansionist elements. Indeed, British officials first assumed Jackson's invasion was unauthorized, that Jackson had acted, as Bagot first reported to Castlereagh, "in open contempt of the Executive Authority of the Country."[121] This interpretation was not comforting: it suggested a fragmented government incapable of fulfilling its duties under treaty and international law. At worst, Britain worried that "Jackson's invasion of Florida and his execution of two Englishmen reflected impatient, self-confident American nationalism," one that could not be contained within acceptable limits.[122] There was no guarantee that the United States would stop its territorial advance in Florida. Far from indicating that the United States had limited aims, the British "feared that the Florida triumph would lead to further American projects."[123] Jackson's invasion, in short, was seen as a costly signal of revolutionary revisionist ambitions.

The situation, as Bagot assessed, was of a "grave character."[124] Although Castlereagh preferred to continue his policy of appeasement, even counseling Bagot to avoid talking about the crisis with Adams for fear of "rupture," the crisis placed serious pressure on the foreign minister's policy. In the face of the invasion, British politicians and papers were calling for a full suspension of diplomatic relations. Lord Liverpool noted to Castlereagh that, in light of "General Jackson's conduct" it is "difficult to draw the closer ties of friendship and connexion between the two countries, by concluding the treaties which are in progress."[125] Spain charged that the invasion was no less than an act of war and demanded a hearing at the upcoming European conference at Aix-la-Chappelle.

By the end of 1818 tensions between the United States and Britain were escalating. Castlereagh and Bagot argued that a suitable justification of the invasion was critical to defusing the crisis. "I look with considerable anxiety to the arrival of the next mail from America," Castlereagh wrote, in hopes that he could assure the Prince Regent that "the conduct of [the American] government and its officers . . . would be found free of reproach." Castlereagh stressed the importance of the Monroe administration providing an appropriate justification for its actions and pressed Bagot to ask for "Mr. Adams' assistance in furnishing me with the means of removing a misconception on a subject which so much interests the public feeling."[126] British newspapers agreed that only a clear justification could signal restraint and diffuse the crisis. The *Courier* outlined the stakes most succinctly when it wrote that "there are so many advantages, political, commercial and territorial, which would accrue to America by her possession of the Floridas, that when we find her grasping at them, we are naturally *suspicious about motives*."[127] It was thus up to "the Washington Cabinet, to satisfy the world *that it had not be actuated by unprincipled ambition*."[128]

What Adams gave to the British was not costly. True that the Monroe administration offered to pull Jackson's troops out of Florida, but it had already demonstrated that the United States could invade Florida at will: demobilization, in short, was hardly credible. Rather it was Adams's appeals to international law—both in his communications in the summer of 1818 and in his infamous Erving letter of November 1818—that "stayed the hand of the British government."[129] Upon reading Adams's defense of Jackson, Castlereagh made no secret of his continued distaste for Jackson's action, that the invasion, and especially the execution of British citizens, was "harsh and unwarrantable."[130] But he agreed that the United States had acted within the confines of international law, that it was Jackson's targets that had engaged in "unauthorized practices" that "deprived them of any claim on their own Government for interference in their behalf."[131]

Bemis argues that in "Europe the effect of Adams's paper was electrical."[132] The once outraged press conceded that the invasion of Florida was within the boundaries international law. If, for example, Adams's charges against Ambrister and Arbuthnot were true, then the *Courier* conceded that "their fate was such as the law of nations warrants."[133] Even more significantly, Adams's justifications were read as a clear signal that the Americans could be bound to the European system, perhaps even more than the so-called "legitimist" states within Europe itself. As the *Morning Chronicle* proclaimed, the American republic, in appealing to international law, had shown itself constrained by institutions, because "if *power alone* were to regulate the issue, nothing could be more easy than for America, particularly in the present embarrassment of Spain, to retain possession of the territory which she has occupied. How different the conduct of this great Republic from the avaricious though purblind Legitimates of Europe!"[134] Through careful justification, Adams had portrayed Jackson's act of war as bound by international law, and a signal that the republic would not mobilize to overturn the existing rules of the international order.

It is difficult to say what might have happened in the absence of Adams's defense, what the counterfactual world would look like if Adams's Erving letter had not appeared. Historians suggest that Castlereagh's warning to Rush that, without Adams's justification, war could have occurred if the ministry had "HELD UP A FINGER" was exaggerated, and neither the cabinet nor British public was eager for another war with the United States. But it is likely that, in the absence of the Erving letter and legal justification for expansion, accommodation would have been far less likely. The British public was clamoring for retribution against the execution of its citizens. The British media was calling for Britain to stand firm against American outrages. It was precisely these conditions that pressed Britain toward war in 1812. Adams's signal of restraint was critical in showing the United States was not mobilizing for revolutionary action: it tamped down dangerous political dynamics and allowed for the pursuit accommodation.[135]

The Monroe administration's rhetoric signaled restraint and constraint in the crisis over South America as well. Exchanges between Castlereagh and his ministers—especially his minister to the United States, Charles Bagot, and minister to Spain, Wellesley—suggest significant uncertainty about whether the United States would uphold international law in South America, or if it would be compelled by its republican ideology to prematurely recognize the revolutionary states. Recognition on revolutionary grounds was deeply problematic. The invocation of republican principles threatened the fabric of the Atlantic order. Such rhetoric suggested the Americans would build in South America a system, as declared by Clay, "animated by an American feeling, and guided by an American policy. They would obey the *laws of the system of the new world*, of which they would compose a part, in contradistinction to that of Europe."[136]

As argued above, Monroe and Adams made it clear to Castlereagh that a policy of recognition was only matter of time, but promised that, when it came, it would be consistent with international law. The British government took notice of the Americans' deliberate language. Bagot wrote to Castlereagh about the "remarkable change that has taken place lately in the language held by the government newspapers," noting specifically the rejection of revolutionary rhetoric in support of the revolting colonies.[137] British observers argued that this language signaled restraint, that the United States was purposively not mobilizing its republican factions. As Castlereagh wrote to Wellesley, if the United States could be steered away from a revolutionary game then "it might be yet *kept within the limits* which ought in good sense and sound Principle to guide the Principal powers of Europe, in any intervention they might take in those concerns."[138] Central to these "sound principles," Castlereagh (and Canning after him argued) was noninterference: to recognize and refrain from violating the rights of sovereign states to determine their own destiny, except when necessitated by self-defense. The principles would bind the United States, not only in the present, but in the future. If the United States could be bound to this principle, Castlereagh believed that "the United States might not only be prevented from breaking loose upon this question, but that the interest and influence of that State might be brought to operate powerfully in repressing order in that Quarter [the Western Hemisphere]."[139]

Likewise when Monroe announced that the United States would recognize the Spanish colonies in 1822, it was a policy deemed not only legitimate, but a signal of continued restraint, a promise to be bound by international principles. Commenting on Monroe's announcement, the *Times* noted that Monroe was right that "the fact of sovereignty is indeed the only *general* test of the right of sovereignty" and thus "the principle which has been adduced to justify [recognition] cannot, we apprehend, be fairly controverted with any regard to common sense, or to the law of nations."[140] Even the Monroe Doctrine that followed was viewed, not as a statement of revolution, but a profound exclamation of restraint. As Bemis argues, Monroe had promised that "while espousing the republican principle, it had not sought by the propagation of its own principles to disturb the peace or to intermeddle with the policy of any part of Europe."[141] It was, as Ernest May argues, both an expression of continental hegemony, and a clear rejection of ideological empire, a sign that the United States would limit its expansion within the boundaries of Britain's Atlantic order.[142]

RHETORICAL COERCION: SILENCING CALLS FOR CONFRONTATION

Not everyone believed the United States could be bound by legitimate principles. Both in Britain and in other European countries, there were those that believed the United States was a rapacious, revisionist power, one that could not be appeased but must be confronted, even at the risk of war. Spain, not surprisingly, protested United States expansion loudly. The United States,

Spain charged, was a danger to the European order, a state "always anxious to promote rebellion and perfidy."[143] Whatever gestures the administration might make to international law, it was clear, as Onís charged in 1817, the United States was a potential juggernaut, stealing land and encouraging settlement that would ultimately spell the doom of the European states. Europe must stand ready to thwart America's plan "of extending the limits of this Republic toward the South, and then of realizing its great Project of reaching the Pacific Ocean. I confess to you that I cannot comprehend how the Powers of Europe fail to awaken from their lethargy on seeing the extraordinary steps of this Republic, and how they can fail to see that it will be too late when they wish to place limits on it, if they allow it to take the flight on which its political actions are rapidly leading it."[144] Within Britain there were fierce critics of appeasement who loudly protested Castlereagh's policy. "I wish, sir, some person would show what quality it is in the disposition of the United States toward Great Britain that gives them a title to become the most favored government on this globe," sniffed a prominent critic of conciliation.[145] It was not merely that accommodation was undeserved; it was dangerous.

But the American government's appeals to international law would, if not persuade their critics, then at least silence them: by invoking institutional norms, the Monroe administration effectively denied their opponents a legitimate basis from which to oppose expansion. As a result, as Gould argues, "the ability of Americans to turn the legal rights of peace to their advantage repeatedly served as a check on the ability of Britain and Europe's other powers to intervene in the Union's affairs."[146] The dynamics of rhetorical coercion are best seen in the Monroe administration's defense of the invasion of Florida. Domestic critics of appeasement pounced at the chance, not only to condemn Jackson's conduct, but to argue that the whole policy of conciliation was based on faulty assumptions of American restraint. In Britain, the *Courier* led the charge, claiming Jackson's actions were consistent with the character of a republican government: "It has pleased the Republican Cabinet to abandon the old fashioned policy of legitimate Monarchies, and to model its proceedings upon the repulsive practice of NAPOLEON, who first invaded, and then condescended to explain."[147] In its invasion of Florida, the United States had violated "the established practices of civilised states with regards to the commencement of hostilities against other powers."[148] The *Times* spat that the United States had taken Florida in a *"fit of aggression* . . . without war or provocation." Adams's words did not impress them; he was engaged only in "political chicanery" to justify Jackson's violence.[149]

In the wake of the invasion, the British opposition demanded Castlereagh and the government defend their policy of appeasing the expanding American power. In the House of Lords, Lord Lansdowne proclaimed that he could not condone Jackson's "departure from the law of nations, and the introduction into warfare of a barbarous practice, subversive of the principles of humanity, by which civilized states were governed." While he did not charge that the U.S. government had sanctioned Jackson's cruel actions, especially the execution of British citizens, he argued that this clear evidence of unbridled expansion demanded a British response. American expansion, he argued, clearly undercut British interest; indeed "no colonial cession so materially affecting the interests of this country had ever before taken place. . . . How did it happen that ministers had been unable to prevent this cession? Why was such an event not guarded against by the treaties concluded at the peace?" By standing by while the United States wrenched Florida from Spain, moreover, it had acquiesced in an act "so violent and unjustifiable, and which tended to establish principles which, if admitted, would produce, a change in the law of nations most unfavourable to humanity."[150]

Adams's rhetoric stripped such assaults of their bite. After hearing Adams's justifications for the invasion, editors at the *Morning Chronicle* chided the *Courier*, noting that they had "told the *Courier* not to pass sentence of condemnation on America, merely because she had a *Republican* government, but to judge of her acts their own merit or demerit."[151] In light of Adams's declarations, the *Morning Chronicle* declared, it was clear that the invasion of Florida was justified. The *Courier*'s charges were not only imprudent, risking an unnecessary conflict with the United States, they were hypocritical, supporting not the rule of law but "crimes of Europe," the unjustified conquest practiced by the so-called "legitimate Monarchies."[152] Lansdowne, too, found himself silenced. His peer, the Earl of Bathurst, argued that Jackson had acted within "a principle admitted by the law of nations, and which in the policy of nations had been frequently adopted." Could his colleague then make a case "which would justify involving the two countries [Britain and the United States] in war"?[153]

Spain too now lacked the rhetorical resources to mobilize a European alliance against U.S. expansion. In the years before the invasion, Spain's ministers had charged the United States with "perverting the clearest sense of treaties" in pursuing its expansion westward and into Florida.[154] In demanding Spanish territory, America had engaged "in manifest violation of the law of nations, employed alternately artifice and violence, and an audacity scarcely comparable to that of Bonaparte during his violent usurpations."[155] Spain hoped to press its case for aid against the United States, galvanizing support both on the North American continent, and in its struggle to retain control over its South American colonies. A flurry of diplomatic correspondence followed the seizure of Pensacola and St. Marks. Jackson's invasion, Pizarro proclaimed, was predicated on nothing but "aggrandizement." In the face of unjustified expansion, Pizarro asked whether it was time for Britain "to interpose in this business in a more effectual manner," either through direct mediation, or by allowing Spain to present its case at Aix-la-Chapelle. Another Spanish representative noted that the Monroe administration was clearly attempting a "total separation affected by that Govt. from the principles which direct the general system of Europe . . . as it lays down a system of its own which begins to develop itself with sufficient rapidity." If Britain did not act on behalf of Spain, it risked appeasing a United States which "in its future extent and projects aims perhaps not only at the humiliation of Spain but at the ruin of the whole system of Europe."[156]

Castlereagh ultimately dismissed Spanish charges against the United States, arguing that Britain had no treaty obligation to come to Spain's aid, and that Aix-la-Chapelle had no reason to take up the issue of Florida or the Spanish colonies. It may be tempting to reduce Castlereagh's response to the pressures of interest. As noted above, Britain had no interest in risking conflict with the United States in the service of Spain. Yet accommodation was hardly assured. Castlereagh had suggested in the past that Britain might want to keep Spain in Florida as a check on growing American power. As he wrote, "Were Great Britain to look to its own interest alone . . . we have an obvious motive for desiring that the Spanish continue to be our neighbours in East Florida, rather than our West Indian possessions be so closely approached by the territory of the United States."[157] Britain might be able to assure this outcome if it insisted on mediating the Spanish-American dispute. Moreover, although Britain sought cooperation with the United States, Castlereagh feared a rupture with Spain or, perhaps more importantly, with the Holy Alliance states more sympathetic to Spain's plight in South America.

As long as the United States was acting legitimately, there was no need for Britain to mobilize against American aggression. Indeed Adams's defense made Castlereagh's ability to mobilize support for accommodation, if not an easy, then a far simpler task. Spain, in the wake of Adams's claims "could not use the situation to gain easy advantage in the court of public opinion."[158] As Bemis argues, "Adams's paper had mollified a hostile reaction of the European government to which Spain had protested the enormity of Jackson's invasion. In England, it had an especially healthy result."[159] And if the U.S. invasion was justified, then Onís and Pizarro had no legitimate grounds on which to ask for European aid—the charge that Spain's rights as a sovereign nation had been violated was its only sound case for European intervention. If Spain could not show that its sovereign rights had been violated, then it had no other reason to ask for support. Indeed, Castlereagh had long castigated Spain for failing to provide sound principles on which to argue for European intervention, either in North or South America.[160] He noted that when Spain had provided cause for intervention—such as when Portugal violated Spain's rights in South America—Europe had been quick to respond.[161] But without a case for intervention, Britain—and the rest of Europe—would stand aside in the conflict.

THE TIES THAT BIND? LIBERAL RHETORIC AND THE POLITICS OF IDENTITY

As argued earlier, scholars suggest that Britain's policy of conciliation stemmed from forces far deeper than those of material power and interest, and was ultimately embedded in a sense of shared identity. But at the start of the nineteenth century, this sense of shared identity was thin. British and Americans believed that their two states shared a common kinship and cultural heritage, but these had been eclipsed by the differences in their nations' social and political systems. The United States, as an article in the *Quarterly Review* declared, was embarked on an "experiment, to see, with how little government, with how few institutions, and at how cheap a rate men may be kept together in a society. Is this a safe experiment? Can it possibly be a successful one?"[162] Travelers' accounts published in the journal described Americans as "civilized barbarian[s]," as a country populated by "swarms of emigrants, renegadoes, and refugees," a nation not "worthy of their parentage."[163] Nor did Americans feel a kinship with their English brethren. Rush declared that England was "no more republican than Turkey" and that its elites were entirely "hostile to republican ideas."[164] Adams, writing to his father from London, warned that "the Royalists everywhere detest and despise us as Republicans. . . . Emperors, kings, princes, priests, all the privileged orders, all the establishments, all the votaries of legitimacy eye us with the most rancourous hatred."[165]

This conflict of identity was not limited to abstract arguments over liberal principles or outburst of nationalist rhetoric; it manifested consistently and clearly in clashes over foreign policy. For example, America's republican identity, Bukovansky argues, pressed the United States into conflict with Britain over the issue of neutral rights, particularly the right of neutral nations to trade with belligerents during wartime.[166] And in the question over the status of the Spanish colonies, questions of identity and principle, at first, seemed to drive the United States and Britain into irreconcilable positions.[167] Britain and the United States shared a commitment to creating a liberal system of trade with the South American colonies, a significant confluence of interest Castlereagh stressed in his negotiations with the United States. But Britain would not—indeed, it could not—support the creation of revolutionary republics. Britain's ideological opposition to republicanism left little room for negotiation with the United States. Reporting on a conversation with Castlereagh about the South American colonies, Rush reported that there was a "fundamental point of difference" rooted in the fact that, for the United States, the policy toward the Spanish American independence must be founded in the "cause of human liberty in the new hemisphere."[168]

At the start of Monroe's administration, this ideological clash meant that containment remained a sound policy. As Castlereagh wrote to Wellesley,

Britain "had the greatest possible interest in faithfully executing the Engagements which bind us to uphold the integrity of the Spanish Monarchy."[169] On the one hand, Castlereagh worked to persuade Spain and the rest of the Concert powers to create a European solution to the rebellion, arguing that Spain's best option was the creation of liberal constitutional monarchies in South America that would remain bound to the Spanish empire. As one historian argues, if this plan "were adopted, South America would be united with the old world rather than with the United States, and a tory government would not have to submit to the painful necessity of recognizing republicanism."[170] At the same time, Castlereagh hoped to "prevent the United States from recognizing a group of new republican nations, so incompatible with the world of restored legitimitist monarchies."[171]

The Monroe administration's rhetoric struck hard at Britain's liberal identity: not only should Britain abandon containment, it should embrace recognition as the only policy consistent with Britain's own principles.[172] From 1818 onward, Adams made multiple approaches to Castlereagh to see if Britain not only would accept U.S. recognition, but if it would work in concert to recognize and uphold the independence of the South American rebels. In his appeals to the foreign minister, Adams argued that Britain must allow the recognition of South America, not merely as a matter of interest, but as a matter of right. The colonies, Adams argued, had achieved de facto independence. They had earned the right of recognition, and any denial of this amounted to unlawful intervention and subjugation.[173]

Perhaps most boldly, Adams suggested that Britain's refusal to recognize the colonies left them in league with the Holy Alliance, the conservative, dynastic alliance of Russia, Austria, and Prussia. Europe, as Adams told Stratford Canning in 1820, was in the midst of a great ideological struggle. "The scepters of all the European continental monarchs were turning to ashes in their hands. . . . Would it be possible for England to witness this in all its consequences and remain quiescent? And how could it act in cases where the struggle, as it now appears, is for free and liberal institutions against absolute power?"[174] This flagrant violation of principles of nonintervention and suppression of liberty, Adams argued, stood contrary to Britain's most valued principles:

> Britain has separated herself from the councils and measures of the alliance. She avows the principles which are emphatically those of the United States, and she disapproves the principles of the alliance which this country abhors. This coincidence of principles, connected with the great changes in affairs of the world, passing before us, seems to me a suitable occasion for the United States and great Britain to compare their ideas and purposes together, with a view to the accommodation of great interests upon which they have hitherto differed.[175]

The more the battle for South America appeared a conflict between "autocracy and parliamentary government," the more the British saw the United States as a liberal partner in the Western Hemisphere. The British domestic audience placed immense pressure on British to support the United States, not merely out of interest, but because it was consistent with Britain's liberal identity. As the *Morning Chronicle* argued, Britain had both interests and principles at stake in South America and while "we have hitherto appealed only to mere profit and loss . . . we say nothing of the infamy of forwarding the plans of the grand confederacy for the destruction of liberty throughout Europe. . . . But surely England is not so low in the moral scale, as to be indifferent to all but mere profit and loss."[176] Rather "the British government, as head of the civilized world, ought to assist rather than oppose the nations who endeavour to render themselves free. . . . In Europe there is at present a conspiracy against the expansion of the human mind, and against the liberties of the human race. By opposing this spirit, England will render her own freedom more secure, and her character illustrious."[177] The more conservative *Times* agreed. The Holy Alliance, they argued, pressured Britain to withhold recognition, yet "to us the struggle of the South Americans has been that of common sense and manifest necessity against blind arrogance and the unteachable spirit of oppression. For England . . . her duties are in accordance with her clearest interests."[178]

Indeed the papers, as the *Morning Chronicle* noted, were almost united in their opinion that recognition was the only policy in line with British principles and interests ("the chief Newspaper warfare is not between Ministerial and Opposition Journals, but between the Ministerial Journals of London and Paris," the editors remarked).[179] Once engaged in a "warfare of the mind," papers now expressed almost universal admiration of the United States, and the Monroe administration's growing willingness to recognize the South American states, and stressed the natural unity between the United States and British causes. The *Morning Chronicle* praised the "example of America, which is fortunately beyond the reach of the Holy Alliance, and with which our connexion is necessarily so intimate, will always remain as a warning and instruction to us." The *Times* exhorted the government to unite with the "confederacy of free states beyond the ocean; and to frustrate those projects which aim at the destruction of a great first principle common to the institutions both of America and England."[180] The Monroe administration's appeals resonated among elites' sense of identity as well. Stratford Canning wrote to his cousin of Adams's appeals, of his insistence that the United States and Britain could move along "parallel lines," champions of constitutionalism and international law in their respective hemispheres.[181]

Even in the wake of the Monroe Doctrine, the British public approved of the liberal principles that underpinned Monroe's proclamation. As the *Times* noted, the British public had anxiously awaited a statement of U.S. policy: "The foreign relations of the United States are at this moment so deeply involved with those of Europe, of South America, and of England, that we turned impatiently to that division of the Message, and it well repaid us." On Monroe's policy, the paper declared that it was "plain speaking, and it is just thinking." Europe had no cause for interference on Spain's behalf, and no cause to disrupt the independence of the colonies.[182] The *Chronicle* likewise declared Monroe's rhetoric "worthy of the occasion and of the people, who seem destined to occupy so large a space in the future history of the world."[183] Britain was not entirely happy with the outcome. They would have preferred to have taken the lead in South America, to work with the United States to show that "the force of blood again prevails, and the daughter and the mother stand together against the world."[184]

Still, in framing their contest with Spain not as a fight for revolution but as a stand against illiberal practices in the Western Hemisphere, the United States had appealed to principles at the core of British identity. It was a language that resonated strongly with the British public and set the stage, if not for partnership, then at least a march along Adams's "parallel lines" in the nineteenth century. The United States might have expanded, but it had done so legitimately. For that reason, Britain could accommodate the emerging power.

On the eve of World War II a journalist and confidant of Roosevelt, Forrest Davis, called on the United States to defend the Atlantic system. "Unlike the Axis blueprints for a New World Order," he wrote "the Atlantic System is old, rational, and pragmatic. Growing organically out of strategic and political realities in a congenially free climate, its roots run deep and strong into the American tradition."[185] The foundations of this system, he argued, rested in shared democracy, and "it was not lost on the Presidents of the Virginia succession, and on Adams, Bolivar, and Canning, that modern democracy was flourishing best in the states of the Atlantic seaboard—in both Europe and America." Laboring together, Britain and the United States built a liberal international regime, "a community believed to be ordinarily at peace, animated by mutually beneficial trade and shared respect for the rule of law, and governed by treaties between states that recognized each other's legitimacy."[186] In partnering to oust the European powers from the Western Hemisphere, the Anglo-American condominium had, as Canning boasted, "called the New World into being to redress the balance of the Old."[187] As Davis wrote, "History, as everyone knows, simulates itself. Substitute Hitler for Czar Alexander, the Nazi New Order for the Holy Alliance, and you have a continental Europe again 'laboring to become the domicil[e] of despotism.' . . . As in Napoleon's time, as in 1823, and also as in 1898, when she balked attempts to revive the Holy Alliance—this time against the United States—England again has placed herself outside a despotic Continental System."[188]

This chapter demonstrates that from 1817 to 1823, Britain would come to see the United States as a vital partner in world politics, a rising power capable of shoring up a liberal system in the Western Hemisphere. British leaders came to see the United States as a partner, despite understanding that American economic growth and territorial expansion could threaten its vital interests in the Caribbean, in Canada, and eventually around the globe. Whatever might the United States could wield, British leaders believed it would be used in the name of what was right. For this reason, it separated itself from its traditional allies, and accommodated, even aided, the rise of American power.

But the story in this chapter rejects the argument that Britain's accommodation was inevitable. Surely social, political, and economic forces were drawing the United States and Britain closer; they had been since the years before the Revolution.[189] But these structural forces were not enough, in and of themselves, to diminish the outright suspicion and hostility that pervaded relations between these two countries in the early nineteenth century. Many in the United States and Britain might have seen each other as family, but family feuds are often the most persistent and bitter of conflicts. Britain still could not trust its revolutionary kin across the Atlantic and, for this reason, even after the War of 1812, Britain remained poised to contain the emerging power. The politics of harm and the politics of interest may have set the stage for accommodation, but for the strategy to move forward required a certainty that the United States would act as a partner, not a revolutionary rival.

And while the chapter here reinforces the narrative of a shared Anglo-American identity, it challenges those who portray that identity as fixed, given, and essential. As demonstrated throughout this chapter, Britain was as likely to see America as a republican, revolutionary upstart as it was to see it as kin. It was only through rhetorical politics, the careful framing of a shared identity, that the "special relationship" took shape. The language of legitimacy proved vital in shaping Anglo-American relations, setting the stage for a condominium that would last for centuries.

CHAPTER 4

Prussia's Rule-Bound Revolution

Europe and the Destruction of the Balance of Power, 1863–64

> The old German adage "right before might" [*Ehrlich warhrt am langsten*] retains its validity in the last analysis.
>
> —Bernhard von Rechberg, foreign minister of the Austrian Empire, 1859–64

> I have beaten them all! All!
>
> —Otto von Bismarck, minister-president, Prussia

In 1815, Europe had been at war with France for almost a quarter of a century. Assembling in Vienna in the wake of the Napoleonic wars, the four major allied states—England, Austria, Russia, and Prussia[1]—established the Concert of Europe, with the aim of an order more stable and peaceful than that of the eighteenth-century balance-of-power system.[2] From 1815 to the 1860s, this European order proved relatively stable. Even after the end of the formal congress system, the European powers sought to manage conflicts and territorial boundaries through the treaties set down by the powers of the Concert of Europe.

Fundamental to this system was the management of German power. As Metternich instructed, "Germany forms the central point of the great ship that is called Europe and it is there that the ballast must rest."[3] Napoleon's wars had left the Holy Roman Empire in shambles. In its place, the European powers constructed a new confederation, composed of small and mid-sized states, with the two great German powers, Austria and Prussia, at its head. Maintaining the balance of power meant keeping Germany peaceful, but divided. A divided Germany could act as a bulwark against France and Russia; at the same time, with neither Prussia nor Austria able to dominate Germany, it could not threaten the rest of the continent. For this reason, throughout the nineteenth century, the European powers took Metternich's advice to heart. Any attempt to unify Germany—such as Prussia's efforts in 1848—was met with containment and confrontation.

Yet from 1863 to 1871, Prussia successfully unified Germany and, in the process, revolutionized the foundations of European order. Over the course of three wars—the Danish-Prussian war of 1864, the Austro-Prussian war of 1866, and the Franco-Prussian War of 1871—Prussia systemically defeated its opponents and consolidated its position as the head of a unified, nationalist Germany. As Prussia expanded, the European powers accommodated Prussia's revisionist aims. Rather than contain Prussian power, the great powers chose either to sit on the sidelines, or even aid Prussia's expanse into new territory. In doing so, the European powers facilitated the growth of Prussian power, German unification, and the transformation of European politics.

The decision to accommodate Prussia's expansion in 1863–64 is of particular historical and theoretical significance. While international politics has all but forgotten about the Danish-German wars over the duchies of Schleswig-Holstein,[4] contemporaries considered the conflict central to the international relations of nineteenth century Europe. European states believed if Prussia were to expand into the duchies, this would have monumental consequences. Each of the major powers recognized that conquest of the duchies could serve as the first step toward German unification under Prussia's rule. As a result, any successful war against Denmark signaled the birth of a continental powerhouse, one that would upset the balance of power in Europe. Prussia's expansion, moreover, was normatively disruptive as well. By invading the duchies, Prussia threatened the treaties of 1815, the foundation of Europe's ideological order.[5]

While some have argued that German unification was the inevitable result of Prussian power and German nationalism, historians have rightly dismissed such explanations as overly determinative and teleological: Prussia's expansion was far from determined and might have been thwarted through great power intervention.[6] In 1848, a similar attempt to conquer the duchies had failed when Britain and Russia threatened to intervene, and in the 1860s, there were signs that Prussia's expansion would once again be checked. In 1863, moreover, Prussia remained relatively weak. In order to expand, Prussia needed to ensure England, Russia, and France would not mobilize against its expansion: no small feat, given that each side seemed poised to align with Denmark if Prussia grew too ambitious. Any successful revision, moreover, would require an alliance with Austria, yet this state firmly opposed upsetting the status quo.[7]

Why then did the powers accommodate Prussia, allowing the rising challenger to expand into Schleswig-Holstein and set the stage for German unification? Ultimately the great powers came to see Prussia's ambitions in the duchies as limited. How the powers reached this conclusion, however, is a puzzle. Neither the politics of harm nor the politics of interest gave a clear view of Prussia's intentions; indeed, both suggested that Prussia could very well pursue an aggressive, revolutionary foreign policy, one that capitalized on nationalist movements to overturn the European order. Its actions in Schleswig-Holstein, taken by themselves, provided the powers with little information about whether Prussia would pursue a conservative or revolutionary path. It was Prussia's legitimation strategies—the way it justified its expansion—that undermined mobilization against its rising might. By invoking reasons that appeared legitimate to the great powers, Prussia's leaders staved off collective mobilization, advancing into the duchies and laying the foundations for German unification.

With a focus on politicians' language, I adopt almost a traditional story of Prussia's rise, placing Bismarck's diplomacy at the center of Prussia's triumph.[8] But Bismarck's success cannot be reduced to genius, charisma, or rhetorical skill. While Bismarck's appeals were critical in mollifying a hostile Europe, the resonance of his rhetoric—the reasons *why* his language proved critical—is to be found as much in the *positions* of the actors, both Prussia and its audience, as they are in the silver tongue of the minister-president. On the one hand, as Prussia prepared to invade the duchies, its leaders adopted a multivocal strategy. To one audience, it framed its actions in the duchies as consistent with the shared rules and norms of the Concert, using the language of treaties purposively designed to resonate with each of the status quo powers. At the same time Prussia deftly used the language of German nationalism to mobilize revisionist coalitions, including both liberal-nationalist factions at home, and revisionist nationalists—such as Napoleon III—abroad. Bismarck and other Prussian leaders could use multivocal language because they were situated at the intersection of traditional dynastic and Concert institutions on the one hand and revolutionary nationalist coalitions on the other. It was this complex position that gave Bismarck and others the capacity to make multivocal claims.

Prussia's audience, moreover, was institutionally vulnerable, and thus likely to listen to Prussia's claims. Key status quo powers, Austria and Russia, were deeply embedded in the traditional networks of the Concert system. In 1863, the Concert system was under threat, and those powers most vulnerable to its demise eager to find a partner to support their vision of global politics. It was this combination of rhetoric and institutions that gave language its power and facilitated an almost costless expansion into the duchies. To Austria, Prussia's language signaled constraint, that Prussia could be bound to international treaties. In Britain and France, Bismarck threatened hypocrisy costs, effectively coercing these governments into supporting Prussia's rise. And in Russia, Bismarck appealed effectively to Russian identity and, in particular, its existential need to preserve conservative principles in Europe.

Table 4 summarizes Prussia's legitimation strategies and its effects on each dyad during the Schleswig-Holstein crisis. While the focus of this chapter is on the events of 1863–64, the figure below also summarizes the

Table 4. European responses to Prussia's rise, 1863–64

Prussia's multivocality		Great powers' institutional vulnerability: Low	Great powers' institutional vulnerability: High
	High	*Weakly resonant* Britain, 1863–64 France, 1863–64	*Strongly resonant* Austria, 1863–64 Russia, 1863–64
	Low	*Weakly dissonant* Britain, 1848 France, 1848	*Strongly dissonant* Austria, 1848 Russia, 1848

great powers' response to the Schleswig-Holstein crisis of 1848. Throughout the chapter, I draw a comparison between the great powers' reactions to Prussia's incursions into Denmark in 1863–64, and its similar advances in the duchies in 1848, where the great powers contained Prussia's expansion, even threatening confrontation, for fear that Prussia was on the verge of creating a revolutionary German national state.

The Prussian-Denmark War: An Overview of the Conflict

By 1863 Denmark and the German powers had shared power over Schleswig-Holstein for almost four centuries.[9] The duchies were a site of persistent territorial disputes. The crisis that would spark Prussia's war with Denmark, and the beginning of its unification of Germany, began in an argument over constitutional rule and dynastic succession. On March 30, 1863, the Danish king Frederick VII issued a royal ordinance, the "March Patent," that attempted to prevent German interference in the duchies. The German states were outraged and claimed Denmark had breached the Treaty of London, the 1852 agreement that had ended the first Danish-Prussian war. In November, the crisis intensified when the Danish king promised to implement a liberal constitution, which would further revise its rule in the duchies. To make matters worse, that month the Danish king died. The accession of Christian IX prompted German nationalists to challenge his right to rule the duchies; the Germans argued that the Duke of Augustenburg was the rightful heir to the Schleswig-Holstein throne. As a German noble, if the duke were to take the throne of the duchies, this would secure Schleswig-Holstein's membership in the German Confederation, and sever its ties with the Danish monarchy.

For all of its complexity, the conflict over the duchies was not simply some obscure dynastic feud. Throughout the nineteenth century the fate of the duchies was intertwined with the larger "German Question," and the future of the fragmented German nation. German nationalists hoped to use expansion in the duchies as a springboard for unification, bringing together all the German-speaking populations under a single state. In Denmark too the dispute had taken on nationalist tones, with the "Eiderdanes"—a coalition of Danish nationalists—refusing to rescind the constitution and calling for the expulsion of all German rule from the duchies.[10] The issue had international significance as well. As Mosse argues, "The fate of the Duchies came to involve the sanctity of treaties and the European balance of power . . . part of a wider conflict between the upholders of public law embodied in international engagements and revolutionary nationalist movements."[11] The conflict over the duchies challenged the treaties of 1815, which established the Danish monarchy as an integral part of the European political equilibrium, as well as the Treaty of London of 1852, which had reaffirmed the status quo of shared sovereignty in the duchies.

For Prussia and its minister-president, Otto von Bismarck, however, the crisis presented an opportunity. If Prussia were to invade Schleswig-Holstein, it could revise the status quo in the German Confederation in its favor. If Schleswig-Holstein became a German state, it would fall in Prussia's sphere of influence, and shift the balance of power in the confederation away from Austria. Moreover Prussia could use the crisis to mobilize the German states: acting on behalf of Schleswig-Holstein would harness the power of nationalism and secure Prussia's place at the moral leader of the German Confederation.[12] But Prussia's leaders understood pursuing its interests would not be easy. Prussia's attempt in 1848 to expand in the duchies had failed. In the wake of the revolutions, a provisional government in the duchies announced it intended to "join in the movement for German unity and freedom with all our might."[13] In the duchies' declaration of unity Prussian leaders saw an opportunity to expand, and immediately proclaimed its support for the German government in the duchies. Within the month Prussia, along with forces from the German states of Hanover, Mecklenburg, Oldenburg, and Brunswick, had invaded the duchies.

In 1848 the European great powers quickly responded, moving to contain and roll back Prussian advances. Britain's prime minister Benjamin Disraeli denounced Prussia and Germany's actions and called for military intervention on behalf of Denmark. The Prussians and Germans, he maintained, were clearly "carried away by that dreamy and dangerous nonsense called 'German nationality,'" and were making an illegitimate attempt to expand.[14] Palmerston cautioned against escalation—he feared a general war on the continent—but agreed that the Prussians had "acted in this matter with unjustifiable violence" and that Britain was bound by treaty to assist Denmark against the advancing Prussian troops.[15] Russia's reaction was even more severe. The Russian diplomat, Baron Peter von Meyendorff, warned Prussia that any invasion of Denmark would "gravely affect the interests of all the Baltic Powers," and Russia would have no choice to respond. By

1849, Russia was readying its fleet to assist the Danes.[16] France too promised to protect the integrity of the Danish monarchy. Austria, once Schwarzenberg had quelled the revolutionary forces in Vienna, threatened Prussia and the German states with force if the states refused to accept the status quo, bringing the confederation to the brink of civil war.

Prussia's revisionist claims in 1848, as Mosse argues, incurred a heavy price, sparking the "cooperation of the other powers and her own complete isolation."[17] And it seemed any expansion in 1863–64 would provoke the same outcome. As Lawrence Steefel argues, "During the summer of 1863, the international situation had been favorable to Denmark." Austria and Prussia were not only deeply divided; Austria "was grouped with Denmark's friends, France and Great Britain."[18] While Russia and Prussia had worked together on issues of conservative rule, Russia had made it clear to Prussia that it would continue its long-standing support of Denmark, and its preference for the status quo in the duchies. In other words, in late 1863 through early 1864 the European powers seemed poised to effectively contain Prussia. Prussia's expansion looked almost impossible.

But ultimately, this balancing coalition collapsed, and as historians have argued it collapsed in a baffling way. Shortly after the outbreak of hostilities, the Danish government "appealed to England, France and Russia for aid in the defense of Schleswig in conformity with the treaties of guarantee made in the 18th century and confirmed in 1848."[19] Yet rather than confront or contain a revisionist Prussia, each of the European powers chose to accommodate Prussia's demands in the duchies. Austria, which had for so long opposed Prussia's rising power in Germany, now *allied* itself with the rising power. At the outset of the crisis, Bismarck approached Austria, arguing that the two German powers should work together to secure the integrity of the duchies against the Danish monarchy. Austria agreed, and by January Austria had committed twenty-three thousand soldiers to an invasion of Schleswig.[20] France too sought cooperation with Prussia; in November 1863 and January 1864 Napoleon III offered, not containment, but an alliance to facilitate Prussia's expansion into Denmark.

Russia and Britain were the two states that had the capacity to mobilize unilaterally and contain Prussian expansion. Both chose to stand aside as Prussia and Austria dismembered their traditional ally. While at first, the British initially seemed poised to intervene on Denmark's behalf, ultimately the cabinet refused to sanction intervention. While the British did serve as the central mediator in the end to the conflict in 1864, Britain simply accepted Prussia's demands for a new status quo in the duchies. Russia, which fifteen years before had mobilized military support for the Danish monarchy, now even seemed sympathetic to Prussia's demands.

In contrast to 1848, then, the European powers failed to mobilize against Prussia's expansion. Their decision not to contain or confront the rising

German power was a significant departure from Europe's policy of keeping Germany divided on the continent, its avowed belief that if Prussia united the German states, the power would become an unmanageable behemoth, capable of overturning the European order. For some, Prussia's uncontested rise demonstrates inherent structural obstacles to collective mobilization. Cooperation, after all, is difficult under anarchy, especially in multipolar systems. In multipolar systems, each state has incentives to free ride on the efforts of others, and as a result each "passes the buck" when it comes to balancing against an emerging power.[21] The inability on the part of the European powers to engage in collective action thus is not at all surprising.

But anarchy was neither an inevitable nor constant obstacle to collective mobilization in 1864. The historical record does not provide strong evidence of buck-passing during the 1863–64 crisis. Indeed, many of the powers—Britain, Russia, and France—seriously contemplated unilateral action. Other states proved willing to take on military costs, but in surprising ways: Austria, for its part, might have prevented Prussian expansion by refusing to support an invasion of the duchies, yet ultimately the German power reluctantly joined forces with the Prussian state. And as noted above, in the 1848 Danish-Prussian war over Schleswig-Holstein, the powers forged a balancing coalition against Prussia, with England, Russia, and Austria intervening to force Prussia to agree to the Treaty of London and return Schleswig-Holstein to its status of shared sovereignty. When the powers saw Prussia as a threat, as they did in 1848, they proved willing and able to mobilize to check the German adversary.

Others suggest that there were domestic obstacles to collective mobilization, that ongoing internal battles about the nature and intensity of the Prussian threat prevented coherent policies of containment or confrontation.[22] But again, such explanations are problematic. In France, Austria, and Russia domestic obstacles to were weak. The Austrian government—save one minister—agreed to support Prussia's actions, even though public opinion was fervently anti-Prussian during the crisis. In Russia and France, the tsar and the emperor controlled foreign policy. In Britain, where divisions were most notable, there were strong voices for containment and confrontation: the British public and media were extremely pro-Danish, and probalancing forces could count on support from the Tories, then in opposition.[23] In 1848, these voices had persuaded the British public that mobilizing against Prussia was necessary to protect British security. Why they failed to do so in 1864 remains a puzzle to be explained.

Overall, it is not that the great powers could not mobilize against Prussia's expansion into the duchies; it is that they chose to stand aside as Prussia conquered the duchies and used its expansion as a springboard for German unification. They did so because they ultimately judged that Prussia held limited aims in the duchies, ambitions that could be contained within the existing European order. And this raises the question: why did the great powers decide Prussia's invasion of the duchies represented only a limited threat? Why did the great powers perceive Prussia's actions in 1863–64 as less revolutionary than they were in 1848, and not worthy of collective mobilization against the adversary?

PRUSSIA AND THE POLITICS OF HARM

As argued in chapter 1, great powers often look to the politics of harm to judge the ambition of a potential adversary: states look to a rising power's behavior for costly signals that a rising challenger can or cannot threaten their security. From this perspective, the answer to the Schleswig-Holstein puzzle might seem a simple one: in 1863 Prussia posed little threat to the European powers.[24] At the onset of the Schleswig-Holstein crisis, Prussia was a weak and fragmented state. On the continent, it was hemmed in on three sides. Austria was arguably still the reigning hegemon in the German Confederation, and more than a match for Prussia's military. Napoleon III's France, which had recently wrested territory from the Austrian Empire, seemed ready to contain Prussia's expansion to the west. And Russia's foreign policy had long constrained Prussia, so much so that some viewed the German power as practically a client state of the tsar. When one adds to this the fact that Prussia's target was Denmark—hardly a great power of note—the reaction of the status quo powers needs no explanation. As Mearsheimer remarks, "It is not surprising that none of the European great powers balanced . . . in 1864 because the stakes were so small."[25]

But the great powers did see the invasion of Schleswig-Holstein as potential threat to their security, a sign that Prussia could become a powerful revolutionary force in European politics. As it became clear that Prussia was going to act in Schleswig-Holstein, the question of how to react to its aggression became the primary focus of all the European governments.[26] Their concern was understandable. Prussia was already a rising power, both in terms of its industrial strength and its military might. During the 1850s and 1860s, Prussia was reaping the benefits of the world's industrial boom. Prussia's industrialization led to an explosion in its railway network, and its growth in critical industries "such as steel smelting and machine-building, was supported by a phenomenal expansion in the extraction of fossil fuels."[27] While the economy slowed briefly in the late 1850s, by 1860 it had not only recovered but grown more robust. In 1865, Bismarck was boasting "that the Danish war had largely been financed out of budget surpluses for the previous two years" and that Prussia "could wage the Danish War twice over" without needing outside financial support.[28] The great powers were thus not sanguine about Prussia's revisionism; they saw the invasion of Schleswig-Holstein as a potential sign of what the German power would do with its newfound might.

Even if Prussia's rising power was concerning, it may be that the invasion of Schleswig-Holstein seemed defensive and limited in scope, prompting no need to mobilize against the potential adversary. Yet Prussia's offensive actions in 1863–64 had the potential to pose a significant threat to the European powers. The invasion of the duchies put Prussia in a position to seize Denmark's ports on the Baltic, and gain a strategic hold where it could threaten both British and Russian security. Those fears helped drive Britain and Russia toward confrontation with Prussia in 1848; their fears that incursions into Schleswig-Holstein would have profound strategic consequences for the European powers had not diminished.[29]

More important, the great powers also understood that Prussia could use the crisis over Schleswig-Holstein as the starting point to reorganize Germany.[30] As Bismarck himself explained to an Austrian envoy, Prussia would "seize the first best pretext to declare war against Austria, dissolve the German diet, subdue the minor states and give national unity to Germany under Prussian leadership." Upon hearing the conversation, Disraeli certainly had no difficulty interpreting Bismarck's meaning. As he remarked, "Take care of that man; he means what he says."[31] Prussia would not remain on the defensive, or forego the use of force. Rather "Prussia must build up and preserve her strength for the advantageous moment. . . . The great questions of the day will not be settled by speeches and majority decisions . . . but by blood and iron"[32]

Schleswig-Holstein would serve nicely as Bismarck's "best pretext" for expansion. If Prussia were to succeed in Schleswig-Holstein, it would become the leader of the German Confederation, and lay the grounds for national unity under its hegemony. Gone would be the multiple middle-states, such as Bavaria and Hanover, that served as a check on Prussian and Austrian power. In its place would be a German industrial behemoth. Indeed, invading Schleswig-Holstein would put Prussia in the position to overturn the very foundations of the European order. In 1815 the Concert treaties had established a unified Danish kingdom as an indispensable part of the European political equilibrium. If Denmark could be invaded with impunity, this might tear apart the last vestiges of the Concert order. Prussia could use the invasion to galvanize a powerful revolutionary coalition against the status quo powers, perhaps even working with France to challenge the existing order.

Given this, it is hard to see Schleswig-Holstein as *inherently* limited and defensive. This should not be surprising: it was precisely because Prussia's invasion of Schleswig-Holstein was such a threat—because it could unleash revolutionary nationalism, increase Prussian strength, and destroy Denmark's integrity—that drove the European powers to mobilize against Prussia in 1848. There was no reason for the great powers to view Prussia's invasion of Schleswig-Holstein as any less revolutionary than they saw it in 1848.

THE POLITICS OF INTEREST

Another possibility is that the politics of interest drove Europe's decision to accommodate Prussia's expansion in the duchies. While Prussia's actions in Schleswig-Holstein could have put the rising challenger in a position to threaten the great powers, Prussia's interests indicated that it would not do so: it would be too costly for Prussia to adopt revolutionary aims in Schleswig-Holstein. Doing so would provoke a fierce balancing coalition and risk the costs of war. If Prussia provoked its European partners, it would incur economic and diplomatic costs as well. As a result, the great powers could remain confident that Prussia would continue on a limited course, both in the duchies and in the future. At most, Prussia would act as a limited-aims revisionist, interested in expanding and unifying Germany, but not at all interested in becoming a continental hegemon.[33]

Such limited aims, moreover, were consistent with the interests of the great powers. For Britain, a strong Germany, united under a Prussian government, could be a boon to its economy and security in Europe. A unified Germany could check France and Russia, and preserve Britain's desired balance of power on the continent; as Castlereagh noted almost fifty years before the crisis, British policy should aim to ensure that "Germany might again be confederated in the same system, to render it an impregnable bulwark between the great States in the East and West of Europe."[34] Later British politicians would proclaim a similar harmony of interests, especially as it came to see a Germany as a potential economic and political ally on the continent. As Palmerston wrote in 1847, "There can be no doubt that it is greatly for the Interest of England to cultivate a close political Connection and alliance with Germany, as it is also the manifest interest of Germany to ally itself politically with England. The great Interests of the two are the same."[35] Russia too had reasons to want the "consolidation of Germany under the leadership of Prussia."[36] It was only Prussia, Russia believed, that could prevent France from wreaking revolutionary havoc in Poland and the German states. For this reason, Meyendorff extolled the virtues of unification under Prussian leadership: "If a chance remains of saving Germany, it is from here [Berlin] that the impulse must come. God grant that the effort be successful. . . . May the Germans, enlightened about their true interests, understand that Russia can wish only to see Germany powerful and united."[37]

From this perspective, then, the Schleswig-Holstein crisis seems to epitomize a successful signaling process, with both Prussia and the great powers communicating their harmonious interests. Yet while there can be no doubt that interests guided the foreign policies of the great powers, they far from determined the response to Prussia's expansion in the duchies. For one, the interests of the great powers were not all that clear. As Mosse argues, whatever attitude the powers had toward a unified Germany, it "was modified by the appearance of the Schleswig-Holstein question."[38] Whatever the benefits of unification, the great powers believed that they had an equal—if not greater—interest in maintaining the integrity of the Danish monarchy. If Prussia were to act to undermine the Danish monarchy, Russia warned, a "rupture between Russia and Prussia was inevitable."[39] Likewise, British politicians feared that the dissolution of the monarchy would have catastrophic consequences and that that they should defend Denmark, even if this stood in the way of German unification. There was no straightforward path for the powers based on interests.

More important, explanations that focus on the politics of interest cannot explain how it is that the European powers resolved their uncertainty about Prussia's aims. For many of these powers, a strong Prussia at the head of Germany could be a valuable ally, but only under specific conditions: the powers' perceptions of their interests turned on what *type* of power Prussia was, and what type Germany would become.[40] For Russia and Austria, the primary concern was whether Prussia would use Schleswig-Holstein to unleash nationalist forces in European politics. It was not clear that Prussia would steer clear of this path—while its own government was conservative, taking the mantle of revolutionary nationalism would give it unchallenged power in the German Confederation. If Prussia turned to such forces to consolidate its power, then Russia would have to resist, as "a unitary national movement in Germany threatened to destroy alike the princely dynasties and the internal divisions which secured Russia's influence . . . the Russian national interest appeared to demand the maintenance of the status quo in Germany."[41] Likewise, Austria remained uncertain as to whether Prussia would toe the conservative line in the duchies. As Elrod writes, "A conservatively inclined Prussia was an invaluable ally for Austria: a Prussia of another persuasion was an uncontrollable rival."[42]

Likewise, for Britain, while a restrained Germany could be a powerful ally on the continent, a revolutionary German power would tip the balance against Britain.[43] And Schleswig-Holstein offered very little clarification of what type of power Prussia was. Commenting on Prussia's behavior, one official wrote, "It is not easy to understand the policy of Prussia," which seemed to waver back and forth between nationalist revolutionary forces on the one hand and traditional conservatism on the other.[44] Likewise, the *Times* complained that "the real difficulty lies in the uncertainty of the future conduct" of Prussia, which they thought might be "already acting under the dictates of revolutionary passion."[45]

In sum, the politics of interest did little in and of itself to answer the great power's questions about their adversary's intentions. As the crisis over Schleswig-Holstein erupted in 1863, the European states remained mired in uncertainty. What was the extent of Prussia's aims? Would Bismarck and his master, Wilhelm, seek simply to guarantee the rights of Schleswig-Holstein, or would they seek to destroy the Danish monarchy? Was Prussia pursuing its goals *within* the treaties of 1815, or was it seeking a revolution, a new European order to take the place of the old? The situation was particularly fraught, because Britain, Russia, and Austria already had one revolutionary on their hands: Napoleon III had proclaimed his ambition to transform the foundations of the European order. A second revolutionary, this one positioned in the heart of conservative Europe, would likely make that revolutionary future a reality. To understand how and why these powers resolved their uncertainty requires analyzing not only the politics of harm and interest but the politics of legitimacy.

Prussia and the Politics of Legitimacy

As the crisis unfolded, most of the powers—save France—decided that Prussia was no revolutionary, and that the rising power would pursue limited aims on the continent. Bismarck was intent on communicating Prussia's "limited" aims: he realized, as historians argued, that the reaction of the great powers to his expansion depended on how they interpreted his ultimate intentions on the continent. And in retrospect it seems that European powers read Prussia's ambitions correctly—by the 1880s, Bismarck was declaring Germany a satisfied power, with no interest in self-aggrandizement and promising to play the "honest broker" of Europe.[46]

Yet the way in which Prussia communicated its intentions should be puzzling for rationalist approaches. Very little of what Bismarck promised was credible, and Prussia's costly signals were often unsettling at best. Certainly a liberal power looked with suspicion even on the appointment of Bismarck to the position of minister-president, which seemed to signal Prussia's conservative commitments. During the Schleswig-Holstein crisis, moreover, British politicians and newspapers pointed to signs of an aggressive and revisionist Germany, ready to dismember the Danish monarchy. As one correspondent noted, the cry of Germany was "Schleswig-Holstein to the rescue," and that the Germans are "to a man eager to see the banners and men-at-arms of Germany crossing their frontiers."[47] Austria was hardly assuaged by Bismarck's desire to undercut its position in the confederation. Not even Russia found Prussia's actions convincing. The Russian diplomat Count Paul Oubril expressed alarm at Bismarck's appointment and believed Prussia had appointed a "dangerous man" to guide a revisionist foreign policy.[48]

When Prussia did promise restraint, as Bismarck did repeatedly during the Schleswig-Holstein crisis, much of what he said was cheap talk: commitments easily broken, private statements that could be denied. The signals were also ambiguous. Indeed, as discussed in detail below, part of Prussia's success depended on the fact that different powers interpreted Prussia's statements differently throughout the crisis. Despite the seeming emptiness and ambiguity of these statements, Prussia's politicians persuaded the great powers that accommodation—not containment or confrontation—was the answer to Prussia's first forays into its revisionist aims.

What is missing in conventional accounts, I argue, is the politics of legitimacy. Prussia's justification of its expansion provided, not a costly, but a *resonant* signal of Prussia's intentions and ensured accommodation of its power in European politics. As argued in chapter 2, legitimation strategies resonate under two conditions: when the rising power is multivocal, able to appeal across broad coalitions, and when the great powers are institutionally vulnerable and susceptible to believing what an adversary says about its actions. It is these two conditions that allowed Prussia's appeals to resonate with the great powers. As a result, these legitimation strategies had powerful effects on the European powers' ability to mobilize against Prussia's revisionism: they convinced the great powers that it had limited aims; they silenced hawks that hoped to confront Prussia in the duchies; and even persuaded some powers, notably Austria and Russia, that Prussia would work to uphold conservative norms in international politics. How this process unfolded is the subject to which we now turn.

THE POLITICS OF LEGITIMACY: PRUSSIA'S JUSTIFIES ITS INVASION OF THE DUCHIES, 1863–64

As the Schleswig-Holstein crisis unfolded, it seemed likely Prussia would face an insurmountable balancing coalition. Russia, Britain, and France all appeared poised to intervene, either unilaterally or as a coalition, and with force if necessary. All Austria had to do, moreover, was stand aside—without Austria's assistance, Prussian elites believed any action against Denmark would fail. If successful action in the duchies was to be possible, Prussia needed to disrupt this collective mobilization and persuade each of the great powers that an invasion would be justified.[49] Prussia's leaders, especially Bismarck, believed that whether these powers would mobilize depended on the *reasons* the German power gave for intervention. As Bismarck explained to his foreign minister, Prussia had at its disposal "means of securing . . . essential objects and interests" if it used the "justification of our efforts to reach our object in a somewhat devious way."[50]

At the outset of the crisis, there were three ways in which Prussia could legitimate its invasion of the duchies. First, it could justify its aggression as a means of upholding the Treaty of London, the 1852 treaty that had reestablished the status quo in the duchies after the revolutions of 1848. In this framing, it was Denmark that had violated the treaty by attempting to sever Holstein from the German Confederation. Prussia, for its part, was resorting to military force as a means to ensure the status quo, allowing the German powers and Denmark to continue to share sovereignty over the duchies, with Holstein in particular remaining a part of the German Confederation. Second, Prussia could claim that it was acting to secure the dynastic rights of the Duke of Augustenburg in Schleswig-Holstein against an illegitimate Danish king and constitution. Doing so, in practice, would sever the two duchies from Danish rule, and undercut the integrity of the Danish monarchy. Finally, Prussia's leaders could embrace the revolutionary rhetoric of German nationalism, arguing that its invasion of the duchies was justified as a measure to protect German minority rights. Here again it was Denmark, not Prussia, that had pushed the powers into this position, by violating the rights of German speakers in the duchies.

Prussia's leaders recognized that only the first of these justifications—appeals to the Treaty of London—would legitimate Prussia's invasion of the duchies to an international audience. As an editorial in the *Times* stated at the outset of the crisis, if Prussia were to invade the duchies to support the duke, it "would violate a solemn Treaty only eleven years old; it would seek to renew the practice of war from the assertion of dynastic rights, and it would do its best to destroy one of the most respectable and inoffensive States in Europe. By attempting this it is most certain that it would draw down on itself not only odium, but retribution."[51] Invading Holstein and Schleswig in the name of the treaty, Bismarck realized, was necessary if Prussia wanted to expand without resistance: only if Prussia appeared to uphold the treaties would Austria, Russia, and Britain stand down.

But legitimation was no straightforward task. Prussia faced a serious revisionist dilemma, where language that would resonate to some audiences would appear illegitimate to other powerful coalitions. Even among the "status quo" powers—Britain, Austria, and Russia—there was some disagreement as to what constituted a legitimate invasion of the duchies. For Austria and Russia, a legitimate foreign policy was one that not only reinforced international treaties, but also protected dynastic rights; in contrast, Britain saw dynastic rights as outdated and took a firm stand on the Treaty of London—only expansion that would reinforce this treaty would be accepted as legitimate. Despite these differences over the status of dynastic rights in international politics, appealing to the Treaty of London would satisfy both of these parties.

More problematic was appealing to revisionist and revolutionaries, both at home and abroad. France's Napoleon III had proclaimed the treaties of Europe irrelevant, that only policies based on nationalism had any legitimacy. France might have been an historic enemy, but it could not be ignored: not only did it have the power to make Prussia's expansion costly, Napoleon III was using nationalist appeals to woo German revolutionaries as well. If France outbid Prussia on German nationalism, Prussia could face a French-led "Confederation of the Rhine" on its border. At home, moreover, Prussia's leaders were wrestling with an impossible situation, with factions eager to undercut Prussia's power in the German Confederation. In 1863, German liberals controlled the German Diet, and its ministers were eager to liberate Schleswig-Holstein in the name of national self-determination. These liberals distrusted Bismarck, who they saw as a conservative reactionary whose greatest ambition was to restore monarchial control. German liberals saw the looming battle over Schleswig-Holstein as opportunity to use nationalist public opinion to outflank Prussia and Austria, to portray the hegemons of Germany as no more than puppets of a status quo that kept the nation divided. And the nationalist Diet seemed unafraid to provoke international condemnation as well. As a *Times* correspondent reported, for example, German nationalists condemned Britain's "brutal attempt at intimidation" and attempts to squelch German rights to self-determination.[52]

Herein then lay a seemingly impossible dilemma: to prevent the mobilization of the status quo powers, Prussia had to appear to uphold treaties that underpinned the European order. To mobilize the revisionist support it needed to pursue its expansion, it needed to appeal simultaneously to revolutionary actors at home and abroad. Legitimating Prussia's actions to multiple coalitions required a *multivocal* legitimation strategy, the capacity to speak to nationalist and conservative principles simultaneously. On the one hand, Prussia's leaders, especially Bismarck, "rested his case against the Western powers on strict adherence to the Treaties of London."[53] In this framing, Bismarck justified Prussia's interest in the duchies as an attempt to uphold the Treaty of London, and the broader principles of a European equilibrium on which it was based. Prussia might be expanding, but its reasons were limited: the state would neither spread revolution nor revise the European order. As epitomized by his well-reported speech of December 1863:

> Our position with respect to the Danish question is determined by a past from which we cannot at pleasure detach ourselves, and which imposes upon us duties towards the European powers. . . . Prussia's position in the affair is in the first place regulated by the London Treaty of 1852. It may be deplored that the treaty was ever signed; but since signed it was, honour and prudence alike command us to allow no doubt to be cast upon our fidelity to treaties.[54]

As Bismarck argued, any intervention in the duchies was only to secure "the essential objects and interests which prevailed in the negotiations of 1851 and 1852."[55] Indeed, throughout the crisis, there is no moment that Bismarck publicly justifies Prussia's actions in Schleswig-Holstein without reference to the treaty.

At the same time, both nationalist and dynastic legitimations for Prussia's actions pervaded the crisis. In this narrative of events, Prussia was justified in taking radical action, overturning the treaties in order to secure

German rights in the duchies. Prussia, as the *National Zeitung* proclaimed, had a right to intervene in Schleswig-Holstein to "vindicate [the duke's] right of inheritance" and protect Schleswig-Holstein from "an unrightful pretender."[56] Protecting the "right of the Duchies to indivisibility and independence was not only justified as securing "hereditary right of the Augustenburg family." It was also a nationalist action, fulfilling the "will of the whole nation."[57]

The multivocal content of Prussia's legitimation strategies persisted throughout the crisis. To trace the content of Prussia's legitimation strategies, I looked at Prussian justifications as reported by the *Times* during the heart of the Schleswig-Holstein crisis, from November 1863 to February 1864.[58] During the crisis, the *Times* reported on the Germany's internal politics surrounding the crisis, communicating to the British public speeches by prominent leaders (including Wilhelm and Bismarck), debates in the German Diet, editorials in German newspapers about the duchies, and other intelligence about Prussia's actions in the duchies. I looked at forty-four articles describing Prussia's position on the duchies, coding legitimating phrases in these articles into three categories: appeals to international treaties and law, appeals to dynastic rights, and appeals to German nationalism. This qualitative content analysis supports the argument that the Prussians consistently used a mix of justifications to explain their actions in the duchies. Appeals to international law dominate discussion of the duchies, especially among Prussian officials: over half of the legitimating phrases references international law, especially the London Protocol, as the reason for Prussia's invasion. But these appeals were mixed with justifications that invoked either dynastic rights or German nationalism, which accounted for the other combined 50 percent of legitimating claims.[59]

There is ample evidence that Prussia's Janus-faced rhetoric was chosen strategically: Prussian elites were careful in formulating their legitimation strategies. For example, fearful of appearing revolutionary at one point, Bismarck urged the German Confederation to drop its nationalist claims and legitimate their actions on grounds of the European equilibrium as set forth in the Treaty of London. Prussia asked that the confederation refer to any military action in Holstein as an "execution" (which would recognize the succession of Christian IX in the duchies as legitimate), not as an "occupation" (which would suggest that Christian IX had no standing in the German Confederation, and thus no legitimate sovereign title within the duchies).[60] In other words, Prussia insisted that the Diet change not their *actions*, but their *justifications*. Likewise Bismarck would constrain other Prussian elites—even Wilhelm—from using the wrong language at the wrong time. Nationalist language might work for French diplomats and German nationalists, but he argued it was to be avoided when speaking to the Austrians or Russians.[61]

At times Bismarck and the king relied on deception to create multivocality, shifting their rhetoric, depending on the audience. Private appeals to France and the German Confederation took on a decidedly nationalist tone, whereas confidential correspondence with Austria, Russia, and Britain emphasized conservative principles and European treaties.[62] Different speakers would rely on different language as well. The German ministers and national parties were more likely to appeal either dynastic rights or German nationalism in justifying actions in the duchies. In contrast, Wilhelm often appealed to German "honor," and Bismarck would consistently express Prussia's role in Europe and obligations to treaties.[63] But multivocality was not merely grounded in deception or inconsistency: individuals would also use multivocal legitimation strategies, even when they were speaking publicly. In the same speech where Bismarck pledged Prussia's obligation to treaties, for example, he also used language that hinted at more aggressive, nationalist actions, noting that the government would reserve decision as to when it was appropriate to free itself from the treaty in the name of German interests.[64] Prussia, Bismarck assured the Diet, would pursue its "highest political duty—care for the honour and security of our own country."[65] A later speech by Wilhelm invoked treaty obligations and national aspirations simultaneously: it argued that Prussia would act in the name of the treaty, yet noted that "that no foot's breadth of German land, that no fraction of German rights shall be sacrificed."[66] Likewise, Wilhelm promised to "conduct the matter of the Duchies in a manner worthy of the honour of Prussia and Germany, while at the same time preserving that respect for treaties required by the right of nations."[67]

As argued in chapter 2, multivocality depends not only on the content of speech but the speaker, and Prussia's leaders were positioned to make multivocal claims: tied to multiple coalitions, ranging from conservative to revolutionary parties, Prussian leaders had the authority to invoke multiple principles to legitimate their actions in the duchies. The complexity of Prussia's position can be seen at the international, domestic, and even individual levels. In the international system, for example, Prussia was nested within both traditional aristocratic coalitions and emerging economic and nationalist networks as well. The Hohenzollern dynasty was historically embedded in dynastic political networks, as well as a "great power" within the European system. As a result, its leaders had the authority to make appeals to conservative principles, to invoke the principles of European treaties in justifying their claims.

At the same time, by the onset of the Schleswig-Holstein crisis, Prussia's coalitions had grown diverse. Prussia's leadership of the Zollverein, a German customs union formed in 1834 to manage tariffs among the German states, forged economic ties with liberal actors in the German states.[68] As the liberal bourgeoisie became more nationalist in their ideology, so too did the Zollverein become a political as well as an economic resource.[69]

Ideologically, both members of the Prussian monarchy and cabinet maintained strong ties with the transnational liberal-nationalist movement; the Crown Prince, Frederick III, and his wife had been particularly sympathetic to the national-liberals.[70] Prussia maintained diplomatic and economic ties with Napoleon III as well, signing a far-reaching free trade agreement with France in 1862.

Domestically, moreover, Prussia was a fragmented state, and it wasn't always clear whether conservative or revolutionary factions had the upper hand.[71] In the wake of the 1848 revolutions, the Prussian monarch had reluctantly conceded to a constitution. Prussia was no democracy, but its elected national parliament made it a competitive, constitutional state. Electoral competition had shifted the balance-of-power away from aristocratic landowners and toward the emerging liberal bourgeoisie. When Bismarck came into office in 1862, liberal factions controlled 230 of the 325 deputies to parliament.[72] So intense was the competition between liberals and conservatives that during a standoff over military reform between Bismarck and Wilhelm on one side and the German parliament on the other Wilhelm almost abdicated to his liberal son. Such fragmentation, often portrayed as a drain on a rising power's grand strategy, gave Prussia an advantage. Unlike conservative powers such as Austria, who struggled to mobilize the German states behind programs of reform, Prussia's government could credibly commit to speaking for both liberal-nationalist and conservative factions.

And then there was Bismarck himself. As Christopher Clark describes, by the time he took office, Bismarck's wide-ranging ties to various parties made him a bit of a sphinx: "Bismarck appeared to stand outside the ideological prescriptions of any one interest. He was not an aristocratic corporatist; nor, on the other hand, was he, or could be, a liberal. . . . The result was a freedom from ideological constraints that made his behavior unpredictable."[73] Contemporary observers agreed with this assessment. As one remarked when Bismarck assumed power, "Bismarck is a chameleon to whom every party lays claim."[74] With a conservative aristocratic lineage, Bismarck was deeply embedded in traditional networks and was close friends with key conservative politicians like Ludwig von Gerlach and Otto Theo von Manteuffel.[75] But Bismarck also cultivated ties with nationalists: as early as 1859, Bismarck was making discreet overtures to the National Verein, suggesting that Prussia might be willing to fulfill its program of a *kleindeutsch* German state.

It was this combination of content and position that gave Prussia's leaders the power to speak multivocally, to portray their actions in Schleswig-Holstein as consistent with several different principles simultaneously. They could use nationalist legitimations to appeal to their revolutionary factions on the one hand, and use the talk of treaties to mobilize their conservative aristocratic coalitions on the other. They could claim to be a state embedded in dynastic lineages, and yet position themselves at the vanguard of a liberal, economic national state on the other. It is not surprising, then, that so many have emphasized Bismarck's remarkable diplomatic skill as the foundation of Germany unification, that is, his ability to persuade and coerce was key to Prussia's expansion in the duchies and beyond. But while Bismarck's rhetoric is central, a focus on the speaker is incomplete: Prussia's justifications resonated, not only because of Bismarck's skill, but because of his audience's position in Europe's governing institutions, positions that left these leaders vulnerable to Bismarck's claims.

BELIEVING THE LIE: GREAT POWERS AND INSTITUTIONAL VULNERABILITY

That Prussia was speaking multivocally was no secret but, despite recognition that Prussia's rhetoric was strategic and ambiguous, that it was as revolutionary as it was conservative, it still resonated with the great powers. Ironically it was in the weakness of the Concert that Prussia's legitimations found their strength: leaders' justifications resonated precisely because so many of the great powers perceived themselves as institutionally vulnerable, and thus eager to hear Prussia's claims.

Not all the members of Prussia's audience were similarly positioned in Concert institutions. On the one hand Austria and Russia occupied a position of extreme institutional vulnerability: both were firmly embedded in dynastic and Concert institutions, and both believed that the normative architecture of the system was becoming increasingly unsettled. Austria, by far, was the state that remained most invested in traditional European networks. As Crankshaw argues, Austria more than any other power had a strong interest in preserving the sanctity of treaties, as "the past development and continued existence of her remarkable empire was based on the strict observance of international agreement."[76] Austria had helped create the Concert institution, and in 1863 Austrian ministers—especially Rechberg—were determined to follow in the "Metternichian" tradition, committed to the "old German adage 'right before might' [*Ehrlichwahrtam langsten*] retains its validity in the last analysis."[77] As Elrod argues, Austria's ideological commitment to treaties coincided with its imperial interests. As Rechberg insisted, any foreign policy "based on the different nationalities would be of incalculable disadvantage to the service of His Majesty the Emperor," sowing discord among the Slavs, Poles, and Italians living in the Habsburg Empire.[78]

Russia's position was more robust than Austria's—it was not by any objective measure a "declining" empire and was not (yet) facing revolution in the core of its territory. Still, Russia's leaders viewed the state as deeply invested in traditional European dynastic and diplomatic networks. Russia might not be able to rebuild the venerated "Holy Alliance" of the early Concert period, but it still hoped for a "moral coalition" that would cement relations among the conservative powers as a bulwark against revisionism.[79] Tsar Nicholas's ministers, moreover, viewed nationalist movements as a serious threat to its position, both for practical and ideological reasons. For a century at least, Russia had struggled to put down nationalist movements in vanquished Poland, and in 1863 was facing renewed challenges to its rule. Nationalism, more broadly, was viewed as an ideological attack on legitimist rule, which Russia had placed at the center of the Concert since its inception. And now such institutions were clearly under threat. With the rise of Napoleon III's nationalist revisionism, Russia's government was actively seeking, as one diplomat reported to Russell, "the formation of a sort of moral coalition against revolutionary conspiracy, Ultra-Democracy, exaggerated nationalism, and Military Bonapartist France."[80] Russia, as Mosse remarks, "would not abandon as lightly as the rest of Europe the defence of the treaty and of the established order."[81]

Of the great powers, Britain and France were the least institutionally vulnerable. By the late nineteenth century, Britain was increasingly distant from the Concert, acting as "offshore balancer" unwilling to become enmeshed in European conflicts. In 1863 France was also disengaged from the Concert institutions, positioned not as a status quo actor, but as a revolutionary. This had not always been the case. Louis Napoleon came to rule by plebiscite in December of 1848; on December 2, 1851, a coup dissolved the Corps Legislatif, placing him at the head of France. A year later, Napoleon proclaimed the Second Empire, giving himself the title of Napoleon III. As an "elected" emperor, he proclaimed both popular support and dynastic legitimate right. It was only in the 1860s that Napoleon III adopted the principles of revolutionary nationalism and launched a frontal attack against the foundations of the European order itself. And in 1863, Napoleon III believed France faced a critical moment: with nationalist movements fomenting across the continent, and Germany poised to unify under its revolutionary banner, Napoleon III saw an opportunity to take the lead in the nationalist movement. If the moment passed, so to would France face decline.

As chapter 2 predicts, this difference in position shaped how Prussia's audience heard its legitimation strategies, and as a result, the intensity of the mechanisms that shaped collective mobilization. In Austria and Russia, evidence suggests legitimation strategies significantly shaped perceptions of Prussian threat, persuading the powers that Prussia's aims were limited and undercutting mobilization against the power. Prussia persuaded an institutionally vulnerable Austria that it was, and would continue to be, limited in its aims, bound by the European treaty order. Austria was particularly susceptible to claims that a partnership with Prussia could shore up its identity as a conservative power. Likewise Russia saw in Prussian claims a bulwark against the existential threat of nationalist movements. Interestingly, rhetorical coercion appears less visible in these cases. This may indicate how deeply vested Russia and Austria were in these institutions, that dissent from conservative legitimation principles was unimaginable.

In contrast, Britain was far less institutionally vulnerable. Given the British position, it is perhaps surprising that Bismarck's rhetoric had as much of an effect on Britain as it did. As detailed in the case below, there is some evidence that Prussia convinced British leaders that its aims were limited. More powerful were the effects of rhetorical coercion, the ability of Bismarck to silence Prussia's opponents. In this case, the overarching outcome in Britain was one of continued uncertainty: most observers advocated for a "wait and see" approach, and the key advocates of containment—Prime Minister Palmerston and Foreign Minister John Russell—were ineffective and largely silenced by Bismarck's claims. In France, Bismarck's appeals were also read through Napoleon III's position: in Prussia's nods to nationalism, France both saw a potential partner for revisionism, and at the same time recognized that Prussia's rhetoric increased the costs of containment. By the end of the crisis, France believed that if they balanced against Prussia, this would delegitimate their policies elsewhere.

Legitimation and the Politics of Collective Mobilization

Throughout the Schleswig-Holstein crisis, Prussia's legitimation strategy had profound effects on collective mobilization, one that takes us beyond the politics of harm and interest, and into the politics of legitimacy. In Austria and Russia, Prussia's rhetoric effectively signaled that it would be bound by international norms, that it would act in the name of a conservative identity, and thus persuaded those powers to accept its expansion in the duchies. In both France and Britain, Prussia's legitimation strategy set rhetorical traps and raised the costs of confronting Prussia's rise.

AUSTRIA'S FATEFUL ACCOMMODATION: THE DECISION TO ALLY WITH PRUSSIA

One of the most significant and yet befuddling effects of Bismarck's legitimation strategies was the fact that Austria was persuaded, not only to refrain from confrontation, but to assist Prussia's expansion in the duchies. This persuasion was critical to Prussia's success: without Austria's help, Prussia feared that it would be left alone to face a balancing coalition of France, Britain, and Russia—a coalition it was far too weak to overcome. For some, Austria's choice is not much of a puzzle. While the state's decision might not have been wise in retrospect, at the time it was a simple calculation of power and interests. These scholars argue that Prussia and Austria had long struggled for supremacy among the German-speaking principalities of central Europe. Each hoped to become the hegemonic power in a unified Germany, and both believed that expanding into Schleswig-Holstein was the first step toward achieving that goal.[82]

But the fact is that in 1863 Austria, far from a willing partner, was a formidable obstacle to Prussia's rise. Austria had no interest in seeing the status quo overturned in the duchies. Indeed, Austria feared that any expansion would be fueled by German nationalism, a movement the state saw as inherently threatening its position in Europe. Austria perceived German nationalism as a threat to its own multiethnic empire, whose position had grown more tenuous in the mid-nineteenth century. If Austria were to appear overly devoted to Germany, then, as Rechberg argued, "the Hungarians, the south Slavs, the Poles, and the Italians would unite in the dictum that they would reject any policy that requires sacrifices of money and blood for Germany."[83] Furthermore, Austria viewed both its international and domestic stability as dependent on the treaties of Vienna and conservative dynastic legitimacy. Austria believed any nationalist attempt to upset these treaties—even if it increased Austria's material power—was a threat to the Habsburg's dynastic legitimacy. As argued by one Austrian minister during the crisis, "The [Austrian] Empire . . . has always been governed upon the sole basis of the principle of legitimacy. It would be a very great blot on its history if this principle should ever be departed from. Supported by the traditions of his House, the Emperor has never abandoned it, and never will abandon it . . . for a departure from them would bring direct injury to members of the Imperial Family."[84]

If expansion into the duchies were justified on nationalist grounds, Austria would reject it. Indeed Austria had already refused one plea for assistance—when the German princes sought out a power to help them invade the duchies, it was initially Austria, and not Prussia, to which they turned. Despite the fact that the occupation would enhance Austria's power, the state refused. For the German Confederation, an invasion of the duchies was a matter of nationalism: "Schleswig-Holstein . . . must not be allowed to suffer the fate of Alsace-Lorraine. Just as their ancestors reconquered East Prussia from Poland, Pomerania from Sweden, and the Rhineland from France, the Germans must reclaim the northern duchies from Denmark."[85] As Clark argues, "No sharper contrast to Austrian desires can be imagined than this program, for the smaller states violently attacked the London protocol, and invoked the principle of nationality, which Austria abhorred."[86] As long as this was the justification for action in the duchies, Austria would refuse to cooperate. As the Austrian diplomat Rechberg argued to Prince Alexander of Hesse, "The demand for the conquest of Schleswig for Germany, which is now so prevalent that it seems even to be catching hold of governments otherwise prudent, differs in no way from the striving of the French people for the Rhine."[87]

Prussia's diplomats recognized that without a legitimate basis for intervention, Austria would effectively block expansion in the duchies. In November and December of 1863, therefore, Bismarck calibrated his language to legitimate an invasion of Schleswig-Holstein on conservative grounds, framing Prussia's interest in the duchies as intricately bound with Treaty of London and the broader principles of a European equilibrium on which that treaty was based. As Bismarck argued, any intervention in the duchies was only to secure "the essential objects and interests which prevailed in the negotiations of 1851 and 1852."[88] So important was this framing that Bismarck pled with Prussian elites—even Wilhelm—to avoid nationalist language when speaking to Austrian diplomats, for fear that "Austria would abandon her and leave her, single-handed, to face a conflict with the other signatory powers."[89]

Bismarck's rhetoric never fully convinced Austria that Prussia was a sated power, one that would shy from attempts to upend the status quo. The Austrian diplomats had no illusions about Bismarck's personal ambitious; they knew the minister-president was interested in using the Schleswig-Holstein dispute to revise the status quo in favor of Prussia. As one Austrian diplomat remarked of Bismarck in 1864, "The task of keeping this man in bounds, of dissuading him from his expansionistic policy of utility . . . surpasses human powers."[90] Likewise, another deputy questioned openly Prussia's intentions, asking, "Is Prussia anywhere our friend? Does she not denounce Austria as the arch-enemy of Prussia . . . she is stretching out her claws to the duchies, while we are leading her into them to the music of our own good regimental bands."[91]

But the Prussian leaders' legitimation strategies still resonated and, as a result, they had two effects: they signaled restraint and constraint, and they allowed Austria to identify with the Prussian government. Most of the Austrian government believed that as long as Bismarck and Wilhelm spoke *as if* they were interested in the sanctity of treaties, the treaties would constrain Prussia's actions, just as it constrained Austria's.[92] Austria's leaders understood that Prussia held an advantage in the German Confederation, that the Prussians could appeal to nationalist principles to mobilize the population and outflank Austria without bearing similar costs. If Prussia's leaders were willing to forgo nationalist language in the Schleswig-Holstein crisis, if they committed to a "European" and not "German" settlement, then this signaled that the Prussians were willing to abandon a nationalist coalition and remain tied to their dynastic claims.

Though the Austrians did not believe that Bismarck would uphold the treaties "any longer than necessary to satisfy the foreign powers," the fact that his rhetoric still used the language of legality encouraged the Austrians, as Rechberg put it, to bind Prussia and "set this down in black and white."[93] In a meeting to discuss the alliance in January 1864, only one minister raised the possibility that Prussia could defect from this rhetoric, that the state might not really be constrained by the treaties. Strange as it may seem, as Clark argues, "no one" in Austria believed Prussia would not be trapped by its own rhetoric, that Prussia might "refuse to place her head in the noose."[94] Thus, as Pflantze argues, the Austrians saw in Bismarck's rhetoric a way to bind Prussia to the status quo, and thus "with each successive step of the dual powers in the Danish affair Rechberg and his colleagues sought to put the Prussians into this restraining harness."[95]

So too did Bismarck's language suggest a shared identity between Austria and Prussia. Bismarck and Wilhelm's gestures to Austria as an equal great power, its promises to colead a conservative German Confederation, were particularly resonant at a time when Austria's very identity as a national great power were under attack. Bismarck's rhetoric appealed to Austria's conservative identity: Austria often appealed to dynastic solidarity among German princes to maintain its position as hegemon in the confederation and create a united front against nationalist-liberal coalitions. Called to reform the Bund in 1863, for example, the German princes asked that Prussia support Austria in building unity; Wilhelm, as Bismarck writes in his memoirs, "favoured the Austrian proposal because it contained an element of royal solidarity in the struggle against parliamentary Liberalism."[96] Prussia's appeals to a shared dynastic identity communicated that Prussia was a brother in counterrevolutionary arms, that it would work with Austria to suppress nationalist impulses in Germany and abroad.

Indeed, working with Prussia was the only way to protect Austria from an existential threat. If Denmark were allowed to claim Schleswig-Holstein, the national-liberals in Prussia might stoke enough outrage to overtake conservative coalitions. Franz Joseph was particularly fearful that the Prussian king "would have to call a liberal ministry if Bismarck fell." Moreover Austria's leaders believed that resisting Prussia's actions, or even failing to actively support them, would come with existential costs to the empire. As Clark writes, Austria's actions became a "crusade for the preservation of the sanctity of treaties and maintenance of the existing power, matters of life and death for the Habsburg power."[97] A victory for nationalist principles would have concrete effects on Austria's position as a great power. It would undercut Austria's attempt to dominate German dynastic princes. It would buoy the position of Napoleon III's France. A triumph of nationalism over conservatism was unthinkable, an outcome that would threaten "her existence as a great power and the continuance of the system of 1815."[98]

In sum, Prussia's legitimation strategies persuaded Austria that Prussia could and would be bound to the treaties, and thus only limited revision would emerge from the invasion. As Baron Ludwig von Biegeleben, then in charge of Austria's German Affairs, argued, if Austria bound Prussia to its rhetoric then Bismarck could not give way to his "lust for the annexation of Schleswig and Holstein."[99] Prussia convinced Austria that it was a counterrevolutionary partner, and that joint action in the duchies, a strategy counter to Austria's interest, was the only way to preserve a conservative identity. Austria's choice would incur disastrous consequences. Ultimately the invasion allowed Prussia to build support among German nationalists, persuading them that only Prussia could ensure unification. Disputes over Schleswig-Holstein, moreover, would provide Prussia with its pretext for war against Austria in 1866. But what Austria misjudged was not Prussia's aims, but its flexibility in the face of its legitimation strategies. Prussia had no reason, ultimately, to keep its head in the noose: unlike Austria, Prussia was positioned to benefit from the nationalist sentiments it was poised to unleash.

RUSSIA'S CHOICE FOR ACCOMMODATION: SEEKING A PARTNER TO STEM REVOLUTION

In order to expand, Prussia had to prevent Russia from mobilizing against it in the duchies. In the summer of 1863, this seemed unlikely. Russia had strong interests in the conflict. In 1848 Russia had shown itself committed to confronting the rise of Prussian power: faced with Prussia's invasion of the duchies, Russia pronounced the expansion would "gravely affect the interests of all of the Baltic Powers and tend in its effects to destroy throughout the north the equilibrium established by the treaties. That was an eventuality which Russia could not admit."[100] A Russian naval demonstration signaled the state's commitment. Russia's interests in 1863–64 looked very much the same. Strategically, Russia "had no more desire in 1863–1864 than before to see a German fleet in the Baltic based in Kiel nor to see Denmark so weakened by the loss of the duchies that it would join with Sweden-Norway in a Scandinavian union."[101]

Despite Russia's interests, the state chose not to contain or confront Prussia's expansion in the duchies. Some international relations theorists have attributed this to Russian weakness after the Crimean War, when, it was claimed, Russia was too weak externally and internally to balance against an expanding Prussia.[102] While Russia was weaker in 1864 than it had been in 1848, it still believed it could, if necessary, contain the Prussian power. It is not that Russia failed to make a credible threat to balance Prussian expansion. It is that it made no threat at all: in the end, Russia declared that it would not "send one soldier or spend one ruble for or against Denmark."[103]

It was Bismarck's framing of Prussia's expansion as an attempt to uphold the European treaties that persuaded Russia to stand aside. On the one hand, Bismarck's language signaled restraint to the conservative power. The Russian leaders held no illusions that Bismarck was a "true" conservative, that he was a principled actor that would embrace conservative principles out of sincere belief alone. But if Prussia would act in the name of dynastic and European principles, this might serve to bind Prussia, not only by strengthening Bismarck's ties with conservative allies, but also through severing its ties with revisionists at home and abroad. As Mosse writes, Russia feared a "revolutionary grouping" between Prussia and revisionist states, and believed that any understanding "between Bismarck and Napoleon might destroy Russian influence in Europe." Binding Bismarck to conservative ideals meant keeping him from allying with revisionist coalitions, both those at home, and the French, Italian, and Hungarian coalitions that were eager to form a nationalist movement abroad.[104]

Moreover, Prussia's language affected Russia's sense of its identity as well. Domestically, Russia held to dynastic principles that were inherently threatened by nationalist and democratic claims. Internationally, Russia believed its legitimacy was integrally tied to the maintenance of the European treaties: without these treaties, revolutionary states—such as France—might feel free to remake the boundaries of the European states, upsetting Russian control in Poland and other volatile territories.[105] Thus Russia would not abandon "the defence of the [European] treaty and of the established order."[106] Nationalism must be treated as a revolutionary force, and as a "constant source of anxiety and disturbance to the other Powers." To protect the status quo, Russia's foreign minister, Prince Gorchakov called for "the formation of a sort of moral coalition against revolutionary conspiracy, Ultra-Democracy, exaggerated nationalism" and any overt attempts to undermine the European equilibrium.[107]

Bismarck's strategically chosen rhetoric resonated with this identity. Bismarck assured Oubril that he "intended to safeguard their interests and would faithfully observe the Treaty of London for the sake of the four-power agreement."[108] As a result Russia informed Prussia that its promise to occupy "Schleswig on 'conservative principles,' maintain the treaty of 1852 and preserve the Danish monarchy" was viewed as a legitimate aim by the Russian government.[109] Strikingly Bismarck's rhetoric also convinced that Russia that Denmark was pursuing an illegitimate nationalist strategy—that it was Denmark's actions, not Prussia's, that posed an existential threat. Prussia's pretext for action in the duchies had been Denmark's imposition of a new constitution, one designed to please Denmark's nationalist "Eiderdane" population. Although Denmark realized Russia would not recognize the legitimacy of a liberal-nationalist constitution in the duchies, the government continued to hope that Russia, because of her strategic interests and adherence to the European order, would support Denmark as she had in 1848.

Instead, Russia informed the Danish government that it could not accept its actions as legitimate. Early in the crisis, in December 1863, the tsar told the Danish government that while "I admit that the movement against you in Germany has at present in part a revolutionary basis . . . on your part, too, there are also . . . symptoms of exaggerated tendencies."[110] As the crisis persisted, the British diplomats noted that Russia believed Denmark was "dangerously excited by democratic and national passions," and as a result, it was increasingly likely that power would stand back from the conflict.[111] As Russian officials noted to the British, while "it was the intention of the Powers to maintain the Treaty of London," if nationalist sentiment was not contained, Russia could not support Denmark in a conflict with Germany.[112]

Prussia's rhetoric, in the end, acted as a "wedge strategy," driving apart the possibility of a Russian-Danish alliance. Indeed even as Austria and Prussia marched through the duchies, Russia refused to accept Denmark's rationale for its actions. On February 11, Russia proclaimed that it would not oppose the occupation of the duchies, as they understood that Austria and Prussia were acting in defense of the treaties. To the Danes, the tsar maintained that while he would do everything to restore peace and order, it was up to the Danish government to act legitimately: if anything, it was the Danes, not the Germans, who were threatening the integrity of the European order. As a Russian diplomat explained to the Danes, "It is not for Denmark's interest that Europe protects its integrity; it is for the European interests, for the treaties that are common to us."[113]

THE BRITISH STAND ASIDE: RHETORIC, HYPOCRISY, AND THE SILENCING OF THE HAWKS

At the onset of the Schleswig-Holstein crisis, the British appeared likely to intervene on the side of Denmark and mobilize against Prussia, just as they had done in the first Schleswig-Holstein war of 1848. In 1863, Palmerston declared in a Parliamentary speech that "I am satisfied with all reasonable men in Europe, including those in France and Russia, in desiring that the independence, integrity, and the rights of Denmark may be maintained. We are convinced . . . that if any violent attempt were made to overthrow those rights and interfere with that independence, those who made the attempt would find in the result, that it would not be Denmark alone with which they would have to contend."[114]

Such threats were more than just cheap talk; as Austria and Prussia threatened to invade Schleswig, British pronouncements became even more severe. In late December, Palmerston wrote to Russell that he believed that any German intervention into Schleswig would be unacceptable, arguing that "Schleswig is not part of Germany, and its invasion by German troops would be an act of war against Denmark, which would in my clear opinion entitle Denmark to our active military and naval support."[115] On the January 8, Russell submitted to the queen telegrams he proposed to send to Paris, St. Petersburg, and Stockholm, inviting the governments to join England in denouncing an invasion of Schleswig as "an act of aggression on non-German territory" that should be met with resistance on the part of the great powers. Germany should be convinced to delay the occupation while England organized a conference to mediate the dispute. These were no idle threats; Russell was preparing to match his words with a significant naval demonstration against Prussia.[116]

That the British appeared eager to support Denmark was not at all surprising. Britain had strategic interests in the region and hoped not only to prevent Prussian enlargement, but a possible catalyst for German unification.[117]

Britain, moreover, saw itself as bound both by the Concert and the Treaty of London to ensure the integrity of the Danish monarchy. Despite these interests, however, in the end Britain made no attempt to confront or even contain Prussia's expansion. Indeed, while lamenting that the conflict over the duchies had escalated to war, Britain ultimately pronounced that Prussian interests were legitimate, whereas the Danes had acted contrary to the dictates of international treaties.[118]

What explains Britain's decision to accommodate Prussia's expansion? Certainly some of this strategy can be explained by domestic confusion, as Schweller's theory of societal divisions and "underbalancing" suggests. For example, while Palmerston, Foreign Secretary Russell, and conservatives such as Benjamin Disraeli were eager to confront Prussia, even at the cost of military action, Queen Victoria's sympathies lay with Germany. She charged Palmerston and Russell's threats were anti-German and overly aggressive, and worked through other ministers—notably Granville—to undermine the prime minister in Parliament.[119] Moreover, the cabinet, although pro-Danish, was strongly pacifist, and ministers such as Granville and Lord Derby loudly criticized Russell's language as the first step toward war.[120]

Although domestic opposition played an important role in stifling Britain's balancing effort, the explanation itself is insufficient. On the one hand, similar disunity had plagued Britain in 1848, yet the British successfully confronted Prussia's expansion into Denmark, joining with Russia to force Prussia to compromise over the duchies. Just as in 1864, in 1848 Palmerston and Russell opposed Prussian expansion, yet faced serious opposition from Queen Victoria, who denounced their efforts as a "direct attack upon Germany."[121] In 1848 radical members of Parliament also criticized Britain's confrontation of Prussia: these members hoped that Prussia's actions would help cement a liberal German unification, leading to a liberal-democratic government who would prove a firm ally on the continent. Palmerston and Russell, however, overcame this disunity to force a confrontation with Prussia.

Moreover, it is unclear why the domestic opposition, in and of itself, led to accommodation and not confrontation. Yes, the queen opposed Russell and Palmerston's aggressive response, but she had limited influence on foreign affairs. Much of her interference, at first, provoked a backlash. The *London Review*, for example, charged that the queen's interference was "despotic."[122] A member of the House of Lords likewise proclaimed that the queen was acting in German interest, and that he hoped the ministers would side with Denmark "as to show to Germany and to the whole world that the policy and feelings of George III—those truly English feelings . . . still animate the Government of this country."[123] Public opinion was also fervently pro-Denmark, and thus solidly behind stopping Prussia's march into the Danish monarchy. The British public had long seen itself as the protector of Denmark; the marriage of the Danish princess Alexandra with the Prince of Wales in March 1863 had further increased the number of popular demonstrations in sympathy of Denmark.[124] Newspapers, such as the *Times*, echoed Palmerston and Russell's policies. An editorial in March 1863, for example, argued that "the maintenance of the independence and constitutional liberty of the Danish empire demands the carrying out of the principle, regardless of possible sacrifice."[125]

Given these strategic interests and public support, then, why did Britain turn away from containment and confrontation, and allow Prussia's expansion into the duchies? In Britain, Bismarck's rhetoric had two significant effects: it signaled restraint and constraint, and it silenced opponents, especially Palmerston and Russell. Following Prussian pronouncements, for example, the Earl of Derby argued there was no reason to mobilize against Prussia in the duchies, noting that "the parties now proceeding against Denmark do not rest their claim on any opposition to the treaty. On the contrary, they proclaim they are proceeding in the spirit of the treaty."[126] Papers such as the *Times* too changed their opinion. Where the paper had once promoted containment, even at the risk of war, they now noted that Prussia's rhetoric—specifically referring to an address by Bismarck earlier that week—signaled "there was no reason to complain of the conduct" and that a force could enter the duchies as long as the Prussians continued to express "a proper feeling of its responsibility to Europe."[127] As the paper noted, "Strange to say, the Prussian ministers who had, it should seem, so obvious an interest in hiding their own delinquencies under the tumult and excitement of a war have shown a respect for Treaties, a good sense, and a moderation that was scarcely to be expected from them."[128] Confrontation was hardly necessary under these circumstances, and politicians who argued for an aggressive strategy were irresponsible at best.

There were those, most notably Palmerston and Russell, who remained convinced that Prussia was an aggressively revisionist state: there were no serious binding effects among those that saw Prussia's interest in expansion. The prime minister maintained to the German powers that their conduct "was unjustifiable"[129] and argued to the Danish government that Prussia's treaty claims were made in "bad faith."[130] Diplomats, such as Sir Andrew Buchanan, warned that he would be shocked if "Bismarck did not seek to obtain more solid advantages for Prussia in return for the losses and sacrifices which the country will have to suffer in the event of war."[131] Throughout the crisis, Russell attempted to organize an alliance against Prussia's actions, to rebuild the coalition that had stymied similar expansion in 1848. As late as February 1864, Russell hoped the Russian and French governments would join Britain in a collective naval demonstration against the Prussian invasion.

These efforts to mobilize support for confrontation fell on deaf ears. In Britain Prussia's legitimation strategies effectively set a rhetorical trap, weakening those who wanted to balance against Prussia, and strengthening the position of those that demanded isolation. Palmerston and those arguing for aggressive containment of Prussia had taken their stand "on the sanctity of the treaties": it was because Prussia was violating the Treaty of London of 1852 that confrontation was necessary.[132] As Palmerston consistently emphasized in conversations with cabinet ministers and the Parliament, the question of British intervention turned on this treaty. If Prussia threw off its obligations, and proclaimed its right to conquest based on might, it would be an "unprovoked and unjustified attack," one that would be met with British resistance.[133]

Having embraced the rhetoric of treaties, however, these politicians now looked like hypocrites for condemning Prussia's policy. Those who wanted to avoid intervention now simply pointed out that Prussia was acting within the boundaries of the treaty Palmerston had promised to protect. The queen chastised Palmerston and Russell for threatening an "*aggressive* war on Germany."[134] Likewise, Palmerston and Russell were forced to admit that the legal restrictions imposed on Prussia applied to Denmark as well, and that if Denmark failed to meet her treaty obligations, Prussia had a right to intervene.[135] The cabinet refused to support Russell's attempts to build an alliance against Prussia and refused to sanction a naval demonstration.[136] Russell was forced to retract messages to France and Russia and to rewrite drafts to dampen Britain's threats of confrontation.

In other words, these domestic leaders could no longer justify confrontation of Prussia's legal action. Both Palmerston and Russell considered resigning from the cabinet in protest of British inaction.[137] Instead, the ministers folded. By February Palmerston was forced to retract his policy, in a move that Temperley calls Palmerston's greatest diplomatic defeat.[138] In acquiescing, he proclaimed that Prussia was acting legitimately, noting that the German powers "are prepared to declare that they abide by the Treaty of 1852, and will maintain the integrity of the Danish monarchy in accordance with the terms of that treaty."[139] Not all critics remained silent. Lord Salisbury raged that "the people whom she [Britain] affected to befriend are in danger of being swept away. One of the most wanton and unblushing spoliations which history records is on the point of being consummated. But as far as effective aid goes, England stands aloof."[140]

Bismarck's language did not entirely stem Britain's efforts to contain Prussia's advances. Of all the European states, it was Britain's leaders who remained most suspicious of Bismarck's aims, even as they remained unable to mobilize support for military action. Throughout the spring of 1864, Russell worked to limit Prussia's expansion diplomatically, forcing the parties to the bargaining table in March 1864. Even here, however, Russell was unable to mobilize a coalition for anything more than mediation. Without a legitimate basis for intervention, Britain stood aside as Prussia expanded on the continent.

FRANCE AND THE SEARCH FOR REVOLUTION IN SCHLESWIG-HOLSTEIN

If any power had reason to contain Prussia's expansion, it was France. Certainly this state had no strategic interest in allowing Prussia to expand into the duchies, to begin a process that could possibly secure a unified Germany on its eastern border. France, moreover, could not rationally want to encourage a national movement that demanded not only territorial revisions in the north, but along the Rhine as well.[141] As one minister noted, "Today Germany, moving toward unity, needs supports: she invades Schleswig. Another day she will want to protect her southwest border: she will claim Alsace and part of Lorraine. The pretext will be the same: German nationality."[142] Public opinion in France during the crisis, moreover, was stridently pro-Denmark. And in terms of power, each of the European states—Prussia and Austria included—believed that France might be the only state who could unilaterally confront against Prussia's expansion. As Russia and Britain both retreated from containment, an 1864 editorial remarked that "the only thing that might, and probably would, even at this point . . . make the great German powers to hesitate is a decided declaration on the part of France."[143]

From 1863 to early 1864, therefore, it looked likely that France would contain Prussia's expansion and offer material assistance to Denmark. In 1863, France proposed a European conference, designed to revise the territorial borders of European states, Schleswig-Holstein included. To Denmark, France signaled that the conference would be conducted in their interest. In a message to the French minister at Copenhagen, Napoleon III instructed his diplomats to "say to King Christian that the best way of inaugurating his relations with the Emperor would be to accept without the delay the invitation of his Majesty. Before Germany, Denmark loses her case; before Europe, she may win it. Her interest, then is to refer it to a European congress."[144] More strikingly, at the beginning of the crisis France indicated it was likely to support a military demonstration against Prussia, to deter its advance into the duchies.[145]

In early 1864, however, Prussia's legitimation strategies set a rhetorical trap for France. From 1860 onward, Napoleon III had argued to the rest of Europe that legitimate rule rested not on the European treaties or on dynastic claims, but on national self-determination.[146] In 1863 he had gone so far as to proclaim, "The Treaties of 1815 have ceased to exist. The force of things has overthrown them or tends to overthrow them almost everywhere." As another French elite, Emile Ollivier, put it, "Balance is a fine word . . . but a conventional balance established against the will of the people is no more balance than silence produced by despotism is order."[147] With the treaties now obsolete, Napoleon III called for a massive redistribution of territory along nationalist lines. France's policy was not only one of words but of might. France pursued this policy of nationalities in 1859, backing Italy against Austria, and the state continued to seek territorial adjustments on Italy's behalf.

Napoleon III believed that Schleswig-Holstein was central to this nationalist redistribution. Rather than address Schleswig-Holstein on the terms of treaties, the French government called on Europe to invoke a principle of nationalities in solving the conflict:

> The cause and distinguishing characteristic of this conflict is clearly the rivalry of the populations that make up the Danish monarchy. There exists in each of them a national sentiment, the strength of which cannot be doubted. What is more natural, then, in default of a unanimously accepted principle, to take as a basis the wishes of the population? This way, in conformity with the true interests of the two parties, seems to us most suited for bringing about an equitable arrangement and to offer a guarantee of its stability.[148]

Here then Prussia had an opportunity: Napoleon III had long hoped that nationalist legitimacy would spread through the German states, and thus cement his own program of political transformation. Prussia's diplomats thus appealed directly to this nationalist ideology. By invading the duchies, Bismarck assured Napoleon that Prussia would "loose the forces of nationalism."[149] If Napoleon III were to oppose Prussia, he would be party to placing Germans under Danish rule, a move that would reveal France as a hypocrite in international politics.

Like Britain and Austria, France was never convinced of Bismarck's motives—Napoleon ultimately felt that a unified Germany would undermine France's strength. Moreover, despite frequent negotiations and attempts to secure territory for France in exchange for the duchies, there was no material benefit to supporting Prussia; as Steefel argues, Napoleon "gained nothing definite from these negotiations."[150] What evidence does suggest, however, is that once Prussia framed its expansion in nationalist terms, Napoleon III deeply feared the cost of appearing to suppress the German people. He believe that, in doing so, he would lose his rationale for a European congress, his foothold in the Italian conflict, as well as domestic legitimacy at home.[151] Indeed, Prussian diplomats even used the language of nationalism to avoid promises of territorial compensation to France. When French diplomats suggested they might keep quiet in exchange for territory on the Rhine, the Prussians simply noted that "it would be a most flagrant contradiction of the policy of nationalities to want to acquire German lands."[152]

In the end, Napoleon refused to contain Prussia. In explaining his policy, he consistently referred to a nationalist rationale and noted his fear of hypocrisy. In a message to the European states explaining his policy, for instance, Napoleon III argued that he had committed himself to the policy of nationalities, especially in his congress proposal and support for the unification of Italy. He "could not, therefore, be party to replacing the Holsteiners under the rule of Denmark which they detested."[153] Moreover, as French diplomats conveyed to Britain, Napoleon III worried that any appearance of inconsistency—of supporting nationalism in one policy and not the other—would undermine his goals. As noted in one diplomatic message, Napoleon III insisted that "as it is his great desire was to see Venetia wrested from Austria and restored to Italy, he could not lay himself open to the charge of pursing one policy on the Eider and a totally different one on the Po [in Italy]."[154]

In short, Prussia's legitimation strategy shaped decisions for accommodation, confrontation, and containment in all four of the existing great powers. In Austria and Russia, mechanisms of restraint and identification loomed large, with each of these states persuaded that Prussia would operate within the boundaries of legitimist principles. In Britain and France, dynamics of coercion dominated, and strategies of containment and confrontation proved untenable

Prussia's power politics were thus the politics of legitimacy. This is not to say that power and interests do not matter. One cannot tell the story of Prussia's rise without reference to its position in a multipolar system in which most of the European states faced multiple threats to their security. Under these conditions, all of the great powers had some incentive to accommodate Prussia's demands. For Austria and Russia, Prussia could prove a bulwark against French revisionism; for Britain, a potential ally on the continent to ensure stability. As long as Prussia's aims were limited, cooperation with the rising power made sense. And certainly for many of the powers, cooperation with Prussia served the politics of interest, creating an important strategic and economic partner on the continent. Yet these explanations do not explain why it was that the powers came to see Prussia as a state with limited ambition, especially given all of the costly signals that indicated otherwise.

But the politics of legitimacy explains why and how each of the great powers came to see the Prussian threat as limited, and even why some of the powers—Austria and France especially—made strategic decisions that ultimately undercut their own interests on the continent. Without a focus on the role of Bismarck's rhetoric, it is difficult to understand how Prussian expansionism—how the invasion of Schleswig-Holstein—was seen as acceptable. It was not that the invasion of Schleswig-Holstein was inherently limited; it was that the great powers came to understand Prussia's aggression as limited. And that decision cannot be decoupled from what Prussia's leaders said about the conflict, the reasons they gave for their expansion.

But the story is not all one of triumph. Throughout this chapter, and indeed throughout the book, I have stressed the advantages of multivocal rhetoric for rising powers. It is true that merging nationalist and conservative rhetoric strategically allowed Prussia's leaders to mobilize broad support for their expansion and undercut the balancing of their opponents. But the story of Prussia's rise also indicates the very real dangers of multivocality as well. In the decades that followed Prussia's rise, Bismarck would come to see his earlier success unleash forces beyond his control. His multivocal rhetoric had brought together a new coalition that joined conservative forces with liberal-nationalist ones. These same factions that brought the minister-president his glory would eventually unseat him. This raises questions about the role of multivocal strategy in expansion, and whether this language, once used, can unleash movements for expansion that wreak havoc beyond their author's intent. It is a subject to which we will return in the concluding chapter of this book.

CHAPTER 5

Germany's Rhetorical Rage

Britain and the Abandonment of Appeasement, 1938–39

> Now I recommend you to go home and sleep quietly in your beds.
> —Neville Chamberlain, September 30, 1938

On September 30, 1938, Neville Chamberlain landed at Heston Airport in London. A crowd awaited his return from his third and final meeting with Adolf Hitler over the fate of the Czechoslovakia. After a month in which Britain believed it was the brink of world war, Chamberlain announced that Britain and Germany had reached a settlement, one that would give Germany the Sudetenland territory of Czechoslovakia. While Chamberlain had conceded to Hitler's demands, the agreement was a victory. It was, as Chamberlain promised, "only the prelude to a larger settlement in which all Europe may find peace." Waving a piece of paper in front of the enthusiastic crowd, Chamberlain announced that he held in his hands a promise bearing his and Hitler's signatures, "symbolic of the desires of our two peoples never to go to war again." Britain was on the cusp of "peace in our time."

Peace, of course, was not to come, and the Munich agreement has come to epitomize the tragedy of the British interwar strategy of appeasement. Few responses to rising powers have been more studied—and more criticized—than Britain's decision to appease Nazi Germany.[1] From 1933 onward Germany seemed determined to upend the status quo established in the Treaty of Versailles.[2] Yet from 1933 to 1938, as Germany grew more belligerent, Britain eschewed confrontation and instead attempted to settle German "grievances through rational negotiation and compromise."[3] For some, British foreign policy was pathological, based, as Winston Churchill bluntly put it, on a "long series of miscalculations, and misjudgment of men and facts,"[4] a policy tantamount to the "complete surrender of the Western Democracies to the Nazi threat of force."[5]

Revisionist historiography has largely rejected the view that appeasement stemmed solely from incompetence. Indeed for some, appeasement was a necessary evil, the only possible response to insurmountable domestic and international constraints.[6] Constrained by limited economic and military resources, Britain's only choice was to buy time, to appease Hitler in the present and prepare to fight in the future. Other scholars are less certain that appeasement was the only or optimal strategy, but argue that it was still a reasonable response to the politics of harm and interest. In the interwar period, there was enough uncertainty about Germany's intentions to undercut collective mobilization and push the British toward accommodation.

Hitler's legitimation strategies shaped Britain's response to German revisionism in the 1930s. Until the Munich crisis, Hitler and other German politicians justified their aims with a multivocal strategy, appealing to German equality and self-determination to justify German expansion. These legitimation strategies proved strongly resonant and had three significant effects on British politics: they signaled constraint, convincing British politicians that Germany could be bound to an existing institutional order; they silenced "antiappeasers" who demanded a more confrontational policy; and they resonated with Britain's sense of self-identity as a liberal, democratic, and neutral state. After Munich, however, German politicians abandoned these legitimation strategies, arguing instead that rearmament and expansion were justified as a matter of German might, not international rights.[7] Hitler threatened to tear apart the foundations of the Versailles order and construct a new, revolutionary order in its place. The more illegitimate Hitler's claims, the more he declared the Versailles system obsolete, the more Britain came to see Germany as an insatiable revisionist, impervious to negotiation, and responsive only to the language of force.

The study of interwar strategy may appear so well developed that additional explanations of appeasement are unnecessary. But this well-trod history still supplies significant puzzles that legitimation theory illuminates. As argued below, a focus on legitimation explains why it was that British politicians, at least until Munich, read Germany's revisionist actions as largely benign. Scholars that emphasize the politics of harm and interests insist that Germany's actions did not provide enough information to prompt mobilization, especially under challenging political and economic conditions. What these theories miss, however, is that Britain consistently responded to costless signals—to cheap talk—while ignoring the more "costly" signs of Germany's ambition. The theory here suggests that it was Germany's rhetorical framing of its actions—how it justified its revisionism—that made what could and should have been seen as aggressive and revolutionary behavior seem relatively benign. Moreover the legitimation theory here sheds light, not only on why Britain chose to appease Germany before the Munich crisis, but also why Britain committed to *confronting* the German state after Munich, mobilizing its still scarce resources to check the German threat. This chapter argues that this change in British policy stems from a shift in Germany's rhetoric: as German actions appeared illegitimate, so too did they seem to be a threat to Britain's very existence, which had to be confronted at all costs. This argument departs from much of the established historiography that sees the Prague coup of March 1939 as the turning point in British appeasement strategy.

Below, I make the case that British leaders' changed their understanding of Germany's intentions months before the Prague coup. As Roger Eatwell argues, "It is *in the two months after Munich* that we are to find the key to the 'sudden' change of opinion in March 1939."[8] It was in the fall of 1938 that the British began intensifying their rearmament, seeking allies, and mobilizing public support for war.[9] Indeed, it was not the Prague coup that changed Britain's perceptions of Germany as a threat; it was the shift in Britain's understanding of Germany as a threat that shaped the meaning of Prague. Had Britain not settled on an interpretation of Nazi Germany as an insatiable revisionist, the Prague coup might have been yet another moment of ambiguous, limited expansion, not terribly different from events in the Rhineland, Austria, or the Sudetenland.[10]

Finally, the legitimation theory adds social and rhetorical context to traditional approaches to British leaders and appeasement. Like the narrative presented in chapter 4, the story told in this chapter resembles an older historiography, which argues that British leaders failed to understand Hitler as the threat that he was.[11] Although Britain took what Germany had to say seriously, the British politicians in the story that follows are not "guilty men," trapped in cognitive blinders of their own making. Rather, both Germany's ability to legitimate its actions, as well as Britain's response, is only explicable in the context of rhetorical politics: it was Germany's capacity to make multivocal appeals, combined with Britain's institutional vulnerability, that explains why Germany's appeals proved so resonant to the British audience. The account here, then, adopts a social framework, rather than a purely psychological one, to explain why Hitler's legitimation strategies were taken seriously, and why they had such powerful effects on collective mobilization.

Appeasement: Tragic Choice or Grim Necessity?

For many scholars, Britain's "choice" for appeasement was no choice at all; it was necessity, a strategy of last resort. Britain politicians, these revisionist scholars argue, recognized Nazi Germany as a significant threat, one that would eventually have to be confronted with force. But from 1933 to 1938, there was very little the British could do to counter Hitler: in the interwar period, Britain was hamstrung by economic depression, military weakness, and domestic fragmentation, all which undercut the state's ability to mobilize against the looming German threat. Economically, Britain was still recovering from the international depression of the 1930s. Militarily, "the fighting strength of the British Empire was weaker in relation to its potential enemies than at any time since 1779."[12] Although Britain had invested in its rearmament since 1935, its land capacity remained anemic: in late 1938 British civilian and military elites estimated they could send no more than two divisions to France, and by September 1939, the British could only deploy four poorly trained divisions to the Continent. By 1939 Britain had made significant improvements in its defensive air power, increasing its fighter strength and deploying the innovative defensive radar, the "Chain Home" system, to protect the nation from German attack. Yet it still had no significant bomber force, considered critical to fighting a war against Germany, and it remained terrified of a (much overestimated) German bomber threat. The British could do nothing to stop German rearmament, the remilitarization of the Rhineland, and the expansion into Czechoslovakia. Far from accommodating the revisionist power, British politicians turned to appeasement as a means to "buy time": it was a strategy, not of conciliation, not of attempting to sate insatiable demands, but of building up strength until Britain could match the rising power.[13]

To make matters worse, domestic fragmentation undercut Britain's ability to mobilize what little resources it had. Kevin Narizny points to the Conservative government that wanted to protect private companies from the costs of confrontation as the source of appeasement.[14] Likewise, Schweller argues that significant divisions in political coalitions, particularly among the Conservatives, Labour, and Liberals, undercut British efforts to form a coherent vision of its interests, and balance the rising German power.[15] Appeasement was a strategy that would allow Britain to get its house in order, to build up its economy, its military, and mobilize its society for the fight that lay ahead.

There is no doubt that, before 1938, the British believed they were ill equipped economically, militarily, and politically, to confront Germany. But to blame structural obstacles for appeasement underplays the extent to which appeasement was a purposive grand strategy, one aimed at securing a lasting peace with Germany. There is copious evidence that British politicians were committed to appeasement, not only as a measure of buying time, but because these leaders believed that it could shape Germany's behavior and avoid conflict.[16] Certainly British politicians worried about Germany's revisionist behavior and denounced Hitler's aggression. But even in the face of Hitler's revisionism, leaders such as Chamberlain questioned whether the "picture was as black" as it appeared, expressing the belief that negotiation, and not confrontation, could bring Hitler to the table.

Concretely these efforts meant that Britain chose to accommodate Germany's demands in most disputes from 1933 to autumn of 1938, even when this required concessions that were one-sided and allowed Germany to increase its economic and military might. The British approach to German rearmament, for example, was not merely or even primarily to rearm itself in response, but to negotiate treaties that would guide and limit its armament.[17] Britain pursued bilateral and multilateral disarmament and arms control treaties with the Nazi regime, such as the Anglo-German Naval Treaty (1935) that limited German naval acquisitions to 35 percent of Britain's own forces and pushed Germany to negotiate an air pact as well.[18] Britain also sought to incorporate Germany into multilateral security and disarmament pacts, in hopes of directing all of European arms procurement toward a goal of collective security. In this spirit, the British hoped to bring Germany into an "Eastern Locarno," which would provide similar guarantees of security between Germany and the Eastern European states that Locarno had established between Germany and its western neighbors. Ultimately, Britain aimed to draw Germany back into the League of Nations.

Britain also tried to satisfy Germany's territorial demands. Both the British politicians and public were sympathetic to claims that Germany had been unjustly stripped of territorial holdings, both on the continent and abroad. To bring Germany back into a European settlement meant accepting, even facilitating, a revision of territorial boundaries. While the British could not support a violent takeover of Austria, for example, it was willing to support unity pursued through "appropriate" procedures, particularly those institutionalized by the League of Nations.[19] As early as 1936 officials were suggesting that Germany be allowed to annex Memel and Danzig[20] and that the British should agree to a "peaceful evolution" of Czechoslovakia's boundaries.[21] The British also considered returning colonies stripped from Germany by the Treaty of Versailles.[22]

Britain's commitment to appeasement helps explain why it was British efforts to rebuild and rearm from 1933 to 1938 were half-hearted at best. If "buying time" were the primary motivation for appeasement, then it is puzzling what little use the British made of the time they bought. Yes, the British pursued a policy of rearmament, but these efforts represented a fraction of what they were capable of: their efforts were guided by the assumption that Britain could conduct "business as usual"—that is to say, without concern of an imminent, significant threat on the horizon.[23] Indeed, the British purposefully *restricted* their own rearmament so as not to undermine an appeasement policy. From 1937 onward, Chamberlain and his cabinet deliberately avoided rearmament measures that they feared would make Germany insecure. Plans to conciliate Hitler meant reigning in land and naval armament, lest he feel encircled. Chamberlain and others argued vehemently that while rearmament might be accelerated, it should not be expanded in scope, "as any increase in the scope of our program" would lead to a "new arms race."[24] Even air rearmament, often considered the crux of the British deterrence strategy, was undercut by conciliatory efforts.

The British also avoided alliances, lest they signal to Germany that she was being encircled.[25]

And while Britain's public might have been divided over general issues, it was largely unified on the issue of appeasement: those that opposed appeasement, such as Churchill, remained marginal to British politics until late 1938. Whatever disagreement there was among the *means* of British policy, there was a broad consensus on appeasement and conciliation as an *end*. For example, during the Rhineland crisis there were divisions between Labour and Conservatives over the utility of economic sanctions and support for the Locarno treaty, but there was broad consensus, among both the public and politicians alike, that the Germans should be conciliated in the Rhineland, and that the end goal of whatever policy was to bring Germany back into the European fold.[26] And the public greeted news of the Munich settlement with unified elation: Chamberlain returned to cheering crowds, and he received notes of congratulations and gratitude from heads of state across the globe.

As a strategy, then, appeasement meant far more than conceding to Germany's revisionist demands in hopes of putting off a conflict. Britain's ultimate goal was not buying time; it was to avoid conflict by ultimately "bring[ing] Germany back into the comity of nations."[27] It was only by integrating Germany back into existing institutions—in particular by letting Germany take its place as a "good European," embedded in revised institutions of collective security—that peace in Europe could be assured.[28] Even after the Munich crisis, the British hoped that appeasement would lay the foundation for a peaceful European settlement. Having pulled back from the brink of war, British politicians and the public agreed that negotiations with Hitler had worked, that revision could be accomplished through talk and not violence, and that there indeed could be "peace in our time."[29]

Yet from November 1938 to March 1939, British grand strategy would transform dramatically, shifting from appeasement to a policy of confrontation. In a cabinet meeting on November 7, officials agreed that rearmament must be not only accelerated but expanded in scope. They authorized the construction of new escort vessels and began planning for a heavy bomber force.[30] By January 1939, the British had begun a voluntary national service campaign, and the cabinet had committed to an expanded bomber force capable of striking Germany, as well as to a substantial expeditionary force that could be sent to France in the case of war—a deployment far beyond the two divisions the British had considered sufficient in years before.[31]

In the months following Munich, the British also pursued alliances in full force. At the end of November 1938, Chamberlain and Halifax met with their French counterparts to discuss provisions for French security. While in November the British would still resist a firm commitment to France's defense, by January 1939 they were engaged in upper-level staff talks with the French. By February 1939, Chamberlain proved ready to make a pronouncement of an alliance with France, noting that while "it is impossible to examine in detail all of the hypothetical cases which may arise . . . I feel bound to make plain that the solidarity of interest, by which France and this country are united, is such at any threat to the vital interest of France from whatever quarter it came must evoke the immediate co-operation of this country."[32]

Overtures to the Soviets came more slowly, but when they began they were pursued in earnest.[33] In October 1938, the British was still wary of a pact with the Soviets, although they urged the French to maintain relations and not to take "any action which appeared to give Russia the cold shoulder."[34] By January 1939, some officials in the Foreign Office, such as Vansittart, were pushing for closer ties with the Soviet Union, arguing that "Anglo-Russian relations are in a most unsatisfactory state. It is not only regrettable but dangerous that they should be in this state, and a continuence of it will become a great deal more dangerous very shortly."[35] The Foreign Office recommended the immediate initiation of high-level civilian talks between Britain and the Soviet Union, with the aim of convincing the Soviets that British and Russian interests were aligned.[36] After the Prague coup in March 1939, attempts to reach an alliance agreement were accelerated, though they ultimately faltered in the summer of 1939, with well-known consequences for international politics.

What explains this sudden shift in strategy? If the British were "buying time," there should be evidence that appeasement was abandoned for strategic reasons, that buying time was either no longer rational or no longer possible. If Britain had gained a strategic advantage over Germany or, alternatively, if it was poised to lose relative power to Germany in the future, then it would have made sense to confront the fascist state in late 1938–39, rather than fight the inevitable war later on. Far from gaining a strategic advantage, however, historians argue that in the post-Munich world, Britain was *worse off* strategically than it had been from 1936 to 1938.[37] As Steiner argues, it was "accepted that there had been little improvement in the numerical ratio of forces [between Britain and Germany]; in some respects, it had worsened."[38] The remilitarization of the Rhineland in 1936 had greatly diminished Britain and France's capacity to take the offensive against Germany. The dismemberment of Czechoslovakia left Britain and France without a valuable ally in Eastern Europe. With the conquest of the Sudetenland, moreover, Britain believed Germany was establishing economic hegemony in Eastern Europe and could possibly extract resources that would allow it to withstand their planned war of attrition.

The strategic picture was gloomy indeed, yet post-Munich cabinet and Foreign Office discussions seem bereft of pessimistic strategic considerations—all the more surprising, since "worst-case scenario analysis" had dominated British grand strategy throughout the 1930s.[39] In cabinet discussions of rearmament, few mention the economic constraints that had once weighed so heavily on Chamberlain's government. Whereas public opinion was once an insurmountable obstacle to deterrence, cabinet and Foreign Office officials now seemed confident they could mobilize their war-weary constituents.[40] Before late 1938 the British government perceived French economic and military weakness as a reason to avoid alliance; now, it became a reason to commit to France in full force. And whereas the cost of empire had once been proffered as a reason to retrench, Britain's imperial holdings were now assumed to be resources that could be mobilized behind its war effort.[41]

Domestically, Britain unified around this turn to confrontation. Whereas throughout the interwar period Conservatives, Liberals, and Labour might have bickered over grand strategy, from late 1938 onward they "converged on a common response to the prospect and eventual reality of war."[42] Elites in all three parties argued that national unity was essential to face the German threat and decreed their willingness to bury party conflicts in pursuit of British security.[43] From October 1938 onward, moreover, public opinion hardened dramatically.[44] The same public that had overwhelmingly supported appeasement now demanded confrontation and believed that any additional demands from Hitler were unacceptable. In the post-Munich world, then, the "structural obstacles" to British mobilization seemed to disappear. One could argue that there was a simple reason for this—Britain now saw Germany as an existential threat. This is the case. But how British leaders became *certain* of Germany's ambitions is not explained by structural theories alone.

The Politics of Harm and the Politics of Interest: Appeasement under Uncertainty

There is another possible explanation for British strategy: while appeasement was not an optimal response to Germany aggression, it was an understandable one given high levels of uncertainty about Germany's intentions during the interwar period. During the interwar period, neither the politics of harm nor the politics of interest provided clear and costly signals of Germany's aims. Appeasement thus made sense not because Britain could not, but because it should not mobilize in response to German aggression: without credible signals of German ambition, the costs of containment and confrontation were unnecessary at best; at worst, they would unleash the very conflict Britain hoped to avoid.

The British understood full well that Germany harbored revisionist demands. Early German rearmament efforts may have been secret, but they were not unknown: debates about how to address German rearmament efforts dominate British cabinet papers and Foreign Office documents from at least 1933 onward. Nor did the British government hold any illusions about Germany's territorial demands. In 1934, for instance, Foreign

Secretary Eric Phipps wrote a concise, prescient summary of Germany's territorial aims: "Germany's foreign policy may be said to comprise the following aims: (1) Fusion with Austria; (2) Rectification of the eastern frontiers; (3) Some outlet for German energy towards the south or east; (4) The recovery of some colonial foothold overseas. The order may vary with the needs of the moment."[45] Yet such ambitions were not in and of themselves problematic. What remained unknown was whether Germany under Hitler was a "limited aims revisionist," intent only on making modifications to the Versailles settlement, or if Germany was in search of hegemony, of destruction of the League system and dominance of the European continent?[46] Without clear and costly signals of revolutionary intentions, there was no reason for Britain to mobilize against the rising power. It was only when it became clear that Hitler was an insatiable revisionist that a policy of confrontation based on expansive rearmament and committed alliances was a rational choice.[47]

There is considerable evidence that British leaders sought information about Hitler's aims. Before Munich, most concluded Hitler harbored limited goals that could be accommodated within a reformed Versailles system. In contrast, evidence from both the Foreign Office documents and newspaper editorials suggests after Munich the British became far more certain that Germany posed a significant threat to Britain, almost universally embracing the view that Hitler sought domination and that Britain and Germany were locked in an existential conflict between democratic and fascist states. Yet British assessments of German ambitions were rarely based on *costly* signals.[48] For example, even when Germany's *actions* in the years before Munich were offensive and aggressive, British politicians (and the public) interpreted the state's *intentions* as largely benign.

And there was much aggressive behavior for the British to interpret. In 1933, Germany walked out of the Disarmament conference, and shortly after, Germany abandoned the League of Nations entirely. In March 1935, Germany officially unveiled their rearmament programs, announcing that they had reconstituted the Luftwaffe (with an alleged strength of 2,500 planes)[49] and would implement universal conscription, with the goal of increasing the army to 36 divisions, or almost 550,000 men. A year later, Germany's newfound strength would be deployed in what was perhaps their most brazen challenge to disarmament—the remilitarization of the Rhineland.

After the Rhineland militarization, Germany's revisionist efforts shifted from rearmament to territorial expansion. The Treaty of Versailles had stripped Germany of 70,000 square kilometers of European territory, much of which now constituted Eastern European states. Millions of Germans now lived outside the boundaries of the German state, many concentrated in Czechoslovakia's Sudetenland, in the free city of Danzig, and in Lithuania's Memel. Under the Nazi regime, Germany first drove into relatively friendly territory, using mostly political mechanisms to secure the Anschluss—the unification—of Germany with Austria in March 1938. Germany then trained its sights on the Sudetenland, where a vocal German minority charged it was being persecuted by the Czechoslovakian government.

Yet however aggressive German actions, the British consistently interpreted German intentions as limited and relatively benign. The remilitarization of the Rhineland, for example, was interpreted as a German attempt to relieve its insecurity over its undefended border. As outlined by the British Foreign Office, while the action might be an attempt to revise Versailles, there was also "a great deal of justification for Germany's thesis that the conclusion of the Franco-Russian pact justified them in remilitarizing, and more particularly, refortifying the Rhineland."[50] When Germany threatened Czechoslovakia, its expansionist aims toward Czechoslovakia were likewise interpreted as limited, as an attempt to ensure German minority rights. Even Munich itself was treated as a sign that German intentions were benign, and appeasement the right strategy. In September 1938, a Foreign Office memo suggested that "international steps of some sort should be taken, without undue delay, to see what *really legitimate* grievances Germany has and what surgical operations are necessary to rectify them. Potential sores should be discovered and treated quickly. If there are genuine cases for self-determination they should be established and remedied, whether by virtue of Article 19 of the League Covenant or otherwise."[51] On October 3, Chamberlain argued to his cabinet that Munich had created space for a solution to the armaments race, and that Britain should not hesitate to open up negotiations with Germany in pursuit of a sustainable peace.[52]

So too was Britain's decision in late 1938 to confront Germany detached from costly signals of harm and interest. Indeed there was very little costly information driving British elites' reassessment of Hitler's ambitions in autumn of 1938. This is not to say that the British did not seek intelligence about intentions, or that their perception of threat was mere fantasy. In late 1938 to 1939, British officials seemed desperate to gather information about Hitler's intentions: they debated where Hitler would strike next (East? West?), whether Germany's demands remained negotiable, and what Germany's ultimate aims might be. But the information they gathered differed little from what they had prior to Munich, and indeed one historian goes as far as to argue that Britain's "revised appraisals had little to do with new sources of information."[53] The "intelligence" the British gathered was primarily reports about Hitler's speeches and propaganda campaign, not costly, insider information that could have been considered a reliable indicator of aims.

What is striking about the period from fall of 1938 to spring of 1939 is that Hitler really didn't *do* much of anything: he did not change his demands, he did not accelerate rearmament, he did not threaten to invade a country that was more dear to Britain's interest than those of Eastern Europe. Eventually of course there were costly signals of Germany's intentions, most notably the Prague coup in March 1939.[54] And indeed it is the Prague coup that is often taken as the turning point in British grand strategy, the moment when Britain committed to defending Eastern Europe against Germany's expansion. But British understandings of Germany's intentions—and its commitment to mobilize against German aggression—were shifting months before the Prague coup. By the time Hitler moved to destroy Czechoslovakia, the British government had already come to believe that Hitler intended to dominate Europe.[55] Indeed, these beliefs shaped Britain's interpretation of what Prague indicated about Germany's intentions: the Prague coup fit easily within the frame that Nazi Germany was a revolutionary state.

In sum, throughout the interwar period, Britain seemed to ignore costly signals of Germany's intentions. Instead, British leaders looked to what Germany's leaders said about Germany's expansion—their legitimation strategies—to judge the extent of German ambition. Germany's rhetoric, as argued below, was not costly; it was, however, resonant. How German leaders justified expansion, and how these legitimation strategies shaped Britain's decisions to appease or confront Germany, is the subject to which we now turn.

Legitimating Revolution: Germany's Rhetoric of Revision, 1935–39

As argued above, the British strategic response to Germany's rising power, both before and after Munich, generates substantial theoretical and historical puzzles. Why, in the face of consistent German aggression, did the British turn to accommodation—why did politicians continue to believe that Hitler could be appeased? Why then, over a period of five months, would the British embrace a policy of confrontation, one that diverged so widely from previous grand strategy that, had it been articulated in September 1938, it would have left most British elites and public "in a condition of stunned surprise"?[56] A simple answer would be that, in late 1938, the British came to understand that Germany posed an existential threat to its security, one that demanded immediate mobilization, both at home and abroad, no matter what the cost. But this raises the question, why is it that the British suddenly came to perceive Germany as a monumental threat? Why did Britain's image of Germany shift so dramatically?

To explain Britain's shifting understanding of the German threat, some scholars have emphasized the role of cognitive frameworks in shaping Britain's decisions for appeasement and confrontation. Yahri-Milo, for example, argues that leaders like Chamberlain were driven more by long-standing beliefs about Germany's intentions and face-to-face interactions with its leaders than they were by costly signals.[57] These frameworks, she argues, led to "selective attention," causing these leaders to privilege costless signals of limited aims over costly signals of revolutionary revisionism. Likewise, Keith Neilson draws attention to existing British worldviews as shaping perceptions of Germany's intentions: so entrenched were the British in a "Versailles" mindset that all signals were interpreted through this framework.

The analysis below follows these psychological approaches in arguing that the British viewed Germany's actions through frameworks that shaped perceptions of intentions. But instead of focusing on cognitive processes, this study takes a rhetorical and social approach. It was German rhetoric that drove British interpretations of Germany's ambitions, that shaped the meaning of its revisionist actions and, as a result, Britain's decisions to appease or mobilize against German might. Drawing from the framework presented in chapter 2, I argue that the resonance of German strategies depended on two conditions: the Germans' capacity to use multivocal legitimation, their ability to speak across a wide range of audiences; and the institutionally vulnerability of the British, which made its leaders prone to hear a rising power's appeals. When German rhetoric resonated, it signaled restraint, silenced opposition, and even appealed to British identity. When German rhetoric grew dissonant, in contrast, it signaled domination, emboldened opposition, and convinced Britain that the Nazi state was an existential threat.

AN UNKNOWN QUANTITY: THE NAZI REGIME AND MULTIVOCAL LEGITIMATION

Throughout the interwar period, each of Germany's aggressive actions—rearmament, the remilitarization of the Rhineland, the Anschluss in Austria, and expansion into Czechoslovakia—was accompanied by a rhetorical campaign, which attempted to justify Germany's actions to audiences at home and abroad. German politicians, most prominently Hitler, but also other high-ranking Nazi officials such as Goebbels and von Ribbentrop, explained Germany's revisionism in public speeches, in interviews with prominent foreign and domestic newspapers, and in its communications with the British government.

From 1933 up through the Munich crisis, Germany's leaders legitimated revisionist actions using a multivocal strategy: by appealing to principles of equality and self-determination, German leaders ensured that it could both undercut mobilization against its expansion abroad, and yet maintain support for its revisionist efforts at home. Germany's leaders understood that to stave off a balancing coalition, they needed to frame their actions as legitimate, consistent with existing European treaties and norms. If it did not do so, Britain would likely see German expansion as a threat and work to mobilize its resources to contain the rising power. But securing international legitimacy was not enough. At the same time, the success of the Nazi government depended on mobilizing nationalist passions at home and revisionist allies abroad. If they appeared too committed to the status quo, they would risk losing these coalitions.

Appealing to these different coalitions required a multivocal legitimation strategy, one that justified German expansion to different audiences. To do this, German leaders invoked two different justifications for German ambitions: the demand for *equality*, and the need for *self-determination*. First, German politicians justified their revisionist acts as legitimate attempts to reinstate "equality" among the great powers of Europe. Germany, in this narrative, was a peaceful state. Throughout the 1920s and 1930s, Germany had "to put up with a status of inferior rights, which was intolerable for an honour-loving people," as Hitler proclaimed in a speech before the Reichstag in March 1936.[58] What appeared to be German "aggression," its leaders argued, was no more than claiming its equal sovereign rights in Europe. In this narrative, Germany wasn't aggressive or even that revisionist; it was returning to the status quo. Germany might have technically violated the terms of disarmament, for example, but it had done so for just reasons: through rearmament, Hess argued, Germany "assumed the right—the most primitive right of every free people—to create the army and the weapons which were necessary for assuring her freedom and independence."[59] Likewise, the remilitarization of the Rhineland was neither an aggressive act, nor did it signal offensive intentions against France. Rather, in claiming its territory and securing it against foreign threats, Hitler aimed to "to bring the German people from its unworthy situation, to secure equality of rights."[60] Remilitarizing the Rhineland was no more or less than a "restoration of German sovereignty."[61]

Second, Hitler and other German politicians legitimated their revisionism with appeals to self-determination. Versailles, German leaders argued, had denied the German people the fundamental right of self-determination, a principle enshrined in the Versailles order. After the coup in Austria, and after Germany annexed the state, Hitler dismissed accusations that Germany was bent on aggressive conquest. Germany had every right to work with Austria to assure the self-determination of the German people: "Germany is ready at any moment, while fully respecting the freedom of will of Austrian Germanism, to stretch its hand out for a real understanding."[62] It was during the Sudetenland crisis that appeals to self-determination reached their full force. Here, Hitler argued that he "shall not suffer the oppression of the Sudeten Germans. . . . The question is one of injured rights. The Germans demand self-determination." Germany was not behaving aggressively, nor seeking domination: "I do not demand that 3500000 French be oppressed inside Germany or 3,500,000 English," Hitler proclaimed. "I demand firm rights of self-determination for 3,500,000 Germans."[63] Hitler claimed that while Germany was compelled to aid its brethren in the Sudetenland, expansion into non-German areas violated National Socialism's commitment to self-determination and racial purity.[64] As Hitler had argued in 1935, the Nazis believed "the forcible annexation of foreign peoples and property [is] a weakening rather than strengthening of the people and property for the annexing party."[65]

These appeals to self-determination and equality dominated German discourse in the pre-Munich period of revisionist behavior. Using qualitative content analysis, I examined German politicians' legitimation of revisionist behavior from 1936 to 1938, with a specific focus on the Rhineland and Munich crises. These speeches were reported in the public press, as well as through diplomatic cables sent to the Foreign Office. In each of these speeches and communications, I coded "legitimating phrases," those parts of the communication that offered reasons to explain why Germany was engaged in revisionist behavior. Throughout the Rhineland and Munich crises, appeals to equality and self-determination dominated German rhetoric. In speeches about the Rhineland, for example, about 43 percent of all legitimating phrases referenced a need for equality; 20 percent of the phrases were claims of self-determination. In the Sudetenland crisis, self-determination accounted for 67 percent of all of the legitimating phrases.

This language of equality and self-determination may seem straightforward, yet it could sate myriad coalitions simultaneously. On the one hand, when German leaders pledged to seek self-determination and demanded equality for the German people, this invoked existing international norms and institutions. Indeed German leaders emphasized the linkage between their drive for equality and self-determination, and the preservation of a European settlement. Germany was peaceful, but it would "not be content with opportunities which are less favourable than those granted to other nations."[66] If Germans were granted equality, in contrast, they would work productively toward the status quo. As von Ribbentrop argued, Europe must accept German territorial expansion, as "lasting agreement can only be concluded in an atmosphere of sympathetic recognition of the equal rights of all nations." The "peoples of Europe," Hitler argued "are a family in this world," but inequity had left one of the family's members, Germany, isolated and inferior.[67] It was because Germany believed in "the sanctity of treaties" that it was revising the status quo, "to create the necessary conditions" for a European settlement.[68] In essence, Germany sought only "the possibility of a reorganization of Europe and the world by peaceful means, provided that this reorganization of Europe and the world take into account the natural vital principles of the nations and does not . . . lead to injustice. We desire the diminution and reconciliation of intolerable tensions in a peace which offers every country equal rights and equal security."[69]

At the same time, German leaders merged appeals to equality and self-determination with nationalist language designed to appeal to revisionist coalitions at home and abroad. German leaders linked their pursuit of equality and self-determination with demands to uphold German honor—a merging of European appeals with nationalist ones. In the Rhineland, Hitler promised that his "peacetime fortifications" were necessary in the name of equality, but simultaneously that he had taken an "oath" to the German people "to yield to no Power or force in the reestablishment of the honour of our nation."[70] He might negotiate, but not on issues where "Germany's honour was involved."[71] German claims to the Sudetenland might be justified by self-determination, but its expansion there was also a "great historic resurrection," and thus Germans should be "filled with pride and happiness. The world must realize that the Italian and German States are old historic phenomena. No one is obliged to love them, but no power under the sun can remove them. Now this rally is over go home and hold your heads high. We shall never bow to foreign will."[72] Certainly Germans who felt their country had been unjustly stripped of territory and power after Versailles embraced Hitler's charge. So too did revisionists in Eastern European countries—Hungary for example—who saw the potential to share in Germany's revisionism.[73]

Hitler's ambiguous position in German and international politics, as an "unknown quantity" to his observers, gave him the capacity to speak across multiple coalitions. Who Hitler and the Nazis were, and what the truly wanted, was anyone's guess. Many in France and Britain viewed the new chancellor as old German nationalism in a new bottle, an updated version of Bismarck.[74] The ambiguity of his aims was enhanced by competing interests within his government and military. As Tooze notes, it is difficult to assess fragmentation in Nazi German with any clarity.[75] That being said, while Hitler purged many he found resistant or disloyal, he kept enough "conventional" ministers and officers in his circle to cloud Germany's position. Foreign minister Konstantin von Neurath, for example, had served in Streseman's government and was appointed minister of foreign affairs before the Nazis took power. Ludwig Beck, a critic of the Versailles system but never a member of the Nazi Party and a vocal critic of what he saw as irrational and extreme party elements, remained chief of the General Staff until 1938 and was believed to wield substantial power over the Wehrmacht. Surrounded by men of conflicting aims, Hitler's own intentions remained uncertain, and he was able to appeal to multiple principles simultaneously.

As described in detail below, this multivocal legitimation was successful: it undercut British mobilization and allowed Germany to rearm and alter territorial boundaries with little resistance. But in the weeks after the end of the Munich crisis, the Nazi regime changed its legitimation strategies during a propaganda campaign aimed at justifying increased armament and an aggressively expansionist foreign policy. During this campaign the substance of German expansionist demands remained the same: Hitler and others claimed the right to revise territorial boundaries, both in Eastern Europe and in the colonies. They pledged to rearm Germany and lambasted others' efforts to arm against them. Yet while Germany did not alter its substantive demands, its *justifications* changed significantly. The justifications of "equality" and "self-determination" almost entirely disappeared from German legitimation strategies. Instead, throughout the post-Munich period, Nazi leaders invoked two reasons to legitimate its ambitions: German expansion was justified in the face of an existential threat from France and Britain, and was justified by its growing power and need for *Lebensraum*. From the weeks after Munich into the spring of 1939, legitimating phrases were equally split between the frame of existential threat and the need for Lebensraum; together, they account for 90 percent of the content of Germany's legitimating strategies. Gone were the references to equality in a family of European nations and self-determination; at most these appeals occurred in less than 3 percent of German legitimations.[76]

The language of existential threat pervaded justifications for German expansion. In October and November 1938, Hitler spoke to massive audiences at Saarbrucken, Weimar, and Munich; in his speech at Saarbrucken on October 9, 1938, which began the propaganda campaign, Hitler noted that an "understanding with Germany [was] desired by leading men in France and Great Britain," but when "they talk of an 'understanding' we don't know what the understanding is to be about."[77] Hitler now condemned League institutions as merely a guise for British domination and warned its leaders that Germany would not accept "a governess-like guardianship of Germany."[78] If Germany were to expand, it was a legitimate response to existential threats. At Munich, Hitler dismissed negotiations as futile: "For 15 years [we] only negotiated and in doing so lost everything. I too am ready to negotiate, but I will not allow any doubt as to the fact that German rights are not to be infringed, either by negotiation or in any way." He warned that Germany faced an existential threat, that there was "everywhere a rearming and threatening world."[79] Faced with such threats, Hitler warned, "The German Reich is not going to put up in the long run, with a policy of intimidation or even encirclement."[80] For this reason, there should be "no ground for surprise that we assert our rights by other means when we could not do so by normal methods."[81]

Goebbels and von Ribbentrop echoed their Fuhrer's warnings of existential threat in rallies at Hamburg, Berlin, and Reichensberg. At Hamburg, Goebbels warned, "The world is against us. The world is always against us. The only question is whether the world can do anything against us."[82] One British observer of Goebbels reported "the whole speech was filled with the glorification of force and its successful employment by the Nationalist Socialist party."[83] Nazi leaders argued that Britain was full of "warmongers" such as Duff Cooper and Churchill, who agitated openly for preventive war.[84] Likewise the German press amplified the regime's calls for arms and expansion. Britain and France were demanding the "annihilation of the Dictatorships," the paper *Volkisher Beobachter* proclaimed. It certainly could not trust the democracies, who had little control over their warmongers, to commit to peace in the future, and thus must be vigilant. Germany had no choice but to arm itself against the Western nations, as force was, the German press intoned, "the only arbiter in world affairs."[85]

German leaders further merged this rhetoric of existential threat with appeals to its growing might and racial superiority. Lebensraum, of course, was not new to Nazi ideology.[86] But it was during the post-Munich propaganda campaign that German leaders increasingly suggested that their demands for land were justified, not only by "self determination" and the rights of language and blood ties, but also by Germany's expanding national power, racial superiority, and overwhelming might. As Hitler proclaimed to the Reichstag in January 1939, the "overpopulation of our living space" continued to be the "cause of all of our economic difficulties." It was a situation that Germany must either "have to put up with or which we must alter," and National Socialism, Hitler warned, "does not know the word 'capitulation.'"[87]

Nazi officials and the press amplified Hitler's claims. In November, Goebbels proclaimed that the German people would demand colonies as their "appetite grows with the eating."[88] At a speech at Essen, one Nazi politician explained that Germany "has reached a political height such as perhaps never was before . . . I see our German people like a mountain-climber who has been trying for hundreds of thousands of years to climb a steep mountain . . . and who had always after every attempt fallen back to the bottom. He had never succeeded in reaching the final summit, and objective which for me means giving to the people space sufficient for its population."[89] The Germans sought, not reform, but revolution: as institutions threatened to strangle the rising German power, they must be overthrown.[90] As Ribbentrop argued in November 1938, the old world would not be accepted; it would be destroyed, and the Germans could not know "what new thing might arise from the collapse of the old order . . . from the ruins of that old declining civilisation. It was, however, their belief and deepest conviction that if this world changed, eternal Germany would still stand united, strong and great as never before."[91] Germany would seek, not equality within institutions, but its own order on the Continent.[92] Germany now faced a "national emergency," one that demanded unity and sacrifice from the Germany people.[93]

Why did Hitler and his allies abandon multivocal rhetoric in 1938 for language that they must have understood would provoke a British audience? As argued in chapter 2, even actors that have the ability to speak multivocally might turn to dissonant rhetoric when leaders perceive a need for radical and extreme mobilization among the domestic population. In 1938, Hitler faced increasing threats to his political position. The first was his concern that Germany's success at Munich would strengthen coalitions that opposed the Nazis at home. Throughout the crisis, a "dangerous fissure" had "threatened to open between various factions within the leadership of Hitler's regime."[94] Leaders within these factions were eager to use the Munich settlement as evidence that Nazi militarism should be set aside for the pursuit of more normal political and economic goals. Reichsbank officials, for example, argued the government must turn toward "not an expansive power politics, but a policy of peaceful construction," especially as it managed its currency.[95] The majority of Germans backed the Munich settlement, seeing it as evidence that Germany could gain equality and self-determination through negotiation.[96] Hitler not only saw his political position threatened, but his chance to expand Germany fading.

By the fall of 1938, all of these trends threatened to shift the balance of power in Germany away from the Nazi Party. To make matters worse, in the fall of 1938 post-Munich Germany found itself on the verge of a dangerous economic crisis. As the Reichsbank reported in October 3, 1938, "The national Socialist state leadership has managed, despite the critical situation of recent times, to avoid a war that would have jeopardized its earlier success. It now faces, after the political turning point has been reached, the further task of avoiding an inflation whose consequences would be almost as dangerous."[97] They argued that the only way to stem inflationary pressures was to cut Wehrmacht spending.[98] In light of these pressures, Hitler saw himself increasingly hamstrung by his own multivocal rhetoric: he had not only promised to rectify Germany's position through negotiation, he had succeeded. In doing so, he put himself and the Nazi Party as a whole in a precarious political situation. Instead of accepting political defeat, he instead chose the path of extreme rhetorical mobilization. Appealing to anti-Semitic and anti-British rhetoric, he could claim that Germany was in a battle for its life against enemies, both at home and abroad. It was not that Hitler's aims had changed. With the increasing precariousness of the Nazi's position, and the pending economic crisis, only a radical attempt to "re-educate the German people psychologically"[99] to jettison any language that suggested the Versailles system was legitimate, would mobilize support. These efforts to mobilize their own public would provoke a confrontation abroad.

BRITAIN AND INSTITUTIONAL VULNERABILITY

It seems stunning, in retrospect, that the British would give any credence to Hitler's claims: why would they listen to German reasons, when the Germans seemed determined to expand on the Continent? German legitimations proved resonant, not only because of Germany's multivocality, but because of Britain's *institutional vulnerability:* Britain believed that its institutional environment was increasingly unsettled and that, as a result, its security was in peril. Recent historical accounts argue that the British continued commitment to appeasement in the face of a growing Nazi threat must be placed in an international context. These scholars push beyond traditional work that suggests British politicians viewed German actions through pathological "cognitive blinders" that obscured the true meaning of Hitler's actions. Instead, the British interpreted Germany's rhetoric through their own position within the Versailles order, which made them more likely to hear Germany's justifications as legitimate.[100]

As Steiner argues, as early as 1933, the international institutional order "was in disarray."[101] While Versailles' institutions were still dominant in 1930s Europe, it was a fragmenting system, one that was under strain well before the Nazi regime came to power in 1933.[102] The leaders of Versailles were consistently condemned for the their selective application of norms. Members of the League of Nations were hardly equal in standing, and principles of self-determination seemed downright hollow in the colonial world. Throughout the 1920s, moreover, great and small powers alike clashed over issues of collective security and disarmament, and even "good friends" could not agree on the terms of disarmament, as evidenced by Anglo-American clashes over naval reductions.[103] Even moments of relative success revealed fragmentation in the Versailles system. While the Treaty of Locarno supposedly solidified collective security, it simultaneously suggested a lack of confidence in the League's ability to provide collective security—if the League were seen as effective, why was an additional multilateral treaty necessary?

British politicians were deeply concerned about a collapse of the Versailles order. Although Britain was not the creator of these institutions, it had stepped in as the primary guarantor of collective security institutions. Britain became the primary mediator—the so-called "honest broker"—of critical follow-on treaties that pushed forward the disarmament process in the late 1920s and early 1930s, and attempted to settle and guarantee Eastern European boundaries in the mid-1930s as well.[104] The extent to which Britain was invested in the Versailles system can be measured not only through treaties and organizational membership, but through the perceptions of the British elite and public as well. Put most simply, "The League," one diplomat wrote, "is the cornerstone of British policy."[105] British elites believed that their security rested on the persistence of the European settlement. It was not, to be clear, that Britain hoped to remain active in Continental disputes. To the contrary, only if peace was secured on the Continent could the British invest their declining resources in key imperial outposts abroad.

Yet to reduce British perceptions to the instrumental and material would not do them justice: as Nielson and others have noted, British politicians had deep ideological commitments to the Versailles institutions as well.[106] The League's substitution of liberal procedure for the balance of power, for example, resonated with a Whiggish tradition in Britain, whose adherents found comfort in the notion that disputes could be solved through reason rather than military force.[107] That being said, there were those politicians, especially among Conservatives, that questioned whether League institutions were a worthwhile investment; many politicians soon saw themselves as highly constrained by their institutional commitments: "The covenant has deprived Britain of room for maneuver."[108] But even these elites saw themselves as constrained by a collective commitment, among politicians and the public alike, to League order.[109] All of this culminated, as Prime Minister Stanley Baldwin put it, with "the vital character of the League of Nations as a fundamental element in the conduct of our foreign affairs."[110]

In sum, it was not individual naïveté or moral failings that gave rhetoric its power. It was Germany's capacity for multivocal action, combined with Britain's institutional vulnerability, that made rhetoric so resonant. Because of this, Germany's rhetoric had significant causal effects. As long as Hitler and other German politicians justified their aims with appeals to collective security, equality, and self-determination—norms central to the European system established by the Treaty of Versailles—they signaled constraint, convincing British politicians that Germany could be bound to an existing institutional order; they silenced "anti-appeasers" who demanded a more confrontational policy; and they resonated with Britain's self-identity as a liberal, democratic, and neutral state. When German politicians abandoned these legitimation strategies, so too did Britain come to see this revisionist state as insatiable, impervious to negotiation, and responsive only to the language of force.

From Appeasement to Confrontation: Rhetoric and British Mobilization

German rhetoric shaped British collective mobilization, both its decision to accommodate Hitler's demands, and its shift toward confrontation in the fall of 1938. Establishing the causal connection between rhetoric and mobilization is a tricky business. At the most basic level, the evidence should show that the change in British grand strategy in late 1938 correlates more closely with rhetorical shifts than it does with changes in the strategic balance, the availability of credible information, or domestic unity. And indeed the shift in British grand strategy from appeasement to confrontation correlates well with the change in German legitimation strategies. As argued earlier in this paper, is was from October 1938 to March 1939 that the British came to embrace a policy of confrontation, and the timing of this shift cannot be explained with reference to the strategic balance or the acquisition of new information about Germany's intentions.

What did change post-Munich, as demonstrated above, was Hitler's rhetoric, as Hitler abandoned his multivocal strategy and moved toward the rhetoric of might. British elites not only noticed but quickly grew alarmed at the shift in rhetoric. "This is most depressing and gloomy reading," remarked one Foreign Office official on Nazi language. The German propaganda campaign was, as Chamberlain put it, having an "unfortunate effect on Anglo-German relations."[111] As Nazi rhetoric hardened, so too did the British see their chances for a negotiated peace dwindle, and that, as Halifax argued "in present circumstances no useful purpose would be served by a resumption at the present time of the contemplated Anglo-German conversations."[112] When Hitler's legitimation strategies seemed to return to earlier tropes, such as they did briefly in December 1938, officials became more optimistic: Hitler must fear that he had "stiffened opposition to German demands," so much so that they were in for a "period of softer words."[113]

Yet a robust explanation should not only predict outcomes but also be able to account for the mechanisms of change—it should be able to explain *how* and *why* British policymakers chose a strategy of appeasement before Munich, and came to abandon a grand strategy of appeasement and embrace a policy of confrontation in the months following the crisis. To examine the effects of rhetoric, I relied on a process-tracing approach to analyze how British policymakers interpreted and responded to German politicians' rhetoric, focusing specifically on the period from 1938 to 1939. The narrative of British policy below relies heavily on primary documentation from the British Foreign Office, the cabinet papers, and the prime minister's papers on relations from Germany from 1936 to 1939. The case draws especially on documents from the Foreign Office, particularly the complete records of the Foreign Office's correspondence about Germany from 1938 to 1939. These papers are composed of incoming intelligence on German foreign policy and contain ongoing discussions about Germany's aims and British foreign policy. Participants in this discussion include key elites, ranging from traditional "appeasers," such as Foreign Secretary Lord Halifax and Britain's ambassador to Germany, Nevile Henderson, to officials skeptical of Germany's intentions such as Permanent Under-Secretary of State for Foreign Affairs Robert Vansittart.

In order to measure the response of the broader public, I also analyzed editorials on British foreign policy from two major newspapers, the *Times* and the *Manchester Guardian*. With the *Times* long associated with the Conservative government, and the *Manchester Guardian* the voice of the Labour opposition, the editorials examined represent a broad spectrum of political opinion. As important as the archival research is to the analysis below, it should be stressed that the argument here is consistent with much of the existing historiography, especially the postrevisionist historiography on 1930s Anglo-German relations. Of course, serious historical debates continue to mark studies of interwar British policy; this chapter is hardly like to settle these debates, though it does hope, at a minimum, to demonstrate the leverage of the legitimation approach to a key moment in rising power politics.

If the theory here is correct, we should find evidence in these documents that British policymakers before Munich believed Germany was signaling constraint. After Munich, we should see these same elites reacting to the change in legitimation strategy, evidence that Hitler's rhetorical shift—not strategic factors or costly signals—convinced British elites that domination was Germany's goal, and mobilization the only reasonable response. Likewise, if rhetorical coercion is at play, then we should be able to find evidence of substantial hypocrisy costs, which evaporate along with Hitler's change in legitimation strategy. And finally, if identity matters, then we should find British elites deeply concerned with how Germany's claims affect Britain's existential status.

FROM RESTRAINT TO DOMINATION

Until October 1938, most of Britain had been persuaded of the legitimacy of Germany's revisionist claims. As a result, most elites thought that some form of compromise with revisionist Germany was possible, that Hitler and his countrymen could be brought into a general European settlement. Despite their concern about German aggression, British elites still counseled appeasement in the face of rearmament as long as Hitler's claims were consistent with Versailles. Faced with Hitler's claims, the British admitted that "Hitler had a tremendous case of grievance,"[114] and that his appeals to League institutions warranted continuing the policy "which we have followed for 15 years—that of coming to terms with Germany . . . so far as they have justice, logic, and reason on their side."[115] As long as Germany articulated its demands in the language of the League, most British elites argued that Germany could be bound to these institutions, *regardless* of its ill intentions. Soon after Hitler announced German rearmament in 1935, for example, the Foreign Office counseled the pursuit of a disarmament treaty with Germany. Even if the ideal—a multilateral disarmament treaty—could not be obtained, then even a "gentlemen's agreement" would be "likely to serve our purpose for binding the Germans for the future."[116]

Likewise the British reaction to territory revisionism was not based on *whether* Germany would expand—that aim, as officials detailed in numerous internal memos, was taken as a given—but *why* it sought to revise the territorial status quo. There was almost a consensus that Germany sought to revise its borders, and would seek unification with Austria; the annexation of the Sudetenland; and the revision of boundaries in Danzig, Memel, and other areas where there was a substantial German minority. Yet if Germany's territorial aims were legitimate, then the British believed that Germany's intentions were ultimately limited and could be accommodated within a general European settlement. As Weinberg notes, Lord Lothian suggested in his 1936 proposal that a "full application of the principle of self-determination . . . would right the alleged wrongs done Germany and, without seriously harming British interests or the national rights of non-Germans, preserve the peace."[117] To this end, in January 1936 no less a realist than E. H. Carr suggested that Germany's union with Austria could be accommodated "with a minimum of danger to British interests," provided it was done within League procedures. Indeed, Carr urged Britain to make Britain's conciliatory position public, as it was "perfectly clear and in accordance with our general principles."[118] Likewise William Strang argued that while German expansion might "be a threat to our interests," if Germany could be bound to pursue such change legitimately, "without undue damage to the cause of international law," then Britain should not oppose it."[119] As long as Germany pledged itself to accepted norms, the British, as Neville Chamberlain, then chancellor of the exchequer, argued, were "prepared to deal with [Germany] on the basis *that she means what she says*."[120]

Even at the height of the Munich crisis, the British argued that successful negotiations depended on Hitler's justifications for demanding the Sudetenland. As Chamberlain noted in cabinet discussions during the crisis, "The crucial question was whether Herr Hitler was speaking the truth when he said that he regarded the Sudeten question as a racial question which must be settled, and that the object of his policy was racial unity and not the domination of Europe. Much depends on the answer to this question."[121] Halifax agreed, arguing that he did not think it "necessary to assume that Hitler's racial ambitions are necessarily likely to expand into international power lust."[122] And if a settlement to the crisis could be achieved on the basis of self-determination, then the British, as Nevile Henderson argued, "could *bind Germany down* to support the principle," more generally and "she would have to admit it in the case of the Polish corridor."[123]

Significantly, when Hitler and others veered from Versailles norms the British abandoned their beliefs that Germany could be contained within existing institutions. When German rearmament progressed without a nod to the Treaty of Locarno, for example, Anthony Eden charged that "the myth is now exploded that Herr Hitler only repudiates treaties imposed on Germany by force," and suggested the League might consider punishing Germany through sanctions.[124] Likewise, when Hitler seemed willing to abandon self-determination, such as in his second meeting with Chamberlain at Godesberg, the British grew far more pessimistic about a general settlement. Halifax and Cadogan notably stiffened their positions, and Halifax warned Chamberlain that Britain had a "moral obligation" to stand against Hitler's outrageous demands.[125] There was, as Steiner argues, a moment when Chamberlain returned from Godesberg, "with all the determinants of power exactly the same, that the majority of the Cabinet was prepared to reject Hitler's terms even at the cost of war."[126] If Hitler was to abandon the principle of self-determination, then his claims were illegitimate, and Britain would mobilize, however reluctantly, for war.[127]

But it was only when German leaders entirely abandoned their appeals to the Versailles order in the fall of 1938, that British grand strategy underwent a dramatic shift. The weeks after Munich found the Foreign Office planning for more appeasement. Even those who stiffened at Godesberg, Halifax and Cadogan, suggested that Britain's best option was, as Lammers argues "to ask Hitler point-blank to say what he wanted, perhaps in connexion with an offer to call a conference to review the Versailles Treaty on the grounds that it had been 'a temporary, and very bad, expedient.'"[128] Grand strategy would continue to revolve around "appeasement: we must aim at establishing relations with the Dictator Powers which will lead to a settlement in Europe and to a sense of stability."[129] The Foreign Office and cabinet began to plan for *more concessions* in hopes of sating Germany. For British elites, then Munich was a promising signal that Germany wanted a peaceful settlement.

Faced with Hitler's rhetorical rage, as one Foreign Office official wrote, it seemed that "The League system, and 'collective security' are, if not dead, in a state of suspended animation."[130] Those that had most fervently argued German could be contained through appeasement—Lord Halifax most notably among them—now made a different argument: no institution could stop Germany from *dominating* Europe. Germany's claims that it deserved revision of the world order as a matter of power, rather than as a matter of right, that it would rearm not out of grievance but for reasons of strength, and expand into territory where it had no ethnic claims, meant that appeasement was no longer possible. Any attempt to bind Germany to institutions, to engage Germany's demands "as a process of revision of the Versailles Treaty, are equally regarded by Hitler as defeatism and weakness on our part."[131] Meeting Germany's drive toward domination with "strength and the ability to fight if necessary" was the only option.[132]

What is particularly astonishing is that once Hitler's *reasons* for his revisionist goals changed, demands that had once been considered negotiable now became casus belli. Even after Munich, for example, the British had seemed ready to negotiate Germany's legitimate claims to self-determination in areas such as the free city of Danzig, the Polish corridor to Memel.[133] It further accepted the need to return at least some colonies to Germany, as recognition of its equal rights as a sovereign power. Once Hitler abandoned the rhetoric of self-determination and equality, however, Britain's policies changed. For example, British elites argued they should be prepared for war if Germany moved into Danzig, and one opinion poll showed 76 percent of the British public believed that if Germany were to demand Danzig, then Britain should fight on behalf of Poland.[134] Likewise, in light of Germany's pursuit of domination, colonial concessions were impossible, and "whatever might have been justifiable and expedient before Munich, to concede any colonial territory now would be regarded both abroad and at home as a sign of our complete decadence."[135] In sum, as German demands became illegitimate, so too did the British come to believe that Germany could be bound within existing institutions, and that German revisionism must be met with force.

RHETORICAL COERCION: FROM RHETORICAL TRAPS TO MOBILIZATION

Not all British policymakers believed Germany could be bound to institutions. Austen Chamberlain argued that under the Nazis, Germany exhibited an "all Prussian imperialism, with an added savagery, a racial pride."[136] Winston Churchill, the most well-known of the "anti-appeasers," argued throughout the 1930s that the government was gravely underestimating the German threat.[137] Antiappeasers presented powerful arguments for ramping up the British rearmament program. As Ralph Wigram commented on the issue of a general disarmament conference, "I do not believe in heroic solutions on policy: only the quiet and methodical building up of our own strength. That alone will make Germany (who covets our positions) reflect."[138] Likewise Vansittart argued that "until we can be quite sure that [Germany] has renounced her evil ways, we must be extremely cautious in strengthening her at the expense of ourselves or our connections."[139] Given Hitler's actions "anything that fails to provide security by 1938 is inadequate and blind."[140] They argued too that only strong alliances could restrain German actions in Eastern Europe. Vansittart, for example, called for closer coordination with France, while Churchill and Austen Chamberlain proposed driving a wedge between Italy and Germany, and securing the former's support. Some even went as far as to suggest an alliance with Soviet Russia as the only means to contain Germany's expansion in the east.[141]

The antiappeasers, in essence, were proposing a hedging grand strategy, a true version of "hope for the best, and prepare for the worst." But Germany's legitimation strategies not only persuaded, but silenced. So long as Hitler could claim that his efforts to rearm and change the territorial status quo appeared legitimate, the British public could not be convinced to mobilize against Germany, and most saw advocates of confrontation as no more than hypocrites. Evidence of rhetorical coercion is evident in internal discussions among antiappeasers, in their public discourse, and in the public's reaction to their policies. Documents show that elites recognized that Germany's claims trapped them in their own rhetoric. For example, in May 1935, leaders within the Foreign Office engaged in what only can be called a "content analysis" of Hitler's rhetoric surrounding rearmament.[142] Hitler's rhetoric, Foreign Office officials like Wigram claimed, was empty and demonstrated only "the extremely clever manner in which Herr Hitler—basing himself on the methods of his master, Bismarck, has been able without falsification but simply by omissions and corrections to alter the tone of the Fourteen Points and the treaty on the rights and wrongs of the discussion of disarmament."[143]

But Wigram and others also realized, whatever the truth of Hitler's statements, they created a problem for antiappeasers: "But the fact remains that this long passage in Herr Hitler's is an able take which . . . will make a strong appeal to English opinion" and indeed "it will weaken the case that can be made for defence against Germany." German rhetoric also undercut calls for a strong alliance against Germany. In Hitler's framing, alliances against Germany were entirely illegitimate: "Germany desires peace and is serving it more than those who are always forming new blocs in order to hurl once more into the abyss the most peace-loving country in the heart of Europe."[144] As with rearmament, proponents of alliances realized their precarious position. According to Vansittart, the Germans were "trying, pretty successfully, to drive wedges between ourselves and our associates."[145] The antiappeasers were frustrated: "We should certainly not let the Germans get away with these distortions and misrepresentations."[146]

But ultimately, antiappeasers could not fight back: dissenters were faced with intense hypocrisy costs. When Churchill called for rearmament to face the German threat, for example, he did so couched in language that commended the League and collective security, saying, "Some people say: 'put your trust in the League of Nations', others say: 'put your trust in British rearmament.' I say we want both. I put my trust in both."[147] Alliances too must be legitimated in the language of collective security. As Vansittart put it, any new treaty "must *be*, and still more—this cynically—must *appear* as part of a general settlement."[148] This meant that "to satisfy a powerful section of public opinion in this country, which would regard a system of defensive alliances as a retrograde step incompatible with the League system of collective security, His Majesty's Government will presumably wish in the first instance to try for agreements on the Locarno principle."[149]

Despite their best efforts, antiappeasers were treated as hypocrites, dangerous warmongers who would return to the fatal policies of 1914. The *Times,* for example, denounced Churchill's calls for rearmament as a return to dangerous "power politics: they have learned nothing from 1914 and nothing from 1919."[150] When Duff Cooper, for example, argued for increased Anglo-French cooperation, "League enthusiasts interpreted it as a call for an Anglo-French alliance and therefore a return to discredited pre-1914 policies." A Commons debate that followed determined that alliances were "counter to the spirit of the League of Nations."[151] As many of the antiappeasers anticipated, then, a call for confrontation was not "practical politics," and as E. H. Carr said, any government that proposed such policies "would be committing suicide at the next election."[152]

So long as German politicians used institutional norms to justify Germany's revisionist program, antiappeasers had no grounds for opposition, no language that could be used to justify a confrontational policy. When Hitler and others shifted their rhetoric after Munich, Britain's antiappeasers discovered they could use Hitler's rhetoric against him, deploying his attacks on collective security and the liberal, democratic order to legitimate a confrontational policy, and mobilize the British public for war. The answer to domestic fragmentation, officials argued in November 1938, would be found in rhetorical mobilization: "The problem before the Government is therefore to find an appeal which will unite the country in resolving upon measures of rearmament so considerable that their achievement may well involve both a curtailment of our liberties and privileges and a reduction of our standard of living."[153] Hitler's increasing attacks on liberal democracy proved one justification for rearmament. As Churchill argued in late October 1938, collective security was not dead but its fate rested on rearmament. Was rearmament "call to war? I declare it to be the sole guarantee of peace. The swift and resolute gathering of forces to confront not only military but moral aggression; the resolute and sober acceptance of their duty by the English-speaking peoples and by all nations, great and small, who wish to walk with them." So too did the fate of Britain, indeed of democratic civilization, rest on alliances. Duff Cooper argued before a British and French audience that "to hold Germanism in check, a much greater effort would now be needed." Germany was "threatening civilization" and the British and French empires must mobilize "the quality of their strength, which was more important than the quantity."[154]

Evidence suggests that antiappeasers' rhetoric was extremely effective at mobilizing the public and parties behind a policy of confrontation. National unity had not been a given after Munich: even in the face of Hitler's threatening language, the public still supported appeasement, and it seemed that the British Labour Party and trade unions would be reluctant to endorse a full mobilization of resources. But antiappeasers' rhetoric proved effective. Scholars have long called attention to Churchill's ability to unite the Conservative, Liberal, and Labour parties in his "War Cabinet," but as Talbot Imlay argues, this unity emerged earlier than is often understood. By January 1939, Britain's parties agreed that "Germany represented an implacable enemy whose defeat required a massive national effort."[155] Antiappeasers' language—that Germany sought domination, that it was a threat to civilization—now permeated each party's documents, laying the foundation for a consensus coalition. Liberals, for example, now decried appeasement as "surrender to Nazi Germany of the dominant position in Europe," and by January 1939, Labour, Imlay reports, was fully committed to the idea that further German expansion meant war.[156]

Public opinion rallied around antiappeasers' rhetoric as well.[157] The same public that had overwhelmingly supported appeasement and condemned the proponents of rearmament as inviting war now demanded the confrontation of Germany. By November 1938, a poll in the *News Chronicle* suggested that a vast majority of the British public—72 percent—now supported a greatly expanded rearmament program, and other polls suggested that any further German expansion should be met with a military response.

Both party leaders and the public pressured leaders to seek alliances, not only with France and the United States, but with Soviet Russia as well.[158] In sum, by early 1939 a once recalcitrant Britain was fully mobilized around a grand strategy of confrontation. Antiappeasers' rhetoric, once dissonant, had yoked together what Anthony Eden called a "new idealism," a nation determined to resist Germany's bid for domination.[159]

FROM EXISTENTIAL COSTS TO EXISTENTIAL THREAT

In the years before Munich, appeasement was seen as preserving Britain's liberal self-identity: it was a grand strategy that was not only expedient and rational, but was a foreign policy—perhaps the only foreign policy—that resonated with Britain's sense of itself as a liberal great power. German politicians' appeals to liberal procedures and equality, their rhetoric of collective security, and their use of self-determination to justify territorial demands thus resonated deeply with British officials, and British politicians believed that any attempt to balance against Germany would delegitimize their identity as protector of the League and collective security. Hitler's claims to equality, for example, challenged Britain's sense that League institutions were fair, that it had mechanisms to accommodate legitimate demands. After meeting with Hitler in 1937, Lord Halifax argued he felt Hitler had "just claims" in seeing League procedures as unfair and, more specifically, as oriented toward maintaining an unjust status quo.[160] The British feared that confronting Germany would delegitimize their identity as a democratic state, committed to the principle of self-determination, a fear most clearly seen during the Sudetenland crisis. During the crisis, Hitler demanded the Sudetenland problem be solved through a plebiscite, a process that would undoubtedly place Czech territory in German hands. While Hitler justified the plebiscite through the rhetoric of self-determination, the British remained deeply disturbed at the idea of handing over portions of Czechoslovakia—a democratic nation and their strongest potential ally in Eastern Europe—to the Nazi regime. Nevertheless, Chamberlain and his cabinet believed that opposing a plebiscite and self-determination would undermine their own identity as a democratic nation. While "some people might take the view that the demands for a Plebiscite should be rejected out of hand," Chamberlain argued, "that was not his view, nor the view of the Foreign Secretary." Instead Chamberlain "thought it was impossible for a democracy like ourselves to say that we would go to war to prevent the holding of a Plebiscite."[161] Ultimately most officials agreed with Nevile Henderson that Britain's strategy must proceed on "moral grounds . . . not allowing oneself to be influenced by considerations about the balance of power. . . . We cannot win the battle for the rule of right versus might, unless and until our own moral position is unassailable."[162] As Chamberlain put it, Britain "had a mission—the mission of peace maker within Europe."[163]

After Munich, Germany's legitimation strategies were nothing less than a frontal attack on British identity. Hitler questioned, even mocked, liberal principles of negotiation and reason as subservient to Germany's emotional and militant identity: "I am convinced I am leader of a manly people. . . . There has been created today a community of spirit throughout our people of power and strength such as Germany never before has known."[164] Germany had once fallen prey to the soft principles of reason, but now "the umbrella-carrying types of our former bourgeois world of parties are extinguished and they will never return. . . . The German is either the first soldier in the world or he is no soldier at all."[165] It was Germany, and not Britain, that represented true democracy, and Hitler proclaimed that while a British politician "may have an electorate of 15,000 or 20,000. I have one of 40,000,000. . . . The only difference is that they represent only a fraction, and I the whole of the nation."[166] Indeed, not only did Hitler claim his identity as an "arch democrat,"[167] he questioned if Britain was truly a democratic state at all. At home, Britain had failed to unify its own people. Abroad, British imperialism "to my mind smells rather of force than of democracy."[168]

Before Hitler's attacks, Britain had deliberately avoided casting disputes with Germany as ideological. British officials argued that European institutions embodied universal principles, and that if institutions like the League "became an ideological bloc it would be as dead as a mutton."[169] As Germany continued to rail against liberal democracy, the British response hardened. It was no longer that fascist Germany (and Italy) might pose a threat to British interests; it was that the very presence of totalitarian states threatened British identity, and indeed the entire existence of Western civilization. As Collier put it in a memo of November 1938, the Foreign Office must insist that "Germany and Italy are not normal states merely claiming the redress of specific grievances, but represent a predatory movement which merely gains momentum with each concession made to it. If this is recognised, the question for decision becomes merely: when and where should the stand against this predatory movement be made?"[170] These states, he continued, were capable of nothing more than "aggressive nationalism and indefinite expansion at the expense of others."[171] They were, in essence, outside the boundaries of reason and civilization.

Britain had no choice but to confront and resist, a theme echoed not only in the Foreign Office but in the British press and politicians' speeches. Churchill proved the most vocal spokesman of British identity. Germany's "combination of medieval passion, a party caucus, the weapons of modern science, and the blackmailing power of air-bombing, is the most monstrous menace to peace order, and fertile progress that has appeared in the world since the Mongol invasions of the fourteenth century."[172] In the face of this existential threat, "either Britain was going to rise again in her strength as a mighty, valiant nation, champion of lawful right, defender of human freedom, or she was going to collapse and be despoiled, plundered, mutilated, and reduced not merely to the rank of a second-rate country but to a dependent condition."[173]

Understanding Britain's response to Hitler's rhetoric as founded in an existential crisis helps explain not only the content and fervor of Britain's shift toward confrontation but its strange lack of strategic calculation. It is not that British politicians became completely irrational; documents continue to be filled with concrete discussions of defense requirements. But gone from the discussion were references to economic costs or domestic constraints—Britain would bear the cost of rearmament and alliances because it must. Likewise, while there was no official coalition between Britain's Conservative, Liberal, or Labour parties, each shared the assumption that "Germany would have to be resisted regardless of cost."[174] Germany's change in rhetoric was no mere conveyor of new information. It signaled nothing less than a paradigm shift, propelling Britain into a world in which its very identity was at stake. Under such circumstances, as Steiner argues, politicians "did not think of balances; they just assumed that Britain and its empire would prevail."[175] Or perhaps more accurately, that Britain, its empire, and its allies *must* prevail.

In sum, Hitler's rhetoric had a profound effect on British strategy, both before and after the fall of 1938. Before the Munich crisis, German rhetoric operated through all three pathways outlined in chapter 2 of this book: it signaled restraint and constraint; it silenced antiappeasers in Britain; and it appealed to British liberal identity. As a result, appeasement seemed a reasonable response to Hitler's demands. Just as Hitler's resonant rhetoric enabled accommodation, his illegitimate rhetoric was dissonant and provoked a dramatic response. In the wake of Hitler's propaganda campaign, British politicians became certain that Hitler was an aggressive, revolutionary revisionist, one that had to be confronted regardless of the cost.

The foundation of this book is that rhetoric shapes strategic choices even during the most dire moments in international politics. Faced with a rising German power, and by the measure of all costly signals, an aggressive one, British elites paid attention not only to power and intentions, but to the substance of Hitler's claims, to the way in which German politicians justified their revisionist demands. Before Munich, Hitler's rhetoric effectively signaled that it would be bound by the existing international order. When critics of appeasement appeared, Hitler's legitimation strategies set rhetorical traps, raising the costs of opposing Germany's expansion. And finally Germany's legitimation strategy persuaded some British politicians that any opposition to expansion would undermine Britain's own legitimacy as a democratic state. But after Munich, the language coming from Germany proved dissonant to British ears. Politicians and the public alike began to see Germany as bent on domination. Antiappeasers could use Hitler's words to create a new mobilizing rhetoric. And far from feeling secure,

British elites began to see Germany as a threat to its very identity. Under these conditions, confrontation was the only reasonable strategy.

But perhaps this study only serves to prove the point that, even if individuals do not always ignore "cheap talk," they *should*: politicians value words over deeds only at their peril. This is of course precisely one of the points Carr strove to make in the *Twenty Years' Crisis*, when he condemned Britain for its naïve embrace of liberal principles and neglect of national interest and power. It is tempting to read the case of 1930s Britain not as a revelation of rhetoric's influence on grand strategy, but as a urgent warning to ignore the sweet words of revisionists and focus instead on their capabilities. This would be a mistake. Whatever processes should guide foreign policy, the effects of language are powerful and hard to escape. Even Carr himself, as noted above, was not immune from the effects of legitimation strategies. In other words, even "realists" proved bound by institutional shackles and willing to listen to resonant rhetoric.

CHAPTER 6

Japan's Folly

The Conquest of Manchuria, 1931–33

Hakku Ichiu [Eight corners of the world under one roof].
—Prime Minister Fumimaro Konoe, January 1940

On September 18, 1931, an explosion shook a Japanese-owned railway in Mukden, Manchuria.[1] Japan's Kwantung Army accused Chinese troops of attempting to destroy Japan's railway; in reality, it was the colonial army itself that had sabotaged the property as a pretext to occupy the city. During the first few weeks of the crisis, Tokyo's government attempted to halt the Kwantung Army's march through Manchuria. While the government's efforts appeared successful at first, by the end of October the Kwantung Army was launching air strikes against Chinchow, where Manchuria's former governor Chang Hsueh-liang had taken refuge. In Tokyo, the voices for restraint receded. By September 1932, Japan's government opted to sever Manchuria from China, recognizing the puppet-state Manchuoko.

This was not the first time Japan had used its increasing might to pursue revisionist ambitions. Throughout the course of its rise, Japan expanded its territory, often using force to achieve its aims. In the wake of the Sino-Japanese War, Japan claimed Taiwan as its own. In 1905, Japan's defeat of Russia gave it control over Korea, which it would formally annex in 1910. Throughout the early twentieth century, Japan sought to dominate Manchuria, pushing aside Russian and Chinese rivals to gain control over the territory. Yet, whatever the scope of Japanese revisionism in the early twentieth century, it was the expansion into Manchuria that proved a tipping point, launching what many scholars call Japan's "fifteen years' war."[2] It was during the Manchurian crisis that Japan became locked into a futile conflict with China. It was in Manchuria that Japan became mired in a nationalist struggle that sucked critical economic and military resources from the struggling Japanese state. Within Japan, the years that followed the

Manchurian crisis would see the military elite wrest seats of power from political parties. By 1937, Japan was dominated by nationalist, pan-Asianist hardliners and military leaders, a coalition driven toward tragically expansionist projects.

Internationally, the Manchurian crisis provoked a sea change in how the United States responded to Japan's might.[3] Throughout the early twentieth century, the great powers had largely accommodated Japan, cooperating with the power as it expanded into Korea and Taiwan, and made early incursions into Manchuria. At the beginning of the Manchurian crisis, the Hoover administration appeared reluctant to steer the United States on a course toward conflict with Japan over Manchuria. It was not immediately apparent to American officials that Japanese actions in Manchuria even amounted to a "crisis." Japan's aggression in China was neither unexpected nor unusual; and this was not the first time a state had used force to quell local disorder. And if Japan's aims were revisionist, most American officials believed the United States had neither the capacity nor interest to contest Japan in Manchuria.

But by late 1931, much of the administration had concluded, as Secretary of State Henry Stimson stated, that "our attempt to solve the Manchurian problem by discussion and conciliation had failed," and that it was time to risk a more confrontational policy.[4] Over the next few months, Hoover, Stimson, and other members of the State Department laid the foundations of what became known as the Stimson Doctrine: the refusal to recognize any treaty between Japan and China that would "impair the treaty rights of the United States or its citizens in China . . . [or] which may be brought about by means contrary to the covenants and obligations of the pact of Paris of August 27, 1928."[5] More broadly, the United States came to see Japan as a state that would and could not be bound by international treaties; Japan, officials argued, would not only take Manchuria; they would strive to overturn the Washington system, the U.S. order in the Pacific. The Manchurian crisis thus pushed the United States from accommodation to containment, laying the foundation for a policy that would shape U.S.-Japanese relations for the next decade.

The central argument of this book is that a rising power's legitimation strategies—its reasons for pursuing revision—shape a great power's response to its expansion. The United States' turn toward confrontation was driven, not only by Japan's growing capabilities or its interests in China, but by Japan's reasons for invading Manchuria. As Japan's forces moved through Manchuria, the great powers demanded Japan justify its aggression. Instead of appealing to existing treaties to legitimate their actions, Japan's officials stated that the norms of the Washington system were irrelevant in Manchuria, arguing instead that it would seek to establish an alternative order, one more suited to the governance of the Asia-Pacific. It was this revolutionary rejection of the dominant order that ultimately pushed the United States toward a policy of confrontation.

Japan's leaders were neither deaf nor dumb; they understood what reasons were legitimate to the Western powers and had successfully used appeals to rules and norms to legitimate their expansion for decades. Why would it now reject these rules and risk appearing a revolutionary state? Japan's failure to legitimate their actions in Manchuria demonstrates the interaction between international and domestic legitimacy, and how attempts to appease one audience can provoke the hostility of another. As a rising power, Japan's leaders faced ongoing tensions between internationalist and nationalist coalitions, with contrasting claims to legitimacy.[6] We've seen such fragmentation in other cases, but what made these dynamics particularly pernicious was Japan's inability to invoke a multivocal strategy. Without the capacity to speak multivocally, Japan's leaders instead turned to hardline rhetoric to shore up their domestic position, which ultimately provoked confrontational strategies. At the same time, Japan's most important audience for its claims—the United States—was an institutionally vulnerable power, one that believed its security rested on the "scraps of paper" that composed the Washington system. As a result, U.S. officials heard Japan's appeals as a revolutionary threat to its own security.

The Manchurian Incident and Japan's Rise in World Politics

In 1853, when Commodore Perry confronted a closed and isolated Japan, it seemed likely the state would suffer the same fate as China, its sovereignty decimated by the imperial powers.[7] Instead, by the end of the nineteenth century, Japan was a rising power itself. Its increasing economic, military, and diplomatic might stemmed from the reforms that followed the Meiji Restoration of 1868, which wrested power away the shogunate and into the hands of the genro, the advisors to Japan's emperor. In the years following the restoration, the genro ordered universal conscription, using European militaries as models for institutional reform.[8] Economically, the genro accelerated industrialization, building infrastructure and the laying the foundations for a trading state. Politically, the genro authored Japan's constitution, created a parliament, the Diet, and a diplomatic corp.[9]

These military, economic, and political reforms formed the foundations of Japan's increasing power. Japan's growing might unleashed an increasingly expansionist foreign policy, as Japan sought to take its place among the imperial powers. Japan's expansion was, in many respects, unremarkable; it was, as one historian remarks, conducted in a "cautious and 'realistic' manner," allowing Japan to "to emerge as a respectable member of the western imperialist community."[10] In the late nineteenth and early twentieth century, Japan was largely concerned with securing "spheres of influence" along its periphery. In the 1870s, Japan's leaders sent three thousand soldiers to Formosa, arguing that China lacked legal jurisdiction over the territory.[11] After defeating China in 1895, Japan took control of Liaotung and Taiwan. As the Qing dynasty faltered, and Russian influence waned, Japan expanded into Korea, gaining formal recognition of its "special interests" after the Russo-Japanese war in 1905, and formally annexing the state in 1910.

Japan's expansion into Manchuria came as no surprise. Japan's leaders consistently argued it should have a sphere of influence in Manchuria, claiming security and economic interests in the region that could be secured only through control over the territory.[12] Some leaders emphasized Japan's historical connection as well, arguing that Japan's connections were "based on the deep and particular relationship between Manchuria and our empire."[13] After the Russo-Japanese War, Japan gained rights to Manchuria's railway network, and in 1906 formed the semigovernmental South Manchurian Railway Company (SMR).[14] The SMR became the "economic spine" of Manchuria;[15] technically a private company, it operated with government support and was protected by Japan's military, the Kwantung Army. The SMR did not merely exert control over the Manchurian railway; it governed the bulk of Japan's economic activity in Manchuria, its "mining, industry, commerce, power supply, foreign trade, and shipping."[16] It controlled the politics of the towns along the seven hundred miles of railway. All of these holdings were protected by Japan's imperial forces, the Kwantung Army.

In 1915, with the European powers engulfed in conflict, Japan attempted to gain formal control over Manchuria, presenting China with "Twenty-One Demands" that, among other claims, pressed China to acknowledge Japan's status in the territory. Throughout the 1920s, Japan sought to secure a sphere of influence in Manchuria by working with political collaborators to exert control over the territory. Concerned by China's growing nationalist movement, Japan threw its support behind a local warlord, Chang Tso-lin, in hopes of governing the territory indirectly.[17] Chang proved an unreliable partner. He sought to expand south against Chinese nationalist forces, risking his control of Manchuria. He built railways to compete with the SMR, and by 1928 was seeking support from China, Great Britain, and the United States.

It was in this context that expansion in Manchuria unfolded. The explosion in September 1931 was not the first time the Kwantung Army used force as a means to command direct control over the territory. In 1928, the army assassinated Chang, blowing up his train and placing the blame on Chinese forces. The imperial forces hoped Tokyo would order its military to secure the territory and establish formal rule. Instead Japan's government, under the leadership of Prime Minister Tanaka Giichi, condemned the army's actions as illegal and imprudent. While Tanaka's government hoped to secure Japan's grip on Manchuria, they also believed blatant military action was counterproductive and risked international condemnation. Tanaka worked to ensure the international response was muted, fervently making "appropriate explanations" to the Western powers for Japan's military actions.[18] His efforts were successful: the army was unable to advance in Manchuria, and the great powers, though concerned, remained quiet.

In 1931, the Kwantung Army's efforts had a much different outcome. Once again, imperial forces staged an attack on the Manchurian railway, blaming Chinese forces and using the attack as a pretext to advance throughout Manchuria. By the end of 1931, the Kwantung Army had taken control of most of Manchuria's major urban centers, and at the start of the New Year, Japanese troops clashed with Chinese forces in Shanghai. In February 1932, the imperial forces declared victory, and demanded Tokyo and the other great powers recognize the independent state of Manchukuo. Yet while Japan may have secured control over Manchuria, it also provoked hostility: Manchuria proved the "tipping point" of Japan's rise, turning the great powers—especially the United States—away from accommodation and toward confrontation.

The United States and the Turn toward Confrontation: The Stimson Doctrine

From 1931 through the attack at Pearl Harbor in 1941, the United States response to Japan's rise was one of containment and confrontation, a policy that aimed to stem and even roll back Japan's expansion in Manchuria. The strategy found its first expression in the Stimson Doctrine, named for the secretary of state who advocated a "firm ground and aggressive stand towards Japan," as he recorded in his diaries.[19] Key to the Stimson Doctrine was "nonrecognition," the principle that the United States would not recognize any political or territorial revisions made in violation of standing treaties, especially the rules codified in the Nine Power Treaty and the Washington system. Any Japanese expansion that attacked China's sovereignty, or aggression beyond what was required for self-defense, was illegitimate. Formulated in the autumn of 1931, the Stimson Doctrine was publicly announced in a note to Japan and China on January 7, 1932. Stimson advertised the U.S. new position in a public letter to Senator Borah in February 1932, and in August 1932, Stimson declared the administration's doctrine in a forceful speech in front of the Council on Foreign Relations.

Some see the Stimson Doctrine was more appeasement than containment, a weak policy that all but acquiesced to Japan's expansion in the Pacific. As Ogata argues, "The effect of the Stimson doctrine has often been minimized on the grounds that it lacked teeth."[20] The Stimson Doctrine did nothing to end the army's expansion in Manchuria, to stop Japan's recognition of Manchuoko in 1932, or halt Japan's expansion into China and Southeast Asia in the late 1930s.[21] Early on the Stimson Doctrine relied only on "moral suasion" and public opinion to stem Japan's expansionist aims. Stimson's attempts to add economic and military teeth to the doctrine initially faltered. When Stimson suggested the United States pursue economic sanctions, Hoover insisted he would remain limited to a policy of "moral pressure."[22] When Stimson further suggested, in his letter to Borah, that the United States might leave the Washington Naval Treaty and increase its own naval might, colleagues pushed back on the possibility of an arms race in the Pacific.[23]

To call the Stimson Doctrine *ineffective* containment is fair. But the doctrine was not insignificant, nor did contemporaries believe that it was an instrument of appeasement, as critics would later maintain.[24] In the 1930s both proponents and critics of the policy in the Hoover administration saw the doctrine as a marked departure from the accommodation of the previous decade. As one historian argues, with the Stimson Doctrine, Hoover "committed the nation to the moral and diplomatic rejection of change except that achieved through mutual agreement. For a democracy which had acquired the highly moralistic outlook of a status quo power, the doctrine of nonrecognition implied firmness, not appeasement."[25] Stimson, for his part, argued his doctrine represented a clear attempt to get "tough" with the Japanese government, having "realized the importance of having Japan fear this country."[26] Chief of the Division of Far Eastern Affairs, Stanley Hornbeck compared the note to the Monroe Doctrine, and many saw Stimson's Doctrine as a "prelude to action" against Japan and thus "tended to obscure Hoover's earlier statement that the United States was not going to get involved in a war."[27] Academic observers, like Quincy Wright, claimed the doctrine was a significant shift in U.S. foreign policy, that "no diplomatic note of recent or even of distant years is likely to go down as of greater significance in the development of international law."[28]

It is true that, at least initially, enforcement of the doctrine was largely diplomatic and symbolic.[29] But ultimately it proved the first, decisive step in a robust plan of containment and confrontation. During his campaign, Franklin Delano Roosevelt promised his policy toward Japan would build on the Stimson Doctrine, arguing that his administration would work to "uphold the sanctity of international treaties. That is the cornerstone on which all relations between nations must rest."[30] When Roosevelt took office, he told Stimson that "he fully approved of our policy in the Far East; that his only possible criticism was that we did not begin it earlier."[31] As the decade went on, the Roosevelt administration added coercive instruments behind the containment policy. In 1933, Roosevelt announced he would use $238 million of "public works" money to rebuild the navy to treaty strength. Throughout the interwar period the Roosevelt administration, both overtly and covertly, aided China in its struggle, exporting grain to China and financing, supplying, and training its air force.[32]

The Stimson Doctrine thus marked the start of the United States' deliberate and dramatic turn toward a policy of containment and confrontation.

The Manchurian crisis pushed international powers toward containment as well. Some describe the Manchurian crisis as a moment of profound Anglo-American disagreement, with the United States pushing for a hard line against Japan and Britain demurring. Early on in the crisis, Sir John Simon, the British foreign secretary, rebuffed Stimson's attempts to produce a joint Anglo-American statement on the doctrine. As described by David Dutton, "Japan was widely seen to have a strong case against China," and Simon informed the cabinet that Japan had the right to send troops into China. But as historians suggest, Britain quickly came around to the United States' position. It was Simon who on March 7, 1932, proposed that the League adopt the Stimson Doctrine's core principles and refuse to recognize any "'changes brought about by means contrary' to the principles of the League covenant and the Kellogg-Briand Pact."[33] In October 1932, the League concurred with Stimson, arguing in the Lytton report that the "recognition of present regime in Manchuria" would not be "compatible with the fundamental principle of existing international obligations."[34]

For their part Japan's leaders certainly believed the Stimson Doctrine was a policy of containment and confrontation.[35] At the outset of the crisis, Japan hoped the Western powers would support its efforts in Manchuria; Tokyo saw the Stimson Doctrine and Lytton report that followed as a rejection of Japan's aims. Ambassador Forbes reported to the Hoover administration that the doctrine had injured relations with Tokyo.[36] Matsuoka Yosuka, who presented Japan's case at the League, lashed out at what he saw as the West's containment, arguing that the "western powers had taught the Japanese the game of poker but . . . after acquiring most of the chips they pronounced the game immoral and took up contract bridge."[37] The United States' strategy, he charged, was "capricious" an attempt to "dictate" terms to the Japanese in an area of their vital interest.[38]

Critics are correct that the Stimson Doctrine, and the shift toward containment, is puzzling. The Stimson Doctrine was weak at its inception, because the United States lacked the material power to contain Japan. No American politician wanted a conflict with Japan over Manchuria; no policymaker believed the United States had the will or the might to confront Japan if that country did not abandon its revisionist aims. Yet Washington still decided to embrace a policy of containment in Manchuria. Why would the United States adopt a strategy that pulled it toward conflict in the Pacific?

An Inevitable Clash? Japan's Rising Power in the Asia-Pacific

To focus on the Manchurian crisis as the wellspring of containment is to portray U.S. strategy toward Japan as contingent, a result of leaders' decisions during the crisis. Yet there is no dearth of scholarship that suggests the clash between the powers was not contingent, but unavoidable. The

Manchurian crisis was insignificant: regardless of what happened in Manchuria, the United States and Japan were headed toward conflict.[39] Japan had been rising since the late nineteenth century. Deeply dissatisfied with the territorial, economic, and political status quo, Japan's revisionist demands were inevitable. Needing to secure its survival in the face of imperial competition, Japan thrust outward toward Korea, China, and Indonesia. The Open Door, long a staple of U.S. foreign policy in East Asia, was an unacceptable obstacle to Japan's expansion. The United States, for its part, could not allow Japan to undermine its core financial and territorial interests. By the early twentieth century, China was already a significant market for U.S. goods, and American businessmen fantasized about future possibilities in its massive market. Japan's expansion inherently threatened U.S. territorial holdings in the Philippines, Guam, and Hawaii. The United States could not—and would not—accept Japan's emerging regional hegemony.[40] Japan's growing power and capacity to threaten the United States would have eventually produced a containment strategy.

What we have in the Manchurian crisis and beyond is thus a tale of two revisionists, both of whom, rightly or wrongly, believed that each other posed a significant threat to vital interests. But these explanations overstate the extent to which the United States viewed Japan as an inherent threat. This is not to suggest that Washington believed the rising challenger was insignificant, of little concern to the United States. For years, the United States had warily watched Japan's growth in the Asia-Pacific. At the end of World War I, the United States took steps to block Japan's Twenty-One Demands towards China, making sure Japan could not threaten its economic interests in China or its territorial holdings in the Pacific.[41] But more often than not, Washington used the tools of accommodation, working with Japan to limit naval procurement, to secure the Open Door and to stabilize China. The Treaty of Versailles recognized most of Japan's formal wartime acquisitions.[42] The United States also actively sought to bring Japan into the Washington system, a series of treaties designed to manage great power competition in the Asia Pacific.[43]

The Americans proved particularly willing to accommodate expansion in Manchuria, accepting that Japan had unique interests in the territory. For example, while the Nine Power Treaty, signed by the United States, Japan, and Britain in 1922, ostensibly called on its signatories to "respect the sovereignty, the independence, and the territorial and administrative integrity of China," the treaty powers informally agreed that Japan continued to have special interests and preexisting treaty rights in Manchuria. As Theodore Roosevelt noted to President Taft, "The vital interest of the Japanese . . . is in Manchuria and Korea. It is therefore peculiarly to our interest not to take any steps as regard Manchuria which will give the Japanese cause to feel, with or without reason, that we are hostile to them."[44] Roosevelt helped mediate the Treaty of Portsmouth in 1905, which gave Japan de facto control over Manchuria. Likewise, the Lansing-Ishii Agreement of 1917, while expressing continued commitment to an open door in China, also recognized that Japan had special interest in Manchuria.

Accommodating Japan's rise made strategic sense. American administrations of the early twentieth century viewed Japan's expansion in Asia—its defeat of China, its annexation of Korea, and its domination of Manchuria—as acceptable, and not at all threatening to U.S. interests. Indeed, officials argued that Japan's domination of China could prove a boon to U.S. security, stabilizing the region during a turbulent civil war. Throughout the 1920s, officials argued, Japan proved a force for order and economic growth in Manchuria. At the beginning of the crisis, much of China was embroiled in conflict, and U.S. officials agreed that "'full control' of Manchuria was 'the best thing which could happen.'"[45] It would not be the first time a great power had acted to protect its interests in the region—Britain and the United States themselves had bombed Chinese troops at Nanking in 1927—and it would undoubtedly not be the last.

If anything, structural logics should have pushed the United States toward accommodation, not confrontation or containment. Even if Japan's expansion did undercut U.S. interests, there was little to be done about it, especially in Manchuria. As Joseph Grew, who would become U.S. ambassador to Japan, argued, "Nothing will divert Japan from Manchuria." In 1931, U.S. naval forces remained well below Washington Treaty levels, and the navy warned Stimson that it lacked the capabilities to check Japan's expansion.[46] In the face of a worldwide economic depression, it seemed impossible that the United States would mobilize the resources to push Japan out of Manchuria. The rapid turn toward confrontation in the Manchurian crisis, seen in this light, is a significant puzzle.

The Politics of Harm, the Politics of Interest: Containing a Revolutionary Japan?

The U.S. turn toward a strategy of containment and confrontation was not a given. Rather, it was only as the Hoover administration began to see Japan as a revolutionary power, one bent not on limited expansion but the domination of East Asia, that it turned toward a more coercive policy. Why was it that Japan's actions in Manchuria signaled revolutionary aims?

THE POLITIC OF HARM

For some, the shift in U.S. strategy may appear a straightforward example of the politics of harm. Up until 1931, Japan's intentions remained uncertain. Japan might have been expansionist, but for the most part, the government seemed willing to cooperate with the great powers in pursuit of its revisionist aims. But Japan's domination of Manchuria revealed its status as an aggressive, revolutionary state. Its offensive push into Manchuria, its bombing of Chinchow, and its incursions into Shanghai revealed a state bent on dominating regions far outside what aims of security and self-defense would mandate. Japan's increasingly militant politicians and population, moreover, signaled a regime uninterested in upholding the rules of the international system. All of this provided clear and credible information about Japan's revolutionary intentions. America and the international community responded appropriately.

There can be no doubt that Japan's actions in Manchuria changed how the United States saw Japan's revisionist intentions. But why was it that the Manchurian crisis proved so decisive in cementing American fears about Japan's aims? As noted above, Japan's control of Manchuria posed no inherent threat to the United States' position in China or in Asia. American leaders did not see its economic interests, even the Open Door, as inherently threatened by Japanese expansion into Manchuria. At the onset of the crisis, Hoover argued for prudence, noting that there was "an absence of any United States interest in China important enough to invite or risk war." Hornbeck likewise argued that U.S. trade and investment in China was "important but not essential."[47] As argued above, throughout the twentieth century officials accepted Japanese control over Manchuria as inevitable, that "Japan must have room for colonization, and that Manchuria and Eastern Inner Mongolia are legitimate fields for her expansion."[48] As Stimson stated in his memoirs, "I do not recall that there was any difference of opinion whatever in our groups at the State department as to the policy we should follow in the face of this diagnosis of the situation in Manchuria."[49]

Even Japan's use of force was understandable. While Washington saw Japan's recourse to violence as unsettling, its aggression was neither unprecedented nor unexpected. In 1928, a similar incident had occurred in the Shandung-leased territory. With Chiang Kai-Shek's forces moving northward, the Kwantung Army advanced into the city of Tsinan, occupying the city for over a year. The Americans remained quiet. Indeed, in a particularly prescient comment, Hornbeck remarked that "Japan evidently intends to draw a dividing line in China with Manchuria on one side and the Middle Kingdom on the other." Hornbeck demonstrated little angst over the issue.[50]

In 1931, U.S. policymakers were far from certain that Japan's military actions in Manchuria signaled revolutionary aims, and indeed many saw Japanese aggression in Manchuria as unproblematic. United States diplomats believed the Manchurian incident was "no cause for surprise; it was only earlier and more drastic" than diplomats had expected.[51] Given the chaos in China, and the state's inability to impose law and order, Japan had to resort to force; its use of military might was likely to prove legitimate. As Ambassador Forbes put it, Japan "had a perfectly good case to take before the League of Nations and submit to any tribunal. They had developed industry, transportation and agriculture for the benefit mostly of Chinese inhabitants. . . . They had not received protection, the bandits were regularly increasing their raids . . . and the Japanese got no protection or redress."[52] The American public concurred. In Manchuria, Walter Lippmann commented, "there is here no such thing as an 'aggressor' and a 'non-aggressor.'"[53] Both China and Japan had been pushed into Manchuria through domestic and international pressures. The *New York Times* editorial board noted that Japan enjoyed "admitted treaty rights" in Manchuria and cautioned against aggressive diplomacy.[54] For these reasons, Stimson assured the Japanese ambassador that the United States would not "be hasty in formulating conclusions or taking a position" in the face of the Kwantung Army's actions.

Not even the continuing offensive outside of Mukden or the attacks on Shanghai communicated clear information about Japan's intentions. Scholars have argued that the spread of violence to Shanghai, for example, exerted a profound effect on the American and British reaction to Japanese aggression.[55] But here again evidence suggests that the powers remained uncertain about Japan's aims. Japan had been aggressive in Shanghai, but had also been willing to accept international mediation and limit conflict over the city. Japan's bombing of Shanghai was brutal, but Japan's efforts here faded so quickly that in April 1932 the *New York Times* dismissed it as "only an episode"; the main action was to be found in Manchuria itself.[56]

The point here is not that Japan's offensive did not cause concern; it is that there was nothing inherent in Japan's actions in Manchuria that signaled revolutionary aims. Japan's expansion into China could be seen a signal of a radically expansionist agenda, or as a limited attempt to impose order on a region central to its economic interest. As a signal, the meaning of Manchuria was indeterminate.

THE POLITICS OF INTEREST

Another possibility is that in Manchuria the United States saw credible signals that Japan would choose to threaten U.S. interests; that there were increasing signs that Japan's government harbored not limited, but revolutionary interests; and that Manchuria would be a springboard toward more expansionist policies. In particular, Manchuria demonstrated that Japan's "liberal internationalists" had lost control of Tokyo's policies. In charge now were revolutionary parties, military leaders and civilians who embraced nationalist and "renovationist" positions, and aimed to challenge Western dominance in Asia.[57] Manchuria was simply the opening salvo of a "fifteen years war," a constant spate of expansion that would propel Japan further into China, Southeast Asia, and ultimately to attack the United States at Pearl Harbor.

As plausible as this explanation sounds, it overstates the extent to which the invasion of Manchuria, in and of itself, provided a clear, costly signal of Japan's regime type and budding revisionist interests. It is true that polarization had long plagued Japan's government, and that Tokyo had taken a militarist turn. From 1931 to 1937, Japan saw eight governments, each seemingly more hardline than the last. Two months after the onset of the crisis, Minseito, the party most associated with Japan's liberal internationalist goals, fell from power. By February 1932, Seiyukai, which had positioned itself as Japan's foremost nationalist party, held the reins of power, but only for three months: in May 1932, an attempted right-wing coup brought about the end of Japan's party competition, and the creation of a unity government under the leadership of a former navy admiral, Saito Makoto. From that point forward, there would be no more democratic party politics.

Yet Japanese politics and aims continued to be mired in uncertainty, not only in 1931 but through the end of the crisis in 1933. Throughout the crisis Japan's domestic politics were far from settled: as Wilson argues, in 1931 "the situation as far more fluid than is often acknowledged, containing the possibility of outcomes other than those which did in fact occur; and that while the Manchurian Incident can be seen as a milestone in Japanese militarism, this is an interpretation which rests heavily in hindsight."[58] As the crisis unfolded, "revolutionary" hardliners—those that advocated expansion outside of Manchuria—were still outside the government. While Minseito was still in power, Shidehara attempted to subdue the army, with some success.[59] Its rival, Seiyukai, might have been a hardline party, but it also fought back against renovationist and military dominance, and ultimately the truce with China quelled the rise of the hardliners. In other words, Manchuria was no clear victory for the hardliners, even at the end of the crisis. As one historian notes, for this reason most scholars "agree that the turning point in Japanese civil—military relations was the 2.26 Incident of 1936," and not the Manchurian crisis itself.[60]

Nor did the United States believe Japan's regime instability was a clear indicator of revolutionary interests. At the outset of the crisis, American officials continued to believe that moderates were driving Japan's policy. Early in the crisis, Stimson reported to Japan's ambassador that the "American government is confident it has not been the intention of the Japanese government to create or be party" to the aggressive expansion in Manchuria.[61] Grew too argued that there was a split between a "young military group" and "older and wiser" elements, most notably foreign minister Shidehara. Many officials in the Hoover administration suspected that the events were a replay of 1928, and that extremist elements in both Tokyo and the Kwantung Army were responsible for actions in Manchuria.

In essence, then, in 1931 there was no clear and costly signal of revolutionary interests. The initial stages of the invasion prompted, not certainty, but increased *ambiguity* about Japan's intentions in Manchuria and beyond.

All of this strengthened, not undercut, the logic of accommodation. Indeed most in Washington thought that if the United States moved to contain Japan, "the Japanese nationalist element would be immensely strengthened and that it would unite Japan behind the military element"; pushing Japan toward more revisionist intentions was the United States' "principal fear."[62] It was better, as Stimson argued, to "help Shidehara, who is on the right side, and not play into the hands of any Nationalist agitators on the other."[63]

As the crisis unfolded, however, the United States became convinced that Japan's invasion signaled unappeasable revisionist aims. These effects of the Manchurian crisis on U.S.-Japanese relations, I argue, cannot be reduced the politics of harm or interest, both of which proved indeterminate. It was not only Japan's actions in Manchuria, but how the United States came to understand the meaning of Manchuria, that pushed it toward a containment strategy. Key to this interpretation, I argue, was Japan's legitimation strategies, the reasons it gave for its expansion. Rather than appeal to existing norms and rules to justify their actions in Manchuria, during the crisis Japan's leaders increasingly turned to the rhetoric of national emergency and Pan-Asianism to legitimate their aims. It was this framing that convinced the United States that Japan harbored revolutionary aims, objectives incompatible with the international order. Under these conditions, accommodation was no longer possible.

Japan and the Politics of Legitimacy: From Liberal Internationalism to a New World Order

In chapter 2, I argued that a rising power's legitimation strategies shape great powers' decision to accommodate, contain, or confront its revisionist ambitions. It is a rising power's reasons for expansion that shape how great powers come to understand the extent of a challenger's revisionist aims. Historians argue that Japan understood the power of language, and that it had, for at least forty years, portrayed its expansion as consistent with the rules and norms of the international system. Much has been written of Japan's remarkable capacity to "assimilate" to Western institutions: its ability to quickly adopt a constitution after the Meiji restoration, to build a "Western-style" foreign ministry and military bureaucracy, is often credited with Japan's success in avoiding China's fate.[64] Japan's skillful use of international rules and norms to justify its early expansion was equally important in securing its role as a great power. Its expansion into Korea, into German holdings, and into Manchuria were accompanied by careful appeals to international treaties and law and, as Conroy argues, the fact that this expansion "was accomplished without opposition from the powers . . . that the Japanese continental position as established by the Twenty-one Demands passed unchallenged . . . indicates how well the Japanese had built its case."[65]

Japan's leaders, moreover, were well aware of the strategic benefits of their conformist rhetoric, and as they expanded they proceeded with "with great caution, with full attention to diplomatic arrangements, with Western arguments and justifications, with full consciousness of the strength of the west."[66] The content of Japan's legitimation strategies can be separated into three phases. In the first phase, from 1895 to 1917, Japan relied on the language of what Iriye refers to as the "old diplomacy," using rationales commensurate with a realist, balance-of-power system.[67] In this argument, Japan's right to claim Taiwan, Manchuria, or Korea stemmed from its growing might. Japan was justified in securing spheres-of-influence to guard against incursions from Russia and or hedge against Chinese instability. Such rights, after all, had been claimed by European nations for at least a century. As an editorial in the *New York Tribune* argued, Japan's right to territorial expansion was "at least as good as that of Russia, France, England, or any other power to deal as they have with subject nations"[68]

At the end of World War I, Japan's legitimations changed, largely in response to the U.S. pursuit of a liberal international order. Under Wilson, the Americans had a much different idea of what counted as "legitimate" expansion in the international order. Balance of power politics were anathema to the Wilson administration, and aggression only justified in cases of self-defense.[69] Nations, moreover, were bound to accept others' rights to self-determination, even if some of those nations, like China, were still struggling to articulate a national identity. It was inevitable, Japan's prime minister Hara Takashi argued, that "America will take the lead in the world."[70] It was thus America that must be convinced that Japan's aims were legitimate. In the second phase of Japan's legitimation strategies, ranging from about 1918 to 1931, Japan adopted this rhetoric of a "new diplomacy" or "liberal internationalism." Some of this change was strategic, a shift designed to convince an American audience that Japan's expansionist aims in Manchuria were consistent with Wilsonsian institutions. As Dickinson argues, "Hara's strategy for coping with a powerful and meddlesome America was to commandeer the moral high ground on the most pressing problem: China's civil war." Other leaders sincerely embraced the principles of the liberal world order; Yoshino Sakuzo, one of the leaders of Japan's democratic movement, applauded that the "rule of morality" was to replace the "rule of power." Likewise, one journal editor proclaimed that Japan must join "Wilson's great diplomatic revolution."[71]

Whatever the intentions that drove rhetoric, throughout the 1920s, Japan would argue that its interests in Manchuria were legal, that Japan sought, not to dominate in the name of security or interest, but to build a secure order in the region consistent with the rules of the international system. While continuing to fight for its "special rights" in Manchuria, Japan agreed to recognize the fundamental norms of self-determination and liberal constraints against aggression. At the Versailles negotiations, Baron Makino Nobuaki, "surprised all in attendance when he spoke on behalf of the new diplomacy," arguing that it was time to "work to expel oppressive and scheming means, tread the path of righteousness, and make helping weak country our principle."[72] Using this liberal internationalist rhetoric, Japan "came into the critical 1930s with a record of successful expansion, accomplished by cautious and methodical means."[73]

And while Japan's leaders entered the decade committed to pursuing a "vigorous policy in Manchuria" they "did not believe that this undertaking would necessarily antagonize the United States or any other power": they continued to believe they had the diplomatic ammunition at hand to justify their revisionist aims.[74] In the Manchurian crisis, however, Japan's legitimation strategy took a third turn: it departed from the language of liberal international order, and turned instead to a nationalist, pan-Asianist rhetoric. To analyze this shift I looked at Japan's legitimating statements from 1931 to 1933 as recorded in the *Foreign Relations of the United States* (*FRUS*). Documents in *FRUS* give a thorough accounting of explanations Japan's leaders offered to the U.S. government about their actions in Manchuria, which were conveyed to the U.S. ambassador in Japan, to the League of Nations, and at times directly to the United States secretary of state. I also supplement this analysis with reference to speeches by Japan's leaders as reported in the *New York Times*.

At the very beginning of the crisis, Japan continued its appeals to treaty law and self-defense as justifications for their actions in Manchuria.[75] To Stimson, Japan's ambassador reported that "it may be superfluous to repeat that the Japanese government harbors no territorial designs in Manchuria. What we desire is that Japanese subjects shall be enabled to safely engage in various peaceful pursuits. It is the proper duty of a government to protect the rights and interests legitimately enjoyed by the nation or individuals."[76] Likewise, speaking in front of the League of Nations, the Japanese representative argued that "her military and other measures in China were justified as being 'wholly defensive in character.'"[77] Over time, these claims of self-defense transformed into the language of existential threat, where any loss of control in Manchuria was an attack to Japan's economic "lifeline." By the end of 1931, the expression *Seimeisen* (the line between life and death) was among the most popular reasons given for expansion in Japan's media.[78]

As the crisis unfolded, this rhetoric of self-defense, while still prevalent, was joined by a more revolutionary legitimation strategy: that Japan had the right to build a new order in the Pacific. Japan's leaders argued that existing institutions of the Washington system—especially the principles of the Nine Power Treaty—had failed in their efforts to bring peace and order. As argued earlier, China's right to self-determination was integral to the Washington system: the ability of China to construct a stable, sovereign government was considered essential to maintaining peace and prosperity in the region. As Nish argues, "In the later stages of the [Manchurian] controversy, Japan tended more and more to rest her case upon the assertion that China had not that degree of political stability and power which would entitle her to claim or to be accorded the usual rights of a sovereign member of the international Society of States or the League of Nations."[79] In response to American demands that Japan justify its actions in terms of international treaties, Japan responded that Western treaties—both the Nine Power Treaty and the League of Nations—simply did not apply in Manchuria and China. As Japan's foreign ministry wrote to Stimson, the Washington system no longer applied to China, as "the present unsettled and distracted state of China is not what was in the contemplation of the high contracting parties at the time of the Treaty of Washington."[80] China, Japan's leaders argued, had not met the basic requirements to be considered a sovereign state.[81] As Stimson observed, these claims that "China was not an organized state and that this fact relieved Japan from the obligation to carry out the covenants of the Nine power treaty . . . was thereafter *regularly put forward* by the Japanese government in its diplomatic utterances."[82] If China was not a state, then, Japan's leaders argued, it was justified in using force in Manchuria beyond the requirements of "self-defense," because of the disunity and disorder that racked the Chinese state.

The answer to the "Chinese problem," Japan's leaders argued, was to replace Western international norms with a new pan-Asianist order.[83] Such pan-Asian rhetoric was not new to Japanese politics. Since at least the early twentieth century, "renovationists" in Japan had argued that Western treaties had done nothing but stymie Japan's growth and that it was incumbent on leaders to revolutionalize the order on the basis of a more traditional identity. But it was during the Manchurian crisis that these legitimations emerged as the dominant justification of Japan's revisionist behavior. Only through expansion could Japan—and the rest of the great powers—secure peace and order in Asia. As Uchida Yasuya, who served as Japan's foreign minister from 1932 to 1933, argued to League investigators, Japan had decades of experience dealing with Manchuria, whereas the Western powers understood little of Chinese politics. Uchida consistently denied that Japan had violated international law, but mixed these denials with frequent appeals to Japan's cultural leadership in Asia. In a speech to the Imperial Diet in January 1933, he argued that the world must come to realize that "any plan for erecting an edifice of peace in the Far East should be based on the recognition that the constructive force of Japan is the mainstay of tranquility in this part of the world."[84]

The entire Washington system itself, Japan's leaders now claimed, was built on a foundation of Western ignorance. The great powers had tried, as Japan's diplomat Mamoru Shigemitsu argued, to impose their rules and norms on Asia: "International relations in the Far East . . . cannot be properly controlled by an idealistic peace treaty or organization that might be suited to Europe."[85] The League, another Japanese official argued, "due to ignorance or otherwise, has done nothing but prolong the sufferings and strife in the Far East, thereby keeping unnecessarily the different countries in the Orient at daggers drawn, while they ought to have remained tied with strong bond of fraternity from both racial and other considerations."[86] As Uchida explained, "It is admitted by those conversant with actual conditions in China that no remedy can be effected by having recourse either to the covenant of the League of Nations or to any other organ of what may be termed the 'machinery of peace.'"[87] Japan, Uchida proclaimed, would work with Asian partners "linked together by a bond of cultural and racial affinities, will come to coperate [*sic*] hand in hand, for the maintenance and advancement of the peace and prosperity of the Far East, as well as for the peace of the world and the civilization of mankind."[88]

This rhetoric of a revolutionary Asian order eclipsed internationalist claims. As Mori Kaku argued, Japan's interest in Manchuria could not be bound by "mere law or treaty." Japan's actions in Manchuria were a proclamation that she "now defiantly rose from her traditional diplomacy characterized by servility" and was building an order that would "return to the Japanese spirit." It was nothing less than the abandonment of "sixty years of blind imitation of Western Materialistic civilization."[89] This pan-Asianist rhetoric would come to dominate how Japan legitimated its expansion, both during and after the crisis. In 1933, a Japanese journalist's monograph was circulated to U.S. senators and representatives, which proclaimed that Japan was engaged in a "great experiment in the reorganization . . . of an ancient nation. . . . For the first time in history, a non-white race has undertaken to carry the white man's burden."[90] In 1934, Japan's infamous Amo Doctrine declared that Japan had a "mission" to "maintain peace and order in that part of the world 'on its own responsibility, acting alone.'"[91] At times, Japan's leaders even suggested that Japan's new system would stretch not only through Asia, but around the globe. In an interview in early 1933, Japan's representative to the League, Matsuoka, declared, "Japan's mission is to lead the world spiritually and intellectually. Japan can offer spirituality to America and the entire Western World. Japan, I am convinced, will be the cradle of a new Messiah."[92] By 1936, Japan was consistently deriding Western order as sterile and obsolete, proclaiming Japan's ideology the order of the future.

In sum, in the half century of Japan's rise, its legitimation strategies changed dramatically, shifting from a rhetoric that first embraced and then rejected the principles of existing Western institutions to one that proclaimed a revolutionary world order. Japanese legitimation strategies had a profound effect on American foreign policy, pushing officials away from a policy of impartiality and even accommodation in the crisis, to a policy of containment through nonrecognition. As one historian argues, while this was not the first time the United States had faced Japanese expansion in the Pacific, yet "if on former occasions the United States had ignored the display of Japanese power, it could hardly do so in 1931. . . . While recognizing both Japan's need for raw materials and foreign markets as well as its special treaty privileges in Manchuria, the president rejected the Japanese *rationale* for the employment of force."[93]

Daft Language and Deaf Ears: The Dynamics of U.S.-Japanese Legitimation

In the sections below, I argue that legitimation strategies had a significant effect on power politics: by signaling that Japan could not be restrained, by galvanizing opponents, and by threatening the United States' sense of its identity, Japan's rhetoric shaped how the United States mobilized in response to its expansion, laying the groundwork for a containment strategy. Why was it that Japan's leaders turned to language that would be illegitimate to its great power audience? Surely Japan's leaders understood such rhetoric would prove illegitimate to an American audience and potentially provoke a response. Likewise, why did Japan's rhetoric have such a profound effect on American strategy? How was it that "cheap talk" pushed the powers toward confrontation?

On the face of it, there is an obvious answer to both questions: Japan's rhetoric was, in fact, a credible signal of its type. As argued in chapter 2, rationalist theory would predict that revolutionary actors will, at least eventually, turn to rhetoric to mobilize their populations behind revolutionary aims. For this reason, illegitimate rhetoric is a costly signal that will rationally provoke a response from its audience.[94] But there are problems with this explanation. There is little to indicate that, in 1931, Japan's leaders were purposively using illegitimate rhetoric to mobilize their population for an expansionist project. Evidence suggests that Japan's expansionist aims remained as limited as they were in the previous decades: there was a dispute, as Iriye puts it "over the execution of policy, not over the policy itself."[95] Some of Japan's leaders were more nationalist in their approach, but as Nish argues, it was "far from united," and many party members shared the belief that cooperation with the great powers remained the best way to advance Japan's interests in Manchuria.[96] Looking only at preferences it would be, as Matsusaka argues, difficult, if not impossible, to have "foreseen the scope and scale of Japanese aggression."[97] While there was plenty of revolutionary rhetoric, there is little evidence of revolutionary aims, that in 1931 Japan had decided to embark on a "fifteen year war" to expand far beyond Manchuria and into southern China and eventually southeast Asia.[98]

It may have been the United States saw Japan's rhetoric as a costly signal of mobilization nonetheless. But here again, there are holes in this story.

The United States took Japan's rhetoric as a clear and credible signal of its type, strong evidence that Japan was revolutionary state, despite the wealth of *costly* signals suggesting Japan's aims might remain limited: its retreat from Shanghai; the government's refusal to recognize an independent Manchukuo for eight months after the Kwantung Army declared independence; its agreement to a truce and the relative calm between Japan and China from 1933 to 1936. Indeed, what we seem to have is a case of what Mitzen and Schweller call "misplaced certainty" where American officials grew strangely confident in their interpretation of signals and ended up overstating the clarity of Japan's aims.[99] Some historians argue that this misplaced certainty was not only irrational but tragic. Convinced of Japan's revolutionary type, the United States adopted "foreign policy that unintentionally weakened those political elements in Japan that favored accommodation with the United States, cooperative membership in the League of Nations, and the peaceful resolution of international tensions."[100] This suggests a troubling counterfactual, that had the U.S. government continued to support Shidehara in late fall of 1931, if Stimson had not announced a formal nonrecognition, more restrained parties may have kept the reins of power in Japan.

We are left then with the twin puzzles of why Japan's leaders abandoned an internationalist legitimation strategy, and why the Americans responded so strongly, perhaps even irrationally, to mere talk. To explain this, the next sections turn to the conditions introduced in chapter 2: the rising power's capacity for multivocal legitimation and the great power's institutional vulnerability. These combined to make Japan's rhetoric strongly dissonant, a potent signal of revolutionary aims.

THE REVISIONIST'S DILEMMA: JAPAN'S RHETORICAL TURN

As argued in the sections above, for decades Japan had successfully legitimated their territorial expansion, conforming to the rules and norms of the international system to explain their actions in Manchuria. Now its leaders rejected these norms and rules, instead appealing to a hyper-nationalist, pan-Asianist, and "renovationist" order to justify their aims. Japan's leaders understood the risks of such rhetoric, and they continued to try to legitimate their claims in Manchuria to an international audience. During the crisis Japan embarked on a campaign of both official and public diplomacy designed to "persuade Western and especially US audiences of the justice of Japan's cause, with an energy which shows that they neither desired nor necessarily expected to be cut off from the international community as a result of the Manchurian crisis."[101] Members of the government spoke directly to American presses, in attempts to convince the public of the legitimacy of Japan's aims.[102] But without the treaty language, Japan's claims fell on deaf ears.

How can we explain this shift in legitimation strategies? As argued in chapter 2, rising powers face a dilemma when rhetoric that appeals to an international audience will sound dissonant to a domestic one. Under these conditions, leaders face an unenviable choice: appealing to an international audience might stem containment and confrontation, but will lead to ruin at home; appealing to a domestic coalition might mobilize masses at home, but provoke outrage abroad. In the 1920s and 1930s, Japan's leaders faced a severe dilemma. On the one hand there were "internationalist" parties, leaders that had largely dominated Japan's government since World War I. These internationalists, such as Foreign Minister Shidehara Kijuro, Prime Minister Hara Takashi, and many of the members of the Kenseikai (later Minseito) Party, embraced the language of Woodrow Wilson's "new diplomacy."[103] Japan, Shidehara argued, would turn the postwar peace "to its good advantage by rectifying the past mistakes of dual diplomacy . . . militaristic politics, and diplomacy dominated by military cliques."[104] Following Versailles, Kenseikai's leaders proclaimed that the "real essence of the 'new thought' was democracy at home and a great attention to world peace over national rights abroad."[105]

In contrast, renovationist coalitions argued that "Western" norms and rules were fundamentally corrupt and incompatible with Japan's national identity.[106] Interestingly the expansionist *aims* of the renovationists differed little from the internationalists, at least in the period before 1936.[107] Like the internationalists, most renovationists were primarily concerned with expanding into Manchuria; they were not seeking a hegemonic, Asian empire. But whatever their aims, renovationists were "contemptuous of Western-style justification for Japan's expansionist activities," and as a result "they developed as the ideological basis of Japanese expansion the mission of the resurrection of Asia, with Japan as the deliverer, the guide, the hero of the Eastern world."[108] During World War I, renovationists such as Yamagata Aritomo argued that Japan must pursue "self-protection of Asians and for the coexistence and co-prosperity of China and Japan," foreshadowing Japan's foreign policy of the late 1930s. After Versailles, renovationists condemned what they saw as Japan's genuflection toward Western institutions. Konoe Fumimaro, who in 1937 would become Japan's prime minister, castigated the League of Nations as a "tool for shoring up Anglo-American power,"[109] and likewise Ito Miyoji argued that the League would only preserve the "status quo of the Anglo-Saxon race" and "restrict the future development" of rising powers.[110]

Scholars have suggested Japan's turn to hardline rhetoric stemmed from this polarization in domestic politics. As Jack Snyder argues, for example, it was the logrolling among Japan's fragmented elites that led to hardline rhetoric.[111] Yet, other cases in this book demonstrate that, under some conditions, leaders can manage polarization: in both the United States and Prussia, leaders resisted the turn to revolutionary rhetoric. It was not only fragmentation, but an inability to use multivocal rhetoric, that doomed the internationalist enterprise. Unlike their counterparts in the United States and Prussia, Japan's leaders did not bridge coalitions; instead they were positioned either as speakers for "liberal-internationalist" coalitions, like Minseito, or as leaders of nationalist and renovationist movements. Japan lacked a Quincy Adams or a Bismarck: leaders did not cross internationalist and renovationist lines.

This meant that the battle for legitimation quickly became a zero-sum game: leaders could *either* appeal to internationalist or renovationist principles to justify their policies, but not both. At the beginning of Japan's expansion, the inability to make multivocal appeals was insignificant: liberal internationalism was the dominant discourse, both at home and abroad. By 1931, however, liberal-internationalism was in the midst of a legitimation crisis. A worldwide depression undercut liberal principles, the claim that commitment to Western economic institutions would ensure continued growth.[112] As Matsusaka argues, "The global economic crisis did more than any imperialist polemic to discredit the claims of the new diplomacy." Liberal-internationalist rhetoric was further discredited as security institutions began to weaken. In the wake of the London Naval Conference of 1930, when the United States and England refused to accept Japan's demands for an increased cruiser fleet, Japan's military saw an opportunity to mount a "public awareness campaign aimed at the 'popularization of national defense thought."[113]

Even before explosions rocked Manchuria, internationalist discourse was in decline. And as "world events made Japanese opinion still more disenchanted with the foreign ministry views of things, the ideas [of the renovationists] put forth in 1917 and 1918 lay ready to offer an alternative."[114] In the face of this legitimation crisis, these internationalists attempted a multivocal strategy, in a last attempt to appease audiences at home and abroad. Japan's liberal leaders—especially Shidehara—realized the dilemma they were in. They hoped to justify their actions to a Western audience, while remaining "conscious of their weakness and the need to cultivate popularity" among the Japanese public.[115] To their domestic audience, liberal internationalist leaders increasingly invoked renovationist rhetoric to justify Japan's presence in Manchuria. In November and December of 1930, for example, the foreign minister decried "Chinese plans to 'encircle' the SMR and drive the company into the 'jaws of death.'"[116] At the same time, Minseito attempted to assure the Americans that Japan's aims in Manchuria were limited, and it had no plans to abandon the Nine Power Treaty or the Washington system in the Asia-Pacific.

Minseito's leaders, however, lacked the resources to make multivocal claims. To Stimson, Shidehara's appeals to renovationist principles now only made him question the sincerity of his intentions. To the Japanese public, Minseito's internationalist appeals suggested the party was, at best, "spineless" in its foreign policy and, at worst, committing "treason."[117]

At home Minseito's leaders had little authority to make claims in the name of renovationist language. As one historian argues, "Shidehara and Minseito had not put down political roots" with renovationist coalitions.[118] If renovationist language was now the dominant legitimation strategy, there were actors with far more authority to speak it than the leaders of Minseito.

Instead of managing cross pressures, Japan's leaders turn to renovationist language opened up space for this rhetoric to dominate politics: by 1932 all of groups in Japan—*regardless* of the extent of their expansionist aims—were using renovationist rhetoric to legitimate their claims in Manchuria. Even if leaders wanted to stave off international mobilization against their efforts, they found themselves locked into a rhetoric that undercut these strategic interests. Seiyukai's prime minister Inukai Tsuyoshi, for example, still hoped to negotiate a settlement over Manchuria, yet was unable to justify working with an international organization or within the boundaries of the Washington treaties. Instead, his speeches were "self-consciously nationalist. In this atmosphere, the liberal and international voices were hardly heard."[119]

Within Japan the rise of renovationist rhetoric had tragic feedback effects: once "moderates" embraced renovationist rhetoric, they legitimated the most extreme positions in Japan's politics. Seiyukai's leaders, for example, found that their reliance on revolutionary language increased the influence of truly renovationist actors—such as Mori Kaku—who were then able to seize power within the increasingly fragmented state. In March 1932, Seiyukai's prime minister was assassinated. While the successor to the premiership was relatively moderate, renovationists seized control of key ministries in Japan's cabinet. Amongst these leaders were those who would formulate Japan's push toward domination in the late 1930s. Hirota Koki, executed after the war for Class A war crimes, was appointed foreign minister in 1933. Konoe Fumimaro now led Japan's house of peers. Matsuoka, who would serve as Konoe's foreign minister, now represented Japan at the League, and would lead the nation out of the institution in 1933.

Japan's political factions had unleashed a tiger they could not control. Whatever the aims of the leaders, the only rhetoric available to legitimate expansion was renovationist, nationalist, and militaristic in its content, and revolutionary in its words if not in its actions. Once committed to a revolutionary rhetoric, Japan's parties left themselves vulnerable to political outflanking by extremists who could claim much more authority and credibility in speaking to domestic constituencies. With internationalism thoroughly delegitimated, there could be no accommodation with the United States. Japan was now locked into a conflict, not only against China but against the international order. And on the rules of the international system, there could be no compromise.

"SCRAPS OF PAPER": THE INSTITUTIONAL VULNERABILITY OF AMERICAN FOREIGN POLICY

The theory developed in chapter 2 suggests that illegitimate rhetoric is not enough to provoke mobilization; legitimation strategies only resonate when a great power sees itself as institutionally vulnerable, dependent on an unsettled institutional order. The argument that the United States was "institutionally vulnerable" in the interwar period might seem strange: many see the United States as a radically isolationist nation after World War I. The United States rejection of the League, for example, is a story known well enough not to be rehashed here. Throughout the Manchurian crisis American officials remained uneasy with League institutions, at times seeming eager to participate in League negotiations, at others purposively eschewing formal institutions and pursuing a unilateral policy.

Yet American rejection of the League was not a rejection of liberal institutional order. At the end of the war, the United States committed itself to building a new institutional structure in the Pacific, one that would replace imperial relations and the balance of power with a system that secured free trade, guaranteed self-determination, and dampened down military competition through arms control agreements.[120] Key to this architecture were the treaties signed at the Washington Conference in fall of 1921. The Washington system, as Iriye argues, was a push toward liberal global governance, an effort to "demolish the existing system of imperialist diplomacy" and put in its place an institutional "mechanisms designed to harmonize the divergent interests of the great powers."[121] The Five Power Treaty between the United States, Britain, France, Japan, and Italy, for example, limited naval forces and banned gas warfare. The Four Power Treaty committed the United States, Britain, France, and Japan to consult with each other in the event of crisis. And the Nine Power Treaty, as described earlier, rearticulated the Open-Door policy and committed states to China's sovereignty.

Far from viewing international institutions as undercutting American isolationism, moreover, the treaties were seen as critical to the United States' economic and security position and its efforts to replace balance-of-power politics with "multinational agreements repudiating expansionism."[122] If states fulfilled the disarmament pledges in the Washington Naval Treaty, for example, the United States could then decrease its own naval spending and commitments, and draw back from projecting power across the Pacific.[123] It was for this reason that Senator Henry Cabot Lodge—a fierce opponent of the League—acted as one of the delegates to the conference and defended the agreement to remaining "irreconcilables" in the U.S. Congress. Likewise, it was through the Nine Power Treaty that the United States could protect its economic access to China, without raising the specter of European imperialism. Without the treaty the United States would have been forced into "a frank acceptance of the full implication of the spheres of interest idea and a resort without reservation to the principles of self-interest and self-help," principles anathema to U.S. foreign policy.[124] And it was only in a world of nonaggression that the United States could eschew alliance structures believed so dangerous for world peace. President Harding pronounced the treaties a "new state of mind" for world politics, where dangerous balance-of-power politics would no longer hold sway.[125]

For all of these reasons, these institutions were no mere "scraps of paper." As Stimson wrote in his diary: "The question of the 'scraps of paper' is a pretty crucial one. We have nothing but 'scraps of paper.'"[126] The United States could not afford to let "Japan run amok and play havoc with its peace treaties."[127] Evidence suggests these treaties had not only elite but broad public support. Congress ratified the treaties with strong majorities, even gaining support from members who had opposed the League (the naval treaty was opposed by only one vote).[128] The *New York Times* praised American leaders' "practical idealism" in negotiating the treaties.[129]

Despite its popularity in the United States, by the late 1920s, the Washington system was seen as increasingly unsettled. Iriye, for example, suggests the system was flailing as early as 1925, when the great powers failed to agree on China's right to tariff autonomy at the Peking Tariff Conference. By the 1930s, the system was under significant strain, as great power policy toward China grew more unilateral.[130] By the close of the decade, the powers were struggling to coordinate on issues of naval power and regional free trade. By 1930, the powers' failure to reach agreement at the London Naval Conference was placing additional strain on the treaty, and the worldwide depression and increasingly protectionist policies tore at the Washington system's liberal economic foundations.

The United States, in other words, entered the Manchurian crisis as an institutionally vulnerable power, committed to a treaty system that was highly unsettled. Under these conditions, any attack on the institutional order—even if symbolic and rhetoric—was unacceptable. Once Japan turned to the rhetoric of a new world order, Stimson feared that at stake was the entire system of international law, and that "great post-war effort to place the world upon a higher level of international life was in jeopardy."[131] As he stated bluntly, "In the light of treaties and principles of world welfare, it is *a challenge to the whole world.*"[132] Hornbeck similarly argued that Japan was taking on the Powers, and "if Japan won, "the principle that 'might is right' will have been substantially reinforced."[133] The same American policymakers who had long urged accommodation of Japan's aims, argued that "our position is clear as crystal: we hold no brief for either side in the Sino-Japanese dispute; we hold a brief for the inviolability of the international peace treaties."[134] As Stimson argued in 1932, the United States might have "no desire to become Japan's rival in Manchuria" but "he and the people of this country felt that this pact was of the utmost importance to the

United States and to the civilized world and in the event that it came to a question between permitting the destruction of that peace treaty on the one hand and annoying Japan on the other, he would unhesitatingly . . . take his stand for the preservation of the treaty."[135]

In sum, it was this configuration of speaker and audience that ensured Japan's legitimation strategies were strongly dissonant. In the midst of a crisis, Japan's leaders found themselves unable to make multivocal claims and, instead, moved toward a revolutionary rhetoric. While a more secure United States might have seen this rhetoric for it was—a desperate attempt to maintain power at home—an institutionally vulnerable United States took cheap talk at its word, moving to protect its "scraps of paper" at great cost.

Japan Unbound: The American Reaction to Japan's Legitimation Strategies

In chapter 2, it was argued that dissonant strategies will have powerful effects on great power mobilization. As argued above, events in Manchuria in 1931 were troubling, but not fatal to U.S.-Japanese relations, so long as Japan could explain why its actions remained within the boundaries of the Washington system. From the outset of the crisis in September 1931, the United States and the international community demanded that the Japanese government provide reasons for its actions, to explain not only *what* it intended in Manchuria, but *why*.[136] Officials claimed Japanese officials could very well have a "good case" for their intervention.[137] As Japan remained silent about its reasons the first few days of the crisis, the American audience grew frustrated. Stimson pressed Japan's ambassador and its foreign minister for an explanation of the invasion, placing the role of the treaties as core to Japan's legitimacy:

> I pointed out to him the seriousness of the situation when treaty promises began to be broken; I reminded him that the nine power treaty was one of a group of treaties mutually dependent . . . I asked him what was left on which we could rest for the stability of the world when treaty obligations began to be broken; I reminded him of the many times I had spoken of Japan as a stabilizing influence in the world and asked him if he thought I could do so now.[138]

The media, too, seemed wary of Japan's silence. As the *New York Times* put it:

> No impartial person who has followed the Japanese course in China . . . can fail to conclude that Japan has lacked what is called 'good publicity.' She had, in many respects, a good case. She was entitled to stand upon her treaty rights. . . . But apparently the Japanese government did not have that decent respect for the opinion of mankind which would have led her to explain and justify her position in the face of hostile criticism.[139]

Japan's reasons for invading Manchuria, in other words, were of tremendous significance to U.S. officials. And because Japan's claims were dissonant, they had three effects on U.S. mobilization: they signaled Japan could not be restrained by treaty; they amplified voices for containment in the United States; and they framed Japan's actions in Manchuria as an existential threat to the U.S. order. All of these effects meant the United States moved toward mobilizing its forces toward containment and confrontation.

SIGNALING REVOLUTIONARY AIMS

As argued above, throughout the early twentieth century, as Japan rose to prominence, the United States harbored no illusions about Japan's revisionist aims. It foresaw that Japan's increasing power meant that it would naturally seek to modify political, economic, and territorial arrangements in its backyard. Already the United States had accommodated, even encouraged, expansion into China and Korea and, in 1931, there was no sign that the United States would push back against further expansion in the region. Economically, many American officials accepted the Japanese government's argument that it must expand in areas like Manchuria in order to secure the resources and territorial necessary to its economic livelihood.[140] Politically, American officials viewed Japan's dominance in Manchuria as the "least of all evils," suggesting that Japanese control of Manchuria might be the only source of stability in a chaotic region.[141]

Whatever Japan's ambitions, however, its language suggested that the country would be constrained through her institutional ties, particularly by its position within the Washington Conference treaties. Much of this signaling of constraint was rhetorical: no leader in Japan ever abandoned or denied Japan's interest in Manchuria, and the United States was well aware of its aims. Yet the rhetoric continued to signal that was not a revolutionary state and would play by the approved rules of the Washington treaties.[142] As John Gittings argues, "Japan was allowed to go so far because the Western powers believed it would keep its imperialist appetite (which they shared) within bounds."[143] Japan, another scholar argues, "had been admitted to the same club as the Western powers and was to be permitted to play the imperialist game by the same rules, so long as open clashes with the treaties were avoided."[144] American officials and media alike referred to Japan as a good citizen of the global order, despite its efforts to exert control over Manchuria. Even opponents of Japanese expansion conceded that Japan was now working within the boundaries of the treaty. MacMurray, for example, suggested that Japanese power in "East Asia must be accepted" as Japan had been "scrupulously loyal in its adherence to the letter and spirit of the Washington conference."[145]

As Japan's rhetorical took a revolutionary turn during the Manchurian crisis, it proved a potent signal of revolutionary ambition. Grew, for example, expressed his frustration with Japan's insistence that the treaties did not apply to Manchuria, arguing that:

> I have a great deal of sympathy with Japan's *legitimate aspirations* in Manchuria, but no sympathy at all with the *illegitimate way* in which Japan has been carrying them out. One can have little sympathy with the . . . typically Prussian methods pursued in Manchuria and Shanghai since September 18, 1931, in the face of the Kellogg Pact, the Nine Power Treaty, and the Covenant of the League of Nations.[146]

As Wilson argues, this was not simply a reaction to Japan's *actions* in Manchuria, its increased use of military might. As Grew noted, even the use of force might have been acceptable if Japan's politicians could have justified it "somehow within the framework of the international covenants."[147]

The commentary of public intellectuals and the media supports this argument as well.[148] At the beginning of the crisis, much of the public discussion suggests uncertainty as to the legitimacy of Japan's actions, and whether or not they could be accommodated within the existing treaty structure. Many Americans, both policymakers and the public alike, were confused by Japan's refusal to invoke the treaties to legitimate their behavior. Japan had considerable justification for going into China. Japan, as the *New York Times* editorial board noted "enjoys admitted treaty rights" in Manchuria and was acting no differently than the United States had in Haiti when unrest threatened core interests.[149] One commentator remarked that Japan "might even have been asked by the power to go in and restore to Manchuria that order and safety which China was not maintaining."[150] As Japanese representatives increased their verbal attacks on the treaties, the papers changed course. Now, they argued that, as James Shotwell put it, "When the Japanese troops stormed Mukden in the early morning of September 19 last, they attacked something more than the ancient capital of the Manchus. The edifice of international peace which had been built upon the ruins of the World War was shaken by the impact of the blow as much as the Chinese republic."[151]

It was because Japan's reasons were illegitimate—because it rejected the rules and norms governing the Washington system—that U.S. officials now saw a rising power unrestrained by treaty obligations. Japan now seemed a power willing to mobilize the most hardline elements in its society. Before the change in Japan's rhetoric, officials, especially Stimson, believed Japanese officials like Shidehara were doing their best to contain radical nationalist coalitions within Japan. Shidehara, Stimson claimed, was in a "very difficult," position attempting to stave off extremist elements in the government.[152] But as Japan's leaders adopted a nationalist rhetoric, so too did U.S.

officials see this as an attempt to concede to, and ultimately mobilize, the hardline revisionists.

More broadly, Japan's legitimation strategies signaled the state would cast off the treaties of the Washington system. For this reason, Japan's expansion in Manchuria, efforts that Americans had earlier found acceptable, were now seen as evidence of Japan's insatiable revisionism. In the face of Japan's rhetorical defiance, the United States began to engage in what LaFeber calls "domino theory" thinking: whereas Japan's rhetoric had once signaled constraint, now it seemed to suggest a power unresponsive to global governance. Hornbeck, for example, proclaimed that Japan could no longer "be deterred by treaty obligations or moral suasion."[153] He argued that "in light of existing circumstances and conditions, it would appear probable that Japan will continue to work for the realization of a Japanese hegemony in Eastern Asia and that the United States will be the leading power most strongly opposed to the consummation of that objective."[154] Japan was not quelling "local disorders," but pursuing "a carefully prepared and far-reaching plan" to dominate South Manchuria.[155] Eventually, by this reasoning, Japan would declare a "Monroe Doctrine" in East Asia; Manchuria was simply the first step in driving the United States out of all of Asia. There was no room for partnership with a revolutionary power. As Grew would remark after the crisis, any new pact would fail: "If you can't find a rock to build your house on, but only sand, it's much safer not to build a house at all."[156] As Iriye argues, this perception of Japan as an unbound and insatiable revisionist greatly exaggerated Tokyo's aims in the Pacific, which, at least from 1931 to 1933, remained consistent with its limited goals of the previous decade. But in the face of illegitimate rhetoric, Japan now appeared a rising power that would and could not be restrained.

RHETORICAL COERCION: AMPLIFYING THE VOICES OF CONTAINMENT

Even before the occupation of Manchuria, some officials were arguing the United States must check Japan's expansion in East Asia. From World War I onward, a segment of the foreign policy establishment, particularly in the State Department, declared that Japan, if left unchecked, would become a regional hegemon, one driven to expel the United States from the Pacific. Japan's critics grew particularly vocal as Japan attempted to formalize its claims to Manchuria in the wake of that war. The U.S. minister to China, Paul Reinsch, denounced the Twenty-One Demands as the "greatest crisis ever experienced in China." If Japan succeeded, the United States would lose the Open Door, and "the independence of China and equal opportunity of western nations are at stake."[157] Another State Department official argued Tokyo's demands signaled an intention "to work out her salvation and that of China as well upon the basis of 'Asia for the Asiatics,'" and would allow Japan to quickly become powerful enough to deprive the United States of its interests in the region.[158] MacMurray, then chief of the Far Eastern division of the State Department, argued that it was necessary for "restoring the equilibrium in the far East which has been so dangerously upset by Japan's process of aggrandizement." Likewise Hornbeck argued that Japan had an informal "Monroe Doctrine" for Asia and that it would expand into all of China, posing a major threat to the United States in the process.[159]

So long as Japan's rhetoric adhered to the "new diplomacy" and the Washington system, such proclamations seemed misguided. Some diplomats, such as Reinsch, were forced to abandon their arguments in the face of Japan's turn to Wilsonsianism. Others, such as MacMurray and Hornbeck, appear to have changed their mind in light of Japan's embrace of the treaties. As Japan moved toward a revolutionary legitimation strategy during the Manchurian crisis, however, these critics of accommodation were emboldened. As Japan adopted a revolutionary rhetoric, Hornbeck began to argue that the United States must provide "some sort of official denunciation of Japan as a lawbreaker."[160] He argued that Japan was waging "two campaigns: one against China, military; the other against the Powers, diplomatic. She has won in the former every battle; and she has at no point been defeated in the latter." The time was thus "fast approaching when the Powers would either have to 'put up or shut up.'"[161]

Still there were factions in the State Department who argued accommodation should continue to dominate American policy. Many of these calls came from self-proclaimed realists, who argued that the United States had neither the will nor the capacity to confront Japan over Manchuria. Even before the crisis in Manchuria, Castle had urged caution in the call to enforce the Washington treaties: Japan's increasing power, Castle suggested, meant that the status quo would have to change. Japan, he argued, was the United States' "one useful friend in the Orient" and advised Hoover to acknowledge Japan's interests in China.[162] Forbes and Grew, both ambassadors to Japan, worked to, in Forbes words, "keep the United States from being *too insistent* upon checking Japan." Again, this was simple realism. As Grew wrote, there was "no treaty which runs counter to the inexorable facts of history and economic necessity can in any case wholly restrain [Japan's] penetration in Manchuria. . . . She is there to stay unless conquered in war. For nations," he argued, "the moral disapproval of others may change their conception of what constitute justifiable aggression, but only if that disapproval threatens to entail social or economic disadvantages or losses of a practical and material nature." If the United States was not willing to "fight" Japan over Manchuria, they should learn to "like it."

But Japan's legitimation strategies undercut these realist arguments. Realists could not deny that Japan had violated the fundamental principles of the Washington system. As much as they encouraged a prudent response, it was difficult to push back against a condemnation of Japan's actions, even if they saw declarations such as the Stimson Doctrine as counterproductive and inflammatory. Castle continued to insist that "I am convinced that selfish interests make it imperative that we have Japan as a friend in the western Pacific," but conceded that this could only happen "so long at least as Japan maintains an ethical code which we can recognize."[163] Grew urged the Hoover administration to remain impartial to China and Japan, but also recognized that the United States could not abandon the treaties.[164]

In essence, the voices of accommodation could no longer make the case that Japan could be treated as a reliable treaty partner. In the face of Japanese rhetoric, Castle could not convince Hoover to reduce the American fleet at Pearl Harbor, a continuing source of tension between the two nations.[165] And certainly they could not stop the policy of nonrecognition, even though many saw it as an overblown bluff, nothing more than "Pusillanimous administrators putting forth words or threats, behind which there is no preparation for deeds," as Forbes described it.[166] Many of these realists expressed frustration at their inability to counter Stimson and Hornbeck's move toward a more confrontational policy. Hugh R. Wilson, the U.S. representative to Geneva and a friend of Grew, argued that he "felt like bursting into tears" over Stimson's nonrecognition:

> Mr. Stimson . . . had every legal right to take and maintain the position which he did. . . . But you know and I know that the endeavor to place humanity within a rigid framework of legal restriction has never yet succeeded. . . . We need not have done any of these things in such a way as to make us . . . the leaders in what Mr. Stimson called "mobilizing world opinion against Japan."[167]

In sum, so long as Japan had invoked liberal institutionalist norms, the voices of containment had been silenced. But as Japan's rhetoric turned revolutionary, it amplified arguments that it was, indeed, a threat to the United States. These actors could now argue that containment was the only policy consistent with the U.S. order. Mobilization against Japan was now necessary.

IDENTITY AND EXISTENTIAL THREATS: JAPAN'S ATTACK ON THE AMERICAN ORDER

Finally, Japan's shift in rhetoric constructed an image of Japan as an existential threat to the United States, a danger to its very identity as a liberal, treaty-abiding nation. In Japan's attack on Manchuria, U.S. officials came to see, not merely aggression against China, but an offensive against the Washington system and even the entirety of the post–World War I governance structure as a whole. As Hornbeck argued, in Manchuria, Japan had taken on two contests: in invading China, it had embarked on a conflict with China, largely stemming from China's failure to "live up to elementary international obligations"; but in denying the force of treaties, Japan was engaging in a contest against "the Powers of the World" by failing "to observe the conventions . . . which now prevail among the members of the "Family of Nations."[168]

As argued above, the belief that Japan posed an existential threat cannot be reduced to its material might.[169] In 1931, Japan had neither the ability nor interest in threatening U.S. holdings in the Philippines or Hawaii, or in undercutting its economic interests in China. For this reason, scholars often emphasize the role that race played in shaping U.S. perceptions of Japan: it was Japan's status a racial "other" that made its revisionist demands so frightening.[170] There is no doubt that race shaped U.S.-Japan relations and diplomacy. Local discriminatory legislation, such as San Francisco's segregation of schools, fueled Japan's resentment toward the United States. As early as 1915, officials in the State Department and the British Foreign Office were warning of a "'Yellow Peril" that threatened to impose "a Japanese Monroe doctrine on China, and a cry of 'the Far East for the Far Easterns.'"[171] Race shaped critical discussions at Versailles when the European powers rejected the racial nondiscrimination clause, cementing Japan's status as a "second-tier" power in world politics. Throughout the Manchurian crisis, race permeated much of the discourse surrounding assessments of Japan as a threat in East Asia. Grew suggested, for example, that Japan was "menacing because of its national spirit": "The force of a nation bound together with great moral determination, fired with national ambition, and peopled by a race with unbounded capacity for courageous self-sacrifice is not easy to overcome."[172] Officials worried that Japan's actions signaled the nation was "working steadily toward the exclusion of . . . the white man from the Pacific."[173]

As powerful as was the role race played in U.S.-Japanese relations, it neither had a determinative effect on U.S. policy toward Japan, nor doomed these two states to confrontation and conflict. Indeed, in the early twentieth century and especially after Versailles, American officials often spoke of Japan as a kindred spirit in institution building, a partner in creating a civilized, liberal order in East Asia. Japan's adherence to Western diplomacy and industrialization had made her "the pioneer of progress in the Orient."[174] As Japan expanded into Korea and Manchuria at the start of the century, Americans extolled the rising power as "the Great Britain of Asia" and the "Yankees of the East."[175] Throughout the 1920s, American officials praised Japan's commitment to the Washington treaties, its willingness to take the lead in promoting the new diplomacy in the Asia-Pacific.[176] And on the eve of the crisis in Manchuria, official correspondence and media reports alike were far more likely to cast Japan as a member of Western "civilization" rather than as a threat.[177]

Moreover Japan's initial incursions into Manchuria did not, on their own, shift the perceptions of Japan as a long-standing partner in the international order: the actions themselves were indeterminate. At the onset of the crisis, Stimson warned against overreaction, arguing that Japan had demonstrated an "exceptional record of good citizenship in the life of the international world,"[178] and was thus unlikely to pose a threat to the United States. Hornbeck built on this in a memo, arguing that "Japan as an *agent of civilization* should have a premier position in Manchuria. . . . If any nation is to be the mandatory for this neglected corner of the earth with its important undeveloped resources, every consideration indicates Japan."[179] Even if Japan were to challenge the Open Door, this might be acceptable, provided Japan continue to act as a reliable member of the liberal order: "If we compel a strict interpretation of the 'open door' in Manchuria may not doors be rudely burst open elsewhere which are now closed to Japanese; say in California?"[180] The media concurred with the official assessment, that Japan was no "other," but a reliable partner in the Washington system. Japan, reminded the *New York Times*, had long sought to take a position "among the civilized nations." Even as violence persisted, the op-ed pages claimed that Japan's officials "must still desire, as for years past they have shown that they do, to stand well with the civilized nations."[181]

But as Japan's rhetoric rejected the norms of Washington system, instead embracing the revolutionary language of a Pan-Asian order, so too did U.S. perceptions of Japan change: Japan became, not a partner in the liberal system, but an existential threat. Japan's pronouncements were in direct contrast with the identity of the United States. As one State Department memo noted, "As Prussian ideals and aspirations were in conflict with the rights and interest of Great Britain, so Japan's ideals and aspirations are today in conflict with those of the United States." Public commentators likewise began to emphasize the threat Japan posed to the international system. Japan's leaders, the *New York Times* remarked, had long stood with the international order, but in Manchuria Japan was "turning back the clock on her own progress," and that even if she had a "good case" in Manchuria, she had justified it in such a "manner as to give offense to the moral judgment of the whole world."[182]

This growing sense that Japan was an existential and moral threat mandated a policy of containment in 1931, even if that policy undercut United States material interests. As Thorne argues, the United States might not have much at stake in the region, but the "new morality of international relations made it imperative" to contain the Japanese threat. Without some form of containment, the liberal international order would suffer irreparable damage. As Stimson argued, "If the fruits of aggression should be recognized the whole theory of the Kellogg Pact would be repudiated."[183] As Hornbeck's "understanding of the cause and nature of the Manchurian crisis" shifted, he "repeatedly opposed restoration of the status quo ante as the solution."[184] Indeed, in light of Japan's attack on the global order, it seemed crucial that "the whole world be brought into line and into action in defense of rights and interests which are common to all in connection with the problems of peace."[185]

So convinced were officials of the existential and dire nature of the Japanese threat that they were willing to advocate for containment policies that flouted American strategic interests. Stimson and Hornbeck pressed for economic sanctions against Japan, even as these were perceived as undercutting financial interests.[186] Hornbeck argued strenuously that "it was not necessary, and it would not serve a useful purpose—but the contrary—publicly to brand Japan a moral culprit and place her on exhibition as such before a world which is divided in opinion with regard to principles of morality."[187] The United States had long preferred a stable China, yet now "Washington, in the interest of principle, preferred that China continue to fight" and that "China suffer . . . than recognize Japanese gains achieved in defiance of the Nine Power treaty."[188] And American resistance to accommodation must now stretch far beyond Asia. Allowing Japan to defy the treaties would mean, as a State Department memo outlined, "we would go back on our treaties." United States concern for the peace structure, Hornbeck argued, "did not relate particularly to the Orient but to the entire world."[189]

In sum, in a period of months the United States went from seeing Japan as a reliable partner in the liberal order to viewing Japan's expansion as an existential threat to the global system of governance. Japan's actions in and of themselves cannot explain this shift: aggression against Manchuria could have been interpreted as a local and reasonable response to ongoing instability in China. It was Japan's legitimation of its actions as a necessary step in introducing a new order, one which did not admit the legitimacy of existing treaties, that changed how the United States perceived Japan's ambition and, as a result, the strategies necessary to deal with the rising power. Once Japan appeared as a power unconstrained by treaties, as attacking, not only China, but the world order, accommodation was impossible. Containment and confrontation were the only answers to Japan's revisionist aims.

Interwar Japan has come to epitomize the revolutionary revisionist, a state whose rise no great power could accommodate. Captured by a military government, driven by ideological zeal, dependent on expansion for its wealth, security, and legitimacy, there was no way to bargain over Japan's increasingly rapacious demands. In 1931, as Japan moved into Manchuria, containment was inevitable; ten years later, war would become unavoidable. It is understandable why we are tempted to tell the story of U.S.-Japanese relations as hinging on Japan's type. For myriad reasons—the political instability that the Meiji restoration unleashed, its late economic development—Japan always seemed vulnerable to revolutionary forces. From this perspective, Manchuria is simply the moment that the United States fully understood the extent of Japan's aims, that it read, correctly, as the revolutionary's true intentions. Yet, the chapter here has attempted to reveal serious silences in this conventional story.

First, why 1931? Why in 1931 would the United States come to see Japan as a revolutionary threat? As maintained throughout this chapter, there was nothing inherent in Japan's invasion of Manchuria that was threatening to the U.S. position. That Japan would control Manchuria had been a given in U.S. policy toward the country since at least the turn of the century. Even as the crisis unfolded, voices within the U.S. government urged accommodation, arguing that Japan had and would continue to act as a source of order in China. What Manchuria came to mean—how it signaled revolutionary intent—is thus a serious puzzle for conventional explanations. As argued here, we cannot understand the meaning of Manchuria without a discussion of legitimation strategies: it was the justification of Japan's leaders, their rhetorical challenge to the international order, which gave significance to the Manchurian signal.

A second implication goes beyond this. Rhetoric was not simply a revelation of Japan's true type. True that there were renovationist, revolutionary forces in Japan clamoring for expansion, and true also that these voices would come to dominate Japan's politics. But in 1931, interests were still very much in flux. There were, as discussed above, credible signals of restraint, whether it was Japan's decision to pull back from Shanghai, in the government's efforts to subdue the Kwantung Army, or the refusal to recognize the state of Manchukuo. As argued here, arguably these costly signals revealed the continued *uncertainty* of Japan's type, the instability of its intentions, even as its language hardened.

Indeed, the case of Japan casts doubt on the literature's fundamental distinction between "revolutionary" and "limited aims" revisionist states. What was it that was essentially revolutionary about Japan in 1931? Not the extent of its aims, which were still quite limited. Not the composition of its government, which remained in flux. Not its society, much of which remained disconnected from the events of Manchuria. What was revolutionary was the rhetoric itself. Indeed it was, arguably, this rhetorical turn that birthed a revolutionary Japan. It emboldened renovationists at home, empowering their position in politics. And abroad, it placed Japan outside the boundaries of the legitimate world order. Rhetoric was not a reflection of type; it was its creator, the engine of revolutionary change. This raises a fundamental question: if signals are shaping intentions—and not the other way around—then this opens up space for a social constructivist turn in studies of strategic interaction, one in which identities are constructed through the signaling process. We'll turn to this question in the conclusion of this book.

Conclusion

Legitimacy, Power, and Strategy in World Politics

There is perhaps no more uncertain time in international politics than when new powers rise.[1] If a potential challenger harbors revolutionary ambitions, it must be contained or confronted before it has the power to challenge territorial boundaries, upend economic systems, and overturn the existing political and normative order. A challenger with limited aims, in contrast, should be accommodated. A benign rising power could provide a bulwark against other threats in the international system. Aiding an emerging power in economic development could result in a stable state with a vibrant population and market. A like-minded emerging power could shore up existing norms, and guarantee the stability of an international order. Elucidating the intentions of an adversary might be a difficult task, but it is an essential one: only by reducing uncertainty over intentions can great powers formulate a prudent response to a challenger's rise.

The cases in this book provide extensive evidence that much of rising power politics involves the search for certainty, with great powers seeking enough information about the rising power's ambitions to form a coherent and reasonable response to its rise.[2] At the same time, the cases here reveal significant silences in existing explanations about how great powers resolve this uncertainty—and resolve it they do, because the great powers in this story do not remain in a constant state of paralysis, unsure as to what strategy they should deploy. Because the meaning of most revisionist behavior is indeterminate—because actions do not speak for themselves—even expansionist behavior is not a clear and objective signal of a rising challenger's ambitions. For this reason, I have argued that rising powers have the ability to shape the meaning of their behavior through their legitimation strategies. Rising challengers will try to persuade the great powers that, even if they increase their might, their ambitions will remain within the boundaries of what is right.

Legitimation strategies are important, I have argued, because they are a crucial component of collective mobilization, both at home and abroad. For this reason they shape perceptions of a rising power's intentions through three mechanisms. First, legitimation strategies can signal restraint and constraint, a willingness to abide by international norms and secure the status quo. Second, legitimation strategies set rhetorical traps: when rising powers frame expansion as legitimate, they deprive opposing audiences of grounds on which to mobilize against them. And finally, legitimation strategies are likely to be successful when they appeal to a state's identity: a rising power can mobilize support for its demands by evoking principles and norms fundamental to a threatened state.

As argued throughout this book, however, the effects of a rising power's legitimation are not constant across time and space. I argue that legitimation strategies only influence outcomes when they resonate, when they are seen as having "pertinence, relevance, or significance" with a targeted audience. This resonance occurs under two conditions: when the rising power uses a multivocal legitimation language, rhetoric that appeals to several legitimating principles, and thus appeals to multiple audiences simultaneously; and when the great power audience is institutionally vulnerable, when the great power believes the normative system it favors is under attack. Combining these two conditions, I suggest that there are four worlds of legitimation, explaining how vulnerability and multivocality either amplify or mute mechanisms of restraint, coercion, and identification.

The politics of legitimation do not diminish the importance of the politics of harm and interest. The argument here accepts that great powers respond to rising challengers based on whether they think that state will undercut its security or interests. Examining the politics of legitimation, however, allows us to explain why and how it is great powers decide that a rising challenger is a reformer or revolutionary: it cuts to that long-standing question of why some states are seen as threats in international politics.[3] A focus on legitimation, moreover, highlights three additional paradoxes of rising power politics. First, the theory here suggests that rising powers might find strength in their fragmentation. It seems intuitive that fragmented states—states divided by party, class, and ideology—would be weak risers, torn apart by conflicting aims. Yet the cases in this book demonstrate that rising powers are most successful when they can make multivocal claims that resonate across multiple audiences. This capacity to speak multivocally lies in fragmentation, in a leader's capacity to speak to multiple and even contradictory interests: Bismarck, for example, used the proliferation of German national and conservative coalitions to create a sphinxlike appearance to his audience, moving back and forth between revolutionary nationalist and dynastic-conservative language. Fragmentation may also be the foundation of a democracy's successful rise. Indeed while conventional theories point to the importance of transparency in a democracy's foreign policy, the theory here suggests that it might be a democracy's capacity to make ambiguous claims that give it the power to undercut mobilization.

Second, legitimation theory suggests that it might be the most powerful actors in the international system that will be most vulnerable to a rising power's claims. As argued throughout this book, a rising power's appeals are likely to resonate when existing great powers are institutionally vulnerable, when they are both embedded within the existing normative structure of the international system, and when they believe that normative system is unsettled. Ironically, the power to create institutional orders might be what makes these states more vulnerable to a rising power's rhetorical claims. It is the powerful that construct these institutional orders. When great powers construct institutions, they may see, or come to see, their own security as inherently connected to the persistence of that institutional order, even when more "material" factors—military might, economic wealth—suggest that a state should be secure. For these reasons, great powers may be more inclined to respond to attacks on legitimacy than weaker powers in the international system.

Finally, my argument suggests that the path to conflict during power transitions might not lie in uncertainty about intentions—which is the conventional wisdom—but in the certainty, however rational, that one's opponent is a revolutionary state.[4] As seen throughout the empirical chapters, great powers struggle to manage rising powers because they are uncertain about what these states will do with their newfound might, either in the present or in the future. But in each of these cases studied here, this uncertainty did not lead to overwhelming fear, or a sense that the great power must adopt "worst case scenario" reasoning and stop a potential adversary's rise at any cost. To the contrary, great powers want to avoid the costs of confrontation when possible and, in the face of uncertainty, will adopt a "wait and see" approach a rising challenger. It is only when states become certain that a rising power is a revolutionary state, that it cannot be contained within existing rules and norms, that confrontation and containment are likely. Whereas uncertainty induces caution, certainty pushes great powers toward action, even at the cost of war.

And focusing on the politics of legitimation allows us to explain why and how great powers become certain that a rising challenger is a reformer or revolutionary: it cuts to that long-standing question of why some states are seen as threats.[5] This approach has implications for our understanding, not only of past and current power transitions, but also for how scholars approach rhetoric and strategic interaction in international politics more generally. In the remainder of this chapter, I take up three implications of my argument: how a focus on legitimacy highlights the role of contingency and path-dependency in power transitions; the implications of this book for U.S.-China relations, especially American understandings of a rising China's "assertiveness;" and finally, what insights legitimation theory bring to our conventional understandings of strategic signaling and power politics.

The Weight of History: Contingency, Path Dependence, and the Myth of the Thucydides Trap

To begin with, my argument challenges narratives that see the outcomes of power transitions as all but determined. This book clearly departs from theories that suggest that when new powers rise, conflict is likely, and only in rare cases can states escape this "Thucydides Trap" where "misunderstandings about each other's actions and intentions" push states toward war.[6] Here I suggest that great powers, far from being inclined to contain or confront a rising power, are sometimes willing if not eager to incorporate new powers into the international order. Indeed, great powers are often seeking partners to shore up their preferred system of governance.[7] In the United States, Britain saw a like-minded power that was capable of upholding rules and norms in the Atlantic. Austria and Russia saw Prussia as a bulwark against a rising tide of revolutionary nationalism. Both the United States and Britain hoped that Japan would act as a force for order in a region where China and Russia threatened to disrupt the system. In all of these cases, the status quo and rising powers were not heading toward an inevitable clash; there was ample room for cooperation and space for the emerging power to shape the outcomes of its rise.

The argument that great powers may cooperate with rising powers is not new. Scholars across a wide array of theoretical traditions argue that there is plenty of room for cooperation between a rising and status quo power.[8] But even in these accounts, the fate of the rising power often seems all but determined, driven by factors outside its control. For some, a rising power's path is determined by geography, or by whether it rises in an offense- or defense-dominant world.[9] A rising power has little control over the timing of its development, its regime type, its strategic and cultural narratives, all of which shape both the intentions of the emerging power and the reactions to its rise. Put these factors together, and rising powers seem to have little control over the world around them. This is a theoretical world where the United States is favored by the gods. It is born blessed, with a liberal, democratic government, an open economic system, and well-timed industrial development.[10] As it consolidated its power, it was protected by oceans, isolated from potential competitors, able to bide its time before it engaged with the world as a great power in its own right. Japan, by contrast, was cursed from birth. It began its rise as a regime wracked by domestic instability and revolution. It developed too quickly, with an industrial revolution left stunted by a lack of natural resources. Its racial status as an "other" meant that it would stand outside of normal Western diplomatic relations. And its rise into a great power occurred, not in isolation, but within a system of suspicious and hostile states. A clash with one of them was inevitable.

The cases in this book instead suggest that the dynamics of rising power politics are both contingent and path-dependent. To take the American example, the argument here is not that hegemonic war was likely between the two powers. But it is not difficult to imagine a counterfactual world where an "enduring rivalry" was likely, where the two powers would have struggled over influence in South America, in Canada, and throughout the Western Hemisphere. Likewise, it is not impossible to imagine a world in which the United States, worried about disorder in China, faced with a potential hegemonic power in Europe, would have bargained with Japan over Manchuria in 1931. Indeed, in drawing attention to contingency, this book suggests that rising powers have considerable agency to influence and manipulate the strategic reactions to their own rise. Without Bismarck's rhetorical management, balancing was a possible, perhaps even probable, outcome. Likewise, without the Monroe administration's commitment to the legal order, it was not determined that the United States would move westward rapidly and without resistance, or secure the Western Hemisphere as its own neighborhood. Had Japan continued to frame Manchuria as an issue within the Washington order, it may have avoided American ire.

This appreciation of contingency has sparked a growing recent interest in diplomacy, negotiation, and leadership in international politics. Brian Rathbun, for example, argues leaders can adopt different diplomatic styles, ranging from coercive statecraft to more cooperative dialogues, and variation in these diplomatic styles ultimately create or destroy space for peaceful negotiation in world politics. Keren Yahri-Milo focuses on the cognitive processing of individuals to explain how they perceive the intentions of their adversaries. Elizabeth Saunders looks to the preexisting beliefs of American presidents to explain why it is some are more likely to intervene than others.[11] Diplomatic historians, too, have brought individuals back into power politics, whether it is the acumen of John Quincy Adams and Otto von Bismarck in managing their countries' expansion, or the naiveté of a Chamberlain in accepting Hitler's appeals.

This book joins these scholars in putting diplomacy back in the center of great power politics. At the same time, it cautions against theories conceiving of world politics as the arena of unfettered agency and individual skill. As noted throughout the chapters, while it might be tempting to read these histories as determined by the speeches of great men or the decisions of fools, each of these individuals worked with the resources at hand. Adams certainly did not get by on his charisma; it was his position that gave him the resources to make resonant claims. Chamberlain's blinders were not his own; they were a function of Britain's vulnerable position in the international system. To put it another way, the theory here is one of structured agency: leaders are important, but they do not operate in worlds of their own making. Contingency is not mere chance, but the outcome of a particular configuration of rules, position, and rhetoric.

And legitimation strategies have path dependent effects as well. When legitimation strategies resonate, they can become institutionalized knowledge, narratives that continue to shape the interpretation of events long after they are first uttered.[12] Once the United States "understood" that Japan was an insatiable revisionist, signals that it might be willing to negotiate or restrain its actions were discounted. Once the British saw the United States as benign, its saber rattling over Oregon was muted. As legitimation strategies become institutionalized knowledge, costly signals inconsistent with the narrative are discounted, and cheap talk that reinforces the dominant story of the power is amplified. Legitimation strategies, though strategic, become settled discursive filters through which events are perceived.

China and the Puzzle of Assertiveness: The Construction of a Social Fact

As argued in chapter 1, while there is near consensus among scholars and policymakers that China is a rising power, there is considerable debate about China's revisionist ambitions. For some, China has, and will continue to pursue, only limited revisionist aims.[13] Yes, China has territorial ambitions, especially in the South and East China seas and toward Taiwan, but these can be contained. China will seek economic institutional reform, but not revolution: it will exert greater influence in existing trade and financial relations, but will not seek to overturn them. Even if China's ambitions grow, its position within the international system will constrain its actions. China's export-oriented economy relies heavily on foreign investment, which while "no guarantee against war," is "still a major force for peace."[14] There may be tensions in the South and East China seas, but these hardly amount to the sovereign claims that drove major wars in the past.[15] And if all else fails, the threat of nuclear war would induce caution in any rising power.[16]

Others suggest China's revisionist ambitions have and will continue to grow with its power. They point to signs that China seeks to replace the United States as the preeminent economic power, not merely reforming but overturning economic institutions.[17] In 2015, China's formed the Asian Infrastructure Investment Bank (AIIB), a multilateral development bank whose membership spans the globe. China's leaders have pursued the One Belt, One Road initiative to invest in infrastructure projects on the land route from China through Central Asia, as well on the southerly maritime routes from China through Southeast Asia and on to South Asia, Africa, and Europe. China has demonstrated its willingness to use its growing military might to coerce smaller powers in the region to cede territorial claims in the South China Sea, and one need only look at China's modernization of its military—its development of power projection capabilities and precision technology capable of disabling American military force—to see its revisionist aims.[18]

As with other cases in this book, China's intentions are likely to remain uncertain, even to its own leaders. What is clear is that, since 2009, United States' *perceptions* of China's intentions are changing: over the last decade the United States has started to see China as a more ambitious, revisionist power.[19] From the late 1990s on, United States leaders treated China as though it harbored largely benign ambitions: while the United States understood China would likely pursue limited revisionist aims, it believed that those aims could be accommodated within the American-led liberal international order. These beliefs about China's intentions drove an American commitment to accommodation, or engagement, as the best means to manage China's rise. The United States wagered that a China integrated into and strengthened by global institutions would be, and will continue to act, as a sated, status quo state.

But beginning in 2009, as Ian Johnston writes, it became "increasingly common in U.S. media, pundit, and academic circles to describe the diplomacy of the People's Republic of China (PRC) as newly or increasingly assertive."[20] That China held more assertive ambitions need not mean the rising challenger had become a threat. Thomas Christensen, for example, argued that China's new assertiveness was a good thing: better a China that was taking responsibility for world order than one that shirked its duties as a great power.[21] More often than not, however, "assertive" was used to suggest China was increasingly acting as a revisionist power. Analysts used a number of synonyms along with assertive: "truculent, arrogant, belligerent, hard-line, tough, bullying, militant, and even revolutionary. The implication is that China's diplomacy was notably more threatening, exhibited more hostile preferences, and expressed these preferences in more conflictual language than at any other time after the end of the Cold War."[22] As an *Atlantic Monthly* article noted, mentions of an "assertive China" increased significantly from 2000 to 2014, from only 9 mentions in the U.S. media in 2000, to 573 mentions in 2014.[23]

Why is it that the United States so quickly came to see China as more assertive in its revisionist aims? One answer would be that China's behavior provided a costly signal of both its ability and willingness to use its power to undercut American interests. China's most assertive actions were in the South and East China seas, where China's claims to various islands and reefs clash with competing claims from Japan, the Philippines, Vietnam, Malaysia, and Indonesia. Beijing maintains it owns any land or features within the "Nine-Dash Line," which extends as far as two thousand kilometers from the Chinese mainland. From 2009 onward, China appeared more willing to use force to aggressively pursue its claims. In early 2012, for example, China engaged in a maritime standoff with the Philippines over the Scarborough Shoal, leading that country to file an arbitration case with the UN. In 2014, China kicked off what one media outlet called an "artificial-island building spree" a move that signaled "more aggressive territorial claims by China in the region."[24]

On the face of it, then, perceptions of China's assertiveness seem driven by the straightforward politics of harm and interests: China's more aggressive behavior provided a costly signal that it has both the capacity and interest in revising the international order. But analysts of U.S.-China relations argue the picture is far more complicated than what appears at first glance. To begin with, it is not clear that China was significantly more "assertive" in the period after 2009 than it was before. As Johnston summarizes, "Much of China's diplomacy in 2010 fell within the range in foreign policy preferences, diplomatic rhetoric, and foreign policy behavior established in the Jiang Zemin and Hu Jintao eras."[25] Moreover, the signals of China's assertiveness are less straightforward than often portrayed. In the South and East China seas, China often undertakes assertive actions in response to the moves of other claimants, raising questions as to whether China sees its own actions as defensive, what Beijing might see "as a logical and necessary response . . . to defend its policies and prevent an adverse change in the status quo."[26] If this is the case, China's motivations are not offensive but defensive and "China's primary motivation in recent South China Sea military activities, then, is to defend what it sees as its island territories which neighboring countries have attempted to usurp."[27] China may have been aggressive in some instances, but has also demonstrated constraint and even a willingness to compromise. China has sought agreements to jointly develop resources in the South and East China seas and has tamped back on domestic fervor over territorial claims.[28]

In other words, China's behavior provides a mixed signal, at best, of increasingly revisionist intentions. Despite this, scholars argue that the dominant narrative in the United States about China's intentions has changed: whether China has become objectively more "assertive" and revisionist may be in question, but U.S. perceptions of China's assertiveness has become a "social fact."[29] Scholars suggest that this narrative might stem from new communication technology—blogs, social media—which has proven integral in spreading the narrative of China's assertiveness.[30] Other suggest that there was already in place a "folk realism" that made the "assertive China" narrative resonate: the "assertiveness narrative fulfilled popular predictions of behavioural change by rapidly rising powers in general and China in particular. The narrative was 'cognitively congruent' with the background knowledge of many people, that is, it was a close fit with what they 'believed and 'knew' before they heard it.' "[31]

The theory developed in this book suggests another pathway toward a narrative of assertiveness, one that was shaped by legitimation politics. On the one hand, China's own rhetoric has pushed the United States toward a new interpretation of its ambitions, especially its shift to the language "core interests" to justify claims in the South China Seas. From the mid-1990s onward China has relied a strategy of reassurance to manage existing great power's reaction to its rise. In the wake of the Cold War, China's leaders realized that the great powers eyed their increasing might with suspicion, worried that China would use its increasing economic and military might to challenge the existing liberal international order. Beijing reassured the United States and its regional neighbors that it harbored no revisionist aims. Its increasing power, after all, depended on a peaceful international order; China would do little to challenge the existing international order. In turn, China's rise to a great power would contribute to international peace, security, and prosperity. China in essence was engaged in "peaceful rise" and "peaceful development."[32]

China's grand strategy of reassurance was not only rhetorical—it also involved significant economic instruments—but it has involved significant rhetorical effort on the part of Beijing. Beijing was particularly careful to appeal to liberal rules and norms when justifying what other powers might see as revisionist behavior in territorial conflicts in the East and South China seas. Beijing's diplomatic rhetoric seemed light-years away from its language of the 1970s, when appeals to legal norms were dismissed as kowtowing to "bourgeois international law."[33] From the 1990s onward, China claimed that it both understood and would abide "by the rules of the international community."[34] Much of this rhetoric was deployed strategically. In territorial disputes with Japan and the ASEAN states, for example, Beijing coopted concepts found in the UN Convention on the Law of the Sea (UNCLOS)—concepts like "straight baseline" or "archipelago baseline" to legitimate their territorial claims.[35] As noted by one legal scholar, Beijing had purposively sought to "weaponize" international law, to legitimate "activities conducted by using the law as the weapon and through measures and methods such as legal deterrence, legal attack, legal counterattack, legal restraint, legal sanctions, and legal protections."[36]

Scholars suggest that China's appeals to international law were largely successful in staving off a balancing coalition.[37] Both the United States and regional powers saw China's appeals to international law as "self-binding," and thus it had "a constitutive effect on its Asian policy by establishing a positive image, shaping the baseline expectation from its neighbors, and laying the foundation for debates in the SCS territorial disputes."[38] By appealing to international law, and particularly framing its claims as consistent with UNCLOS, China undercut collective mobilization against its expansion: if China was willing to act within the confines of institutions, then there was no need for aggressive action on the part of other claimants. This rhetoric reinforced what Fravel has referred to as China's "delaying strategy," helping keep possible challengers demobilized as Beijing pursued territorial claims.[39] China's rhetoric also seemed to provide further evidence that it was becoming socialized into international norms and rules.

From 2009 onward, however, China has shifted its rhetoric, justifying its claims in the South and East China seas as necessary to protect its "core interests." The language of "core interests" is not new: it has long been central to China's legitimation on what it saw as "critical issues on which there is very little room, if any, for negotiation."[40] But it was only in 2010 that this language of "core interests" was applied to the South China Seas. In March 2010, the *New York Times* reported that Chinese officials suggested China's territorial claims to the South China Sea was a "core interest" in a private meeting with two senior U.S. officials.

It's worth noting that, as Swaine argues, there is no corroborating evidence that Chinese officials actually used "core interests" to justify their actions in the South China Seas during this meeting. Yet Beijing took little public action to clarify its stance on "core interests." As both Johnston and Swaine argue, while China feared its reported rhetoric would provoke concern among American officials, it also faced a domestic dilemma back home. Johnston reports that "a senior Chinese foreign policy" explained that "once the story was out, the MFA [Ministry of Foreign Affairs] could not publicly say that the South China Sea was not a core interest—China does not want to preempt the possibility of making such a declaration. Nor could it state publicly that no senior official had said the South China Sea was a core interest, that the *New York Times* source was wrong. This, too, might have raised the ire of nationalists within the population and the elite."[41] However suspect the initial report, after 2010 the legitimation of core interest became tied to China's claims in the South and East China seas. Observers note that references to "core interests" as the justification for China's foreign policy went from being almost nonexistent in the first decade of the 2000s to appearing consistently in Beijing's defense of its claims.[42] In 2015, China officially linked its claims in the South China Seas as a "core interest" in an official security law.

To sum up, China's own rhetoric provides some explanation for why "assertiveness" has become a social fact. But as argued throughout this book, the resonance of legitimation strategy depends, not only on who is speaking, but the audience. China's rhetorical shift provoked a quick response in the United States. As Kai He and Huiyun Feng explained, "If China lists the South China Sea issues as core interests, it means that China is prepared to use force against other claimants in the South China Sea. It will not only deepen regional concerns about China's rise, but also limit possible resolution of the disputes between China and other claimants."[43] The claims of "core interest" spread quickly through American media and were portrayed as a concerning shift in China's foreign policy and a signal of growing assertiveness. "China's aggressive posture toward the South China Sea has been stirring tensions in the region, and a new national security law suggests that Beijing is just getting started," one media outlet argued.[44] A *Christian Science Monitor* story likewise reported that China "speaks of a 'peaceful rise' in Asia and of binding the region with liberal markets," but that its policy in the South China Sea now raised "doubts about its intentions."[45] A report from the Department of Defense noted that Xi had pronounced China's commitment to defending "its core interests and territorial sovereignty" and warned that Beijing's "assertive efforts to advance its sovereignty and territorial claims, its forceful rhetoric, and lack of transparency about its growing military capabilities" was of growing concern to both the United States and its allies in the Asia-Pacific.[46]

Some suggest that the U.S. response to perceptions China's assertiveness was overly aggressive.[47] The administration did "pivot" military resources toward the region and formulated "Air Sea Battle" as an operational doctrine in response to China's growing military capabilities.[48] The Obama administration worked to strengthen its economic ties with allies in the Asia-Pacific, strengthening its partnerships through outlets like the Trans-Pacific Partnership, with Obama arguing that "TPP allows America—and not countries like China—to write the rules of the road in the 21st century."[49] In the South China Sea, the United States also responded by increasing its Freedom of Navigation operations (FONOP).[50]

Yet arguably the Obama administration's response was fairly restrained. Compared to other cases of confrontation and containment in this book, the Obama administration's response to revisionist intentions amounts to a fairly conservative "hedging" strategy, one that continued to pursue engagement and accommodation, while at the same time protesting what it saw as overly ambitious claims. This reaction is consistent with a situation in which the claims of a rising challenger are illegitimate—they flout international norms and rules—but the existing great power believes it is institutionally secure. Under these conditions, legitimation strategies are weakly dissonant: the great power hears that the rising power's claims are illegitimate but sees these claims as only an ambiguous signal of a rising power's intentions. As argued in chapter 2, under these conditions, the great power might see the rising challenger as a revisionist threat, but it will be able to count on the resilience of the dominant order to secure its interests. It will assume that its allies will contain any threat to the order. It will count on international institutions to constrain significant challenges. There is no need, in these circumstances, for rash or costly behavior.

From this perspective, the Obama administration's choice of strategies makes sense: as described above, in response to China's assertiveness, the U.S. government chose to double down on the international order. Alliance relations were strengthened, both through an increase in multilateral economic partnerships and through a strengthening of bilateral alliances in the region. And as discussed earlier, the United States has stated consistently that its FONOPs are not designed as military operations but as attempts by a neutral party to reinforce international law. While the United States may have aimed to stem China's ambitions, then, it also attempted to do so in a way that suggested its goal was not to coerce or threaten Beijing, and that China could continue to pursue its interests, provided it did so within the limits of international order.

But this raises the question as to whether changes in U.S. institutional vulnerability might prompt a different strategy, a turn toward more radical containment and even confrontation in the South China Seas. The United States, arguably, is becoming more institutionally vulnerable. The 2008 financial crisis continues to reverberate, destabilizing economic institutions such as the World Trade Organization, the G8, and the World Bank, among others, that have regulated financial and trade relations since 1945.[51] Security institutions, such as NATO and the bilateral alliance system in Asia, have allowed the United States to project power globally. And there is evidence that the United States sees these institutions as increasingly unsettled. Populist movements in the United States and abroad threaten commitments to collective security institutions. Transnational terrorist groups explicitly challenge the legitimacy of the sovereign state. Revisionist states, such as Russia, seem to flaunt norms of sovereignty. Nuclear proliferation in North Korea places the key U.S. allies of Japan and South Korea under the weight of an existential threat.

The concern here, then, is that, caught in an institutionally vulnerable position, the United States might not only react, but overreact, to China's rhetoric in the South China Seas. Shoring up institutions in the Asia-Pacific, working to reassure existing allies of its commitments, and seeking more robust partnerships with states like Vietnam and Malaysia might be prudent. But there are calls for stronger strategies of containment and confrontation against China's claims. Many applauded when in May 2017, the first FONOP of the Trump administration saw the USS *Dewey* transiting within twelve nautical miles of Mischief Reef, a feature in the South China Sea occupied by China.[52] Calls for mobilization within the American government have grown louder. In 2016, for example, Senator Marco Rubio introduced a bill in the Senate Foreign Relations committee that calling for sanction against Chinese individuals and entities "that participate in Beijing's illegitimate operations in the South China Sea and East China Sea."[53]

If the legitimation theory here is correct, the more vulnerable the United States sees its international order, the more likely it is to respond to China's rhetoric and language like its claims of "core interest" with containment and confrontation. This is not to say conflict is set in stone. China, arguably, still has the flexibility to walk back its rhetoric, and its language on initiatives like the AIIB and One Belt, One Road has arguably remained consistent with liberal international norms. In the United States, the current administration has shown less interest in the liberal international order and might prove less likely to react to illiberal claims. Regardless, the shifting dynamics between the United States and China demonstrate the continued relevance of legitimation strategies in rising power politics.

Legitimacy, Strategic Signaling, and Power Politics

The focus of this book has been on legitimation during power transitions, explaining how great powers look to legitimation strategies as signals of a challenger's ambitions. But the theoretical approach developed here is not limited to rising power politics. The question of how states assess each other's intentions is a foundational question of international politics. The capacity to tell whether a state's aggressive behavior is driven by insecurity or greed is essential for deciding whether to reassure or deter an opponent.[54] The ability to distinguish friend from foe is necessary for sustained cooperation. Deciphering intentions, in other words, lies at the root of war and peace in international politics.

This suggests that a social constructivist approach to signaling should provide insights, not only for cases of power transitions, but in any instance in which a state attempts to divine the intentions of others. As argued in chapter 1, the legitimation theory here accepts, like rationalist accounts, that communication is a strategic process, that actors will signal their intentions in ways designed to best achieve their own interests. At the same time, the process of signaling is deeply social and revolves around formulating and contesting the resonance of particular frames. For this reason, the legitimation theory here has at least three implications for the broader study of signaling and world politics: it questions the centrality of costly information to signaling approaches; it challenges the meaning of "uncertainty" in strategic interactions; and it suggests an endogenous relationship between signaling and an actor's type.

The first and most obvious implication of the legitimation theory here is that a focus on costly signals only gets scholars so far. Throughout this book we see cases where cheap talk is treated as if it were costly signals, as well as ample evidence that leaders often discount, even ignore, costly signals of their opponents' aims. The legitimation theory here suggests signals reduce uncertainty, not only because they are costly, but because they are resonant, and depend on the content and interpretation of legitimation strategies. But the legitimation theory here is only one approach to the question of why certain signals might prove more salient than others. For example, international relations theorists could pay more attention to literature about the cognitive and psychological foundations of resonance to determine why some signals are recognized as significant sources of information and others are ignored.[55] Likewise, theorists could invest more in the study of emotion and salient signals.[56] The point here is not that there is only one approach to the thorny problem of "resonance" and strategic signaling. It is that the reduction of uncertainty cannot be bounded only by the exchange of costly information in international politics; it depends on a host of intersubjective and subjective meanings that have no objective cost.

Second, the legitimation here pushes scholars to unpack their definitions of "uncertainty" in theories of international politics. As Rathbun has argued, the concept of uncertainty is central to every major theoretical tradition in international relations and "is arguably the most important factor in explaining the often unique dynamics of international as opposed to domestic politics."[57] But there are significant differences in how rationalists and constructivists treat "uncertainty." For rationalists, uncertainty is a condition of ignorance—it is a lack of knowledge about the "true" state of the world. To manage uncertainty in the international system thus means acquiring more and better information about the state of the world, so that actors may more efficiently and effectively engage in "updating," about others' intentions. Following from this, if we want to make cooperation more likely, we need to improve the volume and credibility of information in the international system. This could be achieved through international institutions, which establish routine channels of communication, increase transparency, and can independently verify the quality of information.[58]

For rationalists, then, uncertainty is "epistemological": there is an objective, stable, and "knowable" world out there, but human beings have difficulty perceiving it. For the legitimation theory here, in contrast, uncertainty is more fundamental: the world is "'unknowable' given the complexity of the world."[59] This may all sound esoteric, but the implications of this understanding of uncertainty for signaling, and international relations theorizing more generally, are substantial. If uncertainty is ontological, we cannot simply gather information from the world around us, because the state of that world is not fixed and stable. If uncertainty is about indeterminacy, we cannot read intentions off of behavior, because the meaning of that behavior is mutable.

All of this suggests that managing uncertainty in the international system involves, not merely providing information about an objective world, but also constructing and fixing the meaning of events. As with the study of resonant signals, the legitimation theory is only one take on how actors might define the meaning of their social environment. Myriad constructivists have argued that institutions might reduce conflict, not only by communicating information but by establishing "rules of the game" that guide interaction—in other words, by stabilizing meanings and creating shared understandings, institutions manage uncertainty.[60] Others have suggested how existing narratives shape the interpretation of national interests, threats, and grand strategy.[61] In all of these cases, the focus moves beyond the revealing of information about the "state of the world" to the production and creation of that world itself.

Finally, this book calls into question how rationalists have portrayed the relationship between signaling, intentions, and "type" in international politics. For rationalists, signals are almost naturally intertwined with an actor's type. To return to rising power politics, it is unlikely that, over time, limited-aims revisionists will consistently send revolutionary signals or vice versa. Limited-aims revisionists can send costly signals that they will behave: they have no need to mobilize their populations for expansionist aims; they have no need to build offensive forces; they are willing and able to bind themselves to the existing order. Revolutionary states might dissemble for a while but must eventually reveal their true aims: they will mobilize their populations, build offensive forces, and take action to overthrow the international order. At the very least, the cases in this book suggest that the link between type and signals is not so reliable, that while states may seek to discover the type of challenger they face, the answers they find are not as closely linked to signals as the conventional literature suggests.

But I suggest an even more profound departure from rationalist literature: it may be that the signaling process itself that *shapes the type of revisionist a rising power will become*. This reinforces the constructivist argument that actors themselves, their identities and intentions, are not stable or fixed, but are created and transformed through the legitimation process. In other words, type itself is a rhetorical construct.[62] We can see evidence for this throughout the cases in this book. In chapter 4, for example, we saw how Bismarck combined nationalist and conservative legitimations together in an attempt to appeal across these coalitions. Bismarck's goal was instrumental and strategic, to mobilize support for Prussia's expansion at home and diminish resistance abroad. But the effects of his appeals were far reaching, even unanticipated. This moment of legitimation set the foundations for the conservative, romantic, militaristic nationalism that would underpin the nascent German national state. It was an identity, moreover, that would eventually reject Bismarck and his limited vision for the German nation. Bismarck's rhetoric, in essence, did not reflect a type; it constituted German identity itself. These effects are also evident in the case of Japan. As argued above, Japan was a limited-aims revisionist engaged in revolutionary rhetoric. But this process of legitimation would work to construct Japan as a revolutionary type. The language of renovation empowered actors who had long positioned themselves as the vanguard of a new order in Asia. Socially, the legitimation of the new order pervaded the public: Japan's leaders engaged in far reaching propaganda campaigns that would reconstitute society's vision of itself in international politics. All of this suggests that it is not simply that signaling reveals intentions; through the signaling process, intentions may be constructed, and thus actors identities are indeed endogenous to strategic interaction itself.

In sum, the legitimation theory here has implications beyond rising power politics; it challenges conventional understandings of costs, uncertainty, and identity in international politics. To be clear, rationalist theories have much to say about signaling in international politics. But it would be productive to push the field to think about when and under what conditions rationalist theories might be most useful, and where their insights might be more limited. Rational choice theorists themselves have argued that Bayesian approaches are most useful in situations where a "properly understood institutional framework is present," and thus we can reasonably treat the strategic interaction as occurring in a fixed environment.[63] We can imagine moments in which rules, interests, and events are relatively stable and understood. Even where formal institutions are not present, there may be relatively stable and understood meanings, actors, and strategies. There is very little in the way of formal institutions governing nuclear deterrence, for instance, yet agents have developed common knowledge of the relevant actors, the rules of the game, and the issues involved, allowing theorists to fruitfully explain these interactions as "rational deterrence." But at the same time, international politics—and social life in general—is often a complex system.[64] Interactions are not structured, and unexpected and contingent states of the world are likely. If this is the case, then we need to take seriously constructivist insights into strategic signaling in international politics.

Talk matters. Great powers listen to what rising powers say they are going to do, and why they are going to do it. Rising powers understand this and attempt to shape patterns of mobilization against their actions through their legitimation strategies. This book is certainly not the first to call for a rhetorical turn in international politics.[65] But the argument here aims to push those that study power politics—often considered the theoretical stomping grounds of realism—to take rhetoric seriously. Legitimation *is* power politics. Legitimation draws together coalitions, mobilizing the resources necessary for expansion. Rhetoric wedges apart opposition and silences opponents.[66] Earlier realists such as Morgenthau, Carr, and Aron understood this connection between rhetoric, legitimacy, and power, and for that reason treated these factors as significant in their own studies of international politics.[67] Rather than turning away from power, this book calls for a return to a richer understanding of the instruments and mechanisms of power politics in our theories of international relations, one in which battles over rights are essential in the struggle over might.

Notes

1. The Great Powers' Dilemma

1. The literature on intentions, threat, and rising power politics is substantial. See, e.g., Charles L. Glaser, *Rational Theory of International Politics: The Logic of Competition and Cooperation* (Princeton: Princeton University Press, 2010); Glaser, "Political Consequences of Military Strategy: Extending and Refining the Spiral Model," *World Politics* 44, no. 4 (July 1992): 497–538; Glaser, "The Security Dilemma Revisited," *World Politics* 50, no. 1 (October 1997): 171–201; Andrew Kydd, "Game Theory and the Spiral Model," *World Politics* 49, no. 3 (April 1997): 371–400; and Kydd, "Sheep in Sheep's Clothing: Why Security Seekers Do Not Fight Each Other," *Security Studies* 7, no. 1 (autumn 1997): 114–55; Randall Schweller, "Managing the Rise of Great Powers: History and Theory," in *Engaging China: The Management of an Emerging Power*, ed. Alastair Iain Johnston and Robert S. Ross (London: Routledge, 1999), 1–31; David M. Edelstein, *Over the Horizon: Time, Uncertainty, and the Rise of Great Powers* (Ithaca: Cornell University Press, 2017); Edelstein, "Managing Uncertainty": Beliefs about Intentions and the Rise of Great Powers," *Security Studies* 12, no. 1: 1–40; Keren Yarhi-Milo, *Knowing the Adversary: Leaders, Intelligence, and Assessment of Intentions in International Relations* (Princeton: Princeton University Press, 2014).

2. John Searle, *The Construction of Social Reality* (New York: Simon and Schuster, 1995).

3. See e.g., Glaser, *Rational Theory of International Politics*, 35.

4. Charles L. Glaser, "A U.S.-China Grand Bargain? The Hard Choice between Military Competition and Accommodation," *International Security* 39, no. 4 (spring 2015): 49–90, quote at 64.

5. See e.g., ibid.; Hugh White, *The China Choice: Why America Should Share Power* (Collingwood, Australia: Black, 2012). Michael D. Swaine, *America's Challenge: Engaging a Rising China in the Twenty-first Century* (Washington, DC: Carnegie Endowment for International Peace, 2011).

6. On power transitions see, e.g., Robert Gilpin, *War and Change in World Politics* (Cambridge: Cambridge University Press, 1981); Nazli Chouchri and Robert C. North, *Nations in Conflict: National Growth and International Violence* (San Francisco: W. H. Freeman, 1975); Martin Wight, *Power Politics*, ed. Hedley Bull and Carsten Holbraad (Leicester: Leicester University Press, 1978), esp. 144; A. F. K. Organski, *World Politics* (New York: Knopf, 1968); A. F. K. Organski and Jacek Kugler, *The War Ledger* (Chicago: University of Chicago Press, 1980); Douglas Lemke and Jacek Kugler, eds., *Parity and War: Evaluations and Extension of the War Ledger* (Ann Arbor: University of Michigan Press, 1996); Jacek Kugler and Douglas Lemke, "The Power Transition Research

Program: Assessing Theoretical and Empirical Advances," in *The Handbook of War Studies II*, ed. Manus I. Midlarsky (Ann Arbor: University of Michigan Press, 2000), 129–63; Ronald L. Tammen, Jacek Jugler, Douglas Lemke, Allan C. Stam, Mark Abdollahain, Carole Alsharabati, Brian Efird, and A. F. K. Organski, *Power Transitions: Strategies for the 21st Century* (New York: Chatham House 2000); Douglas Lemke, *Regions of War and Peace* (New York: Cambridge University Press, 2002).

7. As Randall Schweller argues (drawing from Kissinger) all revisionists are dissatisfied to some extent; the question is, are these revisionists willing to pursue their aims within the existing order. Schweller, "Managing the Rise of Great Powers: History and Theory," in *Engaging China: The Management of an Emerging Power*, ed. Alastair Iain Johnston and Robert S. Ross (London: Routledge, 1999), 19.

8. John J. Mearsheimer, *Tragedy of Great Power Politics* (New York: Norton, 2002), 31.

9. Dale Copeland, for example, argues that the main concern of states is not present but future intentions. See Dale Copeland, *The Origins of Major War* (Ithaca: Cornell University Press, 2000); Mearsheimer also stresses this point about future intentions.

10. On the rationality of choosing war now rather than later, see James D. Fearon, "Rationalist Explanations for War," *International Organization* 49, no. 3 (summer 1995): 379–414. It is the inscrutability of intentions that leads realists to focus on capability. See Sebastian Rosato, "The Inscrutable Intentions of Great Powers," *International Security* 39, no. 3 (winter 2014–15): 48–88.

11. For an overview of the strategies great powers use to manage rising powers, see Schweller, "Managing the Rise of Great Powers." Schweller offers several strategic options for managing rising powers, ranging from preventive war to engagement. See also Shiping Tang, *A Theory of Security Strategy for Our Time: Defensive Realism* (London: Palgrave, 2010), 101–3.

12. It is for this reason that scholars have long argued that power transitions are inherently dangerous. See, e.g., Mearsheimer, *Tragedy of Great Power Politics*; Gilpin, *War and Change in World Politics*; Copeland, *The Origins of Major War*; Organski, *World Politics*; Organski and Kugler, *The War Ledger*.

13. See especially Copeland, *The Origins of Major War*, on this point.

14. Gilpin, *War and Change*, 191.

15. Like Edelstein, I am interested in cooperation that has "consequences for the balance of power." See David M. Edelstein, "Managing Uncertainty": Beliefs about Intentions and the Rise of Great Powers," *Security Studies* 12, no. 1: 1–40. Likewise Schweller argues that engagement—here, accommodation—is notable through the "promise of rewards . . . to influence the target's behavior." Schweller, "Managing the Rise of Great Powers," 14.

16. Edelstein poses a similar question. Edelstein, *Over the Horizon*.

17. On signaling as a means to convey intentions, see James D. Fearon, "Signaling Foreign Policy Interests: Tying Hands versus Sinking Costs," *Journal of Conflict Resolution* 41, no. 1 (February 1997): 68–90; Andrew Kydd, *Trust and Mistrust in International Relations* (Princeton: Princeton University Press, 2005); and Robert F. Trager, "Diplomatic Calculus in Anarchy: How Communication Matters," *American Political Science Review* 104, no. 2: 347–68.

18. In other words, states can "tie" their hands during bargaining. Some focus on domestic sources of constraint. See, e.g., Thomas C. Schelling, *The Strategy of Conflict* (Cambridge, MA: Harvard University Press, 1980); Fearon, "Signaling Foreign Policy Interests." Most of the focus here is on the use of domestic constituencies to tie one's hands. Other works stresses the role of institutional commitment in generating binding dynamics. See, e.g., G. John Ikenberry, *Liberal Leviathan: The Origins, Crisis, and Transformation of the American World Order* (Princeton: Princeton University Press, 2011).

19. On threat as the driver of grand strategy, see Stephen M. Walt, *Origin of Alliances* (Ithaca: Cornell University Press, 1983).

20. Schweller, "Managing the Rise of Great Powers," 7.

21. Glaser, *Rational Theory of International Politics*, 99.

22. On the distinction between offense and defense dominant worlds, see Robert L. Jervis, "Cooperation Under the Security Dilemma," *World Politics* 30, no. 2 (1978): 186–213; Jack S. Levy, "The Offense/Defense Balance of Military Technology and the Incidence of War," *International Studies Quarterly* 28, no. 2 (June 1984): 219–30; Sean M. Lynn-Jones, "Offense-Defense Theory and Its Critics," *Security Studies* 4, no. 4 (summer 1995): 660–91; Charles L. Glaser and Chaim

Kaufman, "What Is the Offense-Defense Balance and How Can We Measure It," *International Security* 22, no. 4 (spring 1998): 44–82.

23. Scholars who argue the offense-defense balance is key to diving intentions include Glaser, *Rational Theory of International Politics;* Evan Braden Montgomery, "Breaking Out of the Security Dilemma: Realism, Reassurance, and the Problem of Uncertainty," *International Security* 31, no. 2 (fall 2006): 151–85.

24. Glaser, *Rational Theory of International Politics*, 45.

25. Ibid., 64–65.

26. Robert Jervis, *The Logic of Images in International Relations* (New York: Columbia University Press, 1989).

27. Kydd, "Sheep in Sheep's Clothing," 117.

28. Bruce Russett, *Grasping the Democratic Peace* (Princeton: Princeton University Press, 1983), 40.

29. See Mark Haas, *The Ideological Origins of Great Power Politics* (Cornell: Cornell University Press, 2005); John M. Owen IV, "Transnational Liberalism and U.S. Primacy," *International Security* 26, no. 3 (winter 2001–2): 117–52; Charles Kupchan, *How Enemies Become Friends* (Princeton: Princeton University Press, 2011).

30. Kydd, "Sheep in Sheep's Clothing."

31. See, e.g., Judith Goldstein, Miles Kahler, Robert O. Keohane, and Anne-Marie Slaughter, "Legalization and World Politics: An Introduction," *International Organization* 54, no. 3: 385–99; Ikenberry, *Liberal Leviathan*, 184.

32. This is because common knowledge is central to Bayesian updating. Common knowledge among players provides the foundation for all rational action within a game, and thus the basis for strategic interaction in the first place. If this common knowledge assumption is relaxed then any solution to the game that requires a modicum of rational decision-making unravels—what I do is rational only if I know what you will do, what I think you will do, what I think you think I will do, etc. On the role of common knowledge in rationalist models, see Robert Aumann and Adam Brandenburger, "Epistemic Conditions for Nash Equilibrium," *Econometrica* 63, no. 5 (1995): 1161–80; Ken Binmore and Adam Brandenburger, "Common Knowledge and Game Theory" in *Essays on the Foundation of Game Theory*, ed. Ken Binmore (Cambridge: Basil Blackwell, 1990), 105–50.

33. Arthur A. Stein, "The Justifying State: Why Anarchy Doesn't Mean No Excuses," in *Peace, Prosperity, and Politics*, ed. John Mueller (Boulder, CO: Westview, 2000), 235–56.

34. Jervis, *Logic of Images in International Relations*, 139.

35. For a similar critique, see Rosato, "The Inscrutable Intentions of Great Powers," 78–79.

36. Jonathan Mercer, "Rationalist Signaling Revisited," in *Psychology, Strategy, and Conflict: Perceptions of Insecurity in International Relations*, ed. James W. Davis (London: Routledge, 2012), 78–79.

37. Keren Yarhi-Milo, *Knowing the Adversary: Leaders, Intelligence, and Assessment of Intentions in International Relations* (Princeton: Princeton University Press, 2014); Deborah Welch Larson, *Anatomy of Mistrust* (Ithaca: Cornell University Press, 1997).

38. See Mercer, "Rationalist Signaling Revisited," 70–71. For an overview of the distinction between social understandings and subjective meaning, see Brian C. Rathbun, "Uncertainty about Uncertainty: Understanding the Multiple Meanings of a Crucial Concept in International Relations Theory," *International Studies Quarterly* 51, no. 3: 534–35.

39. See, e.g., Jon Elster, "Deliberation and Constitution-Making," in *Deliberative Democracy*, ed. Jon Elster (Cambridge: Cambridge University Press, 1998), 104. See also Ronald Krebs, *Narrative and the Making of U.S. National Security* (Cambridge: Cambridge University Press, 2015); Stein, "The Justifying State."

40. Contributions to this linguistic turn have drawn inspiration from many sources—including Ludwig Wittgenstein's language games: see K. M. Fierke, *Changing Games, Changing Strategies: Critical Investigations in Security* (Manchester: Manchester University Press, 1998); Patrick Thaddeus Jackson, *Civilizing the Enemy: German Reconstruction and the Invention of the West* (Ann Arbor: University of Michigan Press, 2006). For works influenced by Louis Althusser's mechanisms of articulation and interpellation, see Jutta Weldes, *Constructing National Interests: The United States and the Cuban Missile Crisis* (Minneapolis: University of Minnesota Press,

1999); for works influenced by Jacques Lacan's writings on representational force, see Janice Bially Mattern, *Ordering International Politics: Identity, Crisis, and Representational Force* (New York: Routledge, 2005); for works influenced by Jürgen Habermas's model of communicative action, see Thomas Risse, "'Let's Argue!': Communicative Action in World Politics," *International Organization* 54, no. 1 (winter 2000): 1–39; Jennifer Mitzen, "Reading Habermas in Anarchy: Multilateral Diplomacy and Global Public Spheres," *American Political Science Review* 99, no. 3 (August 2005): 401–17; for works influenced by Erving Goffman and symbolic interactionism, see Michael N. Barnett, *Dialogues in Arab Politics: Negotiations in Regional Order* (New York: Columbia University Press, 1998); Austin Carson, "Facing Off and Saving Face: Covert Intervention and Escalation Management in the Korean War," *International Organization* 70, no. 1 (winter 2016): 103–31; Rebecca Adler-Nissen, "The Social Self in International Relations: Identity, Power, and the Symbolic Interactionist Roots of Constructivism," *European Journal of International Studies* 3, no. 3: 27–39; for works influenced by Charles Tilly and relational analysis, see Daniel H. Nexon, *The Struggle for Power in Early Modern Europe: Religious Conflict, Dynastic Empires, and International Change* (Princeton: Princeton University Press, 2009); Stacie E. Goddard, *Indivisible Territory and the Politics of Legitimacy: Jerusalem and Northern Ireland* (New York: Cambridge University Press, 2009)]; and for works influenced by rhetorical pragmatics, see Markus Kornprobst, *Irredentism in European Politics: Argumentation, Compromise, and Norms* (Cambridge: Cambridge University Press, 2008).

41. This discussion appears in Stacie Goddard and Ronald Krebs, "Rhetoric, Legitimation, and Grand Strategy," *Security Studies* 24, no. 1: 5–36.

42. Ann Swidler, "Culture in Action," *American Sociological Review* 51, no. 2 (April 1986): 273–86.

43. Risse, "'Let's Argue!'"; Mitzen, "Reading Habermas in Anarchy"; Harald Müller, "International Relations as Communicative Action," in *Constructing International Relations: The Next Generation*, eds. Karin M. Fierke and Knud Erik Jorgensen (Armonk: M. E. Sharpe, 2001), 160–78; Marc Lynch, "Why Engage? China and the Logic of Communicative Engagement," *European Journal of International Relations* 8, no. 2 (June 2002): 187–230. On the centrality of persuasion to much constructivist international relations scholarship, see Neta C. Crawford, *Argument and Change in World Politics: Ethics, Decolonization, and Humanitarian Intervention* (Cambridge: Cambridge University Press, 2002); Martha Finnemore, *National Interests in International Society* (Ithaca: Cornell University Press, 1996), 141; Martha Finnemore and Kathryn Sikkink, "International Norm Dynamics and Political Change," *International Organization* 52, no. 4 (fall 1998): 914; Rodger A. Payne, "Persuasion, Frames and Norm Construction," *European Journal of International Relations* 7, no. 1 (March 2001): 37–61.

44. See, among many others, Michael J. Shapiro, *Language and Political Understanding: The Politics of Discursive Practices* (New Haven: Yale University Press, 1981); James Der Derian and Michael J. Shapiro, eds., *International/Intertextual Relations: Postmodern Readings of World Politics* (Lexington, MA: Lexington Books, 1989); David Campbell, *Writing Security: United States Foreign Policy and the Politics of Identity*, rev. ed. (Minneapolis: University of Minnesota Press, 1998); Roxanne Lynn Doty, *Imperial Encounters: The Politics of Representation in North-South Relations* (Minneapolis: University of Minnesota Press, 1996).

45. See, e.g., Stacie Goddard and Daniel H. Nexon, "The Dynamics of Power Politics," *Journal of Global Security Studies* 1, no. 1: 4–18.

2. The Politics of Legitimacy

1. Max Weber, *Economy and Society*, vol. 2, ed. Guenther Roth and Klaus Wittich (Berkeley: University of California Press, 1968), 953.

2. See, among others, Martha Finnemore, "Legitimacy, Hypocrisy, and the Social Structure of Unipolarity: Why Being a Unipole Isn't All It's Cracked Up to Be," *World Politics* 61, no. 1 (2009): 58–85; Mlada Bukovansky, *Legitimacy and Power Politics: The American and French Revolutions in International Political Culture* (Princeton: Princeton University Press, 2002); Ian

Clark, *Legitimacy in International Society* (New York: Oxford University Press, 2007); Ian Hurd, "Legitimacy and Authority in International Politics," *International Organization* 53, no. 2 (spring 1999): 379–408; Christian Reus-Smit, *American Power and World Order* (Cambridge: Polity Press, 2004).

3. G. John Ikenberry, *After Victory: Institutions, Strategic Restraint, and the Rebuilding of Order after Major Wars* (Princeton: Princeton University Press, 2001); Ikenberry, "America's Imperial Ambition," *Foreign Affairs* 81, no. 5 (September–October 2002): 44–60; Stephen Walt, *Taming American Power* (New York: W. W. Norton, 2005).

4. The literature on framing is substantial. For an overview see, for example, Robert D. Benford and David A. Snow, "Framing Processes and Social Movements: An Overview and Assessment," *Annual Review of Sociology* 26: 611–39.

5. Ronald Krebs and Patrick Jackson, "Twisting Tongues and Twisting Arms," *European Journal of International Relations* 13, no. 1 (2007): 45.

6. See Jon Elster, "Strategic Uses of Argument," in *Barriers to Conflict Resolution*, ed. Kenneth Arrow (New York: Norton, 1995): 236–57; On how states legitimate their foreign policies, see Stacie Goddard and Ronald Krebs, "Rhetoric, Legitimation, and Grand Strategy," *Security Studies*, 24, no. 1 (2015): 5–36; Ronald Krebs, *Narrative and the Making of U.S. National Security* (Cambridge: Cambridge University Press, 2015); Patrick Thaddeus Jackson, *Civilizing the Enemy: German Reconstruction and the Invention of the West* (Ann Arbor: University of Michigan Press, 2006); Arthur Stein, "The Justifying State," in *Peace, Prosperity, and Politics*, ed. John Mueller (Boulder, CO: Westview Press, 2001), 235–55.

7. Stein, "The Justifying State," 237.

8. Constructivists have long argued that social institutions circumscribe the range of behavior in international politics. See, e.g., Martha Finnemore, *The Purpose of Intervention: Changing Beliefs About the Use of Force* (Ithaca: Cornell University Press, 2003). On institutions and legitimacy more specifically, see, among others, Bukovansky, *Legitimacy and Power Politics*; Hurd, "Legitimacy and Authority in International Politics"; Reus-Smit, *American Power and World Order*; Jens Steffek, "The Legitimation of International Governance: A Discourse Approach," *European Journal of International Relations* 9, no. 2 (June 2003): 249–75; Achim Hurrelmann et al., eds., *Legitimacy in an Age of Global Politics* (Basingstoke, UK: Palgrave Macmillan, 2007); Dominik Zaum, ed., *Legitimating International Organizations* (Oxford: Oxford University Press, 2013).

9. G. John Ikenberry, *Liberal Leviathan: The Origins, Crisis, and Transformation of the American World Order* (Princeton: Princeton University Press, 2011), 12. For other notable discussions of international order, see, e.g., Hedley Bull, *The Anarchical Society* (New York: Columbia University Press, 1977); Robert Gilpin, *War and Change in World Politics* (Cambridge: Cambridge University Press, 1981); Barry Buzan, "China in International Society: Is "Peaceful Rise" Possible?," *Chinese Journal of International Politics* 3, no. 1 (2010): 5–36; Andrew Hurrell, *On Global Order* (Oxford: Oxford University Press, 2007); Christian Reus-Smit, *The Moral Purpose of the State: Culture, Social Identity, and Institutional Rationality in International Relations* (Princeton: Princeton University Press, 1999); Evelyn Goh, *The Struggle for Order: Hegemony, Hierarchy, and Transition in Post-Cold War East Asia* (Oxford: Oxford University Press, 2013).

10. See David C. Kang, "Authority and Legitimacy in International Relations: Evidence from Korean and Japanese Relations in Pre-Modern East Asia," *Chinese Journal of International Politics* 5, no. 1: 55–71; Andreas Osiander, *The State System of Europe, 1640–1990: Peacemaking and the Conditions of International Stability* (Oxford: Oxford University Press, 1994). On the development of norms of intervention and nonintervention, see, e.g., Martha Finnemore, *The Purpose of Intervention;* Luke Glanville, *Sovereignty and the Responsibility to Protect: A New History* (Chicago: University of Chicago Press, 2014).

11. Friedrich V. Kratochwil, *Rules, Norms, and Decisions: On the Conditions of Practical and Legal Reasoning in International Relations and Domestic Affairs* (Cambridge: Cambridge University Press, 1989), 168.

12. For critique, see, e.g., Stephen G. Brooks and William C. Wohlforth, *World Out of Balance* (Princeton: Princeton University Press, 2008), 193–99.

13. Henry Kissinger, *A World Restored: Metternich, Castlereagh, and the Problems of Peace, 1812–1822* (New York: Grosset and Dunlap, 1957), 146.

14. On the construction of "self-defense," see also Kratochwil, *Rules, Norms, and Decision*.

15. For similar discussions of strategy and rhetoric, see Tine Hanrieder, "The False Promise of the Better Argument," *International Theory* 3, no. 3 (November 2011): 409–10; Frank Schimmelfenig, "The Community Trap: Liberal Norms, Rhetorical Action, and the Eastern Enlargement of the European Union," *International Organization* 55, no. 1 (2001): 47–80; Frank Schimmelfenig, *The EU, NATO, and the Integration of Europe: Rules and Rhetoric* (Cambridge: Cambridge University Press, 2004).

16. Goddard and Krebs, "Rhetoric, Legitimation, and Grand Strategy."

17. Stein, "The Justifying State," 242. For a discussion of global power politics as collective mobilization, see Stacie Goddard and Daniel Nexon, "The Dynamics of Global Power Politics: A Framework for Analysis," *Journal of Global Security Studies* 1, no. 1 (2016): 4–18.

18. Benford and Snow, "Framing Processes and Social Movements."

19. Stein, "The Justifying State," 242.

20. Goddard and Krebs, "Rhetoric, Legitimation, and Grand Strategy."

21. Krebs and Jackson, "Twisting Tongues and Twisting Arms," 45.

22. Ibid.

23. Kelly Greenhill, *Weapons of Mass Migration: Forced Displacement, Coercion, and Foreign Policy* (Ithaca: Cornell University Press, 2011), 52. Greenhill's discussion draws from long-standing scholarship that argues that actors bear costs for violating widely accepted reasons in the public sphere. See most notably Jon Elster, "Deliberation and Constitution Making," in *Deliberative Democracy*, ed. Jon Elster (Cambridge: Cambridge University Press, 1998); Daryl Glaser, "Does Hypocrisy Matter? The Case of U.S. Foreign Policy," *Review of International Studies* 32, no. 2 (2006): 251–68; Alexander Cooley and Daniel H. Nexon, "The Empire Will Compensate You," *Perspectives on Politics*, 11, no. 4 (2013): 1034–50. When hypocrisy increases, this has the effect of creating what some refer to as a "legitimacy gap" in world politics. See Reus-Smit, "International Crises of Legitimacy," *International Politics* 44 (2007): 157–74; Tim Dunne, "'The Rules of the Game Are Changing': Fundamental Human Rights in Crisis After 9/11," *International Politics* 44, no. 2–3 (2007): 269–86; Leonard Seabrooke, "Legitimacy Gaps in the World Economy: Explaining the Sources of the IMF's Legitimacy Crisis," *International Politics* 44, no. 2–3 (2007): 250–68.

24. Alexander Wendt, "Collective Identity Formation and the International State," *American Political Science Review* 88, no. 2 (1994): 395.

25. Christian Reus-Smit, *The Moral Purpose of the State*.

26. Brent J. Steele, "Ontological Security and the Power of Self-Identity: British Neutrality and the American Civil War," *Review of International Studies* 31, no. 3 (July 2005): 526. On "ontological security," see Jennifer Mitzen, "Ontological Security in World Politics: State Identity and the Security Dilemma," *European Journal of International Relations* 12, no. 3 (September 2006): 341–70. See also Richard Little, "British Neutrality versus Offshore Balancing in the American Civil War: The English School Strikes Back," *Security Studies* 16, no. 1 (winter 2007): 68–95.

27. Mitzen, "Ontological Security in World Politics."

28. As discussed in chapter 6, arguing that Japan adopted a "pan-Asian" rhetoric is not to argue that race determined U.S.-Japanese relations in the years before World War II. For a more determinist argument, see Zoltán I. Búzás, "The Color of Threat: Race, Threat Perception, and the Demise of the Anglo-Japanese Alliance (1902–1923)," *Security Studies* 22, no. 4 (2013): 573–606; Steven Ward, "Race, Status, and Japanese Revisionism in the Early 1930s," *Security Studies* 22, no. 4 (2013): 607–39.

29. Fred Kniss, "Ideas and Symbols as Resources in Intrareligious Conflict: The Case of American Mennonites," *Sociology of Religion* 57, no. 1 (1996): 7–23. Several constructivists rely on resonance as a key to explaining why some norms are accepted and others rejected. See, e.g., Jeffrey Checkel, "Why Comply: Social Learning and European Identity Change," *International Organization* 55, no. 1 (2001): 553–88; Margaret Keck and Kathryn Sikkink, *Activists Beyond Borders: Advocacy Networks in International Politics* (Ithaca: Cornell University, 1988), 204; Martha Finnemore and Kathryn Sikkink, "International Norm Dynamics and Political Change," *International Organization* 52, no. 4 (1998): 907; Roger Payne, "Persuasion, Frames and Norm Construction," *European Journal of International Relations* 7, no. 1 (2001): 38–39; Richard Price, "Reversing the Gun Sights: Transnational Civil Society Targets Land Mines," *International Organization* 52, no. 3 (1998): 628.

30. Snow and Benford, "Framing Processes and Social Movements."

31. On relationalism, see Rebecca Adler-Nissen, "Relationalism or Why Diplomats Find International Relations Theory So Strange," in *Diplomacy and the Making of World Politics*, ed. Ole Jacob Sending, Vincent Pouliot, and Iver B. Neumann (Cambridge: Cambridge University Press, 2015), 284–308. David McCourt, "Practice Theory and Relationalism as the New Constructivism," *International Studies Quarterly* 60, no. 3 (2016): 475–85.

32. See Goddard, "Brokering Change," *International Theory* 1, no. 2 (2009): 249–81.

33. Schweller notes this in "Bandwagoning for Profit: Bringing the Revisionist State Back In," *International Security* 19, no. 1 (1994): 15n58.

34. John F. Padgett and Christopher K. Ansell, "Robust Action and the Rise of the Medici, 1400–1434," *American Journal of Sociology* 98, no. 6 (1993): 1259–1319.

35. See, e.g., Bethany Albertson, "Dog-Whistle Politics: Multivocal Communication and Religious Appeals," *Political Behavior* 37, no. 1 (2015): 3–26.

36. For a discussion, see Daniel H. Nexon, *The Struggle for Power in Early Modern Europe* (Princeton: Princeton University Press, 2009), 115n37.

37. Snyder, "Dueling Security Stories: Wilson and Lodge Talk Strategy," *Security Studies* 24, no. 1 (2015): 171–97.

38. Quoted in Charles W. Hallberg, *Franz Joseph and Napoleon III, 1852–1864: A Study of Austro-French Relations* (New York: Bookman Associates, 1955), 157.

39. Padgett and Ansell, "Rise of the Medici," 1307.

40. Pierre Bourdieu, *Language and Symbolic Power* (Cambridge, MA: Harvard University Press, 1993), 40.

41. For an extensive discussion, see Krebs, *Narrative and the Making of U.S. National Security*.

42. Schroeder, *The Transformation of European Politics*, 1763–1848 (Oxford: Oxford University Press, 1992), 694.

43. See, e.g., Goddard and Krebs, "Rhetoric, Legitimation, and Grand Strategy."

44. The institutional investment argument is in line with Keck and Sikkink's observation that "once a government commits itself to a principle" it is hard to depart from the institution. Keck and Sikkink, *Activists beyond Borders*, 24.

45. I thank Paul K. MacDonald for this term.

46. See Krebs, *Narrative and the Making of U.S. National Security*.

47. On socialization see, e.g., Jeffrey T. Checkel, "International Institutions and Socialization in Europe: Introduction and Framework," *International Organization* 59, no. 4 (2005), 801–26.

48. To measure power, I relied primarily on measures of the material attributes of the state: table 2 below identifies rising powers by their relative share of great power gross domestic product over a period of ten years, as well as increases in their CINC score, a measure of national military capabilities As MacDonald and Parent argue, while there are drawbacks to using GDP as a measure, GDP is a parsimonious way to capture wealth and avoids problems of endogeneity that occur with other composite measures. See Paul K. MacDonald and Joseph M. Parent, "Graceful Decline," *International Security* 35, no. 4 (spring 2011): 24. First, is there an ordinal transformation among the great powers, or in other words, does a rising power surpass one of the existing great powers? Second, does the rising power ever pass more than 5 percent of the collective GDP of the great powers, a measure that, while somewhat arbitrary, captures the need to identify only those rising powers that might be considered contenders for great power status.

49. Chapter 4 will explore the arguments and critiques of the "revisionist" school of British foreign policy.

50. Stein, "The Justifying State."

51. In some of the cases, rhetoric was coded using the qualitative content analysis software, Atlas.ti.

52. In much of network analysis "between-ness centrality" is another measure of access within a clique, and those actors with more "between-ness" are considered more central to the clique. Here I am interested in actors that bridge cliques, but they may not be the sole occupant of that position (a broker), and they may or may not be central within a particular network subgroup.

53. See, e.g., Raymond Aron, *Peace and War: A Theory of International Relations* (Garden City, NY: Doubleday, 1966), xiii.

3. America's Ambiguous Ambition

1. Henry Cabot Lodge, "Our Blundering Foreign Policy," *The Forum*, vol. 19, March 1895.

2. For some, American expansion was driven by an exceptional ideology, especially by dictates of Manifest Destiny, which drove settlers across the expanse of the North American continent. For an overview of Manifest Destiny, see, e.g., Walter McDougall, *Promised Land, Crusader State: The American Encounter with the World since 1776* (Boston: Houghton Mifflin Harcourt, 1997), especially chapter 4; Anders Stephenson, *Manifest Destiny: American Expansion and the Empire of Right* (New York: Farrar, Straus and Giroux, 1996). For arguments that the United States expanded as any great power would, see Fareed Zakaria, *From Wealth to Power: The Unusual Origins of America's World Role* (Princeton: Princeton University Press, 1998); John J. Mearsheimer, *The Tragedy of Great Power Politics* (New York: Norton, 2001), 238–60.

3. There is a rich historiography on the foreign relations of the early American republic, only a portion of which I will cite here. On U.S. negotiations with Britain over its territorial and economic disputes, see, e.g., Bradford Perkins, *Castlereagh and Adams: England and the United States, 1812–1823* (Berkeley: University of California Press, 1964), especially 196–348; Kenneth Bourne, *Britain and the Balance of Power in North America* (Berkeley: University of California Press, 1967). On the United States and the negotiations over the Transcontinental Treaty (and its relations with Spain more generally), see Samuel Flagg Bemis, *John Quincy Adams and the Foundations of American Foreign Policy* (New York: Knopf, 1950), especially chapters 15 and 16; William Earl Weeks, *John Quincy Adams and American Global Empire* (Lexington: University of Kentucky Press, 1992); Philip Coolidge Brooks, *Diplomacy and the Borderlands: The Adams-Onis Treaty of 1819* (Berkeley: University of California Press, 1939); J. C. A. Stagg, *Borderlines in Borderlands* (New Haven: Yale University Press, 2009); Arthur P. Whitaker, *The United States and the Independence of Latin America, 1800–1830* (New York: W. W. Norton, 1964); James Fred Rippy, *Rivalry of the United States and Great Britain over Latin America* (New York: Octagon Books, 1964). On the conflict with Native American tribes in the early republic, see, e.g., Eliga H. Gould, *Among the Powers of the Earth: the American Revolution and the Making of a New World Empire* (Cambridge: Harvard University Press, 2012); Robert V. Remini, *Andrew Jackson and his Indian Wars* (New York: Penguin, 2002). On the Monroe Doctrine, see Dexter Perkins, *A History of the Monroe Doctrine, 1823–1826* (Cambridge: Harvard University Press, 1927); Jay Sexton, *The Monroe Doctrine: Empire and Nation in Nineteenth-Century America* (New York: Hill & Wang, 2011).

4. Weeks, *John Quincy Adams*, 169.

5. Perkins, *Castlereagh and Adams*, 156.

6. See, e.g., Charles Kupchan, *How Enemies Become Friends: The Sources of Stable Peace* (Princeton: Princeton University Press, 2011); Stephen R. Rock, *Appeasement in International Politics* (Lexington: University of Kentucky Press, 2000), 25–48; Barry Buzan and Michael Cox, "China and the US: Comparable Cases of 'Peaceful Rise'?" *Chinese Journal of International Politics* 6, no. 2: 109–32.

7. Webster argues that this period laid "the foundation of the hundred years peace which few in either country at that time expected or desired." Charles K. Webster, *The Foreign Policy of Castlereagh, 1815–1822: Britain and the European Alliance* (London: G. Bell, 1958), 437.

8. Weeks, *John Quincy Adams*, 106.

9. Quoted ibid., 109.

10. See e.g., Bemis, *John Quincy Adams*, 345.

11. J. C. A. Stagg, *The War of 1812: Conflict for a Continent* (Cambridge: Cambridge University Press, 2012), 168.

12. Bemis, *John Quincy Adams*, 300.

13. See, e.g., Webster, *Foreign Policy of Castlereagh*, 437–58. Perkins, *Castlereagh and Adams*, 196–219.

14. Draft of Castlereagh to Bagot, "Most Secret and Confidential," The National Archives (hereafter TNA), Foreign Office (FO) 5/120, November 10, 1817.

15. On these ongoing disputes, see, e.g., Perkins, *Castlereagh and Adams*, 239–82; even historians, such as Bourne, who emphasize the ongoing competition between the powers through the nineteenth century, argue that a significant change to a policy of conciliation occurred under Castlereagh's guidance. See Bourne, *Britain and the Balance of Power in North America*, 7.

16. For the details of the Convention of 1818, see Perkins, *Castlereagh and Adams*, 259–82; Bemis, *John Quincy Adams*, 278–99.

17. See Gould, *Among the Great Powers*.

18. Bemis, *John Quincy Adams*, 303.

19. See, e.g., Bourne, *Britain and the Balance of Power in North America*, 7.

20. See, e.g., Weeks, *John Quincy Adams*, 77; Webster, *Foreign Policy of Castlereagh*, 415–22.

21. For Castlereagh's discussion of mediation, see, e.g., Castlereagh to Bagot, "Private and Confidential," TNA, FO 5/120, November 10, 1817; Castlereagh to Wellesley, "Mediation with the United States in Favor of Spain," TNA, FO 72/196, April 14, 1817.

22. On the importance of defending Canada, see, e.g., Bourne, *Britain and the Balance of Power in North America*, 57.

23. On British policy during the Civil War, see, e.g., Peter Thompson, "The Case of the Missing Hegemon: British Nonintervention in the American Civil War," *Security Studies* 16, no. 1 (2007): 96–132.

24. Sexton, *The Monroe Doctrine*, 63.

25. Buzan and Cox, "China and the US," 116. See also Mearsheimer, *Tragedy of Great Power Politics*, 234–52.

26. See, e.g., Bourne, *Britain and the Balance of Power in North America*, 11.

27. On the issue of the fisheries and the northern boundary, see Perkins, *Castlereagh and Adams*, 166–67, 263–64; Bourne, *Britain and the Balance of Power in North America*, 7; Webster, *Foreign Policy of Castlereagh*, 51.

28. *Memoirs of John Quincy Adams, Comprising Portions of His Diary from 1795 to 1848*, ed. Charles Francis Adams (Philadelphia: J. B. Lippincott, 1875), vol. 4, 61.

29. This, as MacDonald argues, was a common method of British imperial war and was often successful. See Paul K. MacDonald, *Networks of Domination* (Oxford: Oxford University Press, 2014).

30. Gould, *Among the Great Powers*, 183; Bourne, *Britain and the Balance of Power in North America*, 59.

31. Bourne, *Britain and the Balance of Power in North America*, 59.

32. Gould, *Among the Powers*, 123.

33. See "Protocol of Conference, August 8, 1814," *American State Papers: Documents, Legislative and Executive of the Congress of the United States*, part 1, vol. 3, no. 269. During Ghent, British diplomats demanded that their allies be included in the peace, and that their territory be "definitively marked out as a permanent barrier between the dominions of Great Britain and the United States." Although Britain eventually backed off of its demands for a formal barrier state, it forced the United States to agree that lands taken from the tribes during the war would be returned.

34. Perkins, *Castlereagh and Adams*, 285.

35. Castlereagh would ultimately only make a half-hearted gesture toward mediation. When the United States politely refused the request, Britain decided not to pursue the issue.

36. *Leeds Mercury*, August 8, 1812.

37. On the British case for war in 1812, see Troy Bickham, *The Weight of Vengeance: The United States, the British Empire, and the War of 1812* (Oxford: Oxford University Press, 2012), chapter 2.

38. Castlereagh to Foster, FO/583, April 10, 1812.

39. "Our Announced Commercial Treaty with the United States," *Morning Chronicle*, October 13, 1815. The editors noted that the "transactions of Europe seem entirely to have absorbed all our attention" and in the process had led to Britain unintentionally strengthening its "most dangerous rival." It was thus time to turn to the Western Hemisphere and support both Indian trade and Canada. Likewise, other papers demanded, not only attention, but domination. Two years into the War of 1812, *The Times* growled that any treaty with the United States should have a single aim: "submission."

40. Paul Kennedy, *The Rise and Fall of the Great Powers* (New York: Random House, 1987), 154.

41. See Jeremy Black, *Naval Power: A History of Warfare and the Sea from 1500 Onwards* (London: Palgrave, 2009).

42. This GDP data is drawn from Angus Maddison. See http://www.ggdc.net/maddison/oriindex.htm.

43. Bickham, *The Weight of Vengeance*, 50.

44. Both Mearsheimer and Dale Copeland argue the importance of future uncertainty in power transitions. See Mearsheimer, *Tragedy of Great Power Politics*, 31; Dale Copeland, *The Origins of Major War* (Ithaca: Cornell University Press), 29.

45. *Times*, June 2, 1814.

46. *Morning Chronicle*, October 13, 1815.

47. *Courier*, July 21, 1818.

48. Charles Duke Yonge, *The Life and Administration of Robert Banks, Second Earl of Liverpool*, vol. 3 (New York: MacMillan, 1868), 305.

49. Quoted in Bourne, *Britain and Balance of Power in North America*, 65.

50. Quoted ibid.

51. Here Canning refers to U.S recognition of South American republics.

52. Robert Kagan, *Dangerous Nation: America's Foreign Policy from Its Earliest Days to the Dawn of the Twentieth Century* (New York: Vintage, 2007), 4.

53. Weeks, *John Quincy Adams*, 72.

54. Ibid., 80.

55. Ibid., 44.

56. *Times*, November 28, 1812.

57. Bickham, *The Weight of Vengeance*, 11.

58. Weeks, *John Quincy Adams*, 44–45. For a discussion of the economic foundations of conciliation, see also Perkins, *Castlereagh and Adams*; Bourne, *Britain and the Balance of Power in North America*, 6.

59. Bemis, *John Quincy Adams*, 284.

60. Charles K. Webster, ed., *Britain and the Independence of Latin America*, vol. 1 (Oxford: Oxford University Press, 1938), 42.

61. Castlereagh to Bagot, "Enclosing Project of Commercial Convention," TNA, FO 5/120, March 21, 1817.

62. Kupchan, *How Enemies Become Friends*, 110; Rock, *Appeasement in International Politics*, 35.

63. See, e.g., Bickham, *The Weight of Vengeance*, chapter 2.

64. *Morning Chronicle*, October 8, 1815.

65. See, e.g., Matthew McCarthy, *Privateering, Piracy, and British Policy in Spanish America, 1810–1830* (Suffolk, UK: Boydell & Brewer, 2013); Dorothy Goebel, "British Trade to the Spanish Colonies 1796–1823," *American Historical Review* 43, no. 2: 288–320.

66. Quoted in Rippy, *Rivalry of the United States and Great Britain*, 108–10.

67. Quoted in Kagan, *Dangerous Nation*, 138.

68. Quoted in Perkins, *Castlereagh and Adams*, 294.

69. For Castlereagh's continued uncertainty about American intentions toward Canada, see Bourne, *Britain and the Balance of Power in North America*, 11.

70. See, for example, Lord Lansdowne's comments to Parliament on the threat to the West Indies, *22 Hansard*, vol. 40, 287–302; on Castlereagh's concerns about American expansion into Florida and concerns about the West Indies, see, Castlereagh to Bagot (Draft), TNA FO 115/29, November 10, 1817. On concerns about Cuba, albeit at a later date, see, e.g., Canning to Castlereagh (Draft), FO 115/41, December 5, 1822.

71. For example, Bagot analyzed a trip of Monroe's, taken after the inauguration, for clues as to whether or not he would appeal to "violent democrats" See Bagot to Castlereagh, FO 115/30, August 8, 1817. He later noted that Monroe had appointed one member to the South American commission who was "a man of abilities" but yet "violent in his republican principles." See Castlereagh to Bagot (Draft), TNA, FO 115/30, December 2, 1817.

72. Castlereagh to Wellesley, "Private and Confidential," TNA, FO 72/209, March 27, 1818.

73. Ibid.

74. Perkins, *Castlereagh and Adams*, 174.

75. John Quincy Adams, November 16, 1819. In *Memoirs of John Quincy Adams*, vol. 4, 438–39.

76. Peter S. Onuf, *Jefferson's Empire* (Charlottesville, VA: University of Virginia Press, 2000).

77. Inaugural address, accessed at http://avalon.law.yale.edu/19th_century/monroe1.asp.

78. Paul A. Gilge, *Free Trade and Sailors Rights in the War of 1812* (Cambridge: Cambridge University Press, 2013), 46.

79. See, e.g., ibid., 179.

80. Adams, *Memoirs*, vol. 4, 168.

81. There are questions as to whether Adams wrote the letters, which were published under the pseudonym "Phocion." See Weeks, *John Quincy Adams*, 99. Lewis argues the letters were more likely written by George Hay. Adams himself demurred when asked if he had written the letters (Adams, *Memoirs*, vol. 4, 23). For the purposes of argument here, the European audience treated the Phocion letters as if they were written by Adams (ibid.).

82. There is now an expanding literature on the creation of the Atlantic World, much of which stems from Bernard Bailyn's initial efforts to embed the history of the American revolution in a larger international history. See Bailyn, *Atlantic History: Concepts and Contours* (Cambridge: Harvard University Press, 2005). Among the scholarship that influences the chapter here are Gould, *Among the Great Powers;* Gould, "Zones of Law, Zones of Violence: The Legal Geography of the British Atlantic, circa 1772," *William and Mary Quarterly* 60, no. 3 (July 2003): 471–510; Gould, "The Making of an Atlantic State System: Britain and the United States, 1795–1825," in *Britain and America Go to War: The Impact of the War and Warfare in Anglo-America, 1754–1815*, ed. Julie Flavell and Stephen Conway (Gainesville: University of Florida Press, 2004), 241–65; Gould and Peter S. Onuf, eds., *Empire and Nation: The American Revolution in the Atlantic World* (Baltimore: Johns Hopkins University Press, 2005).

83. Lynn Hudson Parsons, *John Quincy Adams* (Lanham, MD: Rowman and Littlefield, 1992), xvi.

84. Coding was done in Atlas.ti, a qualitative coding program.

85. Weeks, *John Quincy Adams*, 140.

86. "The Secretary of State to George Erving, Department of State," Washington, November 28, 1818. The letter is printed in Adams, *The Writings of John Quincy Adams*, ed. Worthington Chauncey Ford, vol. 6 (New York: MacMillan, 1916), 474–502. The letter was also printed in several media outlets, including the *Times* on January 28, 1819.

87. Gould, *Among the Great Powers*, 197.

88. "The Secretary of State to George Erving," *The Writings of John Quincy Adams*.

89. Ibid., 489.

90. Ibid., 476–77.

91. Ibid.

92. John Quincy Adams, *Writings of John Quincy Adams*, 468.

93. Henry Clay, "On the Independence of South America," *Speeches of the Hon. Henry Clay, of the Congress of the United States*, ed. Calvin Colton, vol. 1 (New York: A. S. Barnes), 69.

94. Ibid., 70.

95. "Speech on the Occupation of West Florida," *Annals of Congress*, 11th Congress, 3d session. For an analysis of Clay and his republican ideology, see Robert V. Remini, *Henry Clay: Statesman for the Union* (New York: W. W. North, 1991).

96. *National Intelligencer*, October 30, 1817.

97. *National Intelligencer*, December 1, 1817.

98. Ibid.

99. *National Intelligencer*, October 30, 1817.

100. Quoted in Frederic Logan Paxson, *The Independence of the South American Republics: A Study in Recognition and Foreign Policy* (Philadelphia: Ferris and Leach, 1903), 159.

101. Monroe, Special Address to Congress, March 8, 1822.

102. As Weeks notes, "The Monroe doctrine was less a hollow threat to the European powers than a formal announcement to Congress of the policy already in place." Weeks, *John Quincy Adams*, 177.

103. Bemis, *John Quincy Adams*, 394.

104. See e.g., *Memoirs*, vol. 6, 195, 198.

105. See e.g., G. John Ikenberry, *After Victory: Institutions, Strategic Restraint, and the Rebuilding of Orders after Major Wars* (Princeton: Princeton University Press, 2001). Even more recent scholarship remains largely concerned with British institution building efforts on the continent. See, e.g., Barry Buzan and George Lawson, *The Great Transformation* (Cambridge: Cambridge University Press, 2015).

106. Gould, "Zones of Law," 481.

107. See, e.g., Castlereagh to Bagot (Draft), TNA, FO 5/129, August 8, 1818.

108. Gould and Onuf, *Empire and Nation*.

109. It was Castlereagh's aim, to put it in his own famous words, to not "collect trophies, but to try if we can bring the world back to peaceful habits." Lord Castlereagh to Liverpool, August 17, 1815. Castlereagh's own commitment to building the Concert and Congress system is well documented. See, e.g., Webster, *Foreign Policy of Castlereagh*; John Bew, *Castlereagh: A Life* (Oxford: Oxford University Press, 2012). Castlereagh's foreign policy is suggested at times to be inconsistent with the Britain's parliamentary system, in particular, favoring order and stability over democratic principles. These contradictions are overdrawn. As Castlereagh argued, only through nonintervention could Britain effectively pursue the spread of liberal, constitutional governments. See, e.g., Castlereagh's statements to Parliament on February 16, 1816, in *The Parliamentary Debates from the Year 1803 to the Present Time, published by T. C. Hansard* (London, 1816), vol. 32, 578–613. Moreover, Castlereagh's ostensibly more liberal successor, Canning, pressed for the very norms of nonintervention that Castlereagh held dear. For Canning on nonintervention, here in the case of Spain, see, e.g., George Canning, FO 115/33, January 10, 1823.

110. Quoted in Barry Alan Shain, *The Nature of Rights at the American Founding and Beyond* (Charlottesville: University of Virginia Press, 2013), 76.

111. See, e.g., Canning to Wellington, FO 115/40, October 1, 1822.

112. Edward L. Cox, "The British Caribbean in the Age of Revolution," in *Empire and Nation*, ed. Gould and Onuf, 275.

113. Some have argued that the divide between constitutional governments, such as Britain, and the Holy Alliance partners is overstated. Yet certainly Castlereagh and Canning worried that Russia, in particular, would pursue an ideological interventionist foreign policy in South America and Spain. For an overview of the divide, see Webster, *Foreign Policy of Castlereagh*; Charles K. Webster, "Castlereagh and the Spanish Colonies, II," *The English Historical Review* 30, no. 120 (October 1915): 631–45; Harold Temperley, *The Foundations of British Foreign Policy* (Cambridge: Cambridge University Press, 1938), 39.

114. As Webster argues, there is a "vast" amount of evidence that the Tsar was thinking about intervention at Troppau. See Webster, "Castlereagh and the Spanish Colonies, II," 639.

115. Castlereagh to Wellesley, TNA, FO 72/209, March 1817.

116. Castlereagh to Wellesley, TNA, FO 72/196, May 27, 1817.

117. Gould and Onuf, *Empire and Nation*, 14.

118. Gould, *Among the Great Powers*, 179.

119. *Courier*, July 28, 1818.

120. "Private Correspondence," *Caledonian Mercury*, January 16, 1819.

121. Bagot to Castlereagh, TNA, FO 5/132, June 29, 1818. See also statements by the *Courier*, July 30, 1818; and the *Times*, June 29, 1818.

122. Perkins, *Castlereagh and Adams*, 294.

123. Ibid., 295.

124. Bagot to Castlereagh, TNA, FO 5/132, June 29, 1818.

125. Lord Liverpool to Castlereagh, September 18, 1818. Printed in *Correspondence, Dispatches and Other Papers of Viscount Castlereagh*, ed. Charles Vane (London: Shoberi Press, 1851), 38.

126. Castlereagh to Bagot, TNA, FO 5/129, August 18, 1818.

127. *Courier*, July 28, 1818. Emphasis added.

128. Ibid. Emphasis added.

129. Bemis, *John Quincy* Adams, 328. As argued here, it is not, to be clear, that Adams's rhetoric was solely responsible for averting an Anglo-American conflict. His rhetoric did, however, appease Castlereagh and give the foreign minister ammunition to support the continuation of his policy of accommodation. See Weeks, *John Quincy Adams*, esp. 138–50.

130. Castlereagh to Bagot, TNA, FO 5/141, January 2, 1819.

131. Castlereagh to Bagot, TNA, FO 115/34, January 2, 1819.

132. Bemis, *John Quincy Adams*, 328.

133. *Courier*, July 1, 1818.

134. *Morning Chronicle*, September 5, 1818.

135. For this assessment, see, e.g., Perkins, *Castlereagh and Adams*; Bemis, *John Quincy Adams*; Weeks, *John Quincy Adams*.

136. *Annals of Congress,* 15th Congress, 1st Session, 1817–18, II, 1482.

137. Bagot to Castlereagh, TNA, FO 115/30, November 9, 1817. Note that the *National Intelligencer* was (rightfully) considered the official voice of the Monroe administration, so that a change of rhetoric in this newspaper was considered a change in governmental rhetoric as well.

138. Castlereagh to Wellesley, "Private and Confidential," TNA, FO 72/209 March 27, 1818. Emphasis added.

139. Ibid.

140. *Times,* April 22, 1822.

141. Bemis, *John Quincy Adams,* 395.

142. See Ernest May, *The Making of the Monroe Doctrine* (Cambridge: Harvard University Press, 1975).

143. Quoted in Stagg, *Borderlines in Borderlands,* 75.

144. Quoted ibid., 90.

145. William Sabatier, *A Letter to the Right Honorable Frederick J. Robinson . . . on the Relative Situation of the British North American Possessions, with the United States of America and Great Britain* (London, 1821), 14–15. Quoted in Perkins, *Castlereagh and Adams,* 199.

146. Gould, *Among the Great Powers,* 218.

147. *Courier,* July 30, 1818.

148. Ibid.

149. *Times,* April 22, 1818.

150. Lord Lansdowne, in T. C. Hansard, *The Parliamentary Debates from the Year 1803 to the Present Time,* vol. 40 (London: TC Hansard, 1819), May 11, 1819, quotations from 288, 291, 293, 294.

151. *Morning Chronicle,* September 5, 1818.

152. Ibid.

153. *The Parliamentary Debates from the Year 1803 to the Present Time,* vol. 40, 295, 296.

154. Pizarro to Wellesley, TNA, FO 115/29, April 26, 1817.

155. Pizarro to Wellesley, "Differences between Spain and the United States," TNA, FO 115/29, July 12, 1817.

156. The Duke of St. Carlos to Lord Castlereagh, "Differences with the United States," TNA, FO 72/216, July 23, 1818.

157. Castlereagh to Bagot, TNA, FO 115/29, January 22, 1818.

158. 1Weeks, *John Quincy Adams,* 119.

159. Bemis, *John Quincy Adams,* 327.

160. See e.g., Castlereagh to Wellesley, TNA, FO 72/209, March 1817.

161. Castlereagh to Wellesely, "Slave Trade, Mediation between Spain and her Colonies, between Spain and Portugal," TNA, FO 72/196, February 14, 1817.

162. Quoted in Perkins, *Castlereagh and Adams,* 178.

163. Ibid., 185.

164. As described ibid., 217.

165. Adams, *The Writings of John Quincy Adams,* 61.

166. Mlada Bukovansky, "American Identity and Neutral Rights from Independence to the War of 1812," *International Organization* 51, no. 2 (March 1997): 209–43.

167. As Rush put it, there was "an immense and growing rivalry . . . at all points, in all quarters." Quoted in Perkins, *Castlereagh and Adams,* 217.

168. Rush, in Perkins, *Castlereagh and Adams,* 296.

169. Castlereagh to Wellesley, TNA, FO 181/15, April 1, 1817.

170. Webster, "Castlereagh and the Spanish Colonies II, 1818–1822," 641.

171. Bemis, *John Quincy Adams,* 343.

172. See e.g., Adams, *Writings,* vol. 6, 318. For a discussion, see Perkins, *Monroe Doctrine,* 49.

173. It was in January 1819 that Adams informed the British government that the United States was considering recognition and invited that government to join them in recognition. For a description of the approach, see Adams to Rush, May 20, 1818 in Adams, *Writings of John Quincy Adams,* vol. 6, 319–27. Adams assured Stratford Canning, then representative in Washington, that the United States and Britain were moving along parallel lines in South America. See, e.g., Canning to Castlereagh, TNA, FO 115/36, October 3, 1820.

174. Adams, *Memoirs,* vol. 5, 195.

175. Adams, *Memoirs,* June 1823, vol. 6, 152.
176. *Morning Chronicle*, July 5, 1823.
177. *Morning Chronicle,* August 8, 1822.
178. *Times*, November 8, 1823.
179. *Morning Chronicle*, November 2, 1822.
180. *Times,* November 8, 1823.
181. Stratford Canning to Castlereagh, TNA, FO 115/36 October 3, 1820.
182. *Times*, December 27, 1823.
183. *Morning Chronicle*, December 27, 1823.
184. Quoted in Perkins, *Castlereagh and Adams*, 319.
185. The full text of Forrest Davis, *The Atlantic System,* is online at http://penelope.uchicago.edu/Thayer/E/Gazetteer/Places/America/United_States/_Topics/history/_Texts/DAVATL/Foreword*.html. All quotations are from this version.
186. Gould, "Making of the Atlantic State System," 242.
187. "Canning's Parliamentary Triumph, 12 December, 1826." Text of Canning's speech to parliament in Harold Temperley, *The Foreign Policy of Canning 1822–1827: England, the Neo-Holy Alliance, and the New World* (London: G. Bell and Sons, 1925), 381.
188. http://penelope.uchicago.edu/Thayer/E/Gazetteer/Places/America/United_States/_Topics/history/_Texts/DAVATL/Foreword*.html.
189. Gould, "Making of the Atlantic State System," 242.

4. Prussia's Rule-Bound Revolution

1. France joined the Concert as a member of the Quadruple alliance in 1818.
2. For the complete text of the treaties of Vienna, see Edward Hertslet, *The Map of Europe by Treaty: Showing the Various Political and Territorial Changes Which Have Taken Place since the General Peace of 1814*, 3 vols. (London: Butterworths, 1875), 1:60–147. The literature on the Concert of Europe, both in history and political science, is immense. A small selection includes Edward W. Gulick, *Europe's Classical Balance of Power: A Case History of the Theory and Practice of One of the Great Concepts of European Statecraft* (Westport, CT: Greenwood Press, 1982); Enno Krahe, "A Bipolar Balance of Power," *American Historical Review* 97, no. 3, 707–15; Robert L. Jervis, "From Balance to Concert: A Study of International Security Cooperation," *World Politics* 38, no. 1: 58–79; Henry Kissinger, *A World Restored* (New York: Grosset and Dunlap, 1964); Charles K. Webster, *The Congress of Vienna* (Oxford: Oxford University Press, 1919); Paul W. Schroeder, *The Transformation of European Politics, 1763–1848*. (Oxford: Oxford University Press, 1992); G. John Ikenberry, *After Victory* (Princeton: Princeton University Press, 2001); Celeste Wallander and Robert O. Keohane, "Risk, Threat, and Security Institutions," in *Imperfect Unions: Security Institutions over Time and Space*, ed. Helga Hftendorn, Robert O. Keohane and Celeste A. Wallander (Oxford: Oxford University Press, 1999), 21–47. For recent work on the Concert, which considers the Concert a significant movement toward great-power global governance, see Jennifer Mitzen, *Power in Concert* (Chicago: University of Chicago Press, 2013); Mark Jarrett, *The Congress of Vienna and Its Legacy: War and Great Power Diplomacy after Napoleon* (London: I. B. Taurus, 2013).
3. Metternich to Rechberg, quoted in Richard B. Elrod, "Bernhard von Rechberg and the Metternichian Tradition: The Dilemma of Conservative Statecraft," *Journal of Modern History* 56, no. 3 (1984): 442.
4. For exceptions, see James Davis, *Threats and Promises: The Pursuit of International Influence* (Baltimore: the Johns Hopkins University Press, 2000), 44–74; Branislav L. Slantchev, "Territory and Commitment: the Concert of Europe as Self-Enforcing Equilibrium," *Security Studies* 14, no. 4 (2005): 565–606.
5. On Schleswig-Holstein in European politics, see, e.g., Lawrence Steefel, *The Schleswig-Holstein Question* (Cambridge: Harvard University Press, 1932); William E. Mosse, *The European Powers and the German Question 1848–71* (Cambridge: Cambridge University Press, 1958), 146–212; William E. Mosse, "Queen Victoria and Her Ministers in the Schleswig-Holstein Crisis, 1863–1864," *English Historical Review* 78, no. 307 (1963): 263–83; Chester Wells Clark, *Franz*

Joseph and Bismarck: The Diplomacy of Austria before the War of 1866 (Cambridge: Harvard University Press, 1934), 55–122; William E. Echard, *Napoleon III and the Concert of Europe* (Baton Rouge: Louisiana State University, 1983), 203–8; William Carr, *Schleswig-Holstein 1815–48* (Manchester: Manchester University Press, 1963).

6. Mosse, *The European Powers*, 148–52; Steefel, *The Schleswig-Holstein Question*, 110–68.

7. See, e.g., Chester Wells Clark, *Franz Joseph and Bismarck: the Diplomacy of Austria before the war of 1866* (Cambridge: Harvard University Press, 1934); Charles W. Hallberg, *Franz Joseph and Napoleon III 1852–1864* (New York: Bookman Associates, 1955); Roy A. Austensen, "Austria and the Struggle for Supremacy in Germany, 1848–1864," *Journal of Modern History* 52, no. 2 (1980): 195–225; Richard B. Elrod, "Rechberg and the Metternichian Tradition," 430–55.

8. One might argue that there is no more "great man" in international diplomatic history than Otto von Bismarck. For examples, see Otto Pflantze, *Bismarck and the Development of Germany* (Princeton: Princeton University Press, 1963); Pflantze, "Bismarck and German Nationalism," *American Historical Review* 60, no. 3 (1955): 548–66; Edward Crankshaw, *Bismarck* (New York: Viking, 1981); Lothar Gall, *Bismarck: The White Revolutionary*, 2 vols. (Allen and Unwin, 1986). Henry Kissinger, "The White Revolutionary: Reflections on Bismarck," *Daedalus* 97, no. 3: 888–924. However, out of fashion "great man" history has become, the centrality of Bismarck persists. See, e.g., Jonathan Steinberg, *Bismarck: A Life* (Oxford: Oxford University Press, 2011).

9. This description draws from Steefel, *The Schleswig-Holstein Question*, 3–8.

10. On nationalist movements in Denmark and Germany, see Carr, *Schleswig-Holstein 1814–1848*; Steefel, *The Schleswig-Holstein Question*, 22–32; John Breuilly, *The Formation of the First German Nation-State, 1800–1871* (London: Macmillan, 1996).

11. Mosse, *The European Powers*, 146.

12. Steefel, *The Schleswig-Holstein Question*, 105. See also Otto Pflanze, *Bismarck and the Development of Germany* (Princeton: Princeton University Press, 1963), 234–40.

13. Quoted in Mosse, *The European Powers*, 18. Government in Schleswig-Holstein composed of "conservatives, national liberals, and radicals to protect the rights of the duchies" (51).

14. Speeches of Mr. Disraeli and Lord Palmerston in the House of Commons, the 19th April, 1849, on the Danish Question. In Kenneth Bourne and D. Cameron Watt, eds., *British Documents on Foreign Affairs: Reports and Papers from the Foreign Office Confidential Print* (hereafter *BFDA*) (University Publications of America), part I, vol. 17, Series F, Europe, Denmark 1848–1914, Doc 6, p. 15.

15. Palmerson to Bloomfield, May 18, 1848. Quoted in Herbert C. F. Bell, *Lord Palmerston* (London: Longmans, Green, 1936), vol. 2, 8.

16. Nesselrode to Meyendorff, April 26, 1848, printed in F. de Martens, *Recueil des Traites* (St Petersburg, 1888), vol. 8, 375.

17. Mosse, *The European Powers*, 43.

18. Steefel, *The Schleswig Holstein Question*, 110.

19. Mosse, *The European Powers*, 170.

20. For a description of Austria's policy, see Clark, *Franz Joseph and Bismarck*, 236–56.

21. John J. Mearsheimer, *The Tragedy of Great Power Politics* (New York: W.W. Norton, 2001), 269–72; Thomas J. Christensen and Jack L. Snyder, "Chain Gangs and Passed Bucks: Predicting Alliance Patterns in Multipolarity," *International Organization* 44, no. 2: 137–68; Thomas J. Christensen, "Perceptions and Alliances in Europe, 1865–1940," *International Organization* 51, no. 1: 65–97.

22. See e.g., Randall Schweller, *Unanswered Threats: Political Constraints on the Balance of Power* (Princeton: Princeton University Press, 2006), chapter 1.

23. Mosse, "Queen Victoria and Her Ministers."

24. Mearsheimer, *The Tragedy of Great Power Politics*, 268. See also Christensen, "Perceptions and Alliances in Europe, 1865–1940." While Christensen's coding starts in 1865, he argues that Prussia was not perceived as a threat in the 1860s.

25. Ibid., 291.

26. Mosse, *The European Powers*, 159.

27. Christopher Clark, *Iron Kingdom: The Rise and Downfall of Prussia, 1600–1947* (Cambridge: Belknap Press of Harvard University Press), 530.

28. Quoted ibid., 531.
29. Steefel, *The Schleswig-Holstein Question*, 130.
30. Ibid., 110–68; Carr, *Schleswig Holstein*; Mosse, *The European Powers*.
31. Quoted in Steinberg, *Bismarck*, 174.
32. Quoted ibid., 180–81.
33. Schweller, *Unanswered Threats*, 32. Similarly, David Edelstein describes Prussia's intentions as "uncertain" but "malleable." Edelstein, "Managing Uncertainty: Beliefs about Intentions and the Rise of Great Powers," *Security Studies* 12, no. 1 (2002): 18–31. See also Edelstein's discussion of Prussia's intentions, which covers a later period that I've covered here, in *Over the Horizon: Time, Uncertainty, and the Rise of Great Powers* (Ithaca: Cornell University Press, 2017).
34. Extracts from a speech in the House of Commons, March 20, 1815. In Charles Webster, *British Diplomacy 1813–1815* (London, 1921), 397.
35. Palmerson to Prince Albert, September 16, 1847. In Theodore Martin, *The Life of H.R.H. the Prince Consort* (London, 1875), vol. 1, 447.
36. Mosse, *The European Powers*, 16.
37. Quoted ibid.
38. Ibid., 18.
39. Nesselrode to Meyendorff, April 26, 1848, in Martens, *Recueil des Traits*, 375.
40. On this question, see also Edelstein, "Managing Uncertainty."
41. Mosse, *The European Powers*, 5; R. H. Lord, "Bismarck and Russia in 1863," *American Historical Review* 29, no. 1 (1923): 24–48.
42. Elrod, "Rechberg and the Metternich Tradition," 444.
43. See, e.g., Mosse, *The European Powers*, 15–17; Frank G. Weber, "Palmerston and Prussian Liberalism, 1848," *Journal of Modern History* 35, no. 2 (1963): 125–136. Edelstein, "Managing Uncertainty."
44. *BFDA*, 139.
45. *Times*, February 5, 1864.
46. See W. L. Langer, *European Alliances and Alignments, 1871–1890* (New York: Knopf, 1931), 145.
47. *Times*, December 2, 1863.
48. Quoted in Mosse, *The European Powers*, 135.
49. On wedge strategies, see Timothy W. Crawford, "Preventing Enemy Coalitions: How Wedge Strategies Shape Power Politics," *International Security* 34, no. 4 (Spring 2011): 155–89.
50. Bismarck to Bernstorff (Communicated to Earl Russell by Count Bernstorff, October 30), Berlin, October 27, 1862, *BDFA*, 103.
51. *Times*, November 20, 1863.
52. *Times*, December 2, 1963.
53. Steinberg, *Bismarck*, 215.
54. Bismarck's address, as reported in *Times*, December 4, 1863.
55. Bismarck to Bernstorff (Communicated to Earl Russell by Count Bernstorff, October 30), Berlin, October 27, 1862, *BDFA*, 103.
56. *Times*, November 23, 1863.
57. *Times*, December 17, 1863.
58. Using the qualitative content analysis program Atlas.ti.
59. At the beginning of the crisis, German politicians were more likely to appeal to dynastic rights than nationalism. Over time, appeals to support the Duke of Augustenburg's claims became a matter, not of dynastic principle, but of German national rights.
60. *Times*, December 17, 1863. See also Pflanze, *Bismarck and the Development of Germany*, 242.
61. Steefel, *The Schleswig Holstein Question*, 107.
62. E.g., Otto Pflanze, *Bismarck and the Development of Germany*; and Pflanze "Bismarck and German Nationalism," *American Historical Review* 60, no. 3 (1955): 548–66.
63. The *Times* noted the discrepancy between Bismarck's language and Wilhelm's. See, e.g., *Times*, December 2, 1863, which notes that, while the king "was inclined to place himself at the

head of the anti-Danish policy in Germany," it was Bismarck who pulled Prussia to the legal course of action.

64. *Times*, December 3, 1863.

65. *Times*, December 4, 1863.

66. *Times*, December 21, 1863.

67. *Times*, January 2, 1864.

68. See, e.g., W. O. Henderson, *The Zollverein* (Cambridge: Cambridge University Press, 1939).

69. See, e.g., Immanuel Geiss, *The Question of German Unification, 1806–1996* (New York: Routledge, 2013), 44.

70. On Frederick III, see Andreas Dorpalen, "Emperor Frederick III and the German Liberal Movement," *American Historical Review* 54, no. 1 (1948): 1–31.

71. See, e.g., John Breuilly, *Formation of the First German Nation-State;* James Joll, "Prussia and the German Problem: 1830–1866," in *The New Cambridge Modern History,* vol. 10, *The Zenith of European Power, 1830–70,* ed. J. P. T Bury (Cambridge; Cambridge University Press, 1960), 493–521.

72. Clark, *Iron Kingdom*, 516.

73. Ibid., 521.

74. Quoted in Pflantze, *Bismarck and the Development of Germany*, 178.

75. Indeed some saw Bismarck's appointment in 1862 as nothing more than an attempt to bring in Manteuffel's influence without completely alienating the liberal parliament.

76. Crankshaw, *Bismarck*, 166.

77. Rechberg to Bach, November 9, 1859. Quoted in Elrod, "Rechberg and the Metternichian Tradition," 450.

78. Rechberg to the Council of Ministers, February 11, 1861. Quoted ibid., 438.

79. See, e.g., Mosse, *The European Powers*, 145.

80. Napier to Russell, most confidential, December 30, 1863. Quoted in Mosse, *The European Powers*, 165.

81. Ibid., 163.

82. See e.g., Heinrich Friedjung, *The Struggle for Supremacy in Germany, 1859–1866* (London: Macmillan, 1935). Cf., Austensen, "Austria and the Struggle for Supremacy in Germany, 1848–1864."

83. Quoted in Elrod, "Rechberg and the Metternichian Tradition," 438.

84. Count Belcredi to Conte Malaguzzi, October 25, 1865. Quoted in Clark, *Franz Joseph and Bismarck*, 27.

85. In Pflanze, *Bismarck and the Development of Germany*, 235.

86. Clark, *Franz Joseph and Bismarck*, 57.

87. Quoted ibid., 58.

88. Bismarck to Bernstorff (Communicated to Earl Russell by Count Bernstorff, October 30), Berlin, October 27, 1862, *BDFA*, doc. 34, 103.

89. Steefel, *The Schleswig-Holstein Question*, 106.

90. Quoted in Elrod, "Rechberg and the Metternichian Tradition," 451.

91. Quoted in Crankshaw, *Bismarck*, 171.

92. E.g., Steefel, *The Schleswig-Holstein Question*, 79–109; J. V. Clardy, "Austrian Foreign Policy during the Schleswig-Holstein Crisis of 1864: An Exercise in Reactive Planning and Negative Formulations," *Diplomacy and Statecraft* 2, no. 2: 254–69; Clark, *Franz Joseph and Bismarck*, esp. chapter 2.

93. Clark, *Franz Joseph and Bismarck*, 58–59.

94. Ibid., 60.

95. Pflantze, *Bismarck*, 241–42.

96. Bismarck, *Bismarck, the Man and the Statesman*, vol. 1 (London: Smith, Elder, 1898), 370.

97. Clark, *Franz Joseph and Bismarck*, 24.

98. Ibid., 60.

99. Ibid.

100. Nesselrode to Meyendorff, 26 April 1848. Printed in Martens, *Recueil des Traités*, 375.

101. Steefel, *The Schleswig-Holstein Question*, 130.

102. E.g., Slantchev, "Territory and Commitment: the Concert of Europe as Self-Enforcing Equilibrium," 603–4.

103. Quoted in Clardy, "Austrian Foreign Policy during the Schleswig-Holstein Crisis," 264. See also Mosse, *The European Powers*, 72.

104. Mosse, *The European Powers*, 72.

105. See, e.g., Lord, "Bismarck and Russia in 1863."

106. Mosse *The European Powers*, 164.

107. Napier to Russell, no 823, most confidential, 30 December 1863, RA I 92/175. Quoted ibid., 65.

108. Ibid., 167.

109. Ibid., 168. For a discussion, see also Steefel, *The Schleswig-Holstein Question*, 200.

110. Quoted in Steefel, *The Schleswig-Holstein Question*, 131.

111. Quoted ibid., 200.

112. "Memorandum of the Transaction which preceded the war between Denmark and Germany," *BFDA*, 132.

113. Mosse, *The European Powers*, 172. My translation.

114. *Hansard Parliamentary Debates*, 3rd ser. 172, col. 1252, July 23, 1863.

115. In Sir Spencer Walpole, *The Life of Lord John Russell*. (New York: Greenwood, 1968), 388.

116. See, e.g., Temperley, *Foundations of British Foreign Policy*, 367.

117. Steefel, *The Schleswig-Holstein Question*, 110–68; Mosse, *The European Powers*, 146.

118. Denmark was in breach because, by administering Schleswig separately from Holstein, it was violating the principle that the duchies were indivisible.

119. Mosse, "Queen Victoria and Her Ministers"; Bell, *Lord Palmerston*, vol. 2, 373–80.

120. See e.g., Bell, *Lord Palmerston*, vol. 2, 376–77.

121. Quoted ibid., 11.

122. Quoted in Mosse "Queen Victoria and Her Ministers," 278.

123. *Hansard Parliamentary Debates*, clxxv, col. 609.

124. Steefel, *The Schleswig-Holstein Question*, 61.

125. *Times*, March 30, 1863.

126. *Times*, February 5, 1864.

127. *Times*, December 3, 1863.

128. *Times*, December 4, 1863.

129. Palmerston to Russell, 1 May 1864. In *Foundations of British Foreign Policy, 1792–1902*, ed. Harold Temperley and Lillian M. Penson (Cambridge: Cambridge University Press, 1938), 269.

130. Palmerston to Hall. Quoted in Steefel, *The Schleswig-Holstein Question*.

131. Quoted in Crankshaw, *Bismarck*, 170.

132. William M. Sloane, "Bismarck's Apprenticeship," *Political Science Quarterly* 14, no. 3 (September 1899): 437; Bell, *Lord Palmerston*, vol. 2, 376–77; Mosse, "Queen Victoria and Her Ministers."

133. *Times*, February 9, 1864.

134. Quoted in Mosse, "Queen Victoria and Her Ministers," 271. Emphasis in original.

135. Ibid., 268.

136. Palmerston to Duke of Somerset (first lord of the admiralty), 20 Feb. 864, printed in Evelyn Ashley, *The Life of Henry John Temple, Viscount Palmerston* (London, 1876), vol. 2, 247.

137. Granville to the queen, 5 May 1864, TNA, RA I 97/I6.

138. Temperley, *Foundations of British Foreign Policy*, 248.

139. *Hansard Parliamentary Debates*, CLXXII, col. 107, col. 111.

140. Quoted in Crankshaw, *Bismarck*, 170.

141. See e.g., Echard, *Napoleon III and the Concert of Europe*; Ann E. Pottinger, *Napoleon III and the German Crisis 1865–1866* (Cambridge: Harvard University Press, 1966); Jennings, "French Diplomacy and the First Schleswig-Holstein Crisis."

142. Quoted in Lawrence C. Jennings, "French Diplomacy and the First Schleswig-Holstein Crisis," *French Historical Studies* 7, no. 2 (Autumn 1971): 216.

143. *Times*, February 3, 1864.

144. Steefel, *The Schleswig-Holstein Question*, 115.

145. Ibid., 179.
146. See, e.g., Echard, *Napoleon III and the Concert of Europe*; Pottinger, *Napoleon III and the German Crisis;* David Baguley, *Napoleon III and His Regime* (Baton Rouge: Louisiana State Press, 2000).
147. Quoted in David Wetzel, *Duel of Giants: Bismarck, Napoleon III, and the Franco-Prussian War* (Madison: University of Wisconsin Press, 2001), 28.
148. *Les Origines diplomatique de la guerre de 1870–1871*, vol. 2, no. 349.
149. Mosse, *The European Powers*, 128.
150. Steefel, *The Schleswig-Holstein Question*, 216.
151. See ibid., 183; Mosse, *The European Powers*, 186–89; Hallberg, *Franz Joseph and Napoleon III*, 314–41; Echard, *Napoleon III and the Concert of Europe*, 193–210.
152. Quoted in Steefel, *The Schleswig-Holstein Question*, 183.
153. Walpole, *The Life of Lord John Russell*, 390.
154. Ibid.

5. Germany's Rhetorical Rage

1. The literature on appeasement is too voluminous to cite in its entirety. It can be divided into three schools of historiography: a traditionalist school, which largely condemns appeasement as irrational; a "revisionist" school, which sees appeasement as, if not completely effective, a generally rational response to Germany given strategic constraints; and a "postrevisionist" school, which questions the rationality of appeasement. For a traditionalist account, see Winston S. Churchill, *The Second World War*, vol. 1, *The Gathering Storm* (Boston: Houghton Mifflin, 1948); "Cato" [Michael Foot, Peter Howard, Frank Owen], *Guilty Men* (London: Penguin, 1998). Revisionist historiography is often argued to have begun with A. J. P. Taylor's, *The Origins of the Second World War* (New York: Simon and Schuster, 1995). Other revisionist accounts, more steeped in documentary evidence, include W. N. Medlicott, *British Foreign Policy since Versailles, 1919–1963* (London: Methuen, 1968); D. C. Watt, "1939 Revisited: On Theories of the Origins of Wars," *International Affairs* 65, no. 4 (autumn 1989): 685–92; David Dilks, "Appeasement Revisited," *University of Leeds Review* 15 (1972): 28–56; Dilks, "'We Must Hope for the Best and Prepare for the Worst': The Prime Minister, the Cabinet and Hitler's Germany, 1937–1939," *Proceedings of the British Academy* 73: 309–52; Paul M. Kennedy, *Strategy and Diplomacy, 1870–1945* (London: George Allen and Unwin, 1983): 99–100; Brian McKercher, "'Our Most Dangerous Enemy': Great Britain Pre-eminent in the 1930s," *International History Review* 13, no. 4 (1991): 751–83. For examples of the counterrevisionist school see R. A. C. Parker, *Chamberlain and Appeasement: British Policy and the Coming of the Second World War* (New York: St. Martin's Press, 1993); Parker, *Churchill and Appeasement: Could Churchill Have Prevented the Second World War* (New York: Macmillan, 2000); Neville Thompson, *The Anti-Appeasers: Conservative Opposition to Appeasement in the 1930s* (Oxford: Oxford University Press, 1971). For a succinct recent overview of the historiography, see Patrick Finney, "Introduction," in *The Origins of the Second World War: A Reader*, ed. Patrick Finney (London: Bloomsbury, 1997), 12–17.

2. Nazi Germany's aims, including the extent of Hitler's expansionism and his willingness to bear the cost of a World War, are still somewhat disputed. A. J. P. Taylor's provocative claim that Hitler was a mere opportunist, expanding without any set revisionist aims, have been largely rejected by historians. There is still disagreement over whether Germany's foreign policy stemmed entirely from Hitler's racial ideology, as articulated in *Mein Kampf*, making both expansion into Soviet Russia and the war in the West inevitable, or if Hitler's ideology set broad parameters for German foreign policy. For an example of the former, see Gerhard Weinberg, *Hitler's Foreign Policy, 1933–1939: The Road to World War II* (New York: Enigma Books, 2010); on the latter, see Ian Kershaw, *Hitler: Nemesis, 1936–1945* (New York: W. W. Norton, 2001). The chapter here tends toward the latter approach but, ultimately while this debate is significant in its own right, it is not central to the study here. What matters to this case study is Britain's response to Germany's justification of its aims, not the precise aims of Germany (or Hitler) itself. If it could be shown that Germany's rhetoric stemmed directly from its foreign

policy interests, then the aims would be central, but no historian that I am aware of makes this argument.

3. Paul M. Kennedy, "The Tradition of Appeasement in British Foreign Policy, 1865–1935," *British Journal of International Studies* 2, no. 3 (autumn 1976): 195. See also Paul W. Schroeder, "Munich and the British Tradition," *The Historical Journal* 19, no. 1 (spring 1976): 223–43.

4. Churchill, *Gathering Storm*, 293.

5. Ibid., 273. For accounts that blame individuals, and particularly Chamberlain's, assessment, see Churchill, *Gathering Storm*. For more recent accounts, see Erik Goldstein, "Neville Chamberlain, the British Official Mind, and the Munich Crisis," *Diplomacy and Statecraft* 10, no. 2–3 (1999): 276–92; Keren Yahri-Milo, "In the Eye of the Beholder: How Leaders and Intelligence Communities Assess the Intentions of Adversaries," *International Security*, 38, no. 1 (2013): 7–51. For a general theory of domestic politics and "underbalancing," see Randall L. Schweller, *Unanswered Threats: Political Constraints on the Balance of Power* (Princeton: Princeton University, 2006). On domestic constraints in Britain and their influence on grand strategy, see Schroeder, "Munich and the British Tradition"; Kevin Narizny, "Both Guns and Butter, or Neither: Class Interests in the Political Economy of Rearmament," *American Political Science Review* 97, no. 2 (2003): 203–20.

6. See for example Norrin M. Ripsman and Jack S. Levy, "Wishful Thinking or Buying Time? The Logic of British Appeasement in the 1930s," *International Security* 33, no. 2 (2008): 148–81; Ripsman and Levy, "The Preventive War that Never Happened: Britain, France, and the Rise of Germany in the 1930s," *Security Studies* 16, no. 1 (2008): 32–67; John J. Mearsheimer, *Tragedy of Great Power Politics* (New York: W.W. Norton, 2001), 185; Christopher Layne, "Security Studies and the Use of History: Neville Chamberlain's Grand Strategy Revisited," *Security Studies* 17, no. 3 (2008): 397–437.

7. As discussed in detail below, historians have attributed this change to British revulsion at a number of events in Germany, including the events of *Kristallnacht* and increasing persecution of the Jews. Here, I focus on the rhetoric that emerged from Hitler's propaganda campaign following Munich. My focus on language is thus consistent, though perhaps more narrow, with the counterrevisionist historiography on the change in British foreign policy. See, e.g., Zara Steiner, *Triumph of the Dark: European International History, 1933–1939* (Oxford: Oxford University Press), 679–80; Weinberg, *Hitler's Foreign Policy*; Roger Eatwell, "Munich, Public Opinion, and Popular Front," *Journal of Contemporary History* 6, no. 4 (1971): 131.

8. Eatwell, "Munich, Public Opinion, and Popular Front," 139.

9. Talbot C. Imlay, *Facing the Second World War: Strategy, Politics, and Economics in Britain and France, 1938–1940* (Oxford: Oxford University Press, 2003), chap. 4; Adam Tooze, *The Wages of Destruction: The Making and Breaking of the Nazi Economy* (New York: Penguin Books, 2006).

10. I thank Talbot Imlay for this insight.

11. See, e.g., Winston S. Churchill, *Gathering Storm*.

12. Kennedy, *Strategy and Diplomacy*, 99–100.

13. Ripsman and Levy, "Wishful Thinking or Buying Time," 156.

14. Narizny, "Both Guns or Butter."

15. Schweller, "Unanswered Threats: A Neoclassical Realist Theory of Underbalancing," *International Security*, 29, no. 2 (fall 2004): 159–201.

16. As discussed below, this view of appeasement as an end in and of itself is a cornerstone of the postrevisionist historiography on British grand strategy. See, e.g., Steiner, *Triumph of the Dark*; Parker, *Chamberlain and Appeasement*.

17. Steiner, *Triumph of the Dark*, 83.

18. See "British Policy Towards Germany," FO 371/19885, February 20, 1936; "Germany's Return to the League of Nations," FO 371/18848, July 18, 1935; "German Foreign Policy," FO 371/19884, January 22, 1936.

19. "Germany Foreign Policy," PRO, FO 371/19884, January 22, 1936.

20. See, e.g., Lord Lothian's proposal to cede these territories on June 3, 1937, published in J. R. M. Butler, *Lord Lothian, 1882–1940* (London: Macmillan, 1960), 215, 354–62. Nevile Henderson, the British Ambassador to Berlin, also promoted territorial concessions in the East. See Sir Nevile Henderson, "Anglo-German Relations," FO 371/20736, July 12, 1937. For a discussion about these proposals, see "Anglo-German Relations," FO 371/20736, July 20, 1937.

Halifax would raise the possibility of altering the boundaries of the Sudetenland, Memel, and Danzig in his meetings with Hitler in November 1937. See the summary of these meetings in "Foreign Office: Private Office Papers of Sir Anthony Eden, Earl of Avon, Secretary of State for Foreign Affairs," FO 954/10A. As discussed below, questions about whether to cede Eastern European territory to Germany would continue after Munich.

21. "Foreign Office: Private Office Papers of Sir Anthony Eden, Earl of Avon, Secretary of State for Foreign Affairs," FO 954/10A, November 1937. For a discussion of this conversation, see also Steiner, *Triumph of the Dark*, 338.

22. See, e.g., "Germany's Contributions towards General Appeasement," PREM 1/330, January 22, 1936; "Peace Plan of the German Government of March 31, 1936 handed to the British Government by Ambassador von Ribbentrop on April 1, 1936," FO/954/10A, April 2, 1936; "German Foreign Policy," FO 371/19884, January 22, 1936.

23. One of the animating arguments of the counterrevisionist school is that, even in the face of economic and domestic constraints, Chamberlain and his cabinet had policy choices available to them other than appeasement, and that, more specifically, armament could have been accelerated and expanded had Chamberlain seen the need for such measures. See, e.g., Steiner, *Triumph of the Dark*, 297; Peter Jackson, *France and the Nazi Menace: Intelligence and Policy Making, 1933–1939* (Oxford: Oxford University Press, 2001), 273; Parker, *Chamberlain and Appeasement*, 275; For a summary of postrevisionist work, see Patrick Finney, *Remembering the Road to World War II* (New York: Routledge, 2011), 188–25. This counterfactual seems to be born on out in the British acceleration and expansion of rearmament in late 1938 and early 1939.

24. CAB 23/96, October 1938.

25. "What Should We Do," FO 371/22659, September 1938.

26. Sarah Wilkinson, "Perceptions of Public Opinion: British Foreign Policy Decisions about Nazi Germany, 1933–1938," Ph.D. diss., University of Oxford, 2000.

27. See "Germany Foreign Policy," PRO, FO 371/19884, January 22, 1936.

28. On the possibility of making Hitler a "good European," see, e.g., PRO PREM 1/330; FO 371/21658.

29. On the unity of British opinion after Munich, see, e.g., Eatwell, "Munich, Public Opinion, and the Popular Front."

30. "Conclusions of a Meeting with a Cabinet Held at 10 Downing Street on Monday, 7 November," CAB 23/96, November 4, 1938 (note the document is dated as November 4, which must be an error).

31. On the voluntary national service campaign, see "Germany and the Return of Colonies," *Times*, January 24, 1939. On expansion of the rearmament effort, see, e.g., Cabinet Meeting 8(39), FO 371/22929, February 22, 1939. For a discussion see Weinberg, *Hitler's Foreign Policy*, 683.

32. *Hansard*, House of Commons Debate, February 6, 1939, vol. 343, col 623.

33. Some scholars argue that the British remained reluctant to form an alliance with the Soviet Union, even through the summer of 1939. See, e.g., Michael Jabara Carley, *1939: The Alliance that Never Was and the Coming of World War II* (Chicago: I. R. Dee, 1999); and Louise G. Shaw, *The British Political Elite and the Soviet Union* (New York: Taylor and Francis, 2007). Certainly part of the reason an alliance was not pursued more fervently was British distrust of Soviet motives. Yet, Nielson and others make a convincing argument that impediments to an Anglo-Soviet alliance rested, not only or even primarily in anti-Bolshevism, but in more mundane quarrels about alliance structure, particularly issues concerning guarantees to the Eastern European states. For a summary of difficulties with the Eastern European states, see "Negotiations between His Majesty's Government and the Soviet Government, March–May 1939," FO 371/23065, May 7, 1939. For an analysis, see Keith Nielson, *Britain, Soviet Russia, and the Collapse of the Versailles Order* (Cambridge: Cambridge University Press, 2006), 315.

34. Phipps to Halifax, quoted in Nielson, *Britain, Soviet Russia, and the Collapse of the Versailles Order*, 262.

35. See ibid., 265.

36. See e.g., Minute, Cab 27(39), CAB 23/99, May 10, 1939.

37. See Williamson Murray, *The Change in the European Balance of Power, 1938–1939* (Princeton: Princeton University Press, 1984). As Steiner states, "The existing balance of power in terms of comparative military strength had moved against Britain and France." Zara Steiner, "British Decisions for Peace and War," in *History and Neorealism*, ed. Ernest May, Richard Rosecrance, and Zara Steiner (Cambridge: Cambridge University Press, 2010), 137.

38. Steiner, *Triumph of the Dark*, 772.

39. As Steiner argues, when debating the merits of confrontation, most elites "did not think of balances; they just assumed that Britain and its empire would prevail." Steiner, *Triumph of the Dark*, 1035.

40. On the shift in public opinion, see Daniel Hucker, *Public Opinion and the End of Appeasement in Britain and France* (Ashgate, UK: Farnham, 2011); Sarah Wilkinson, "Perceptions of Public Opinion," 282–319.

41. For an example of this shift in cabinet discussions, see Halifax, "Cabinet: Committee on Foreign policy," FO 371/21658, November 23, 1938. For a discussion about the lack of strategic thinking in post-Munich Britain, see Steiner, *Triumph of the Dark*, especially 772, 1035; Weinberg, *Hitler's Foreign Policy*, 682–83.

42. Imlay, *Facing the Second World War*, 187.

43. Ibid.

44. See the analysis ibid.; Daniel Hucker, "Public Opinion between Munich and Prague: The View from the French Embassy," *Contemporary British History* 25, no. 3 (2011): 407–27; Wilkinson, "Perception of Public Opinion," 282–319.

45. Sir E. Phipps to Sir John Simon, FO 408/64, January 31, 1934.

46. For an argument about Britain's rational uncertainty about Hitler's intentions, see Layne, "Security Studies and the Use of History."

47. See James D. Morrow, "The Strategic Setting of Choices: Signaling, Commitment, and Negotiation in International Politics," in *Strategic Choice and International Relations*, ed. David A. Lake and Robert Powell (Princeton: Princeton University Press, 1999), 77–104.

48. Yahri-Milo makes this point as well. Yahri-Milo, "In the Eye of the Beholder."

49. As discussed below, German military strength was consistently exaggerated. For example, in terms of air rearmament, of existing planes only about eight hundred were actually combat ready.

50. "The German Danger," April 7, 1936, TNA, FO 371/19889.

51. "What Should We Do?," TNA, FO 371/21659, September 18, 1938.

52. Wilkinson, "Perceptions of Public Opinion," 283.

53. Steiner, *Triumph of the Dark*, 771.

54. As Finney summarizes, these historians argue that "when Hitler proved in March 1939 that he could not be trusted, Chamberlain's policy became one of deterrence and resistance, and his careful handling of affairs through his whole premiership ensured that war came at the best possible conjuncture with the nation united and prepared." Patrick Finney, "The Romance of Decline: the Historiography of Appeasement and British National Identity," *Electronic Journal of International History* 1 (2000), http://sas-space.sas.ac.uk/3385/1/Journal_of_International_History_2000-06_Finney.pdf. Security studies scholars have adopted this timeline as well. Layne, for example, argues that Hitler's real aims remained "shrouded in ambiguity until the period between Munich and Prague," without explaining what costly action revealed Hitler's intentions during that time period. Layne, "Security Studies and the Use of History," 33.

55. See, e.g., Imlay, *Facing the Second World War*, 111.

56. Donald Lammers, "From Whitehall after Munich: The Foreign Office and the Future Course of British Policy," *Historical Journal* 16, no. 4 (winter 1973): 856.

57. Yahri-Milo, "In the Eye of the Beholder"; Yahri-Milo, *Knowing the Adversary: Leaders, Intelligence, and Assessment of Intentions in International Relations* (Princeton: Princeton University Press, 2014).

58. "Herr Hitler's Speech," *Times*, March 9, 1936.

59. Ibid.

60. Ibid.

61. "German Case Stated in London," *Times*, March 20, 1936.

62. "Extract of Speech by Herr Hitler," FO 408/64, January 30, 1934.
63. "Herr Hitler's Speech," *Times*, September 10, 1938.
64. "Extracts from Speeches and Press Interviews with German Foreign Ministers on the Aims of German Foreign Policy," FO 371/19885, February 13, 1936.
65. Ibid.
66. "Herr Hitler's Speech," *Times*, March 9, 1936.
67. Ibid.
68. "Peace Not Gestures: Herr Hitler's Speech," *Times*, March 28, 1936.
69. General von Blomburg, FO 371/19885, March 17, 1935.
70. "Herr Hitler's Speech," *Times*, March 9, 1936.
71. "Anglo German Relations," TNA, FO 371/21659, November 25, 1938.
72. "Herr Hitler's Speech," *Times*, September 13, 1938.
73. In Hungary there were disputes as to how close to draw to Hitler, not surprisingly between more moderate factions and right-wing revisionists. See Thomas L. Sackmyster, "Hungary and the Munich Crisis: The Revisionist's Dilemma," *Slavic Review* 32, no. 4 (December 1973): 725–40.
74. For comparisons of Hitler to Bismarck, see, e.g., FO 371/18844, May 30, 1935.
75. Tooze, *Wages of Destruction*, 273.
76. This relies on a qualitative analysis of "legitimating phrases" in thirteen speeches after Munich (five by Hitler and eight by other high-ranking Nazi officials) and articles from German papers that were translated and recorded in the Foreign Office. See FO 371/21658 and FO 371/21659. Steiner goes further, arguing that "Hitler had abandoned his lip-service to self-determination, and made clear his intention to challenge whatever restraints still existed to the fulfillment of his ambitions in the east. Steiner, *Triumph of the Dark*, 752. See also Weinberg, *Hitler's Foreign Policy, 1933–1939*, 632–27.
77. For reporting and analysis of Hitler's speech, see Foreign Office Memorandum, "Anglo-German Relations," FO 371/21659, November 23, 1938.
78. "Text of Chancellor Hitler's Speech at Saarbruecken," *New York Times*, October 9, 1938.
79. "Herr Hitler on Democracy," *Times*, November 9, 1938.
80. "Herr Hitler's Speech," *Times*, April 3, 1939.
81. "Herr Hitler on Democracy," *Times*, November 9, 1938.
82. "Relations with Germany," *Times*, October 27, 1938.
83. Sir G. Olgive-Forbes, "Anglo-German Relations," TNA, FO 371/21659, November 23, 1938.
84. Speech at Weimar. For general British reactions to Hitler's speeches after Munich, see TNA, FO 371/21659, the discussion in "Anglo-German Relations: Recent Anti-British Statements," November 23, 1938.
85. Henderson to Halifax, TNA, FO 371/21658, October 24, 1938.
86. Weinberg, *Hitler's Foreign Policy*.
87. "Herr Hitler's Speech," *New York Times*, January 31, 1939.
88. "Anglo-German Relations," November 25, 1938.
89. Ibid.
90. Hitler's speech at Weimar can be accessed at http://www.humanitas-international.org/showcase/chronography/speeches/1938-11-06.html. For reporting of the speech at the Foreign Office and analysis of Hitler's rhetoric, see Foreign Office Memorandum, "Anglo-German Relations," FO 371/22659, November 25, 1938.
91. "Anglo-German Relations," TNA, FO 371/21659, November 25, 1938.
92. Ibid.
93. Steiner, *Triumph of the Dark*; Tooze, *Wages of Destruction*, 302.
94. Tooze, *Wages of Destruction*, 268.
95. Ibid., 286.
96. Weinberg, "Munich after 50 Years," *Foreign Affairs* 67, no. 1 (1988): 170.
97. Quoted in Tooze, *Wages of Destruction*, 287.
98. Ibid., 300. Steiner, *Triumph of the Dark*.
99. Quoted in Steiner, *Triumph of the Dark*, 673.

100. Recent historical accounts, such as Steiner's and Nielson's, talk about Britain's commitment to the League as shaping "mental maps" or "frames of reference" through which Hitler's and other German politician's rhetoric was interpreted. Much like the analysis here, these interpretations seem largely shaped by institutional arrangements, although both Nielson and Steiner tend to use the language of individual psychology rather than institutional position. I posit that the institutional explanation is better able to explain why most British politicians read Germany's legitimation strategies as binding—one would assume that, if this were purely an individual-level phenomenon, there would be far more variation in how elites interpreted Germany's claims. See Steiner, *Triumph of the Dark;* Keith Nielson, *Britain, Soviet Russia, and the Collapse of the Versailles Order.*

101. Steiner, *Triumph of the Dark,* xv.

102. Steiner, *The Lights that Failed: European International History 1919–1933* (Oxford: Oxford University Press, 2007) provides a sweeping discussion of the creation and dissolution of the Versailles order.

103. Steiner, *The Lights that Failed,* 565–601.

104. For a discussion of Britain's perception of itself as mediator, see M. L. Roi and Brian McKercher, "'Ideal' and 'Punch-Bag': Conflicting Views of the Balance of Power and Their Influence on Interwar British Foreign Policy," *Diplomacy and Statecraft* 12, no. 2 (2001): 38; "Disarmament and Future British Foreign Policy," FO 371/18527, June 13, 1934; "Tendencies at Geneva," FO 371/21243, October 21, 1937; Lord Cranborne, "Applications of Principles of Covenant of League of Nations," FO 371/21243, September 11, 1937.

105. Sir Eric Phipps, "Security Problems," FO 371/19884, February 11, 1936.

106. See Nielson, *Britain, Soviet Russia, and the Collapse of Versailles.*

107. Joseph Charles Heim, "Liberalism and the Establishment of Collective Security in British Foreign Policy: The Alexander Prize Essay," *Transactions of the Royal Historical Society* 5 (1995): 91–110; Nielson, *Britain, Soviet Russia, and the Collapse of the Versailles Order*; G. Bruce Strang, "The Spirit of Ulysses? Ideology and British Appeasement in the 1930s," *Diplomacy and Statecraft* 19 (2008): 481–526.

108. William Strang, "Possible Future Course of British Policy," TNA, FO 371/21569, October 10, 1938.

109. See Steiner, *Triumph of the Dark,* 106.

110. Quoted ibid.

111. Foreign Office to Ogilvie-Forbes, "Anglo-German Relations," FO 371/21658, November 23, 1938. Olgivie-Forbes to Halifax, "German Press Comments on British Rearmament," FO 371/21658, October 24, 1938. See also "German Press Comments on Prime Minister's Speech and German Press Attack on Mr. Greenwood," FO 371/21658, November 4, 1938. "German Press Comments on British Press reaction to German Chancellor's Speech," FO 371/21658, November 7, 1938; "Anglo-German Relations," FO 371/21659, November 25, 1938.

112. Halifax, "Cabinet: Committee on Foreign policy," FO 371/21658, November 23, 1938.

113. Minute by William Strang, "Anglo-German relations," FO 371/21659, December 3, 1938.

114. "Meeting of the Cabinet to be Held at No. 10, Downing Street," CAB 23/81, March 20, 1935.

115. Sargent and Wigram, *Documents in British Foreign Policy,* 2, 15.

116. Foreign Office Minute, "Anglo-German Naval Conversations," FO 371/18735, June 12, 1935.

117. Weinberg, *Hitler's Foreign Policy,* 336.

118. "German Foreign Policy," FO 371/19884.

119. William Strang (in response to memorandum from Henderson), "Anglo-German Relations," FO 371/20736, July 20, 1937.

120. *Lord Lothian Papers,* GD 40/17/445/47. Quoted ibid. Emphasis added.

121. Quoted in Parker, *Chamberlain and Appeasement,* 169.

122. Letter from Halifax to Henderson, Henderson papers, FO 800/269, March 19, 1938.

123. Henderson to Halifax, Prem 1/330, April 1938. Emphasis added.

124. Eden himself, however, remained suspicious of sanctions in this case.

125. Quoted in Adam Roberts, *The Holy Fox: the Life of Lord Halifax* (London: Weidenfeld and Nicholson, 1991), 116.

126. Steiner, "British Decisions for Peace and War," 136.

127. See, e.g., Wilkinson, "Perceptions of Public Opinion," 277.

128. Quoted in Lammers, "From Whitehall after Munich," 838. As Lammers notes, these collections of memos were sent to Halifax who, although was suspicious of Hitler, was still willing to pursue appeasement if it allowed Britain to avoid war.

129. "Meeting of the Cabinet to Be Held at No. 10 Downing Street, S.W.!, on Monday 31st October, 1938," CAB 23/96, October 31, 1938. See also "Joint Declaration between German Chancellor and Prime Minister," FO 371/21658, October 4, 1938, "Interview between Mr. Chamberlain and Dr. Seibert," FO 371/21658. While the House of Commons debate on October 3 and 6 had been more contentious than Chamberlain had hoped, he left the debate convinced of the continuing support for appeasement.

130. Cadogan "Possible Future Course of British Policy," FO 371/22659, October 14, 1938.

131. "Two Memorandum Communicated to the Foreign Office by Prominent Germanophiles," FO 371/22961, January 1939.

132. Ibid.

133. Discussions of British grand strategy in the Foreign Office after Munich are outlined in "Possible Future Course of British Policy," FO 371/22659, October 1938, and contain memoranda from Cadogan, Collier, and Strang, among others. For an analysis, see Lammers, "From Whitehall After Munich." Cabinet discussions are outlined in "Cabinet: Committee on Foreign policy," FO 371/21658, November 23, 1938.

134. Steiner, *Triumph of the Dark*, 766.

135. Collier to Cadogan, "Possible Future Course of British Policy," TNA, FO 371/21659, October 29, 1938.

136. Parker, *Churchill and Appeasement*, 32.

137. Ibid., 96.

138. Wigram, note on "Disarmament and Future British Foreign Policy," FO 371/18527, May 23, 1934.

139. Robert Vansittart, PRO, FO 371/19852/C 1906, March 22, 1936.

140. Vansittart "Reorientation of the Air Defense System," (attached note to "Germany's Return to the League of Nations"), FO 18/18848, July 19, 1935.

141. Most of the calls for an alliance with the Soviet Union came from the Northern Office, those officials charged with analyzing relations with the Soviet Union. While the Northern Office was deeply suspicious of Stalin's motives, the office's close work with the Soviet Union made them more likely to see opportunities for cooperation in the face of the German threat.

142. The following discussion draws from Foreign Office Memorandum, "Herr Hitler's Reichstag Speech of 21 May, 1935." FO 371/18844, May 30, 1935.

143. Note by Wigram ibid.

144. "Extracts from Speeches and Press Interviews with German Foreign Ministers on the Aims of German Foreign Policy," FO 371/19885, February 13, 1936.

145. "Anglo-German Naval Conversations," Minute by R. Vansittart, FO 371/18735, June 12, 1935.

146. Note by Vansittart in "Herr Hitler's Reichstag Speech of 21 May 1935." FO 371/18844, May 30, 1935.

147. Quoted in Parker, *Churchill and Appeasement*, 78.

148. Foreign Office Memorandum, "Regional Pacts and the Extent to which the United Kingdom Should Participate," (note by Vansittart), FO 371/19910, July 8, 1936.

149. Ibid.

150. Quoted in Thompson, *The Anti-Appeasers*, 49.

151. Parker, *Churchill and Appeasement*, 94.

152. Minute by Ralph Wigram, FO 371/19910, July 8, 1936.

153. The discussion below draws primarily from the exchange found in "Possible Future Course of British Policy," FO 371/21659, October 1938.

154. Phipps, "Relations with Germany: Mr. Duff Cooper's Lecture on International Affairs in Paris on 7th December," FO 371/22659 December 8, 1938.

155. Imlay, *Facing the Second World War*, 197.

156. See, e.g., ibid., 196, 198.

157. The discussion in this paragraph draws from Steiner, *Triumph of the Dark*, 766.

158. Ibid.

159. Bodleian, Conservative Party Archive, CRD 1/737, Clarke to Director, 26 January 1939, with attached note: the Election Programme. Quoted in Imlay, *Facing the Second World War*, 196.

160. Lord Halifax in "Record of the Foreign Office of an Anglo-French Conversation," FO 371/20736, December 1, 1937.

161. "Czechoslovakia Crisis," September 14, 1938, FO 371/21738.

162. Henderson to Halifax, FO 371/21743, April 7, 1938.

163. Quoted in Parker, *Chamberlain and Appeasement*, 273.

164. "Text of Chancellor Hitler's Speech at Saarbruecken," *New York Times*, October 9, 1938.

165. Text of Hitler's speech at Weimar reprinted in "Hitler Assails 'War Agitators,' Calls on World to Disarm Them," *New York Times*, November 7, 1938.

166. *Times*, "Herr Hitler on Democracy," November 9, 1938.

167. Ibid.

168. Ibid. German politicians, for example, constantly attacked British policy in Palestine as violent and flagrantly undemocratic.

169. "Foreign Office Minute: Tendencies at Geneva," minute by Lord Cranborne, FO 371/21243, October 21, 1937.

170. Collier to Cadogan, "Possible Future Course of British Policy," TNA, FO 371/21569, October 10, 1938.

171. Ibid.

172. "Text of Address by Winston Churchill Replying to Chancellor Hitler: Prospects Would Be Different," *New York Times*, October 17, 1938.

173. "Mr. Churchill and Germany," *Times*, November 26, 1938.

174. Steiner, *Triumph of the Dark*, 1033.

175. Ibid., 1035.

6. Japan's Folly

1. On Manchuria, see for example, Yoshihisa Tak Matsusaka, *The Making of Japanese Manchuria, 1904–1932* (Cambridge: Harvard University Press, 2001); Ian Nish, *Japan's Struggle with Internationalism: Japan, China, and the League of Nations, 1931–33* (London: Kegan Paul International, 1993); Sandra Wilson, *The Manchurian Crisis and Japanese Society, 1931–1933* (London: Routledge, 2002); Wilson, "Containing the Crisis: Japan's Diplomatic Offensive in the West, 1931–33," *Modern Asian Studies* 29, no. 2 (May 1995): 355–58; Sadako N. Ogata, *Defiance in Manchuria: The Making of Japanese Foreign Policy, 1931–1932* (Berkeley: University of California Press, 1984); Louise Young, *Japan's Total Empire: Manchuria and the Culture of Wartime Imperialism* (Berkeley: University of California Press, 1998); Richard N. Currant, "The Stimson Doctrine and the Hoover Doctrine," *American Historical Review* 59, no. 3 (1954): 513–42.

2. Wilson, *The Manchurian Crisis*, 2. Some scholars have placed the "tipping point" of U.S.-Japanese relations later, from 1937 to 1940. See, e.g., Charles Kupchan, *Vulnerability of Empire* (Ithaca: Cornell University Press, 1994). Some historians see larger processes, such as capitalist and imperialist competition or domestic processes as driving containment, though still mark the Manchurian crisis as the critical moment in U.S.-Japanese relations. Walter LaFeber, *The Clash: U.S.-Japanese Relations throughout History* (New York: W. W. Norton, 1997), esp. 160–81; W. G. Beasely, *Japanese Imperialism* (New York: Oxford, 1987), esp. 174–97. See, e.g., Nish, *Struggle for Internationalism*; Wilson, *The Manchurian Crisis*; Harry Wray, "Japanese-American Relations and Perceptions, 1900–1940," in *Pearl Harbor Reexamined: Prologue to the Pacific War*, edited

by Hilary Conroy and Harry Wray (Honolulu: University of Hawaii Press, 1990), 1–16; Ogata, *Defiance in Manchuria.*

3. Ian Nish, *Japan's Struggle for Internationalism: Japan, China, and the League of Nations 1931–1933* (New York: Kegan Paul, 2000), viii. Nish argues that this shift also occurs in Britain, although more slowly and reluctantly than in the United States. See also Christopher Thorne, *The Limits of Foreign Policy: the West, the League and the Far Eastern Crisis of 1931–1933* (London: Hamish Hamilton, 1972), 202–72. For a discussion of disagreements between the United States and Great Britain over how to respond to the crisis, see Keith Neilson, "Perception and Posture in Anglo-American Relations: The Legacy of the Simon-Stimson Affair, 1932–1941," *International History Review* 29, no. 2 (2007): 313–37.

4. Henry Stimson, *The Far Eastern Crisis* (New York: Harper and Bros, 1936), 82; Currant, "The Stimson Doctrine and the Hoover Doctrine."

5. The Secretary of State to the Ambassador in Japan (Forbes), January 7, 1932, in *Foreign Relations of the United States* (hereafter *FRUS*), Japan, 1931–1941, vol. 1, 76.

6. See for example Jack L. Snyder, *Myths of Empire: Domestic Politics and International Ambition* (Ithaca: Cornell University Press, 1991); Nish, *Struggle with Internationalism*; Nish, *Japanese Foreign Policy in the Interwar Period* (Westport: Praeger, 2002); Frederick Dickinson, *War and National Reinvention: Japan in the Great War, 1914–1919* (Cambridge: Harvard University Press, 1999).

7. See, e.g., Michael R. Auslin, *Negotiating with Imperialism: The Unequal Treaties and the Culture of Japanese Diplomacy* (Cambridge: Harvard University Press, 2006).

8. Japan turned to Prussia, for example, as a model for its army organization, and Britain for the navy. See LaFeber, *The Clash*, 35.

9. Ibid., 23–24.

10. Akira Iriye, *After Imperialism: The Search for a New Order in the Far East, 1921–1931* (Cambridge: Harvard University Press, 1965), 6.

11. LaFeber, *The Clash*, 44.

12. See, e.g., Beasley, *Japanese Imperialism*, 187. See also Matsusaka, *The Making of Japanese Imperialism*; Wray, "Japanese-American Relations," 9; Iriye, *After Imperialism*, 160.

13. Matsusaka, *The Making of Japanese Imperialism*, 248.

14. For the development of the SMR, see Ramon H. Myers, "Japanese Imperialism in Manchuria: The South Manchurian Railway Company, 1906–1933', in *Japanese Informal Empire in China, 1895–1937,* edited by Peter Duus, Ramon H. Myers and Mark R. Peattie (Princeton: Princeton University Press, 1989), 101–32.

15. Wilson Roger Louis, *British Strategy in the Far East 1919–1939* (Oxford, Clarendon Press, 1971), 175.

16. Wilson, *The Manchurian Crisis*, 15.

17. For a discussion of Japan's imperialism and work with collaborators in the 1920s, see especially Matsusaka, *Making of Manchuria*, 312–48. On imperial collaborators, see MacDonald, *Networks of Domination*.

18. Beasley, *Japanese Imperialism*, 187.

19. *The Diaries of Henry Lewis Stimson* (hereafter, *Stimson Diaries*), Manuscripts and Archives, Yale University Library, New Haven, Connecticut, October 8, 1931.

20. Ogata, *Defiance in Manchuria,* 144.

21. Mearsheimer, for example, argues that U.S. policy toward Japan was nothing more than buckpassing. See *The Tragedy of Great Power Politics* (New York: W.W. Norton, 2001).

22. See, e.g., Norman A. Graebner, "Hoover, Roosevelt, and the Japanese," in *Pearl Harbor as History*, ed. Dorothy Borg and Shumpei Okamtoto (New York: Columbia University Press, 1973), 28.

23. Ibid., 30. For discussions on threats about strengthening the U.S. naval presence, see James B. Crowley, *Japan's Quest for Autonomy: National Security and Foreign Policy, 1930–1938* (Princeton: Princeton University Press, 1966), 165; Richard N. Current, "The Stimson Doctrine and the Hoover Doctrine," *The American Historical Review* 59, no. 3 (1954): 513–42.

24. For the reaction of American policymakers, see, e.g., Graebner, "Hoover, Roosevelt, and the Japanese"; Current, "The Stimson Doctrine and the Hoover Doctrine"; Nish, *Struggle with Internationalism,* 66; Wilson, *The Manchurian Crisis,* 84–85.

25. Graebner, "Hoover, Roosevelt, and the Japanese," 32.

26. *Stimson Diaries,* January 26, 1932.

27. Thorne, *Limits of Foreign Policy,* 212.

28. Wright, "The Stimson Note of January 7, 1932," *American Journal of International Law* 26, no. 2 (April 1932): 342.

29. See Crowley, *Japan's Quest for Autonomy,* 165; Current, "The Stimson Doctrine and the Hoover Doctrine," 526–27.

30. "The Secretary of State to the Ambassador in Japan (Grew)," *FRUS, Japan,* vol. 1, January 18, 1933.

31. *Stimson Diaries,* January 3, 1933.

32. LaFeber, *The Clash,* 177.

33. Ogata, *Defiance in Manchuria,* 144.

34. "China's Claim Is Upheld: Return of the 3 Provinces Is Urged, with Autonomy under Nanking," *New York Times,* October 3, 1932.

35. See, e.g., Banno Junji, "Diplomatic Misunderstanding and the Escalation of the Manchurian Incident," *Annals of the Institute of Social Science* (University of Tokyo) 27 (1985): 100–24; Nish, *Struggle with Internationalism,* chapter 3; Wray, "Japanese-American Relations," 11.

36. Ambassador Forbes to Secretary Stimson, Tokyo, *FRUS, Japan,* vol. 1, February 27, 1932.

37. Quoted in John A. S. Grenville, *History of the World from the 20th to the 21st Century* (New York: Routledge, 2005), 207.

38. "Matsuoka Regards U.S. as Capricious," *New York Times,* February 26, 1933.

39. For example, LaFeber argues that United States-Japanese relations were doomed to become a "clash of two capitalisms:" "The United States was determined to push for an open Japan and, beyond that, an open Asia. The Japanese were determined to break free of Western constraints and exert maximum control over their foreign relations." LaFeber, *The Clash,* 396–97.

40. See, e.g. Mearsheimer, *Tragedy of Great Power Politics,* 172–81. Likewise, James Crowley argues that the pursuit of national security drove much of Japan's policy through the 1930s, including the Manchurian crisis. See Crowley, *Japan's Quest for Autonomy: National Security and Foreign Policy, 1930–1938* (Princeton: Princeton University Press, 1966).

41. See, e.g., LaFeber, *The Clash,* 112.

42. See Burton F. Beers, "Robert Lansing's Proposed Bargain with Japan," *Pacific Historical Review* 26, no. 4 (November 1957): 391–400; Sadao Asada, "Japan's 'Special Interests' and the Washington Conference," *American Historical Review* 67, no. 1 (October 1961): 62–70.

43. Asada notes that some scholars, such as A. Whitney Griswold, have characterized the Nine-Power Treaty as "the most dynamic and the most comprehensive attempt" to roll back Japan's expansion; Griswold, *Far Eastern Policy of the United States* (New Haven: Yale University Press, 1972), 331. See also Ikuhiku Hata, "Continental Expansion, 1905–1941," trans. Alvin D. Coox, in *Cambridge History of Japan* (Cambridge: Cambridge University Press, 1988), 271–314. As Asada argues, archival evidence suggests that neither side saw the Washington system as one of rollback.

44. Quoted in W. G. Beasley, *Japanese Imperialism, 1894–1945,* 100. See also Michael Hunt, *Frontier Defense and the Open Door, 1895–1911* (New Haven: Yale University Press, 1973), 221.

45. Hornbeck memo, undated, "The Case for Japan in Manchuria," Hornbeck Papers, Hoover Institution Archive, Stanford University, Box 242.

46. *Stimson Diaries,* March 8, 1932.

47. Quoted in Graebner, "Hoover, Roosevelt, and the Japanese," 34.

48. Stanley Hornbeck, *Contemporary Politics in the Far East* (New York: D. Appleton, 1919), 351. For a discussion, see Richard Dean Burns, "Stanley K. Hornbeck: The Diplomacy of the Open Door," in *Diplomats in Crisis,* ed. Richard D. Burns and Edward M. Bennett (Santa Barbara, CA: Clio Press, 1974), 97.

49. Stimson, *Far Eastern Crisis,* 34–37.

50. Memo by Hornbeck, May 17, 1929, State Department Archives, National Archives, 893.00/9970.

51. Wilson, "Containing the Crisis," 355.
52. Journal of William Cameron Forbes, vol. 8, December 3, 1931; 2 (p. 4), Speeches and Articles, Forbes Papers, Houghton Library.
53. Quoted in Thorne, *Limits of Foreign Policy*, 139.
54. "Friendly and Impartial," *New York Times*, October 14, 1931.
55. For a discussion of the impact of Shanghai, see Thorne, *Limits of Foreign Policy*, 210–25; Nish, *Japan's Struggle with Internationalism*, 90.
56. "Back to Manchuria," *New York Times*, April 17, 1932.
57. On Japan's domestic politics, see Richard D. Burns and Edward M. Bennett, eds., *Diplomats in Crisis* (Santa Barbara, CA: Clio Press, 1974); Ogata, *Defiance in Manchuria*; Nish, *Japanese Foreign Policy*; Matsusaka, *The Making of Japanese Manchuria*; Wilson, *The Manchurian Crisis*.
58. Wilson, *The Manchurian Crisis*, 5.
59. See ibid., 84–85. Banno, "Diplomatic Misunderstanding."
60. Shigeki Mori, "The Washington System and Its Aftermath: Reevaluating after Imperialism from the Perspective of the Japanese Historiography," *International Journal of Asian Studies* 3, no. 2 (2006): 268n19.
61. "Memorandum by the Secretary of State," September 22, 1931, in *FRUS, Japan*, vol. 1, 7.
62. "The Secretary of State to the Minister in China," ibid., September 24, 1931.
63. *Stimson Diaries*, September 23, 1931.
64. See, e.g., LaFeber, *The Clash*, chapter 2.
65. Conroy, "Government versus 'Patriot': The Background of Japan's Asiatic Expansion," *Pacific Historical Review* 20, no. 1 (February 1951): 38n13, 42.
66. Ibid., 31–32.
67. Iriye, *After Imperialism*, 6.
68. Quoted in Hilary Conroy, *Japanese Seizure of Korea, 1868–1910* (Philadelphia: University of Pennsylvania Press, 1960), 350.
69. See, e.g., Dickinson, *War and National Reinvention*, chapter 4; Iriye, *After Imperialism*, 20.
70. Quoted in Dickinson, *War and National Reinvention*, 221.
71. Asada, "Between the Old Diplomacy and the New," 85.
72. Quoted in Dickinson, *War and National Reinvention*, 225.
73. Conroy, "Government versus 'Patriot,' " 42.
74. Iriye, *After Imperialism*, 186.
75. Wilson gives an extensive overview of these rhetorical themes in Manchuria. See Wilson, *The Manchurian Crisis*, 55–70.
76. "The Japanese Embassy to the Department of State," September 24, 1931. *FRUS, Japan*, vol. 1, 11.
77. Westel W. Willoughby, *The Sino-Japanese Controversy and the League of Nations* (Baltimore: Johns Hopkins Press, 1935), 52–53.
78. Wilson, "Containing the Crisis," 56.
79. Nish, *Struggle with Internationalism*, 55.
80. "The Ambassador in Japan (Forbes) to the Secretary of State," *FRUS, Japan*, vol. 1, January 16, 1932.
81. Ibid.
82. Stimson, *The Far Eastern Crisis*, 107.
83. See, e.g., Nish, *Struggle with Internationalism*, chapter 12.
84. "The Address of Count Uchida, Minister for Foreign Affairs, at the 64th Session of the Imperial Diet, January 21st, 1933." Quoted in Rustin B. Gates, "Pan-Asianism in Prewar Japanese Foreign Affairs: The Curious Case of Uchida Yasuya," *Journal of Japanese Studies* 37, no. 1 (2011): 1–27.
85. Quoted in Usui Katsumi, "The Role of the Foreign Ministry," in *Pearl Harbor as History*, 136.
86. *Manchurian Daily News*, February 1, 1933. Quoted in Nish, *Japan's Struggle with Internationalism*, 201.
87. "Text of Uchida's Speech: Japan Bids League not to Interfere," *New York Times*, August 25, 1932.
88. Ibid.
89. Question of Mori Kaku at the 62rd Session of the Diet, August 25, 1932. Quoted in Ogata, *Defiance in Manchuria*, 60.

90. K. K. Kawakami, *Manchukuo: Child of Conflict* (New York: MacMillan, 1933), v–vi.

91. Iriye, "The Role of the U.S. Embassy in Tokyo," in *Pearl Harbor as History*, 108.

92. "Matsuoka Claims for Japan a 'World Spiritual Mission": Tokyo's Envoy at Geneva Declares the Advance of His Country into Manchuria May Mean Regeneration in the Far East," *New York Times*, January 8, 1933. See also Barbara Teters, "Matsuoka Yosuke: The Diplomacy of Bluff and Gesture," in *Diplomats in Crisis*, 284.

93. Graebner, "Hoover, Roosevelt, and the Japanese," 25. Emphasis added.

94. See Andrew Kydd, "Sheep in Sheep's Clothing," Why Security Seekers Do Not Fight Each Other," Security Studies 7, no. 1 (1997): 147–48.

95. Iriye, 'Introduction,' in James William Moreley, ed., *Japan Erupts: The London Naval Conference and the Manchurian Incident, 1928–1932* (New York: Columbia University Press, 1984), 236.

96. Nish, *Struggle with Internationalism*, 74; See also Wilson, *The Manchurian Crisis*, 5.

97. Matusaka, *The Making of Japanese Manchuria*, 385.

98. Wilson, *The Manchurian Crisis*, chapter 4.

99. Jennifer Mitzen and Randall Schweller, "Knowing the Unknown Unknowns: Misplaced Certainty and the Onset of War," *Security Studies* 20, no. 1 (2011): 2–35.

100. Wray, "Japanese-American Relations," 8.

101. Wilson, "Containing the Crisis," 333.

102. See "Matsuoka Finds Us Inconsistent in Entangling Ourselves in the Far East," *New York Times*, April 2, 1933.

103. On the "new diplomacy," see Asada, "Between the Old Diplomacy and the New"; Nish, *Japan's Struggle with Internationalism*, introduction.

104. Quoted in Asada, "Between the Old Diplomacy and the New," 89.

105. Quoted in Dickinson, *War and National Reinvention*, 237.

106. Conroy, "Government versus 'Patriot' "; Iriye, *After Imperialism*, 6.

107. Historians warn that it is inappropriate to see "expansionists" and "internationalists" as entirely opposed. See, e.g., Sidney De Vere Brown, "Shidehara Kijuro," in *Diplomats in Crisis*, edited by Richard Dean Burns and Edward M. Bennett (Santa Barbara, CA: ABC-CLIO, 1974), 213; Iriye, *After Imperialism*, 143, 169.

108. Conroy, "Government versus 'Patriot,' " 39.

109. Nish, *Japanese Foreign Policy in the Interwar Period*, 21.

110. Quoted in Dickinson, *War and Reinvention*, 225.

111. Snyder, *Myths of Empire*.

112. Matsusaka, *The Making of Japanese Manchuria*, 379.

113. On the military's public relations campaign, see Matsusaka, *The Making of Japanese Manchuria*, 378; Wilson, *The Manchurian Crisis*, chapter 3.

114. Matsusaka, *The Making of Japanese Manchuria*, 121.

115. Nish, *Struggle with Internationalism*, 36.

116. Matsusaka, *The Making of Japanese Manchuria*, 374.

117. Crowley, *Japan's Quest for Autonomy*, 137; on accusations of treason, see Wilson, *The Manchurian Crisis*, 85.

118. *Diplomats in Crisis*, 221.

119. Nish, *Struggle with Internationalism*, 76.

120. For an overview of the United States attempt to build a "new order" in the Asia-Pacific, and the importance of Japan as a partner, see, e.g., Iriye, *After Imperialism*; Sadao, "Between the Old Diplomacy and the New."

121. Iriye, *After Imperialism*, 14, 22.

122. Ibid., 20.

123. Hence, Stimson made clear that observance of the Nine Power Treaty was deeply tied to continued disarmament in the Pacific. See Stimson, "Letter to Senator Borah, Committee on Foreign Relations," February 23, 1932, text printed in Stimson, *The Far Eastern Crisis*, 166–67.

124. Stanley K. Hornbeck, "Principles and Policies in Regard to China," *Foreign Affairs* 1, no. 2 (December 15, 1922): 135.

125. "Treaties Embody 'New State of Mind," *New York Times*, February 11, 1922.

126. *Stimson Diaries*, "The Essential Role of the Far Eastern Treaty Structure."

127. Ibid., October 8, 1931. For a discussion, see Current, "Hoover Doctrine and Stimson Doctrine," 517.
128. "Harding's Prestige Grows as Leader," *New York Times*, March 25, 1922.
129. "Practical Idealism by Treaty," *New York Times*, March 30, 1922.
130. Iriye, *After Imperialism*, Chapter 2.
131. Stimson, *The Far Eastern Crisis*, 56.
132. "The Secretary of State to the Minister in Switzerland (Wilson)," *FRUS, Japan*, vol. 1.
133. Hornbeck, "The Case for Japan in Manchuria."
134. Joseph Grew, *Ten Years in Japan: a Contemporary Record Drawn From the Diaries and Private and Official Papers of Joseph G. Grew, United States Ambassador to Japan, 1932–1942* (New York: Simon and Schuster, 1944), 30.
135. "The Acting Secretary of State to the Minister in China (Johnson)," August 17, 1932, *FRUS, Japan*, vol. 1, 101.
136. See, e.g., "The Japanese Embassy to the United States," *FRUS, Japan*, vol. 1, September 21, 1931; see also "Mukden and Nanking," *New York Times*, December 18, 1931.
137. Grew, *Ten Years in Japan*, 30.
138. "Memorandum by the Secretary of State," *FRUS, Japan*, vol. 1.
139. "Both in the Wrong," *New York Times*, 1/19/32.
140. As Thorne argues, most officials saw Manchuria as central to Japan's national interests, and argued that Japan would, like "any nation when faced with intolerable disorder, to take some measures to cure them." Thorne, *Limits of Foreign Policy*, 195.
141. See, e.g., Castle diary, September 29, 1931. In William R. Castle diaries, 1918–1960, holdings in Houghton Library, Harvard University. For a discussion, see Iriye, *After Imperialism*, 300; Thorne, *Limits of Foreign Policy*, 156.
142. On the general role of "Western" justifications in Japan's rise to power, see Conroy, "Government versus 'Patriot,'" 31–42. On Japan's use of Wilson's "new diplomacy" after World War I, see, e.g., Asada, "Between the Old Diplomacy and the New"; Iriye, *After Imperialism*, 6; Dickinson, *War and National Reinvention*, 224; Nish, *Japan's Struggle with Internationalism*.
143. John Gittings, "'Rules of the Game,' review of Christopher Thorne, *Limits of Foreign Policy*," *New York Review of Books* 20, no. 8, (May 17, 1973): 10.
144. Wilson, "Japan's Diplomatic Offensive," 365.
145. MacMurray, "Developments Affecting American Policy in the Far East," November 1935, John Van Antwerp MacMurray Papers, Princeton University.
146. Grew, *Ten Years in Japan*, 14. Emphasis added.
147. Papers of United States diplomat and author, Joseph Clark Grew, August 27, 1932, vol. 58, 198, Diary, Houghten Library, Harvard University. For a discussion, see Wilson, "Containing the Crisis," 363.
148. This discussion is based on an analysis of fifty-nine op-eds published in the *New York Times* from the onset of the crisis in September 1931 to April of 1933.
149. "Friendly and Impartial," *New York Times*, October 14, 1931.
150. Quoted in Wilson, "Containing the Crisis," 360.
151. James Shotwell, "Peace Machinery," *New York Times*, March 20, 1932.
152. See e.g., "Memorandum by the Secretary of State," *FRUS, Japan*, vol. 1, October 12, 1931.
153. Hornbeck, "Memorandum on the Manchurian situation, Department of State," December 5, 1931, printed in *The Diplomacy of Frustration: The Manchurian Crisis of 1931–1939 as Revealed in the Papers of Stanley K. Hornbeck*, compiled by Justus D. Doenecke (Stanford: Hoover Institution Press, 1981), doc. no. 19, 91.
154. Hornbeck, Memo "Manchuria Situation: United States and Japan: Conflict of Policies: Japan's 'Monroe Doctrine for Asia,'" January 14, 1932, printed in *Diplomacy of Frustration*, doc. no. 28, 126–28.
155. Walter Lippmann, *Interpretations* (New York: MacMillan, 1932): 191–92. For a discussion, see LaFeber, *The Clash*, 170.
156. Quoted in Edward M. Bennett, "The Diplomacy of Pacification," in *Diplomats in Crisis*, 74. The perception that Japan could no longer be bound by treaty only increased in the late 1930s. As Grew noted in 1937, "Plenty of machinery existed . . . to prevent aggression—the Kellogg Pact, the League Covenant, and the Nine and Four Power treaties, but Japan had disregarded them all."

157. Quoted in LaFeber, *The Clash,* 111.
158. Quoted ibid., 136.
159. Quoted in Burns, "Stanley K. Hornbeck," 97.
160. Ibid., 103.
161. Hornbeck, Memorandum on the Manchuria Situation, December 5, 1931, printed in *Diplomacy of Frustration*, doc. no. 91.
162. Alfred L. Castle, *Diplomatic Realism: William R. Castle, Jr., and American Foreign Policy, 1919–1953*, ed. Michael E. MacMillan (Honolulu: University of Hawaii Press, 1997), 74.
163. Quoted in Iriye, *After Imperialism*, 300.
164. See, e.g., Wilson, "Containing the Crisis," 361.
165. Castle, *Diplomatic Realism,* 85.
166. W. Cameron Forbes, "American Policy in the Far East," *Proceedings from the American Academy of Arts and Sciences* 73, no. 2 (1944): 5–28.
167. Quoted in Thorne, *Limits of Foreign Policy,* 348.
168. Hornbeck, "Memorandum on Manchuria and Geneva," October 25, 1931, printed in *Diplomacy of Frustration*, 80.
169. As Thorne argues, no one in the Hoover administration saw vital U.S. interests at stake. Thorne, *Limits of Foreign Policy,* 163.
170. See e.g., Steven Ward, "Race, Status, and Japanese Revisionism in the Early 1930s," *Security Studies* 22, no. 4 (2014): 607–39.
171. This specific quote comes from the British Foreign Office. See Minute by Alston, TNA, FO 371/2323, April 3, 1915.
172. Grew's report of May 11, 1933. Quoted in Graebner, "Hoover, Roosevelt, and the Japanese," 33.
173. Ibid.
174. Quoted in Dickinson, *War and National Reinvention,* 205.
175. Quoted in LeFeber, *The Clash*, 50.
176. See Iriye, *After Imperialism,* 25–26; Asada, "Between the Old Diplomacy and the New," 84–105.
177. See, e.g. Wilson, "Containing the Crisis," 355–58; Current, "The Stimson Doctrine and the Hoover Doctrine," 515.
178. Stimson, *Far Eastern Crisis,* 36.
179. Hornbeck, "The Case for Japan in Manchuria," quoted in Shizhang Hu, *Stanley K. Hornbeck and the Open Door Policy, 1919–1937* (Westport, CT: Greenwood Press, 1995), 133.
180. Ibid.
181. "Mightier than the Sword," *New York Times*, February 28, 1932.
182. "Whither Japan," *New York Times,* February 23, 1933.
183. Quoted in Graebner, "Hoover, Roosevelt, and the Japanese," 38.
184. Hu, *Stanley K. Hornbeck and the Open Door Policy*, 133.
185. Hornbeck, "Manchuria Situation: Action upon the Lytton Report," October 4, 1932, printed in *Diplomacy of Frustration*.
186. See, e.g., Grew's warning about sanctions in John K. Emmerson, "Principles versus Realities: U.S. Prewar Foreign Policy toward Japan," in *Pearl Harbor Reexamined*, 38. For the Hoover administration's discussion of sanctions, see Current, "The Stimson Doctrine and the Hoover Doctrine."
187. Hornbeck, "'Respect for Treaties': Ideals and Facts," November 21, 1931, printed in *Diplomacy of Frustration*, 87.
188. Graebner, "Hoover, Roosevelt, and the Japanese," 35.
189. Quoted ibid., 34.

Conclusion

1. E.g., Robert Gilpin, *War and Change in World Politics* (Princeton: Princeton University Press, 1983); Dale C. Copeland, *The Origins of Major War* (Ithaca: Cornell University Press, 2000.
2. See Sebastian Rosato, "The Inscrutable Intentions of Great Powers," *International Security* 39, no. 3 (winter 2014–15): 48–88.

3. E.g., Stephen M. Walt, *Origin of Alliances* (Ithaca: Cornell University Press, 1983).

4. Jennifer Mitzen and Randall L. Schweller, "Knowing the Unknown Unknowns: Misplaced Certainty and the Onset of War" *Security Studies* 20, no. 1 (2011): 2–35; David M. Edelstein, *Over the Horizon: Time, Uncertainty, and the Rise of Great Powers* (Ithaca: Cornell University Press, 2017).

5. E.g., Walt, *Origin of Alliances*.

6. See Graham Allison, "The Thucydides Trap," *Foreign Policy*, June 9, 2017. For similar arguments about the dangers of power transitions see Gilpin, *War and Change*; Copeland, *Origins of Major War*; John J. Mearsheimer, *Tragedy of Great Power Politics* (New York: Norton, 2002).

7. Recent literature on retrenchment, for example, suggests declining powers look to robust alliances with partners, rather than engage in fights. See, e.g., Paul K. MacDonald and Joseph M. Parent, "Graceful Decline," *International Security* 35, no. 4 (spring 2011): 7–44.

8. See, e.g., Paul K. MacDonald and Joseph Parent, *Twilight of the Titans* (Ithaca: Cornell University Press, 2018).

9. See, e.g., Charles L. Glaser, *Rational Theory of International Relations: The Logic of Competition and Cooperation* (Princeton: Princeton University Press, 2010); Glaser, "Political Consequences of Military Strategy: Extending and Refining the Spiral Model," *World Politics* 44, no. 4 (July 1992): 497–538; Charles L. Glaser, "The Security Dilemma Revisited," *World Politics* 50, no. 1 (October 1997): 171–201.

10. Charles Kupchan, *Vulnerability of Empire* (Ithaca, NY: Cornell University Press, 1994); Kupchan, *How Enemies Become Friends* (Princeton: Princeton University Press, 2011); Jack L. Snyder, *Myths of Empire* (Ithaca, NY: Cornell University Press, 1991).

11. See e.g., Brian C. Rathbun, *Diplomacy's Value: Creating Security in 1920s Europe and the Contemporary Middle East* (Ithaca: Cornell University Press, 2014); Keren Yarhi-Milo, *Knowing The Adversary: Leaders, Intelligence Organizations, and Assessments of Intentions in International Relations* (Princeton: Princeton University Press, 2014); Elizabeth Saunders, *Leaders at War: How Presidents Shape Military Interventions* (Ithaca: Cornell University Press, 2011).

12. Ronald R. Krebs, *Narrative and the Making of US National Security* (Cambridge: Cambridge University Press, 2015).

13. See e.g., Charles L. Glaser, "A U.S.-China Grand Bargain? The Hard Choice between Military Competition and Accommodation," *International Security* 39, no. 4 (spring 2015): 64–66; Thomas J. Christensen, *The China Challenge: Shaping the Choices of a Rising Power* (New York: W.W. Norton, 2015), 93–96.

14. Christensen, *The China Challenge*, 46.

15. Jessica Chen Weiss, "China and the Future of World Politics," *Perspectives on Politics* 15, no. 2 (June 2017): 488.

16. David Richards, "Thucydides Dethroned," in *The Next Great War? The Roots of World War I and the Risk of U.S.-China Conflict*, ed. Richard Rosecrance and Steven Miller (Cambridge, MA: MIT Press, 2015), 82.

17. Aaron L. Friedberg, *A Contest for Supremacy: China, America, and the Struggle for Supremacy in Asia* (New York: W.W. Norton, 2012), 2; Zachary Keck, "China's Growing Hegemonic Bent," *The Diplomat*, June 26, 2014.

18. John J. Mearsheimer, "The Gathering Storm: China's Challenge to US Power in Asia," *The Chinese Journal of International Politics* 3, no. 4 (2010): 381–96.

19. See, e.g., Alistair Ian Johnston, "How New and Assertive Is China's New Assertiveness?" *International Security* 37, no. 4 (spring 2013): 7–48; Wu Xinbo, "Understanding the Geopolitical Implications of the Global Financial Crisis," *Washington Quarterly* 33, no. 4 (October 1, 2010): 155–63.

20. Johnston," How New and Assertive Is China's New Assertiveness," 7.

21. Thomas Christensen, "The Advantages of an Assertive China: Responding to Beijing's Abrasive Diplomacy," *Foreign Affairs*, February 21, 2011.

22. Johnston, "How New and Assertive Is China's New Assertiveness," 9.

23. Kathy Gilsinan, "Cliché of the Moment: 'China's Increasing Assertiveness,'" *The Atlantic*, September 25, 2015, https://www.theatlantic.com/international/archive/2015/09/south-china-sea-assertiveness/407203/.

24. Gordon Lubold And Adam Entous, "U.S. Says Beijing Is Building Up South China Sea Islands," *Wall Street Journal*, May 9, 2015.

25. Johnston, "How New and Assertive Is China's New Assertiveness," 7.

26. M. Taylor Fravel and Michael D. Swaine, "China's Assertive Behavior—Part Two: The Maritime Periphery," *China Leadership Monitor* 35 (summer 2011): 15.

27. Greg Austin, "Why Beijing's South China Sea Moves Make Sense Now," *National Interest*, December 16, 2015.

28. Johnston, "How New and Assertive Is China's New Assertiveness," 26.

29. Ibid., 46–47; Bjorn Jerdén, "The Assertive China Narrative: Why It Is Wrong and How So Many Still Bought into It," *The Chinese Journal of International Politics* 7, no. 1 (March 2014): 47–88.

30. Johnston, "How New and Assertive Is China's New Assertiveness," 47.

31. Jerdén, "The Assertive China Narrative," 81.

32. See, e.g., Zheng Bijian, "China's 'Peaceful Rise' to Great-Power Status," *Foreign Affairs* 84, no. 5 (Fall 2005): 18–24; Bonnie S. Glaser and Evan S. Medeiros, "The Changing Ecology of Foreign Policy-Making in China: The Ascension and Demise of the Theory of 'Peaceful Rise,'" *China Quarterly* 190 (June 2007): 291–310.

33. Jerome Alan Cohen and Hungdah Chiu, *People's China and International Law: A Documentary Study*, vol. 1 (Princeton: Princeton University Press, 1974), 29.

34. Wang Zonglai and Hu Bin, "China's Reform and Opening-Up and International Law," *Chinese Journal of International Law* 9, no. 1 (2010): 9.

35. H. S. Kim, "The 1992 Chinese Territorial Sea Law in Light of the UN Convention," *International and Comparative Law Quarterly* 43, no. 4 (1994): 894–904.

36. Jonathan G. Odom, "A China in the Bull Shop? Comparing the Rhetoric of a Rising China with the Reality of the International Law Of the Sea," *Ocean and Coastal Law Journal* 17, no. 2 (2012): 224.

37. See, e.g., Christina Lai, "Talk Is Not Cheap: China's Assurance and Reassurance Strategy in East Asia," Ph.D. diss., Georgetown University, 2015; Simon Andrew Leitch, "The Power of Rhetoric: China's Search for Legitimacy, 1989–2009," Ph.D. diss., Griffith University, 2012.

38. Christina Lai, "Rhetorical Traps and China's Peaceful Rise: Malaysia and the Philippines in the South China Sea Territorial Disputes," *China and the World Bulletin Board*, August 16, 2017.

39. M. Taylor Fravel, "China's Strategy in the South China Sea," *Contemporary Southeast Asia* 33, no. 3 (2011): 292–319.

40. Edward Wong, "Security Law Suggests a Broadening of China's 'Core Interests,'" *New York Times*, July 2, 2015, sec. Asia Pacific, https://www.nytimes.com/2015/07/03/world/asia/security-law-suggests-a-broadening-of-chinas-core-interests.html.

41. Johnston, "How New and Assertive Is China's New Assertiveness," 19.

42. Swaine, "China's Assertive Behavior."

43. Kai He and Huiyun Feng, "Debating China's Assertiveness: Taking China's Power and Interests Seriously," *International Politics* 49, no. 5 (2012): 641.

44. Christopher Woody, "The South China Sea Is Now a 'Core Interest' of Beijing—And That's a Problem for Its Neighbors," *Business Insider*, June 2, 2015.

45. Peter Ford, "China in the South China Sea: Has Beijing Overstepped the Mark?" *Christian Science Monitor*, July 22, 2015.

46. Office of the Secretary of Defense, "Military and Security Developments Involving the People's Republic of China 2017," *Annual Report to Congress*, May 15, 2017.

47. John Ford, "The Pivot to Asia Was Obama's Biggest Mistake," *The Diplomat*, January 21, 2017.

48. For an overview of Air Sea Battle, see "Air Sea Battle: Service Collaboration to Address Anti-Access and Area Denial Challenges," Department of Defense, May 12, 2013; Jan van Tol, Mark Gunzinger, Andrew F. Krepinevich, and Jim Thomas, "AirSea Battle: A Point-of-Departure Operational Concept," Center for Strategic and Budgetary Assessments, May 18, 2010. ASB was renamed Joint Concept for Maneuver and Access in the Global Commons (JAM-GC) in January 2015.

49. Ford, "The Pivot to Asia Was Obama's Biggest Mistake."

50. For a discussion of FONOPS, see, e.g., Lynn Kuok, "The U.S. FON Program in the South China Sea: A Lawful and Necessary Response to China's Strategic Ambiguity," East Asia Policy Paper No. 9, Center for East Asia Policy Studies, Brookings, June 2016; Mira Rapp-Hooper, "All in Good FON: Why Freedom of Navigation Is Business as Usual in the South China Sea," *Foreign Affairs*, October 12, 2015, accessed at https://www.foreignaffairs.com/articles/united-states/2015-10-12/all-good-fon.

51. See, e.g., Jonathan Kirshner, *American Power after the Financial Crisis* (Ithaca: Cornell University Press, 2014), chapter 1; Rebecca Liao, "The End of the G20: Has the Group Outlived Its Purpose?," *Foreign Affairs*, September 14, 2016, https://www.foreignaffairs.com/articles/2016-09-14/end-g-20

52. "Better Late than Never: Trump Launches First FONOP in South China Sea," *American Interest*, May 25, 2017.

53. "Rubio Introduces Bill Targeting Chinese Aggression in South China Sea," Press release from the office of Senator Mark Rubio, December 6, 2016.

54. See, e.g., Robert L. Jervis, *Perception and Misperception in International Politics* (Princeton: Princeton University Press, 2017), chapter 3; Glaser, *Rational Theory of International Politics*; Andrew Kydd, "Game Theory and the Spiral Model," *World Politics* 49, no. 3 (April 1997): 371–400; and Kydd, "Sheep in Sheep's Clothing: Why Security Seekers Do Not Fight Each Other," *Security Studies* 7, no. 1 (autumn 1997): 114–55.

55. Yahri-Milo, *Knowing the Adversary*.

56. See, e.g., Stuart Kaufman, *Nationalist Passions* (Ithaca: Cornell University Press, 2015).

57. Brian C. Rathbun, "Uncertainty about Uncertainty: Understanding the Multiple Meanings of a Crucial Concept in International Relations Theory," *International Studies Quarterly* 51, no. 3 (September 2007): 534–35, 533.

58. Robert Keohane, "International Institutions: Two Approaches," *International Studies Quarterly* 32, no. 4 (December 1988): 379–96.

59. Schweller, "Realism," in *Psychology, Strategy, and Conflict: Perceptions of Insecurity in International Relations*, ed. James W. Davis (London: Routledge, 2012), 26. Edelstein refers to this as "true uncertainty." See Edelstein, *Over the Horizon*, 18–19.

60. See e.g., Martha Finnemore, *National Interests in International Society* (Ithaca: Cornell University Press, 1996), 29; Paul Schroeder, "Reflections on System, System Effects, and 19th Century International Politics as the Practice of Civic Association," in *Psychology, Strategy, and Conflict*, 155–80.

61. Krebs, *Narrative and the Making of US National Security Policy*, chapter 2.

62. This is of course at the foundation of much of constructivist theorizing. See, e.g., Alexander Wendt, *Social Theory of International Politics* (Cambridge: Cambridge University Press, 1999).

63. Kenneth Binmore, *Essays on the Foundation of Game Theory* (Cambridge: Basil Blackwell, 1990), 9.

64. Robert L. Jervis, *Systems Effects: Complexity in Political and Social Life* (Princeton: Princeton University Press, 1997).

65. See the discussion of this literature in chapters 1 and 2.

66. See, e.g., Stacie E. Goddard and Daniel H. Nexon, "The Dynamics of Power Politics," *Journal of Global Security Studies* 1, no. 1 (2016): 4–18.

67. For a discussion, see, e.g., Vibeke Schou Tjalve and Michael Williams, "Reviving the Rhetoric of Realism: Politics and Responsibility in Grand Strategy," *Security Studies* 24, no. 1 (2015): 37–60.

Index

Page numbers followed by an italic *t* indicate a table.

CPSIA information can be obtained
at www.ICGtesting.com
Printed in the USA
LVHW031808030119
602642LV00005B/66/P